THE DOLL & TEDDY BEAR DEPARTMENT

Memorable Catalog Pages from the legendary
Sears Christmas Wishbooks of the 1950's and 1960's

Edited by Thomas W. Holland

Windmill Press

Copyright © 1997

WINDMILL PRESS
P.O. Box 56551
Sherman Oaks, California 91413

First Edition

Manufactured in the United States of America

Published by Windmill Press, P.O. Box 56551, Sherman Oaks, California 91413
Telephone (818) 995-6410   FAX (818) 995-3590

ISBN: 1-887790-03-9

LC: 96-61341

Publisher's Cataloging in Publication
(Prepared by Quality Books Inc.)

The Doll & teddy bear department : memorable catalog pages from the
legendary Sears Christmas wishbooks of the 1950's and 1960's /
edited by Thomas W. Holland.
p. cm.
ISBN: 1-887790-03-9

1. Dolls--Catalogs--History. 2. Teddy bears--Catalogs--History.
3. Manufactures--Catalogs. 4. Sears, Roebuck and Company--
Catalogs.   I. Holland, Thomas W. II. Title: Doll and teddy bear
department.

NK4893.D65 1997   688.7"221
                                   QBI96-40461

*Front cover photograph: A young girl is delighted by the wondrous dolls and teddy bears
available in Sears' 1956 Christmas Wishbook.*
*Rear cover photographs: Sears Department Store, Canoga Park, California as it looked in 1964;
"Think Pink" catalog advertisement circa 1960. (Photos courtesy Sears, Roebuck and Co.);*

Sears makes it easy for you...
to make your family's Christmas wishes come true

Have you ever thought what a simple matter it would be to buy ALL your gifts from Sears Catalogs on Sears Easy Terms? You can order everything you want now, before Christmas, and spread the payments over the months ahead. You don't need all ready cash—and you don't have to disturb your savings. It takes only a small down payment to buy for *everyone* on your gift list.

If you have a Sears Easy Payment Account you can "add-on" your Christmas purchases with NO down payment. Your present monthly payment will not be increased unless your new balance requires a larger payment according to Sears Payment Table. (See page 373 for complete details about Sears Easy Payment Plan, or contact the Credit Department of your Sears Catalog Sales Office.)

For Will and Emily

Acknowledgments

Many people worked behind the scenes to bring this book to fruition and I am most grateful for all the help I received.

Most importantly, I want to thank Sears, Roebuck and Company and their archivist Vicki Cwiok. Without their help this book simply would not have been possible.

Thanks also to Doug Roth, Eleanor Holland and Frank Thompson for their moral support and invaluable advice.

Tracking down all these rare catalog pages was a logistical ordeal and required the kind assistance of numerous people. I want to particularly thank catalog experts Jerry Harrington, Ed Osepowicz, Tim Goss, and Rich Hesson.

Harold and Ruth Feldman, owners of The Doll Shoppe in Sherman Oaks, California were a huge help in compiling information about the individual dolls featured in this book. They truly love dolls and kindly spent many hours advising me on the project in their beautiful shop.

Thanks to Betsy Annas for photographing the cover, Elizabeth Goetzman for modeling, and Carolyn Porter and Alan Gadney who helped me with design and the complex job of reproducing the delicate old original catalog pages.

Introduction

As I began compiling the pages for this book, I was amazed to see the huge number of dolls and teddy bears that Sears, Roebuck and Company sold over the years. The Wishbooks of the 1950's and 1960's featured some of the greatest dolls and teddy bears ever made.

If you ask a collector what the "Golden Age" of dolls was you are likely to get varying answers. Certainly, spectacular dolls and teddy bears were made in the United States and abroad prior to the 1950 Wishbook. And there have been many wonderful dolls made after 1969. But this book focuses on the twenty years during which most Baby Boomers would have received their first doll or teddy, and so I prefer to think of these years as the "Golden Age."

As the Fifties began, the combination of postwar affluence and lots of new children needing toys meant more and better dolls and teddy bears were offered in the Wishbook's pages. Manufacturers began to make elaborate dolls that looked and felt like real babies. Ideal's 1950 Kiss Me doll made various facial expressions with the push of a hidden plunger. The legendary Tiny Tears cried, wet and blew bubbles. But all this was just a hint of the walking, talking wonders to come in future catalogs.

By the mid-Fifties, interactive dolls were the rage. Toni let girls give her a Permanent Wave. Honey Walker could actually walk with you and turn her head at the same time. New plastic formulas like Vinyl allowed dolls to kneel, sit and move realistically.

It was during this period that marketers saw the value in merchandising character dolls from hit movies, and later television. Shirley Temple, Howdy Doody, Mary Hartline, Ricky Ricardo, Jr., Annie Oakley and even American Bandstand's Dick Clark all had dolls modeled after them. Big stars like Piper Laurie, Dorothy Lamour, Betty Hutton... even Miss Frances from Ding Dong School... began to endorse dolls.

Dolls and teddy bears were always good business since there was always a new crop of children needing them, but the toy industry would never be the same after the 1959 release of Mattel's Barbie. Although not seen in the Wishbook's pages until 1960, and then just briefly, this thin, busty fashion model would change everything.

Barbie's base price was reasonable, just $2.26 in 1960, and she was so different from the popular, but Fifties-looking, Miss Revlon and Betsy McCall. Soon Barbie had homes, sportscars and accessories galore. She had boyfriend Ken and pals Midge and Stacey and on and on. Barbie quickly filled up the Wishbook's doll pages and continues to make doll history to this day.

But there are other many other obscure and long forgotten dolls and teddy bears in these old pages too. Surely they all made some child happy, somewhere. I hope, as you look through this book, that you will discover a long forgotten childhood friend and perhaps some happy memories too.

Thomas W. Holland

The Sears Catalog

The roots of the famous Sears Catalog began in 1886 when Richard W. Sears, then a railroad station agent for the Minneapolis and St. Louis Railway in North Redwood, Minnesota, began selling watches and jewelry and later offered them through printed mailers which grew into catalogs. In those years the railroads literally moved America, taking people to work, settlers to new homes and delivering the clothing and supplies they would require. Thanks in large part to the railroad's ability to move things virtually anywhere in the country cheaply and quickly, Sears, Roebuck and Company grew into one of the nation's leading corporations.

In 1896 Sears produced its first large general merchandise catalog featuring 753 pages of merchandise targeted to America's farmers and their families with a variety of items for sale -- from apparel to plows -- watches and jewelry -- even dolls and toys. The specialized Sears Christmas Catalogs -- nicknamed the "Wishbook" -- began in the mid-1930's. It became a holiday staple in virtually every American home.

Not realized at the time, of course, the Sears catalogs were recording the changing scene in America and represented the daily lives and work of thousands of Americans. Edgar Rice Burroughs, author of the famed "Tarzan" series, was at one time a copywriter for Sears catalogs. Jean Arthur, Lauren Bacall, Joan Caulfield, Anita Colby, Susan Heyward, Fredric March, Norma Shearer and Gloria Swanson all appeared on the pages of Sears catalogs as models in years past.

The famous Sears catalogs have been a barometer of the time, reflecting events, the way people lived and how they perceived their surroundings. For example, within months after the destruction of the U.S.S. Maine in Havana harbor in 1898, the catalog offered a complete "stereopticon lecture outfit" on that subject and the Cuban war.

Its easy to forget how far back the Sears catalog really does go. Sears sold the pioneers "Covered wagon covers" and in 1889, before the West was fully settled, the catalog stated: "Cash in full must accompany all orders from points in Washington, Oregon, California, Idaho, Nevada, Utah, Arizona, New Mexico, Montana and Wyoming -- if you live in one of the ten states and territories named." But C.O.D. orders were accepted from the more settled Eastern States.

Even wars and depressions are reflected in the catalog's pages. Song hits sold in the Spring 1918 catalog included "It's a Long Way to Berlin," "Keep the Home Fires Burning," and "Good-Bye Broadway, Hello France." And in the Fall 1942 catalog, Sears announced that its subsidiary, Allstate Fire Insurance Company, sold "the New U.S. Government War Damage Insurance Plan to protect homes and farms against war damage due to enemy attack or resistance by U.S. armed forces." In 1943 the catalog proclaimed: "Silvertone radios have gone to war. Tomorrow they will be back -- better than ever."

For anyone who recalls the Great Depression of the 1930's, perhaps the single most telling proof of its effect appeared in the 1933 Sears catalog which offered a book titled "Understanding the Stock Market" for 87¢. Called "a simple, yet thorough explanation of how the mysterious stock market operates," it had been marked down from $2.50.

Certainly, if anyone wishes to trace the rise of the automobile and the decline of the horse-drawn buggy, the Sears catalog documents the entire process. Taking note of the Tin Lizzie for the first time, the 1894 catalog listed automobile caps and books. But the horse still ruled the roads, with the catalog devoting eight full pages to such items as buggy boots, bridles, cruppers, harness, tops and whips. By 1929 the tables had turned. The buggy offering was down to half a page, and disappeared entirely thereafter. The catalog index, at the same time, listed 266 separate items under auto accessories.

In January 1993, Sears discontinued most of its catalog operation. But the old pages that still exist, such as those reproduced in this book, offer a rare peek through a window to the past, documenting virtually everthing about we Americans and our lives. For readers interested in the wonderful dolls and teddy bears of the 1950's and 1960's, the Sears Wishbook documents the era in a visual way no other historical text can.

As the decade of the Fifties began, the Sears Christmas catalog of 1950 was packed with more items for sale than ever before. The post war baby boom had begun and this new youthful population would need lots of toys and dolls. The economic prosperity that followed the war also meant more affluent buyers, resulting in more elaborate and expensive toys.

The 1950 Christmas catalog featured a large number of dolls, many made by Ideal for Sears and sold under Sears' house brand "Happi Time." These included several with "Magic Rubber Skin" which closely simulated real skin texture to make the doll feel like a real baby. Unfortunately, the rubber skin on these dolls tended to rot over the years. Finding one today in excellent condition is quite rare. Fixing the rubber skin is virtually impossible.

Ideal, a leading American doll manufacturer, made many of the dolls and teddy bears which appeared in the catalog this year including Kiss Me, Baby Coos, Snoozie (available with "an imported Swiss music box right inside her tummy") and a doll which would become a best seller -- Tiny Tears.

A NEW, BIGGER THAN EVER STOREHOUSE FOR SANTA

GIFTS FOR

SEARS 1950 *Christmas Book*

SEARS, ROEBUCK AND CO., 925 S. HOMAN AVE., CHICAGO 7, ILL.

Satisfaction guaranteed or your money back . . Index starts on page 279

Sears Christmas
Wishbook

1950

HAPPI-TIME *Dolls*
REG. U.S. PAT. OFF.

with voices! Our best values in 7 years!
Richly dressed Babies with magic rubber
skin .. molded rubber wetting Dolls

(DESCRIBED ON FACING PAGE)

ORDER EARLY! Shopping is easy the catalog way

Every price reduced on these Happi-Time Dolls with soft, life-like Magic Rubber Skin!

(ILLUSTRATED ON OPPOSITE PAGE)

Finely detailed durable molded plastic heads · **Sparkling go-to-sleep eyes . . . real lashes!** · **To clean, just sponge doll off with soapy water** · **Petal-soft skin of rubber; arms, legs jointed**

We sincerely believe these Happi-Time Dolls with Magic Rubber Skin are the finest money can buy! Priced far lower than a year ago! Everything little "mothers" look for in a doll.

Was $3.98
$379
49 N 3650

- Wonderfully warm, cuddly body, arms and legs are covered with petal-soft magic rubber skin that's just like real.
- Washable! Sponge dolly off with soapy water to keep her clean.
- Soft cotton and foam rubber stuffed body; jointed arms, legs.
- Durable molded realistically detailed plastic head tilts and turns.
- Expressive go-to-sleep glassene eyes; realistic long, silky lashes.
- Caress her . . . hear the sob or cry of her sensitive coo-type voice.
- Each doll beautifully attired in richly trimmed organdy dress . . . wears cotton slip, diapers, rayon socks, imitation leather shoes.

[A] Our finest Happi-Time Magic Rubber Skin Doll with curly mohair wig, lustrous spun rayon coat, etc.

49 N 3670—14-inch doll.
Shpg. wt. 1 lb. 12 oz.
(Was $7.98) $7.45

49 N 3671—16-inch doll.
Shpg. wt. 2 lbs. 4 oz.
(Was $9.98) $8.45

[B] Happi-Time Magic Rubber Skin Doll with curly mohair wig.

49 N 3660—14-inch doll.
Shpg. wt. 1 lb. 8 oz.
(Was $5.98) $4.79

49 N 3661—16-inch doll.
Shpg. wt. 2 lbs. 6 oz.
(Was $7.98) $6.69

[C] Happi-Time Magic Rubber Skin Doll with molded hair.

49 N 3650—14-inch doll.
Shpg. wt. 1 lb. 10 oz.
(Was $3.98) $3.79

49 N 3651—16-inch doll.
Shpg. wt. 2 lbs. 4 oz.
(Was $5.98) $5.45

Happi-Time Mohair Wig Magic Skin Baby with Layette, Case

[D] *PRICES REDUCED!* You save 44c on 14-inch size, 23c on 16-inch size! Each of these mohair wig dolls has a complete wardrobe packed in canvas-effect carrying case. Petal-soft magic rubber skin body is stuffed with foam rubber and cotton. Jointed arms and legs. Nicely molded plastic head tilts and turns. Expressive sleeping eyes of glassene; realistic lashes.

Same quality was $9.39
$895
14-inch size

Press her tummy gently and she sobs . . . press hard and she cries! She wears a knit shirt and diapers. *Layette* consists of beautiful organdy dress with matching frilly bonnet, cotton slip, rayon socks, imitation leather shoes, cotton jacket, bar of soap, six clothespins, stomach band, cotton nightie and 3 powder puffs.

49 N 3680—14-in. doll.
Wt. 5 lbs. (*Was $9.39*) . . $8.95

49 N 3681—16-in. doll.
Wt. 6 lbs. (*Was $10.98*) . . $10.75

Prices cut on Happi-Time Drink-Wet-Cry Baby with Layette, Case!

She cries; listen to her life-like voice! · **She drinks; you can feed her from bottle!** · **She wets. Change her diaper, bathe her.**

- A wonderful gift for any little girl!
- She drinks . . . wets . . . cries when you fondle her!
- Life-like molded plastic head turns, is almost unbreakable.
- Flesh-like molded rubber body; jointed arms, legs.

Was $8.79
$695
13½-inch size

[E] Feed her from her own little bottle and she wets. Change her diapers, bathe and powder her. Dolly wears cotton shirt and diapers, has her own nursing bottle and layette in handsome canvas-effect fiberboard case with two snap locks and carrying handle. Little girls love taking dolly's layette with them when they travel. And, the case is ever so handy to store dolly's clothes.

Layette consists of sheer organdy dress and bonnet, cotton slip, two diapers, rayon socks, imitation leather shoes, six clothes pins, plastic spoon, saucer, three powder puffs, four safety pins.

49 N 3078—13½-inch doll with layette, case. Shpg. wt. 4 lbs. (*Was $8.79*) $6.95

49 N 3079—15-inch doll with layette, case. Shpg. wt. 5 lbs. (*Was $10.79*) $8.95

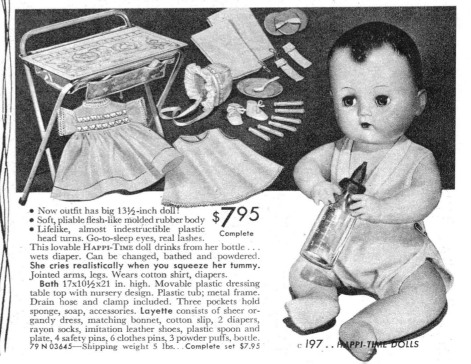

HAPPI-TIME Miniature Dolls

Doll turns as music box plays, making truly a lovely picture! Order a music box with your doll!

New Happi-Time Miniatures with sleeping eyes!

Luxuriously dressed realistic miniature dolls that girls of all ages love to collect. About 7½-in. tall. All-plastic bodies; movable arms. Plastic heads tilt and turn; have realistic go-to-sleep eyes. Painted shoes. All except nun and groom have curly mohair wigs. All girl dolls wear pantalettes and petticoats, have exquisite dresses with full-gathered billowy skirts. All stand without support. Music box [L] below not included.

[F] **Little Red Riding Hood.** All ready to visit grandmother! Wears cape, attached hood over rayon dress. Carries basket.
49 N 3111—Shipping weight 12 oz. $1.79

[G] **Nun.** Wears rosary beads imported from Italy. Black rayon garment, black veil, white collar, head piece. Metal cross.
49 N 3109—Shipping weight 12 oz. . . . $2.29

[H] **Lovely Bridesmaid.** Wears beautiful rayon dress with embroidery trim. Net hat has artificial flowers. Carries bouquet.
49 N 3110—Shipping weight 12 oz. $1.79

[J] **Handsome Bridegroom.** Wears felt hat, coat, striped trousers and tie. White vest and shirt front. Gold-color metal watch chain. Has white felt flower in his coat lapel.
49 N 3103—Shipping weight 12 oz. $1.79

[K] **Radiant Bride.** White rayon satin dress, lace peplum net bodice, net-veil with artificial orange blossoms. Has bouquet.
49 N 3112—Shipping weight 12 oz. $1.79

[L] **Finest imported Swiss Music Box.** Turntable revolves as music plays. Assorted popular tunes. Rubber attachment holds miniature dolls. Plastic 4¼-in. diam. base.
49 N 3094—Dolls not included. Wt. 8 oz. $2.39

She drinks, wets, cries . . has her own bath, layette!

- Now outfit has big 13½-inch doll!
- Soft, pliable flesh-like molded rubber body.
- Lifelike, almost indestructible plastic head turns. Go-to-sleep eyes, real lashes.

$795 Complete

This lovable HAPPI-TIME doll drinks from her bottle . . . wets diaper. Can be changed, bathed and powdered. **She cries realistically when you squeeze her tummy.** Jointed arms, legs. Wears cotton shirt, diapers.

Bath 17x10½x21 in. high. Movable plastic dressing table top with nursery design. Plastic tub; metal frame. Drain hose and clamp included. Three pockets hold sponge, soap, accessories. **Layette** consists of sheer organdy dress, matching bonnet, cotton slip, 2 diapers, rayon socks, imitation leather shoes, plastic spoon and plate, 4 safety pins, 6 clothes pins, 3 powder puffs, bottle.
79 N 03645—Shipping weight 5 lbs. . . Complete set $7.95

c 197 . . HAPPI-TIME DOLLS

Her lips move when she "gives you a kiss" .. real affection!

She puckers her lips and cries when you push plunger in back

Ideal

Blessed Event "KISS ME" Baby Doll

This new-born infant puckers her lips and..

She actually gives a kiss

$998

Most lifelike Doll-Baby we've ever seen . . . so tiny, so new her eyes are only partly open! When visiting grownups first see her, they'll probably think she's an honest-to-goodness baby. Brings untold joy to her little "mother" . . . for, whatever her mood, she looks perfectly adorable. Her sweet mouth is open, revealing a tiny pink tongue . . . and, though it's a bad habit, she sometimes puts her finger in. When you want her to cry, pout or pucker her lips "for a kiss," you simply push the plunger in her back. Her turning head, arms and legs are made of soft, cuddly vinyl plastic; her plump cotton-stuffed body is cloth-covered. Baby is dressed in a flannelette shirt and panty combination; baby-style flannelette gown. To keep her warm, there's a fluffy outer blanket with a wide ribbon bow.

49 N 3653—About 21 inches tall. Shipping weight 5 pounds . . . . Only $9.98

Ideal

"Snoozie" with Swiss Music Box

Lullaby time is sure to come often for this little one . . . she has an *imported Swiss music box* right inside her tummy! She's 16 inches tall—a fine size for cuddling. Beautifully shaped vinyl head, hands and legs; soft cotton-stuffed body. Wears long flannelette wrapper and diaper. Comes in fluffy outer blanket with big ribbon bow. Plays a sleepy lullaby tune.

$6.95

49 N 3624—Shpg. wt. 2 lbs. 4 oz. $6.95

11-inch "Snoozie"

"New-born" baby—so soft and sweet-looking, she inspires a world of tender care. Rubber skin body, arms, legs; cotton and foam rubber stuffed. Flexible vinyl turning head has shell-like ears, rosebud mouth, painted eyes. Jointed arms. Press her tummy, she cries. Flannelette wrapper, diaper. Blanket, bow.

$3.27

49 N 3608—Shpg. wt. 1 lb. . . . $3.27

SHE SHEDS BIG TEARS like a real baby

SHE BLOWS BUBBLES when playtime comes

SHE TAKES BATHS in water up to her neck

New "TINY TEARS" weeps, sleeps, drinks, wets and blows bubbles!

Out of dreams and into reality . . . a doll which actually *weeps big wet tears* that well up in her eyes and roll down her cheeks! Not only can you *hear* and *see* her crying lustily . . . but she also sleeps, drinks from her bottle, wets her diaper, blows bubbles with her cute little bubble pipe . . . and bathes like a real infant. Caring for "TINY TEARS" is practically a full-time job . . . but her young "mother" is bound to enjoy every minute of it. Doll has a turning plastic head (practically unbreakable); shining go-to-sleep eyes with thick lashes; molded, tinted hair. Her body, legs and movable arms are molded rubber. "TINY TEARS" comes in a knit cotton shirt and panties. Her layette includes: sheer organdy dress and bonnet, cotton slip, diaper, bootees, soap, towel, sponge, bottle, bubble pipe, pacifier and cleansing tissues.

$745

49 N 3009—13 inches tall. Shipping weight 3 lbs. . . . . Complete set $7.45

Look at the hair on these two dolls!

Popular Sparkle Plenty, daughter of B. O. Plenty and Gravel Gertie, with long, wavy blond wig and crying voice. Her rubber-skin body is stuffed with foam rubber. Jointed arms; legs can be sponged off. Plastic head; sleeping eyes with lashes. Cotton and rayon yarn hair. Coveralls, rayon socks, imitation leather shoes. About 14 in. tall. (Copyright Chicago *Tribune.*)

$5.69

49 N 3015—Shpg. wt. 2 lbs. . . $5.69

NEW "Tousle-Head." Her hair is a mop of soft fur (lambskin, really)—and it's forever in need of a good combing. Has her own plastic brush, comb and mirror. Rubber-skin body, foam-rubber stuffed. Arms are jointed and she cries when you squeeze body or legs. Plastic head turns; glass-like eyes close. Cotton knit shirt, diaper. About 16 inches tall.

$4.98

49 N 3628—Shpg. wt. 3 lbs. . . $4.98

198 . . SEARS, ROEBUCK AND CO. CPB

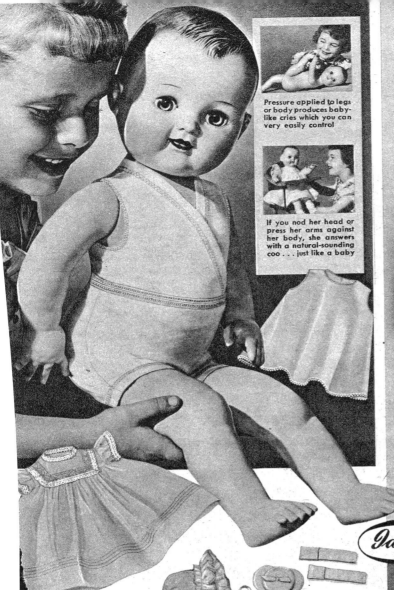

Pressure applied to legs or body produces baby-like cries which you can very easily control

If you nod her head or press her arms against her body, she answers with a natural-sounding coo . . . just like a baby

Pals! Life-size Baby Coos is almost as big as a 1-year-old child

Price cut $6.00 on lifesize Baby Coos

Was $22.95

$16⁹⁵

Lifesize Baby Coos—wears real baby clothes

As big as a real live baby—wears 6 to 12-month size baby clothes—yet lightweight. Has all features of BABY COOS doll at left. Magic Skin rubber body stuffed with foam rubber . . . practically unbreakable plastic head. "Go-to-sleep" eyes with silky lashes. Can be bathed and powdered. Wears corduroy coveralls with straps that unbutton, matching tam, cotton shirt and panties, rayon socks, real leather baby shoes.
79 N 03076—27 inches tall. Shpg. wt. 7 pounds. *(Was $22.95)* . . . . Now $16.95

Ideal

NEW LOW PRICES on nationally famous

"Baby Coos"

She's the most sensational baby in all dolldom

- She coos if you cuddle her
- She complains if pinched
- She sobs if you paddle her
- She has "go to sleep" eyes

Prices greatly reduced to make it easier for BABY COOS to become a member of your household. She's a real celebrity . . . has appeared on television and radio. Newspapers have shouted the BABY COOS story all over the country.

BABY COOS looks, feels and even makes sounds like a real, live baby. Caress her gently and she'll coo affectionately. Pinch her and she'll give a plaintive sob. And, if you squeeze her roughly, she'll scream to let you know it hurts! Her smooth Magic Skin rubber body is stuffed with soft foam rubber—she's warm and cuddly—almost human to touch. Like any infant, she must be bathed, powdered and dressed. Her head is practically unbreakable plastic. Go-to-sleep Lucite eyes have a bright sparkle—long, silky lashes. BABY COOS wears rib-knit cotton shirt and panty. Comes with complete outfit: a sheer, prettily-trimmed organdy dress with matching bonnet, cotton slip, rayon socks, imitation leather shoes, 3 powder puffs and 6 clothespins.

Was $5⁴⁷

$4⁹⁷
14-inch

49 N 3040—14 inches tall. Shipping wt. 2 lbs. . . . . *(Was $ 5.47)* . . . . Now $ 4.97
49 N 3042—18 inches tall. Shipping wt. 2 lbs. 8 oz. . . . . *(Was   9.47)* . . . . Now   8.95
49 N 3061—22 inches tall. Shipping wt. 4 lbs. . . . . *(Was 12.95)* . . . . Now 12.45

NEW—Baby Coos with mohair wig and complete layette in carrying case . . . ready to go visiting

Now has a lovely mohair wig, an outstanding value due to Sears' economical distribution methods. Wears knit cotton shirt and panties. Her de luxe layette includes: organdy dress, bonnet, slip, lace-trimmed cotton bed jacket, cloth coat and bonnet, rayon socks, imitation leather shoes, 3 powder puffs, soap, miniature plastic dishes, tummy band and 6 clothespins. Doll has all features of BABY COOS at left. You can bathe, powder and dress her. Lucite eyes "go to sleep."
49 N 3696—14-in. doll. With layette and case. Shpg. wt. 5 lbs. $10.75

$10⁷⁵

Be sure to see page 283 for full details on Sears Easy Terms

CPB **PAGE 199 . . BABY DOLLS**

Give a Toni Play-Wave Doll!

Wave her lustrous Nylon hair again and again
What fun for your little "hairdresser!"

Ideal

ORDER EARLY! Do your gift shopping now

$9.49

14½-in. size

Now **Dolly** has the Toni! And your little girl can be the imaginative hairdresser to design new and different hair stylings for this glamorous doll. Toni's hair-dos will never go out of style. Dolly keeps pace with changing fashions because her hair can be waved over and over again. Toni's gloriously soft nylon hair is specially applied so it won't wash loose from her head. Frequent shampooing and play waving won't harm its texture, either.

Toni Doll comes with a complete play-wave kit—contains comb, curlers, papers, shampoo and Toni Play-Wave formula with a bottle to hold the waving solution. Mother will be happy to know that this play-wave formula makes a harmless sugar and water solution. (To make solution, mix 1 teaspoon of sugar with ⅛ cup of water.) It's always easy to keep a supply on hand.

Toni's plastic, so it won't matter if she gets wet during shampooing. Just wipe her dry and go ahead with the "beauty treatment." Practically unbreakable, too. Jointed arms and legs move with lifelike grace. Head turns and tilts just like a lively girl's; sparkling go-to-sleep eyes have real lashes. Wears dainty cotton dress (assorted styles, sorry no choice). Cotton half-slip and panties have lace trim. With rayon socks, imitation leather shoes. Wears attractive ribbon bow in her nylon wig.

49 N 3374—14½ in. tall.
Shpg. wt. 1 lb. 14 oz....**$9.49**

49 N 3375—16 in. tall.
Shpg. wt. 2 lbs. 4 oz.... **$11.49**

$5.67 $5.45 $6.59 $8.98

Dolls with special personalities. She'll treasure them for years

A **Howdy Doody—the Television Cowboy.** Here's a happy-go-lucky hombre who's taking the country by storm! Sturdy plastic turning head. Jaws move like ventriloquist's dummy. Go-to-sleep glass eyes; soft, cotton-stuffed body, vinyl hands. Wears cotton bandana, bright shirt, frontier pants, imitation leather cowboy boots, belt. About 20 inches tall.
$5.67

49 N 3571—Shpg. wt. 2 lbs.. $5.67

B **Pigtail Doll.** All practically unbreakable plastic, finely detailed. Jointed arms and legs; head turns and tilts. Rich mohair pigtail wig frames lifelike plastic head. Go-to-sleep eyes with lashes. Wears wide-brimmed straw hat, lace and embroidery trimmed cotton dress, half slip, panties. Rayon socks and imitation leather shoes. Shipping weights 2 pounds, 3 pounds.
$5.45
14½-in. size

49 N 3345—14½-in $5.45
49 N 3346—17-in 6.98

C **Judy Splinters,** sparkling new television personality. Turning head of flexible vinyl plastic finished in excellent detail. Special ring on back of her neck controls head movement secretly. Pigtail yarn wig with ribbons. Soft body stuffed with cotton and foam rubber. Rubber skin arms and legs. Authentic television costume of lovely broadcloth: dress, jacket, panties. Rayon socks, imitation leather shoes. About 17 inches tall.
$6.59

49 N 3564—Shpg. wt. 2 lbs...... $6.59

D **Doll Bride with Satin Gown.** Enchantingly beautiful in traditional white. Rayon satin wedding dress with veil cap trimmed with silver-color metallic braid. Long, flowing net bridal veil. Carries bouquet of artificial flowers, which also decorate her gown. Wears cotton half slip over crinoline underskirt and panties. Rayon socks and imitation leather shoes. All plastic body. Jointed arms and legs. Head turns and tilts; go-to-sleep eyes; mohair wig. Bride doll makes an ever popular gift. Shipping weight 2 pounds 8 ounces.
$8.98

49 N 3360—18 inch doll $8.98

Order all your Christmas needs on Sears Easy Terms. For complete details see page 283 of this catalog.

[A] $8.95 14½-in. size

[B] $7.98

[C] $6.98

[D] $7.69

[E] $2.98

[F] $3.29

Mme. Alexander Dolls

Your little girl dreams about enchantingly "alive" dolls like these by Mme. Alexander . . . famous for amazingly lifelike detail. Truly the finest quality dolls we could find in America. These beauties will satisfy your girl's fondest wish. All except Baby Doll molded of practically unbreakable plastic, have jointed arms and legs. Baby Doll of lifelike rubber skin, movable arms and legs. Heads turn and tilt. Glass-like go-to-sleep eyes with real lashes. Luxurious outfits of assorted fine quality fabrics, carefully sewn and finished. Rayon socks, imitation leather shoes. (Cinderella wears no socks.)

Wendy Ann with Human Hair Wig

[A] You can comb or set her lovely human hair. Rayon dress, ruffle skirt, flower, lace trim. Rayon half slip, panties. Wts. 1 lb. 6 oz., 1 lb. 12 oz. **$8.95** 14½-in. doll
49N3391–14½ in. tall..$8.95
49N3392–17½ in. tall..10.95

Famous Amy of "Little Women"

[B] Rayon dress has contrasting collar and sleeves, velvet belt. Ribbons in blonde shiny yarn wig match belt. Lace trimmed half slip has stiff hem to fluff skirt. Cotton pantalets. **$7.98** 14-in. doll
49N3361–Wt.1 lb.8 oz. $7.98

Poor Cinderella in Kitchen Dress

[C] Wears cotton peasant costume with patched skirt. Contrasting apron and kerchief, lace-trimmed cotton panties. Net keeps shiny yarn wig neat. Old-fashioned broom. Wt. 1 lb. 4 oz. **$6.98** 14-in. doll
49N3340–14-in. tall..... $6.98

Squeeze Her Body She cries Ma-ma!

[D] Soft latex rubber skin body. Lace-trimmed rayon dress; cotton half slip, panties. Bonnet is trimmed with lace and flowers. Plastic head, molded, tinted hair. 16 in. tall. **$7.69** 16-in. doll
49N3697–Shpg.wt.2 lbs.. $7.69

Big value Girl Dolls

[E] **Outdoor girl** . . . dressed to frolic in the sun. Wears cotton play dress (asst'd styles), matching bonnet with wide brim, ribbon tie. Rayon socks, imitation leather shoes. Composition body; tinted hair. Jointed arms, legs . . . head turns, tilts. Sleeping glass eyes with real lashes. **$2.98** 16½-in. doll
49 N 3548—Shipping weight 2 lbs.... $2.98

[F] **Majorette Doll.** Leads the parade with her snappy uniform, wood baton. Red skirt and visored cap with plume, gold color trim. Cotton blouse. Cotton panties. Rayon socks, imitation leather shoes. Molded plastic arms, head, legs are jointed. Sleeping eyes. **$3.29** 12-in. doll
49 N 3327—Shipping wt. 1 lb...... $3.29

This pert 16-inch charmer has 6 stylish outfits

[1] 4-piece cotton snow suit. Trousers have knit cuffs, jumper has plaid front. Cap, plastic belt.

[2] Floral organdy evening gown with lace trimmed hem and collar. Sewed-on organdy half slip.

[3] Cotton "shortie" coat with lace trimmed plaid collar, cord tie at neck. Cap with ribbon.

[4] Print cotton pajamas with lace trimmed front.

[5] Pert print cotton play suit with sun back ties around neck. 2 plastic hangers included.

[6] Wears rayon taffeta dress, cotton panties, rayon socks and imitation leather shoes.

Your little girl will have the best dressed "daughter" in the crowd when you give her this charming plastic doll . . . and every girl wants to have a dolly with lots of pretty clothes. This graceful doll comes complete with a 6-outfit wardrobe . . . has clothing for every occasion.

Party clothes, winter and summer play clothes and pajamas. Doll about 16 inches tall is made entirely of molded plastic with a lifelike rosy color . . . practically unbreakable. Arms and legs fully jointed, head turns, tilts. Wears ribbon bow in her lustrous, fine quality mohair wig. Sleeping eyes with real lashes. 49 N 3373—Shipping weight 2 pounds...... Doll, 6 outfits $8.95

$8.95 with 6 outfits

[1] [2] [3] [4] [5] [6]

He begs

He's an alert guard

Tail squeals when squeezed

Fully-jointed Pup with squealer tail

"Snuggles" is a bright-eyed, "well-trained" dog. He's always ready to do his many tricks . . . beg, sit up, play dead, "speak," shake hands or strike amusing poses. Legs are fully jointed—head moves. Two-tone rayon plush coat, softly stuffed with cotton. About 9½ inches long overall.
49 N 4074—Shpg. wt. 1 lb. .$2.89

$2.89

make soft, safe pets

NEW. Plush Lamb. This $1.79 lambkin will inspire a world of juvenile affection. His soft, cotton-back rayon plush coat is snowy white with black hoofs. Rayon ribbon collar has a tinkling bell. Has sewed-in button eyes. Assorted styles. About 9 in. tall.
49 N 4006—Shpg. wt. 14 oz. . . $1.79

PRICE CUT. Adorable Was $1.19 White Kitten. She'll be **$1.09** cherished by any child. Soft, cotton-stuffed body covered with rayon plush. Sewed-in, glass-like button eyes, whiskers, felt tongue. Ribbon collar with bell. About 6 inches long. Shpg. wt. 5 oz.
49 N 4003—Was $1.19 . . . Now $1.09

Friendly, plush-coated animal playmates—all improved

[A] **Gold-color fully-jointed bear.** $3.59 13½-inch *Now has American music box.* As handle is turned, merry chimes tinkle. Cotton-back rayon plush, cotton-stuffed. Shiny eyes. Wts. 1 lb. 12 oz., 2 lbs. 4 oz.
49 N 4376—13½-inch .$3.59
49 N 4377—16½-inch. 4.59

[B] **"Kuddles Kitten"—** $2.85 *now has squeaker voice added at last year's low price.* She's yearning to be your youngster's playmate. Fluffy, white mohair plush, cotton stuffed. Sparkling eyes, whiskers, ribbon bow. About 11 inches tall.
49 N 4015—Wt. 1 lb. . .$2.85

[C] **Sleepy Head Pup** $2.89 *—now has squeaker voice at no increase in price.* Sears exclusive. A fine companion for a quiet rest. Cotton-back rayon plush . . . cotton-stuffed. Felt nose, eyes and tongue. Head turns. About 12 in. long.
49 N 4066—Wt. 1 lb. . . $2.89

PRICE CUT! Plush Horsie . . easy to ride, steer

● Handsome, two-tone plush coat . . . New, felt-lined open mouth Was $8.95
● He holds up to 100 pounds . . . takes plenty of punishment
● Mounted on strong steel frame—rubber-tired steel disc wheels **$8.45**

This frisky horse is saddled and bridled . . . ready to be ridden by his lucky owner on Christmas morning. You can guide him in any direction . . . to the left, right or around in circles . . . by turning shaped wood handle. He's docile when led by the reins, too. Strong, husky body; cotton-back, rayon plush coat. Stuffed with cotton and excelsior. Imitation leather saddle, 13 in. from floor; metal stirrups. Your youngster will find him "good-natured" and easy to handle.
79 N 04366—18x9¾x21 in. high overall. Shpg. wt. 8 lbs. $8.45

This lovable Sleepy-head Doll makes baby's naps more pleasant . . . her play hours happier

She's very soft, with a sweet face that will make her baby's favorite play and crib companion. Kitten-smooth, cotton-back rayon plush in pastel colors, stuffed with cotton. Rosy face of easy-to-clean plastic, painted features. Cotton yarn ringlets.

$2.87 14½-in. size

Zipper-pocket Sleepy-head 16½-inch Doll. Pocket in back for holding hankies, etc.
49 N 3528—Shpg. wt. 1 lb. 8 oz. $4.79

Sleepy-head Doll without pocket. 14½-in. size.
49N3527—Wt. 1 lb. $2.87

Large-size doll has 5-inch zipper pocket

PRICE CUT!
Was $3.89
$2.94
13-in.

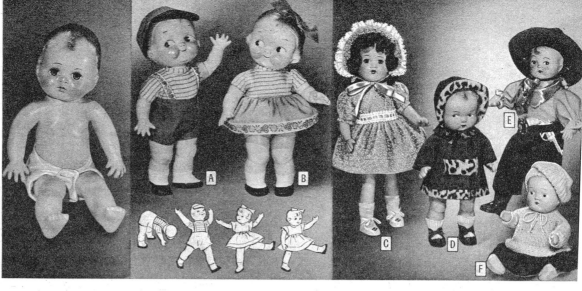

Bundles of Joy..Low Priced Dolls

Diaper Baby with go-to-sleep eyes, jointed arms and legs. *Priced far lower than a year ago!* Practically unbreakable plastic head; realistic molded facial features. Drinks from bottle, wets diaper. Flesh-like molded rubber body, arms and legs—washable, unbreakable. Head turns.
$2.94
13-in. size
49 N 3611—13-in. doll. Shpg. wt. 2 lbs. 8 oz. (*Was $3.89*)...$2.94
49 N 3612—15-in. doll. Shpg. wt. 3 lbs. (*Was $4.89*).......$3.89

NEW "Baby Gurglee." **$1.99** Squeeze her plump body or her dimpled legs—she'll sigh or sob. She has plastic head which turns, go-to-sleep glass-like eyes and long lashes. Washable rubber-skin body, arms and legs are all one piece, stuffed with cotton and foam rubber. 13 in. tall. Shpg. wt. 1 lb.
49 N 3089.........$1.99

The Campbell Kids in person! **$2.49** These saucy, captivating imps stepped right out of the Campbell soup ads—ready to win your heart with their coy painted eyes and rosy apple cheeks. Stand without support . . . take dozens of lively poses, to the endless delight of every child. Durable composition; jointed arms and legs; turning, tilting heads. Pert bobbed hair is molded, tinted composition; socks and shoes painted on. Dressed in colorful cotton. 12¼ inches tall. Shpg. wt. each 2 lbs.
A **Campbell Boy** 49 N 3430—$2.49
B **Campbell Girl** 49 N 3431—$2.49

C **Big Sister.** **$2.59** Composition. Tilting head, go-to-sleep eyes. Curly mohair wig. Arms, legs move. Cotton dress, bonnet, undies. Shpg. wt. 1 lb. 8 oz. 49 N 3321—15 in. tall..$2.59

E **Cowboy.** **$1.79** Composition head, arms; stuffed body. Cotton outfit, metal gun, plastic boots. Wt. 1 lb. 4 oz. 49 N 3315—14 in. tall..$1.79

D **Toddler.** **$1.37** Composition. Stands alone; arms, legs move. Cotton flannel coat, leopard cloth trim; lovely bonnet. Shipping weight 1 pound.
49 N 3314—12½ in. tall..$1.37

F **8½-in. Baby.** **94c** Composition. Movable arms, legs; painted eyes. Knit cap, sweater; skirt, panties, bootees.
49 N 3311—Wt. 12 oz....94c

Doll Clothing

HOW TO ORDER: Measure doll from head to foot. On your order, state catalog number and length of doll in nearest even inches.

G **Coat Set for Baby Doll.** Coat and matching bonnet made of soft cotton flannel, prettily trimmed. Tasseled rayon cord tie. Shpg. wt. 6 oz.
Low as **$1.10**
49 N 3415—Size 10 to 13-in..$1.10
49 N 3416—Size 14 to 17-in.. 1.29
49 N 3417—Size 18 to 21-in.. 1.59

H **Dainty Dresses for Baby Doll.** Assorted styles, fabrics; charming lace or ribbon trim. On hangers—ready for dolly's wardrobe. Shpg. wt. ea. 6 oz.
Low as **59c**
49 N 3418—Size 10 to 13-in....59c
49 N 3419—Size 14 to 17-in.... 67c
49 N 3420—Size 18 to 21-in....79c

J **Snowsuit Set for Baby Doll.** 1-pc. rayon fleece suit has zipper front, snug knit anklets, all-around belt at waist, rayon cord at neck. Matching bonnet. Shpg. wt. 8 oz.
Low as **$1.45**
49 N 3423—Size 10 to 13-in.$1.45
49 N 3424—Size 14 to 17-in. 1.69

N **Evening Gown for Girl Doll.** Fine organdy print dress—hem, sleeves and neck trimmed in lace; ribbon sash. Includes long, lace-trimmed petticoat. Shpg. wt. 10 oz.
Low as **$2.47**
49 N 3447—Size 12 to 15-in. .$2.47
49 N 3448—Size 16 to 19-in. 2.77

P **4-pc. Roller-Skating Set for girl doll.** Striped cotton jersey shirt, slacks, matching bonnet. Doll-size skates attached to imitation leather shoes. Shpg. wt. 10 oz.
Low as **$1.47**
49 N 3451—Size 12 to 15-in. .$1.47
49 N 3452—Size 16 to 19-in.. 1.57

K **5-pc. Outfit for Baby Doll.** Cotton dress, bonnet, slip; rayon socks; imitation leather shoes. Shpg. wt. 8 oz.
Low as **$1.17**
49 N 3425—Size 10 to 13-in. .$1.17
49 N 3426—Size 14 to 17-in.. 1.45
49 N 3427—Size 18 to 21-in.. 1.94
49 N 3428—Size 22 to 25-in.. 2.14

L **Pajamas for Baby Doll.** On plastic hanger. Cuddly cotton flannel, floral design. Snug knit anklets to assure neat fit. Dolls sleep soundly in these! Shpg. wt. ea. 6 oz.
Low as **59c**
49 N 3421—Size 10 to 13-in....59c
49 N 3422—Size 14 to 17-in....73c

M **Corduroy Set for Baby Doll.** Full-gathered suspender skirt of velvety pin-wale corduroy; matching beret. Striped jersey shirt has ribbed neckband and wrists. On hanger. Shpg. wt. 8 oz.
Low as **$1.49**
49 N 3429—Size 10 to 13-in.$1.49
49 N 3433—Size 14 to 17-in. 1.79
49 N 3434—Size 18 to 21-in. 1.97

R **Carriage Cover Set.** 19x24-inch cover, pillow to match. Cotton; rayon ruffle; bow trim.
$1.79
49 N 3537—Shpg. wt. 1 lb. . .$1.79

S **Zippered Doll's Garment Bag.** Holds up to 8 doll outfits! Transparent plastic film. Cloth binding. Metal top frame, hook. 14x12x4 in.
49 N 3438—Shpg wt. 8 oz......89c

T **Doll Dress Hangers.** Made of plastic. Shpg. wt. set 6 oz.
8-pc. Set **43c**
49 N 3575.........Set of 8 for 43c

U **3-pc. Rain Outfit** for girl doll. Cotton plaid coat, bonnet, rubber boots. Shipping weight 1 lb.
Low as **$1.12**
49 N 3445—Size 12 to 15-in. .$1.12
49 N 3446—Size 16 to 19-in.. 1.37

The early Fifties brought a migration to the suburbs and new cities like Levittown were springing up on previously rural farms and ranches. Buying a new home in a shiny new community became the American Dream for millions of people, so it was not surprising that the 1951 Sears Christmas Wishbook showed numerous doll houses along with the dolls and teddy bears.

For just $7.98 a young girl could have the ultimate home for herself and miniature family. The De Luxe Colonial Doll House had five big rooms and 57 pieces of plastic furniture "including ironing board, iron and automatic dishwasher."

Most of these impressive and large tin lithographed doll houses were manufactured by the Marx Toy Company for Sears' Happi Time house brand. Marx was a major toy maker of the day, producing many items for Sears. The best remembered of these are Marx's electric trains and tin playsets, which usually included a lithographed building like a farm or fort, small human figures and various accessory items.

Dolls of note in the 1951 Wishbook were a 20-inch Howdy Doody ventriloquist's dummy and Sparkle Plenty, glamorous daughter of B.O. Plenty and Gravel Gertie of Dick Tracy fame.

Knickerbocker Toy Company offered one teddy bear along with a plush-coated kitten and puppy. The teddy bear "with squeaker voice" was available in either a 13 1/2-inch or 16-inch height.

Sears Christmas
Wishbook

1951

Low Priced Beginner's Doll House With Furniture

$3.39

- 5-room house is 19½ in. long, 9 in. wide, 15½ in. high overall
- 36-pieces of bright plastic furniture scaled to fit the doll house

Specially designed for little "beginner" homemakers to keep make-believe house.
Little girls . . . and, little boys, too, have loads of fun rearranging furniture to suit their fancy in this charming Colonial. Youthful homemakers prefer cozy, compact rooms and beautifully styled miniature furniture . . . just the right size. Order one today for the little girl or boy on your shopping list. Steel house has turned edges for safety. Colorfully lithographed exterior, interior . . . 2 fireplaces, gay curtains, rugs in every room, pictures . . . just like a real home. Living room has sofa, cocktail table, 2 arm chairs, radio, dining room, 4 chairs. Kitchen: refrigerator, sink, stove, table, 4 chairs. Bedroom: bed, vanity; bench, night table. Bathroom: tub, lavatory, toilet, hamper. Nursery: crib, training chair, play pen and others.
Shipped flat . . . easy to assemble without tools. Instructions included.
49 N 1459—Shipping weight 5 pounds. . . . . Complete set $3.39

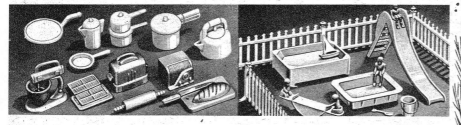

NEW.. Set of Doll House Appliances

89c

What could be more fun than playing with these miniature plastic appliances? Set of 16 includes toaster, waffle iron, bread board with knife, mixer, mixer bowl, radio, frying pan, coffee pot and cover, tea kettle, pressure cooker, double boiler, griddle, etc. Scaled to fit doll houses.
49 N 1467—Shipping wt. 6 oz. . . . Set of 16; 89c

Doll House Playground Set

95c

Her doll house isn't complete without a playground. Plastic wading pool actually holds water. Also, sail boat, plastic ladder-slide, teeter-totter, sand box, pail, shovel, 4 fence sections. 4 vinyl plastic dolls in set: boy, girl, 2 babies. 2½-in. high fence . . . other pieces in proportion.
49 N 1454—Shpg. wt. 1 lb. . . . Complete set 95c

Big Charm Craft Jewelry Kit

$2.29

Over 50 charms, colored plastic beads, clasps, plus jewelry chain, thread with which to make necklaces, bracelets, earrings, lapel pins and many other jewelry items. Attractive 14½x11½-inch box. Instructions included.
49 N 1207—Shpg. wt. 1 lb. 12 oz. $2.29

Gold-plated Lapel Pins

$1.00

Disney-design pins represent GLAMOUR to any little girl. Six sturdy pins all in gold plate with safety clasps. Mickey and Minnie Mouse, Pluto, Donald Duck, Practical Pig and Jiminy Cricket . . . each about 1½ inches tall. 8x5-inch box. Shipping weight 1 pound.
49 N 1308E—(20% Fed. Tax included) . . . $1.00

Special Value . . Doll House with Breezeway, Furniture, Baby Dolls, Cadillac-type Sedan

$4.99

- 5-room house with rumpus room; garage, sun deck
- Metal doll house is 38x9½x15½ inches high
- 53 pieces plastic furniture scaled to fit house

[A] Make this her happiest, proudest Christmas ever with a beautiful suburban style Colonial doll house. It's a gift loaded with play value . . . full of fun and excitement. She'll never tire of re-arranging furniture and playing with her doll family in this home of her own. Complete furnishings include: television set; piano; chaise lounge; juke box and ping pong table. Living room sofa is about 3⅝ in. long, other pieces in proportion. Interior is decorated with brightly lithographed draperies, rugs, fireplace, book shelves. Walt Disney characters on nursery wall; sports equipment in rumpus room; tools in garage. Outside is finished to represent stone and clapboard. Flower boxes, bright green shutters, decorate the windows. House and rumpus room are connected by breezeway with "flagstone" floor. Three little doll figures . . . boy, girl, and baby . . . are molded of flexible vinyl plastic. Sturdy construction features . . . floor sections are ribbed, walls double turned for extra strength. Has no rough edges to cut or scratch. A doll house promises long hours of play throughout the year. It's a toy that never goes out of date. Shipped flat; can be set up in just a few minutes, no tools needed.
79 N 01460—Shipping weight 8 lbs. . . . . Complete set $4.99

Completely Furnished Metal

Doll Houses..

De Luxe Colonial Doll House Now with 11 piece Utility Room Larger rooms and furniture

- 5 big rooms. House is 33½x12x18¾ inches high overall
- Special utility room . . . chuck full of modern appliances
- 57 pieces of large plastic furniture, scaled to fit house
- Colorful lithographed interior and exterior in vivid colors
- Sturdy metal house, safe turned-in edges, cut-out windows

[B] See how luxuriously this spacious, ultra-modern Colonial "manor" is furnished. 5 **$7.98** big rooms filled with 57 pieces of larger furniture, with extra-fine details. She'll thrill with pride as make-believe hostess in this Toy Town mansion . . . so beautifully decorated, so perfectly furnished . . . truly a little girl's dream home. New utility room fully equipped with laundry appliances . . . including ironing board, iron, automatic washer. And, she'll have grand fun decorating furniture with 27 decals. Sofa is 5¼ in. long, other pieces in proportion. Outside of whitewashed brick and clapboard; inside has colorful rugs, drapes, fireplace (all lithographed). Shipped flat . . . easy to set up. No tools needed.
79 N 01461—Shipping weight 12 lbs. . . . . Complete set $7.98

[C] **Plastic Carry-All and Make-believe Make-up Kit.** Thrilling gift for little girls who love to $1.29 imitate mother's make-up routine. Plastic set **Complete set** contains no actual cosmetics. Compact with mirror, eyebrow pencil, lipstick, memo pad with make-believe pencil, change purse, key holder, comb, earrings, ring and rouge case. Colorful carry-all kit with shoulder strap is about 2⅞x4⅞x3¼ in. high overall. Order one for the little girl on your shopping list.
49 N 1325—Shipping weight 8 oz. . . . . Complete set $1.29

[D] **Family of 8 Dolls for her Doll house** . . . molded **79c** in lifelike color. Playing "make-believe" house is loads more fun with a real doll family. Father is **Set of 8** 3¼ inches tall, other dolls in proportion. Molded of flexible, soft vinyl plastic in realistic sitting and standing positions. Fit furniture above and any standard-size doll house.
49 N 1468—Shipping weight 6 oz. . . . . Set of 8; 79c

[E] **NEW.. 3 Electric Doll House Lamps** . . that really **83c** light. Add to the play value of her doll house with these decorative plastic table lamps. Just give **Set of 3** a slight twist and they light up. Bases and shades in assorted styles; various color combinations (no choice). Flash light bulbs and batteries included. Lamps are 2½ inches high; diameter of shades 1½ inches.
49 N 1466—Shipping weight 6 oz. . . . . Set of 3; 83c

A $4.99

with rooms full of year round fun!

B $7.98

C Plastic Toy Make-up Kit $1.29

D Plastic Doll Family 79c

E Set of 3 Toy Lamps That Really Light 3 for 83c

POPULAR DOLLS .. moderately priced

[A] **Tiny Baby** is only 11½ inches tall. Warm, cuddly body is all composition. Has jointed arms, legs, wears fleecy snowsuit and cap. $1.45
49 N 3305—Shpg. wt. 10 oz........$1.45

[B] **Big Sister.** 15 inches tall. Go-to-sleep glassene eyes; curly mohair wig. Fully jointed composition body. Rayon dress; asst'd. styles. $3.32
49 N 3320—Shpg. wt. 1 lb. 8 oz.....$3.32

[C] **Toddler.** $1.75 All composition. Stands; arms, legs move. Rayon coat, bonnet; cotton dress; diaper, shoes. Wt. 1 lb.
49N3304—12½ in. tall.$1.75

[D] **Cowboy.** $1.99 Composition head, arms. Cotton-stuffed body. Head turns, rattles. Cotton outfit; tiny gun. Wt. 1 lb. 4 oz.
49 N 3315—14 in. tall $1.99

[E] **Saucy Sally Lou.** Press $3.29 soft rubber-skin body; she cries. Plastic head; go-to-sleep eyes. Bright cotton jersey outfit. Wt. 2 lbs.
49 N 3024—14 in. tall . . $3.29

Beautiful Dolls

17-inch Curlyhead Wears Coat . . . $5.45 ready to "go bye-bye." She has pretty mohair curls, sleep-or-wake glassene eyes, lashes. Open mouth shows teeth, tongue. Hard-to-break plastic head turns. Rubber skin arms and legs; cotton-stuffed body. Crying voice. Wears lustrous rayon satin coat and bonnet, sheer cotton dress, slip, rubber pants, cotton socks, imitation leather shoes.
49 N 3140—Shpg. wt. 1 lb. 8 oz...$5.45

16-inch Curlyhead Baby. $3.99 Sweet face framed with shining mohair curls. Turning plastic head is practically unbreakable; has sparkling go-to-sleep glassene eyes, thick lashes. Soft, flesh-like rubber skin arms and legs; plump cotton-stuffed body. Rubber panties, filmy organdy dress with lace trim, matching ruffled bonnet, cotton slip, socks, imitation leather shoes. Crying voice.
49 N 3135—Shpg. wt. 1 lb. 8 oz. . . $3.99

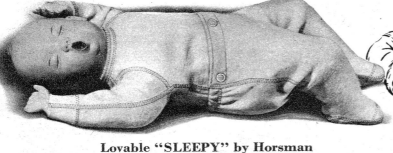

Lovable "SLEEPY" by Horsman

Youngsters aren't likely to object to nap-time if they can take "Sleepy" along. Snuggly soft body stuffed with cotton; head and arms are vinyl plastic . . . washable, pliable, practically unbreakable! Sleeps peacefully on her tummy; cries when flipped over on her back. Washable, removable, cotton-knit sleeper with Gripper Fasteners. $5.89 17-inch
49 N 3637—17-in. Shpg. wt. 2 lbs. $5.89   49 N 3649—21-in. Shpg. wt. 2 lbs. 6 oz. $7.85

Bright, go-to-sleep eyes with lashes

Tilt her body and she cries softly

Life-like rubber skin arms and legs

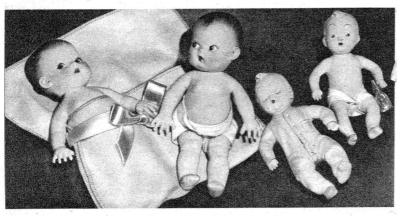

Littlest of all our Baby Dolls .. little prices, too

Pete and Repete Twins. A mere 9¼ in. tall. Turning heads; Magic Skin rubber bodies. Squeeze them and hear them cry. Each in diaper. Fleecy outer blanket, bow trim.
49N3607—Shpg. wt. 1 lb. $2.93

Adorable Sleepy-Baby. She whistles when she's squeezed. Molded of washable rubber. About 10½ inches tall. Shpg. wt. 12 oz.
49 N 3004........$1.15

Diaper Baby. Drinks from her bottle; wets her diaper. Squeeze her, she whistles. Soft rubber. 10 inches tall. Shipping wt. 12 oz.
49 N 3602........$1.19

BARGAIN .. 24-inch Crying Baby .. 2 styles

If your little girl's notes to Santa specify "A great big doll, please", here's just the doll for her. She's a large, lovable armful for any child . . . and amazingly low priced, considering how nicely she's made. She has *glossy mohair curls* . . . and her shining glassene eyes close for sleep. She cries softly when you lay her down. Easy-to-wash rubber skin arms and legs; soft cotton-stuffed body. Plastic turning head is very nearly unbreakable; has finely molded features. Wears: Rubber panties, dainty dress with lace trim, matching bonnet, cotton slip, rayon socks and imitation leather shoes. $6.88 With wig

79 N 03183—With mohair wig. Sheer Ninon dress.
Shipping weight 4 pounds.....$6.88

79 N 03182—With molded hair. Organdy dress.
Shipping weight 4 pounds...$5.85

SHE SHEDS BIG TEARS like a real, live baby

SHE BLOWS BUBBLES when playtime comes

SHE TAKES BATHS in water up to her neck!

27-inch "Sweetie Pie" . . 2 styles

She's a dimpled coquette with tousle wig to brush. She cries when you lay her down. Her lustrous glassene eyes are fringed with long lashes, and they close for sleep. What's more, her lamb's wool hair can be combed and brushed! Her turning, tilting head is hard-to-break plastic; teeth and tongue show. Arms and legs are soft vinyl plastic; body cotton-stuffed, jointed arms. Wears rayon taffeta dress, bonnet and panties; rayon socks, imitation leather shoes. A doll that any little girl would be thrilled to find under her Christmas tree.

$14.95
With fur wig

With tousle wig (Lamb's wool).
79 N 03299—Shpg. wt. 7 lbs. $14.95

With molded hair (no wig).
79 N 03298—Shpg. wt. 6 lbs. . . $12.89

"Tiny Tears" with layette and carrying case . . 2 styles

Big wet tears well up in her eyes and roll down her cheeks. Not only can you **see** and **hear** her crying lustily . . . she also sleeps, drinks her bottle, wets her diaper, blows bubbles with her tiny bubble pipe . . . and bathes like a real infant. Turning plastic head is hard to break; glassene eyes have thick lashes. Body, jointed arms, legs are molded rubber, 11½ inches tall. Wears knit shirt, panties. **Layette includes** sheer cotton dress, bonnet, cotton slip, diaper, bootees, soap, wash cloth, sponge, bottle, bubble pipe, Kleenex, cardboard case with handle.

$9.49
With fur wig

Deluxe has tousled Fur Wig (lambs wool really). Can be combed and brushed. Added flannelette robe in Layette.
49 N 3017—Shpg. wt. 3 lbs. 3 oz. $9.49

With molded hair. Has Layette and all the features described above (no robe); smaller case.
49 N 3014—Shpg. wt. 2 lbs. 10 oz. . . . $7.29

Charming Tousle-Head

Her hair is a mop of soft fur (lambs wool, really) . . . and it's forever in need of a good combing. She's ready for you to do it, too . . . has her own plastic brush, comb and mirror handy. But she'll cry if you so much as squeeze her body or legs. Chubby rubber-skin body is cotton and foam rubber stuffed; has jointed arms. Hard-to-break plastic head turns; glassene go-to-sleep eyes have thick, pretty lashes. Wears regular baby-style cotton knit shirt and pants. About 16 inches tall.

$4.98

49 N 3628—Shpg. wt. 1 lb. 12 oz. $4.98

Howdy Doody

Here's a freckled face that's familiar to all young TV fans. Lower jaw moves to simulate speech movements, like those of a ventriloquist's dummy. Sturdy plastic head turns; glassene eyes close for sleep. Soft body is cotton-stuffed; hands are vinyl plastic. Wears bright cotton bandana, plaid shirt, frontier pants, imitation cowboy boots and belt, elastic arm bands. Measures about 20 inches tall.

$7.49

49 N 3571—Shpg. wt. 2 lbs. $7.49

Sparkle Plenty

Glamorous daughter of B.O. Plenty and Gravel Gertie . . . with her long, gleaming blond "wig." She has a coo-type voice. Rubber-skin body is foam rubber stuffed; can be sponged off. Arms are jointed. Plastic head turns; has cotton, rayon yarn wig. Glassene go-to-sleep eyes with lashes. Wears cotton coveralls, rayon socks, imitation leather shoes. About 14 inches tall. (Copyright Chicago Tribune.)

$6.49

49 N 3015—Shpg. wt. 1 lb. 10 oz. . . $6.49

Newborn Bonny Braids

Cooing baby of Dick Tracy, Tess Truehart. Has 1 tooth, toothbrush. Turning vinyl head, 2 tufts washable, brushable Saran hair. Rubber-skin body, foam rubber stuffed; jointed arms. Rayon dressing sacque, organdy dress, cotton slip, diaper, boots. 14 in. (Copyright Chicago Tribune).

$6.69
14 in. size

49 N 3662—Shpg. wt. 2 lbs. $6.69

11 in. Bonny Braids (not shown). 1-pc. body. Blanket, undies, gown.
49 N 3659—Wt. 1 lb. 7 oz. $3.89

HAPPI·TIME
REG. U.S. PAT. OFF.

Miniature Dolls

NEW! 7½ inches tall
Go-to-sleep eyes with eyelashes

Dressed Dolls
$1⁷⁹ Each

TRULY EXQUISITE . . . gems to shine in any girl's doll collection. They're all plastic . . . with arms that move, heads that tilt and turn, glassene eyes that sleep! Every one stands alone. Shoes are painted on. All except nun, groom and cowboy have curly mohair wigs. Why not order a music box (H) along with the doll?

[A] **Cowboy.** Ready for round-up. Wears fringed imitation leather chaps, bright felt vest, bold-checked cotton shirt, big felt hat. Metal gun in holster.
49 N 3115—Shpg. wt.12oz.$1.79

[B] **Cowgirl.** Little Westerner all set for rodeo-time. In fringed imitation leather vest and skirt, cotton shirt, big felt cowgirl hat. Metal gun.
49 N 3116—Shpg. wt.12oz.$1.79

[C] **Nun.** Black rayon taffeta habit, soft black veil, white collar and headpiece. Silver colored metal crucifix on cord. Shpg. wt. 12 oz.
49 N 3114 . . . . $1.79

[D] **Mannequin.** Needs a complete wardrobe . . . for she comes without any clothes at all. Lots of fun to sew for! Dress any way you like.
49 N 3556—Shpg. wt. 5 oz..63c

[E] **Little Red Riding Hood.** On her way to visit grandmother. Flowing cape, hood attached; full-skirted rayon dress. Carries basket.
49 N 3104—Shpg.wt.12oz.$1.79

[F] **Bridegroom.** Handsome fellow in formal attire. Felt hat, striped trousers, "tails" and tie. White vest and shirt front. Gold color metal watch chain.
49 N 3102—Shpg.wt.12oz.$1.79

[G] **Bride.** Radiantly lovely in her traditional gown. It's white rayon satin, net trimmed; veil is net, too. Artificial orange blossom bouquet.
49 N 3101—Shpg.wt.12oz.$1.79

[H] **Imported Swiss Music Box.** Turntable revolves as music plays. Rubber attachment holds doll. Asstd. tunes. Plastic; 4¼-in. diam. base.
49 N 3094—Shpg. wt. 8 oz.$2.44

REVOLVING MUSIC BOX
[H] displays doll beautifully while music plays. Sold separately

Doll Clothing.. SMART STYLES

HOW TO ORDER: Doll clothes are sold according to height. Measure doll from head to foot. On your order, state catalog number and length of doll in nearest even inches

[J] **Coat Set for Baby Doll.** Coat and bonnet made of soft cottons. Shpg. wt. 6 oz.
Low as **$1.10**
49 N 3464—Size 10-11 in..$1.10
49 N 3465—Size 12-13 in.. 1.10
49 N 3466—Size 14-15 in.. 1.29
49 N 3467—Size 16-17 in.. 1.29
49 N 3468—Size 18-19 in.. 1.42
49 N 3469—Size 20-21 in.. 1.42

[K] **Baby Doll Layette.** Dress, slip, bonnet; socks, shoes. Shpg. wt. 8 oz.
Low as **$1.17**
49 N 3492—Size 10-11 in..$1.17
49 N 3493—Size 12-13 in.. 1.17
49 N 3494—Size 14-15 in.. 1.49
49 N 3495—Size 16-17 in.. 1.49
49 N 3496—Size 18-19 in.. 1.94
49 N 3497—Size 20-21 in.. 1.94
49 N 3498—Size 22-23 in.. 2.14
49 N 3499—Size 24-25 in.. 2.14

[L] **Dainty Dress for Baby Doll.** Assorted styles, assorted cotton fabrics . . . attractively trimmed. On hanger. Wt. 6 oz.
Low as **59c**
49 N 3402—Size 10-11 in. . .59c
49 N 3403—Size 12-13 in.. .59c
49 N 3404—Size 14-15 in.. .69c
49 N 3405—Size 16-17 in.. .69c
49 N 3406—Size 18-19 in.. .79c
49 N 3407—Size 20-21 in.. .79c

[M] **Pajamas for Baby Doll.** Cuddly, soft flannelette in neat floral design. Snug knit anklets assure good fit. Dolls sleep soundly in them! On plastic hangers. Shpg. wt. 6 oz.
Low as **59c**
49 N 3408—Size 10-11 in.. .59c
49 N 3409—Size 12-13 in.. .59c
49 N 3410—Size 14-15 in.. .77c
49 N 3411—Size 16-17 in.. .77c

[N] **Snowsuit Set for Baby Doll.** Rayon fleece suit, knit anklets, belt, tassel around neck. Matching bonnet. Shpg. wt. 8 oz.
Low as **$1.45**
49 N 3435—Size 10-11 in..$1.45
49 N 3436—Size 12-13 in.. 1.45
49 N 3437—Size 14-15 in.. 1.69
49 N 3438—Size 16-17 in.. 1.69

[P] **Corduroy Set for Baby Doll.** Suspender skirt made of velvety pinwale corduroy; matching beret. Striped jersey shirt. Shpg. wt. 8 oz.
Low as **$1.49**
49 N 3453—Size 10-11 in..$1.49
49 N 3454—Size 12-13 in.. 1.49
49 N 3455—Size 14-15 in.. 1.79
49 N 3456—Size 16-17 in.. 1.79
49 N 3457—Size 18-19 in.. 2.14
49 N 3458—Size 20-21 in.. 2.14

[R] **Evening Gown for Girl Doll.** Organdy dress, lawn slip. Shpg. wt. 10 oz.
Low as **$2.14**
49 N 3460—Size 12-13 in..$2.14
49 N 3461—Size 14-15 in.. 2.14
49 N 3462—Size 16-17 in.. 2.44
49 N 3463—Size 18-19 in.. 2.44

[S] **Layette for "newborn" Baby Doll.** Sheer cotton dress and bonnet, cotton slip, rayon socks, shoes. Wt. 10 oz.
Low as **$1.44**
49 N 3470—Size 10-11 in..$1.44
49 N 3471—Size 12-13 in.. 1.44
49 N 3472—Size 14-15 in.. 1.73
49 N 3473—Size 16-17 in.. 1.73

[T] **Doll's Garment Bag.** Transparent plastic. Hanger. Zipper. Metal top frame. 14x12x4 inches.
98c
49 N 3438—Shpg. wt. 8 oz . . .98c

[U] **Roller-Skating Set for Girl Doll.** Doll-size skates on imitation leather shoes. Slacks, matching bonnet; striped jersey shirt. Shpg. wt. 10 oz.
Low as **$1.37**
49 N 3440—Size 13-14 in..$1.37
49 N 3441—Size 15-16 in.. 1.37
49 N 3442—Size 17-18 in.. 1.57
49 N 3443—Size 19-20 in.. 1.57

[V] **Dude Ranch Outfit for Girl Doll.** Sun Valley overalls; gay cotton shirt; imitation leather play shoes. Shpg. wt. 6 oz.
Low as **$1.18**
49 N 3474—Size 14-15 in..$1.18
49 N 3475—Size 16-17 in.. 1.24
49 N 3476—Size 18-19 in.. 1.24

[W] **Hangers for Doll Dresses.** Made of plastic. Shpg. wt. 6 oz.
8 for 43c
49 N 3575—Set of 8

Buy everything you need for a happy holiday season on Sears Easy Terms . . . see page 313 for complete details

Plush horsie .. for young cowpokes to ride

- Glossy two-tone plush coat . . . cotton and excelsior stuffed
- Will hold up to 100 pounds, takes plenty of punishment
- Mounted on strong steel frame . . rubber tire steel disc wheels

$8.45

This horse will bring a sparkle to some youngster's eyes on Christmas morning. He's good-natured, easy to handle, and a star performer in all cow-puncher activities . . . stands up even under days of long, hard riding. He's docile when his young rider dismounts and leads him by the reins, too. Rubber-tired, steel disc wheels are easy rolling, sturdy. Cotton-backed rayon plush coat is soft and smooth to the touch . . . firmly stuffed with cotton and excelsior. Colorful, long-wearing plastic bridle, harness and reins. Durable imitation leather saddle is shaped for comfort. Sparkling eyes. Horse is 19x9¾x20 in. high overall. Metal stirrups. Height from saddle to floor 13 in.

79 N 04364—Horse on wheels. Shipping weight 8 lbs. $8.45

Our finest quality plush-coated Pets

[A] Gold-color jointed bear $2.99 13½-in. size
with squeaker voice climbs right into your toddler's heart, for every child loves a teddy bear. Cotton-back rayon plush. Cotton stuffed, fully jointed. Has a friendly face with bright, shiny eyes. Felt nose, yarn mouth.
49 N 4321—13½ inches high.
Shpg. wt. 1 lb. 8 oz.. . . . . $2.99
49 N 4322—16 inches high.
Shpg. wt. 1 lb. 14 oz.. . . . . $3.99

[B] "Mohair" Kitten. $2.89 An adorably soft little kitty with bright eyes and a squeaking voice that endears her to children. She's yearning to be your youngster's playmate. Fluffy, mohair plush, stuffed with cotton. Realistic whiskers, ribbon bow. Shpg. wt. 1 lb.
49N4015-11½ in. tall $2.89

[C] Sleepy-head Pup. $2.89 Perfect companion for sleepy-time hours. Makes naps more pleasant, play hours happier. Has a squeaker voice . . . cuddly as a real live puppy. Cotton-back rayon plush. Felt nose, eyes and tongue. Cotton stuffed. About 12 in. long.
49 N 4066—Wt. 1 lb. $2.89

Stuffed Animals

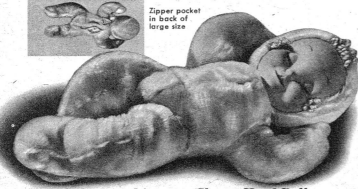

Zipper pocket in back of large size

Soft as a whisper .. Sleepy-Head Doll

Soft, lovable doll with an impish face to capture your heart. She'll be baby's favorite play, crib companion. Kitten-smooth, cotton-back rayon plush in pastel colors, stuffed with cotton. Rosy face of easy-to-clean plastic, painted features. Yarn ringlets.

$4.79 17-in. size

De luxe 17 in. Zipper-pocket Sleepy-head. Pocket in back to hold trinkets.
49 N 3528—Shpg. wt. 1 lb. 8 oz. $4.79

Sleepy-head doll without pocket. 15-inch size.
49N3527—Shpg. wt. 1 lb.. . $2.89

Jointed "Speaking" Dog

This cunning little pooch is a bright-eyed, well-trained dog. He speaks when his tail is squeezed and strikes all sorts of amusing poses. Legs are fully jointed and movable, head moves, too. Finest quality, two-tone cotton back rayon plush coat, stuffed with cotton. Plastic harness with bell and leash keeps him close to home. About 10 in. long.
49 N 4080—Wt. 1 lb. 10 oz.. $4.84

$4.84

Popular "cuddlers" for bedtime or playtime hours

[D] Leaping white plush $1.89
Lambkin—to inspire a world of juvenile affection. His soft cotton back rayon plush coat is snowy white—set off by jet black button eyes and feet. Legs can be bent to make him stand or sit. Tinkling bell attached to ribbon collar. Yarn nose, felt tongue. Cotton stuffing. 9 in. long. Wt. 14 oz.
49 N 4012. . . . . $1.89

[E] Adorable two-tone $1.37
kitten. She'll be cherished by any child. Soft, cotton-stuffed body covered with cotton back rayon plush. Expressive eyes, perky whiskers and felt tongue. Matching ribbon collar. Stands about 6 inches high—just right for a little child to cuddle and hug. Takes hard wear. Shipping wt. 8 oz.
49 N 4009. . . . . $1.37

[F] Circus Monkey. $3.59
Provides lots of fun for everyone. Legs, arms, tail, bend to any position . . . he can even *hang* by his tail. Cotton-back rayon plush. Cotton stuffed. He's gaily dressed . . . as though he just escaped from a circus. Colorful felt jacket and cap. Smiling face. Felt hands, feet. About 15 in. long.
49 N 4040—Wt. 1 lb. $3.59

NEW Vinyl Nose Bear and Panda, Amazingly Realistic

Two-tone Honey Bear. New vinyl plastic nose makes him look more lifelike than any toy bear we have ever seen. Soft and unbreakable. A playtime pal for your youngster to hug and pet. He'll take lots of rough treatment and never complain a bit. His bright eyes are safely anchored—and with his new plastic nose, he can almost smell! Cotton-back rayon plush coat in two-tone brown. Cotton stuffed. 12-inch size has stub feet; shaped feet on others.

$1.97
12-in.

49N4347—About 12 in. Shpg. wt. 1 lb..... $1.97
49N4348—About 15 in. Shpg. wt. 1 lb. 3 oz. 2.79
49N4349—About 19½ in. Shpg. wt. 3 lbs... 4.65

Squealer voice in tail. Irresistible Panda—a sure bet to win the heart of any child. A cuddly toy made to be hugged . . . the perfect crib companion or active playmate. His new nose and big black, friendly eyes make him just that much more wanted. His coat is cotton-back rayon plush with panda markings. Cotton stuffed to stand up under hard wear. The kind of toy that becomes more lovable with wear. 12-inch size has stub feet; shaped feet on others.

$2.14
12-in.

49N4380—About 12 in. Shpg. wt. 1 lb. 4 oz. $2.14
49N4381—About 15 in. Shpg. wt. 1 lb. 6 oz. 2.90
49N4382—About 17 in. Shpg. wt. 3 lbs..... 3.93

Make Lovable Pets

Fully Jointed GROWLING Teddy Bear

This roughish-looking fellow actually GROWLS—has lots of the same appeal that brings crowds out to see real bears at the zoo. He'll assume just about any pose you can imagine. Arms and legs are fully jointed, his head moves and he has a deep growler voice. Your tot will be delighted to see this new playmate under the tree on Christmas morning. He'll be a faithful companion . . . go anywhere and everywhere with your youngster, share his naps and playtime hours. His perky, friendly face has sparkling eyes and a plastic nose that looks almost real enough to twitch. Brown, cotton-back rayon plush coat . . . soft cotton stuffed makes him the most huggable, lovable animal you've seen in a long time.

$3.79
13½ in. tall

49 N 4352—About 13½ inches tall. Shpg. wt. 1 lb. 4 oz............ $3.79
49 N 4353—About 18 inches tall. Shpg. wt. 1 lb. 12 oz............. 5.79

NEW! "Twisty" Cat

$3.79

Here's a brand new twist in stuffed animals—an adorable plush cat that you can twist into hundreds of delightful poses. This versatile kitty will provide hours of amusement for the youngsters—and Mom and Dad will have fun, too. Has an impish look on his expressive vinyl plastic face—with big mischievous eyes. Two-tone cotton-back rayon plush with cotton covered multicolor striped tummy. A colorful pet for your tot's playroom or crib. About 17 inches tall.

49 N 4054—Shpg. wt. 2 lbs. 4 oz....... $3.79

Dear Santa: For Christmas this year I want a . . .

[A] Popular-priced Panda. Santa has many, many calls for this inexpensive little pet. Cotton-back rayon plush "coat" . . . cotton stuffed. Shiny eyes, plastic nose, yarn mouth, big rayon ribbon. White and black Panda markings. 12 inches tall.

$1.87

49 N 4360—Shipping weight 1 lb........ $1.87

[B] Swiss Music Box Bear. Has real imported Swiss music box in his cotton stuffed middle. Wind key in his back—he takes great pleasure in singing lullabys to little sleepy heads. Two-tone cotton-back rayon plush, bright eyes, plastic nose.

$4.78

49N4384—About 12 inches. Shpg. wt. 1 lb..$4.78

[C] Puppy-dog with turning head. In two vivid colors with painted eyes and nose. Cotton stuffed body. His coat is a plastic material. Washable—jam and jelly stains wipe off easily with a damp cloth—safe and sanitary for young children.

$1.45

49N4030—About 8½ in. high. Shpg. wt. 12 oz. $1.45

[D] Washable plastic fabric kitty. This kitty is just as practical as she is pretty for those baby smudges wash right off with a damp cloth. Made of Wataseal plastic fabric; soft cotton stuffed body. Painted eyes and mouth. Jingle bell on collar.

$1.09

49N4027—About 10 in. long. Shpg. wt. 8 oz. $1.09

Plush Puppy wants a home

$2.79

Here's just the sort of puppy every child wants. He has big soulful eyes—just yearning to be some lucky child's playmate. Thickset, two-tone cotton back rayon plush, plastic nose, felt tongue. Soft cotton stuffed body. Has a stubby little tail and floppy ears that fairly shout his urge to be friendly. Listens attentively to children's chatter—an all 'round companion. Sits about 10½ inches high.

49 N 4053—Shpg. wt. 2 lbs...... $2.79

Interest in dolls exploded in 1952. The Wishbook's pages were jammed with popular dolls from previous years and brand new franchises like Mary Hartline (based on the television character) and Betsy McCall ("replica of the famous McCall's Magazine mannequin") which would remain an extremely popular doll until the Barbie invasion of the 1960's.

The popular 14 1/2-inch Toni doll was featured prominently again this year, priced at $11.29. A 16-inch version could be had for $12.98. The catalog copy stated that "your little hairdresser can wash and permanently wave Toni's hair as often as she likes, yet it retains its lovely texture." Isn't it a shame that real hair didn't! Today, Toni dolls are very collectible. A Toni doll in excellent condition in the original box is worth $250 to $350.

Honey Walker, which was fully jointed and walked when guided, was sold in both 15-inch and 19-inch heights. This doll was made by the Effanbee Company, which is still in business today. In fact, based on collector interest the doll has been re-issued this year.

Other dolls of note in 1952 included the Campbell Kids, made famous by the soup company's TV commercials; Sara Lee, a "colored doll" designed "with the help of noted colored educators"; and Saucy Walker which was authorized by Dorothy Lamour.

Lots more teddy bears filled the 1952 Wishbook pages too. A bendable, growling teddy bear was available in either a 13 1/2-inch or 18-inch height.

Sears Christmas
Wishbook

1952

Give FAMOUS "TONI"—a Toni Permanent Wave

Toni is the queen among dolls. Her crowning glory is her soft, shining nylon hair; it's the finest quality doll wig we know of. Your little "hairdresser" can wash and "permanent wave" Toni's hair as often as she likes, yet it retains its lovely texture. Toni comes with a complete Play Wave Kit, containing Toni creme shampoo, play wave solution (harmless), curlers, comb, end-papers and directions. To make a refill for the play wave solution, mix 1 teaspoon of sugar with ⅓ cup water.

$11.29
14½-inch size

Toni's all plastic, so water won't harm her. She's practically unbreakable, too—a fascinating companion for active play. Jointed arms and legs move with lifelike grace. Head turns and tilts to all sorts of poses, just like a lovely little girl's. Sparkling go-to-sleep eyes are fringed with thick lashes. Wears richly-trimmed dress of fine cotton material (assorted styles). Includes a cotton half slip, panties, rayon socks, shoes to match her outfit.

49 N 3374—14½ inches tall Shipping weight 1 pound 14 ounces.................$11.29
49 N 3375—16 inches tall. Shipping weight 2 pounds 4 ounces....................12.98

"SAUCY WALKER" walks, sits and cries

Take Dolly by the hand, help her to walk, step by step, just like a real mother does in teaching her own baby. Sparkling glassene eyes have thick dark lashes .. and roll flirtatiously as she walks .. go to sleep when she's tired.

$14.79
22-inch size

Of rare quality .. she's fashioned completely of hard-to-break plastic .. perfectly shaped, from the tip of her cute little nose to the ends of her realistically formed fingers. Her head turns and tilts coyly, and her parted red lips reveal two tiny pearl-like teeth. Her glamorous long braids are of Saran hair that can actually be shampooed and set. It's soft, shining and manageable. Wears a colorful waffle-weave cotton pinafore with dainty lace-trimmed organdy blouse, cotton half slip, panties, rayon socks, vinyl plastic shoes. 3 doll curlers.

79 N 03397—De Luxe 22-inch Doll .. the most popular size (illustrated). Shipping weight 5 pounds...$14.79

49 N 3362— 16-inch Doll. Has features described; eyes go to sleep, do not roll. Shipping weight 3 pounds. $9.29

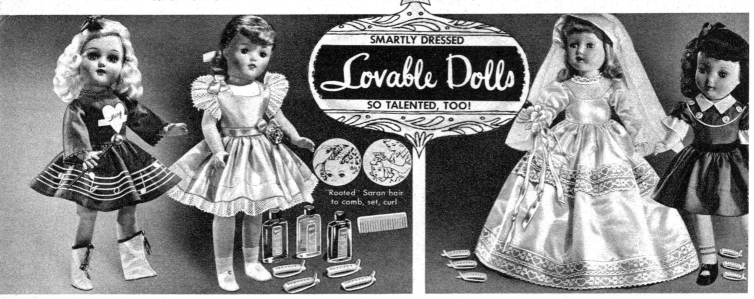

SMARTLY DRESSED *Lovable Dolls* **SO TALENTED, TOO!**

Mary Hartline. Lovely all plastic doll, dressed like the famous television star. She's 16 inches high, has jointed arms and legs, and turning head. Glamorous go-to-sleep eyes are edged with flattering lashes. Beautiful long blonde Saran wig. Smart majorette costume, complete with boots and baton. Doll hair curlers included.
$11.29
49 N 3357—Shpg. wt. 1 lb. 8 oz..$11.29

A Real Beauty with "rooted" Saran hair to wash, comb, and curl .. and a toy wave kit to keep it lovely. Washable plastic from head to toe .. head of realistic soft vinyl plastic. Dark lashes fringe her go-to-sleep eyes. Head turns, arms and legs are fully jointed. 18½ inches tall. Wears rayon dress, cotton half slip, panties, socks, and shoes. Kit of toy shampoo, tonic, lotion, curlers, bobbie pins, and comb.
$9.98
49 N 3335—Shpg. wt. 3 lbs......$9.98

All Plastic Bride Doll is radiantly lovely. Saran wig can actually be combed, brushed and curled. Her beautiful bridal gown is of white rayon satin and lace. Net veil, artificial flower. Panties, rayon socks, shoes. Go-to-sleep eyes have lashes. Movable head, arms and legs. Doll hair curlers included. Shpg. wt. 1 lb. 6 oz.
$4.99
49 N 3338—14 in. tall....$4.99

Betsy McCall Doll .. replica of the famous McCall's Magazine mannequin. She's made of plastic, and her legs are jointed. Her head and arms are of soft vinyl plastic, feel ever-so-lifelike. Lovely sparkling eyes close for sleep .. and are edged by long lashes. Wears a bright cotton dress, half slip, panties, rayon socks, and shoes. 14½ inches tall.
$7.49
Doll
49 N 3355—Shpg. wt. 1 lb. 4 oz.........$7.49
McCall Paper Patterns for two complete outfits, designed to fit Betsy McCall doll above.
49 N 3419—*Postpaid.* (Shpg. wt. 2 oz.)....70c

Saran Wigs on these three dolls can be combed, brushed, curled . . arranged in a variety of hairdos

Life-size "Sweetie Pie" . . 27 inches tall

A special purchase makes this great value possible . . similar doll with less costly fur wig sold for $14.95 last year. She's a dimpled coquette . . a real beauty with wonderful Saran wig to wash, comb, set. She cries when you lay her down, and her lustrous go-to-sleep glassene eyes have long lashes. Her turning, tilting head is hard-to-break plastic. Arms and legs are soft vinyl; body is cotton-stuffed, arms are jointed. Organdy dress, cotton undies. Fine quality shoes and socks, usually found only on costly dolls.

$995

79 N 03197—27 inches tall. Shipping weight 6 pounds. $9.95

89c **Rayve Toy Permanent Wave Kit.** Includes toy shampoo, curling solution and hair tonic, 6 soft plastic curlers, bobby pins, plastic comb and mirror on lid of box.

49 N 3543—Shpg. wt. 7 oz. 89c

New Lifelike Soft Vinyl Heads

Cute, cuddly Curlylocks has Saran hair to be washed, brushed, combed, and curled. She's irresistible to look at . . to care for! Head is soft, fleshlike vinyl plastic. Go-to-sleep glassene eyes have real lashes; open mouth reveals small tongue. Soft rubber-skin arms and legs; cloth-covered, cotton-stuffed body. Tilt her, and she cries. Wears organdy dress with buttons and bonnet, cotton slip, panties with lace, rayon socks, imitation leather shoes. Shpg. wt. 3 lbs.

$699

49 N 3171—About 20 inches tall . . .$6.99

This Baby Doll with soft vinyl head is a better-than-ever bargain this year . . she's 15% bigger, costs 15% less than in 1951. Her curly Saran wig can be brushed and curled. Soft vinyl face feels and pinches like a real baby; she coos when squeezed. Go-to-sleep eyes, head turns. Her body is soft washable rubber skin, arms are jointed. Wears dainty ninon dress, bonnet, cotton slip, panties, rayon socks, shoes. Shpg. wt. 3 lbs.

$589

49 N 3678—18 in. tall. $5.89

Fully jointed

Walks when guided

Sits by herself

Saran wig to comb, brush, curl

Turn crank . . Dolly dances in rhythm to music of your own record player or radio.

"Honey Walker" . . and a real honey she is, too! As she walks, her lovely head turns with each step. Sits without support. Her all plastic body is beautifully detailed, and her eyes close for sleep. Saran wig can be shampooed, waved and set, like any child's. Smartly costumed in ripplesheen dress with braid trim; matching panties, black patent snap shoes, rayon socks.

$9.49 **19-in. size**

49 N 3324—15 in. tall. Shpg. wt. 2 lbs. $7.49
49 N 3325—19 in. tall. Shpg. wt. 3 lbs. 9.49

New! Unique Arthur Murray Dancing Doll circles her revolving dance floor with graceful half turns, full turns, and whirls . . both left and right. Lovely detachable doll is unbreakable plastic with movable eyes. Saran wig can be washed and combed. Velveteen frock, slip, panties, evening shoes, stockings, lace gloves, evening bag. 12x12x5-in. sturdy decorated platform. Turn crank to operate. Shpg. wt. 10 lbs.

$15.95

79 N 03399—Doll is 14 in. tall. $15.95

Sister-Brother Duet have soft lifelike rubber skin bodies, cotton stuffed. Soft molded fleshlike vinyl head moves; coo-type voice.

$3.89 **Boy Doll**

49 N 3687—16 in. Boy Doll wears cotton blouse, gabardine pants, bow tie, sports jacket, socks, shoes. Shpg. wt. 2 lbs. $3.89

49 N 3688—19 in. Big Sister Doll wears percale dress with sheer pinafore, panties, socks, shoes. Shpg. wt. 3 lbs $4.89

Press legs or body—nod her head or press arms against body and she'll sob

Famous "Baby Coos" .. new low price!

Miss Popularity herself *is greatly improved, but her price is cut!* Baby Coos is more precious than ever . . . because she now has a soft vinyl plastic head . . . as well as warm, cuddly Magic rubber skin body, stuffed with cotton and foam rubber. Her sparkling go-to-sleep eyes have long lashes, and she coos when you cuddle her, cries and sobs when squeezed harder. She loves to be sponged clean, and although she wears only a sunsuit, she comes with a complete outfit including: pretty organdy dress, matching ribbon-tied bonnet, slip, diaper, booties, 2 safety pins, 3 powder puffs, 6 clothes pins, wash cloth and soap.

Was $5.79
$4.99

49 N 3041—14 inches tall. Shipping weight 1 pound 6 ounces $4.99

This Baby drinks, wets, cries, has Layette

$5.98

Lifelike and lovable . . . this Happi-Time Baby comes with complete layette and carrying case! She drinks from her bottle, wets her diaper . . . and of course she needs to be bathed, changed and powdered, just like any baby. When you squeeze her tummy, she cries. Practically unbreakable molded plastic head, with go-to-sleep glassene eyes and dark lashes. Body of flesh-like molded rubber with jointed arms and legs. Wears cotton diaper, and her layette includes: dainty organdy dress, matching bonnet, cotton slip, 2 diapers, 4 safety pins, shoes, socks, 6 clothes pins, 3 powder puffs, bottle and nipple. (Extra bottle and nipple are tied to baby's arm). All in handy cardboard carrying case, with plastic handle and metal clasp. Our large quantity purchase makes this low price possible.

49 N 3081—11¾ inches tall. Shipping weight 2 pounds 4 ounces $5.98

SHE WANTS ONE OF THESE
Baby Dolls
TO CUDDLE AND LOVE

Sparkle Plenty

New Low Price on famous comic strip baby. Long blonde yarn wig. Rubber-skin body, foam rubber stuffed. Arms, plastic head move. Coo-type voice, go-to-sleep eyes. Wears coveralls, socks, shoes. About 14 in. tall. (Copyright *Chicago Tribune*).Wt.1 lb.10 oz.

Now
$4.89

49 N 3015—Was $6.49 . . **$4.89**

Wee One Wets, Sleeps

Feed her from her bottle and she'll wet her diaper. Then tuck her in bed and she'll close her eyes for a nap. Though very young, she's already learned to sit alone. Her plastic head is almost impossible to break. Her body, arms and legs are soft, molded rubber . . . washable and almost unbreakable. Head turns, jointed arms and legs take all sorts of positions. Young tots will love to bathe and care for this lovable baby . . . she seems almost human. Shipping weight 3 pounds.

$3.25

49 N 3612—15½ inches tall **$3.25**

30-inch BABY COOS .. Biggest doll value in years

$8.79

She's always been a big bundle of joy . . . but now she's even more real, and three inches longer, with a soft life-like vinyl plastic head. *Sensationally low priced, too* (last year she was $12.98 and only 27 inches tall)! Can be dressed as Boy or Girl. This original undressed "Baby Coos" wears actual size baby clothes . . . size 6 to 12 months . . so dress her in your own tot's outgrown clothes . . or order the layette below.

Washable, soft, smooth Magic Skin rubber body, cotton and foam rubber stuffed, go-to-sleep eyes with lashes . . . baby-like coo-type voice.

79 N 03072—Doll only 30 inches tall. Shipping weight 7 pounds **$8.79**

Layette to fit "Baby Coos" above. Dressed in this outfit *last year, the 27-in. "Baby Coos" sold for $19.98* . . . now "Baby Coos" (above) and the layette are just $12.28. Layette includes: cotton trousers, tam, jacket, shirt, socks, leather baby shoes.

49 N 3418—Layette only. Shipping weight 1 pound **$3.49**

Happi-Time Baby with "rooted" hair

$7⁹⁸

She's the very newest in doll development—the most realistic ever, with miracle Saran hair rooted directly in her soft vinyl plastic head. Strands of Saran hair are securely anchored in her scalp, so it can actually be washed, combed, waved, curled and brushed over and over, just like any child's. She carries her own plastic comb, brush, mirror and curlers right with her, too!

Her large lustrous eyes, fringed with dark lashes, close for sleep when Dolly tires of play. Soft, huggable vinyl plastic head, body, arms and legs are washable; feel like a real baby . . . she coos when you squeeze her, too. Head turns, arms are jointed. Finely detailed knuckles, palm lines, etc. Dressed in dainty outfit of fine ninon and lace, huge hair bow, slip, knitted panties, new-style vinyl plastic shoes and rayon socks.

49 N 3620—18 inches tall. Shipping weight 3 pounds $7.98

"Tiny Tears" cries, wets, blows bubbles

$9⁴⁵
With fur wig

Big wet tears well up in her eyes and roll down her cheeks, and she'll need to be pacified, just as any baby does. She cries lustily . . . and she also sleeps, drinks her bottle when she's hungry, wets her diaper, blows bubbles at playtime with her tiny bubble pipe . . . and bathes like a real infant.

Her turning plastic head is hard to break; bright glassene go-to-sleep eyes are accented by silky lashes. Body, jointed arms, and legs are soft molded rubber. She wears a knit shirt and panties, but brings a layette including sheer organdy dress, bonnet, cotton slip, diaper, bootees, soap, wash cloth, sponge, bottle, bubble pipe, Kleenex.

De luxe has tousled fur wig to comb, brush and wash. Added robe in layette. 11½ in. tall. Cardboard carrying case. Shpg. wt. 3 lbs. 3 oz.
49 N 3032 . . . . $9.45

With Molded Hair but larger doll. Layette and all features described above (no robe). In cardboard box. 13½ inches tall. Shipping weight 3 pounds.
49 N 3031 . . . . $7.45

Tousle Head . . Jointed

$4.98

Her hair is a mop of soft fur . . . forever in need of a good combing. AND . . . this year she has fully jointed head, arms and legs, too, to make her more realistic than ever before. She brings her own plastic brush, comb, and mirror with her. She'll cry if you squeeze her. Chubby rubber skin body is cotton and foam rubber stuffed. Hard-to-break plastic head. Glassene go-to-sleep eyes have lashes. Wears knit shirt and pants. About 15 inches tall. Shpg. wt. 1 lb. 12 oz.
49 N 3623 . . . . $4.98

Famous Bonny Braids

$6.69

Cooing baby of Dick Tracy and Tess Truehart, comic strip characters. Has one tooth and toothbrush. Soft vinyl plastic head turns. Two tufts washable, brushable Saran hair. Rubber skin body, foam rubber stuffed; jointed arms. Rayon dressing sacque, organdy dress, cotton slip, diaper, boots. (Copyright Chicago Tribune.) Shipping weight 2 pounds.
49 N 3662—14 inches tall $6.69

11-inch Bonny Braids (not shown). Complete with blanket, undies, gown.
49 N 3659—Shpg. wt. 1 lb. 7 oz . . $3.79

Four Novelty Dolls . . amusing playmates

[A] **Dotty and Scottie.** 12½-in. all-plastic doll has sleeping eyes, Saran wig. Jointed head, arms, legs. Vinyl pique dress, panties, hooded rain cape, bootees. 6-in. black felt doggie has leash, cape. **$4.89**
49 N 3339—Doll has plastic stand. Shipping weight 1 lb . . . . Both for **$4.89**

New 10½-inch vinyl "character" dolls. Head and arms move. Wt. 1 lb.
[B] 49N3416—Girl wears dress, apron, undies, shoes. Basket, flowers. **$2.89**   [C] 49N3417—Boy wears shirt, pants, jacket, hat. **$2.89**

[D] **Crawling Bonny Braids.** Crawls on hands, knees like real baby. Molded plastic, flesh-colored. Tiny tufts of hair. Key-wind motor.
49 N 3506—12 inches long, 7¼ inches high. Shipping weight 1 lb . . **$2.89**

CUDDLY, LIFELIKE DOLLS WITH *Saran Hair*

- Saran Hair wigs sewn in layers .. easy to comb, brush, se
- Almost unbreakable plastic heads .. go-to-sleep eyes
- The biggest doll values we have offered in over 10 year

Here's an armful of baby that any little girl will love to cuddle. She's 22 inches of softness with such an appealing crying voice. Her cotton covered body is stuffed with soft cotton and her rubber skin arms and legs feel real as life . . . are easy to keep clean with a damp cloth. She wears a beautiful lace-trimmed ninon dress and bonnet, cotton slip, rubber panties, rayon socks, and artificial leather shoes.
79 N 03192—22-in. size. Shpg. wt. 4 lbs. . . $6.88

$6.88

A wonderful gift for any little girl and a wonderful buy, too . . . *in 2 sizes. Her washable all-Latex rubber skin feels so lifelike . . . is easy to keep clean, too.* She has a sweet coo voice and jointed arms. Wears a lace-trimmed ninon dress and bonnet, lace-trimmed panties, cotton slip, socks, artificial leather shoes. An outstanding value for an all-rubber skin doll.
49 N 3655—19-in. size.
Wt. 2 lbs. 8 oz. . . $5.98
79 N 03677—22-in. size.
Shpg. wt. 3 lbs. . . $7.79

$5.98
19-in. size

A 17-inch bundle of joy, with washable Latex skin, soft foam rubber stuffed body and appealing coo voice that will win her young "mother's" heart. And she's a low-priced special. She wears a ninon dress and bonnet; cotton slip and panties; rayon socks; artificial leather shoes.
49 N 3676—Shpg. wt. 2 lbs. . $4.98

$4.98

15 inches of sweet cuddly baby. She has a soft cotton-stuffed cotton c ered body, washable Latex a and legs. She cries when hold her up. Her head is alm unbreakable plastic. Wears ninon dress and bonnet, slip, panties, rayon socks, artificial leather shoes.
49 N 3232—Wt. 1 lb. 4 oz. . . . $3.79

$3.7♦

Pete and Repete

$2.79 Cuddly twins are just right for the littlest mother to hold. A mere 9¼ inches of soft, snuggly babies, with turning heads, Magic Skin rubber bodies. Squeeze them and they cry in a baby voice. Each in a soft diaper. Fleecy outer blanket with pretty bow trim.
49N3607—Shpg. wt. 1 lb. $2.79

New . . Drink Baby

$1.69 **All Vinyl Plastic Baby.** Wide-eyed adorable little baby is all ready for her dinner. 12 inches of lovable doll with unbreakable vinyl skin . . . feels so real and is easy to keep clean. She moves her arms and legs, too. Comes complete with flannelette diaper and bottle . . . ready for her new "mother" to love.
49N3613—Shpg.wt. 14 oz. $1.69

Campbell Kids

$2.99 This famous Camp-
Each bell duo are a pair of mischievous twins that steal your heart. Their all-vinyl plastic bodies feel so real; are easy to keep clean, too. They're 13 inches of impish charm with beautifully detailed faces, arms, legs; molded hair. Heads and arms are easily turned. Shpg. wt. ea. 1 lb. 2 oz.

A 49 N 3564—Chef in cotton outfit—apron, hat.. $2.99
B 49 N 3565—Girl wears cotton dress. $2.99
49 N 3568—Set of Boy and Girl. Wt. 2 lbs. 4 oz. $5.79

LITTLE DOLLS FOR LITTLE GIRLS
Priced so you can order several

C **Topsy Doll.** This new 12-inch doll has composition body, movable arms and legs. Her face has carefully painted details and she has the cutest yarn pigtails. Her pretty dress is made of cotton.
49 N 3414—Wt. 14 oz. . . . $1.09

$1.09

D **Tiny Baby** is only 12 inches tall. Realistic molded body is composition. Her jointed arms and legs are movable. She wears a soft, fleecy snow suit and cap. A wonderful surprise for your little girl.
49 N 3305—Wt. 10 oz. . . . $1.39

$1.39

E **Big Sister** is 15 inches tall, has go-to-sleep glassene eyes and a curly mohair wig. Composition body with movable arms, legs and head. She wears a pretty rayon dress . . . in assorted styles.
49 N 3320—Wt. 1 lb. 8 oz. $3.19

$3.19

F **Toddler** . . Has composition body. She stands alone, has movable arms and legs. Wears adorable dress and coat with bonnet of poodle cloth; diaper; imitation leather shoes. 12½ in. tall.
49N3303—Shpg. wt. 1 lb. $1.69

$1.69

G **Cowboy.** 14 inches of real western he-man. Has composition head and arms . . cotton-stuffed body. Head turns. Wears a colorful western outfit made of cotton. Has a tiny gun and plastic boots.
49N3315—Wt. 1 lb. 4 oz. $1.94

$1.94

H **Saucy Sally Lou.** 14 inches of perky little doll. Press her rubber-skin body and she cries. Plastic head; go-to-sleep eyes Bright cotton jersey outfi A cuddly doll to make you little girl happy.
49N3024—Shpg. wt. 2 lbs. $3

$3.19

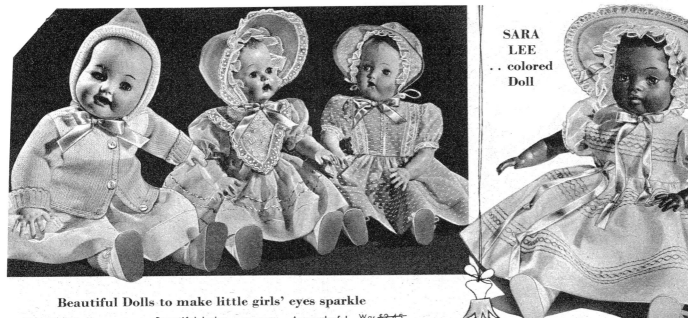

SARA LEE .. colored Doll

Beautiful Dolls to make little girls' eyes sparkle

Adorable 18-inch baby wears knitted jacket and bonnet made of soft wool, just waiting for her new "mother" to take her out. Her cuddly one-piece washable Latex rubber skin body is cotton stuffed. She has a soft, flesh-like vinyl plastic head and a sweet coo-type voice to make her a bundle of charm every little girl will love. She has sleeping eyes with long lashes and wears an organdy dress with slip and panties, rayon socks and artificial leather shoes. A wonderful Christmas surprise.
49 N 3632—Wt. 3 lbs... **$4.97**

Beautiful baby doll . . . *in two sizes.* This cuddly doll has washable Latex skin body, arms, legs. Her head is beautifully molded plastic, almost impossible to break; and she has a charming coo-type voice. Her go-to-sleep eyes have long lashes. Jointed arms and movable head. Wears lacy ninon dress, bonnet to match, cotton slip, panties, rayon socks, artificial leather shoes.
49 N 3621—14½-inch baby. Shpg. wt. 1 lb. 8 oz..... **$3.39**
49 N 3622—De luxe 17-in. Shpg. wt. 2 lbs........ **$4.49**

$3.39
14½-in. size

A wonderful value *just in time for Christmas giving.* This baby now has washable Latex arms and legs instead of composition arms, yet the price has been drastically cut. Her turning plastic head has go-to-sleep eyes. Soft, cloth covered body is cotton stuffed. She has crying voice. Wears sheer cotton dress and bonnet, rubber panties, rayon socks, artificial leather shoes. 15 inches tall. Shipping weight 1 pound 6 ounces.
49 N 3109 . *Was $2.45* **$1.98**

Was *$2.45*
$1.98

POPULAR-PRICED Dolls WITH MOLDED HAIR

Notice that the fine facial features are true to life. Sara Lee, with the help of noted colored educators, designed this new baby for youngsters who have always wanted to own a truly beautiful colored baby doll. She cries in a sweet baby voice when tilted, has go-to-sleep eyes. Her vinyl plastic head, arms and legs feel so lifelike. Cotton-stuffed body. She wears a pretty organdy dress, bonnet, undies, rayon socks, imitation leather shoes. About 18 in. tall. Shpg. wt. 2 lbs. 8 oz.
49 N 3273—*Was $6.89*............ **$5.99**

Was *$6.89*
$5.99

De luxe selection of DOLL CLOTHING for *your* dolls
Smart styles for every occasion . . accessories too!

HOW TO ORDER: Doll clothes are sold according to height. Measure doll from head to foot. On your order, state catalog number of size nearest height of your doll.

A **Coat Set for Baby Doll.** Coat and bonnet made of soft cottons. Shpg. wt. 6 oz.   Low as **$1.07**
49 N 3464—Size 10-11 in..$1.07
49 N 3465—Size 12-13 in.. 1.08
49 N 3466—Size 14-15 in.. 1.18
49 N 3467—Size 16-17 in.. 1.18
49 N 3468—Size 18-19 in.. 1.42
49 N 3469—Size 20-21 in.. 1.42

B **Baby Doll Layette.** Dress, slip, bonnet; socks, shoes. Shipping weight 8 oz.   Low as **$1.17**
49 N 3492—Size 10-11 in..$1.17
49 N 3493—Size 12-13 in.. 1.17
49 N 3494—Size 14-15 in.. 1.49
49 N 3495—Size 16-17 in.. 1.57
49 N 3496—Size 18-19 in.. 1.79
49 N 3497—Size 20-21 in.. 1.79
49 N 3498—Size 22-23 in.. 2.14
49 N 3499—Size 24-25 in.. 2.19

C **Dainty Dress for Baby Doll.** Assorted styles, assorted cotton fabrics . . . attractively trimmed. On hanger. Wt. 6 oz.   Low as **57c**
49 N 3402—Size 10-11 in.... 57c
49 N 3403—Size 12-13 in.... 59c
49 N 3404—Size 14-15 in.... 65c
49 N 3405—Size 16-17 in.... 65c
49 N 3406—Size 18-19 in.... 79c
49 N 3407—Size 20-21 in.... 84c

D **Pajamas for Baby Doll.** Cuddly, soft flannelette in neat floral design. Snug knit anklets assure good fit. Dolls sleep soundly in them! On plastic hangers. Shipping weight 6 oz.   Low as **57c**
49 N 3408—Size 10-11 in.... 57c
49 N 3409—Size 12-13 in.... 59c
49 N 3410—Size 14-15 in.... 69c
49 N 3411—Size 16-17 in.... 69c

E **Snowsuit Set for Baby Doll.** Rayon fleece suit, knit anklets, belt, tassel around neck. Matching bonnet. Shipping weight 8 oz.   Low as **$1.45**
49 N 3435—Size 10-11 in..$1.45
49 N 3436—Size 12-13 in.. 1.45
49 N 3437—Size 14-15 in.. 1.69
49 N 3439—Size 16-17 in.. 1.69

F **Corduroy Set for Baby Doll.** Suspender skirt made of velvety pinwale corduroy; matching beret. Striped jersey shirt. Shipping wt. 8 oz.   Low as **$1.39**
49 N 3453—Size 10-11 in..$1.39
49 N 3454—Size 12-13 in.. 1.45
49 N 3455—Size 14-15 in.. 1.61
49 N 3456—Size 16-17 in.. 1.61
49 N 3457—Size 18-19 in.. 1.98
49 N 3458—Size 20-21 in.. 1.98

G **Evening Gown for Girl Doll.** Organdy dress, lawn slip. Shpg. wt. 10 oz.   Low as **$1.98**
49 N 3460—Size 12-13 in..$1.98
49 N 3461—Size 14-15 in.. 1.98
49 N 3462—Size 16-17 in.. 2.47
49 N 3463—Size 18-19 in.. 2.47

H **Glamour Box by Mme. Alexander.** Plastic comb, mirror, lipstick, hairpins, curlers, etc. Plastic fiber braid for braided wig, chignon. Shipping weight 1 pound.   Was *$2.87* **$1.98**
49 N 3501—*Was $2.87*.... **$1.98**

J **Doll's Garment Bag.** Transparent plastic. Hanger. Metal top frame. 14x12x4 inches.   **89c**
49 N 3438—Shpg. wt. 8 oz... 89c

K **Roller-Skating Set for Girl Doll.** Skates on imitation leather shoes. Slacks, bonnet; jersey shirt. Wt. 10 oz.   Low as **$1.29**
49 N 3440—Size 13-14 in.$1.29
49 N 3441—Size 15-16 in.. 1.33
49 N 3442—Size 17-18 in.. 1.45
49 N 3443—Size 19-20 in.. 1.45

L **Dainty Girl Doll Dress.** Assorted styles, cotton fabrics. Hanger incl. Wt. 6 oz.   Low as **86c**
49 N 3596—Size 14-16 in...86c
49 N 3597—Size 17-18 in...98c
49 N 3598—Size 19-20 in.. $1.12

M **Hangers for Doll Dresses.** Made of plastic. Shpg. wt. 6 oz.   8 for **43c**
49 N 3575—Set of 8

Soft face

BETTY HUTTON, starring in a Paramount production, "Somebody Loves Me," color by Technicolor, says: "I can just hear these lovely dolls say 'Somebody loves me. Buy me for that sweet little somebody'".

I SAY 'MAMA-PAPA'

Wig to comb and brush

"Mama"-"Papa" Doll .. always a favorite child, now has a Saran wig and soft vinyl head

This famous HAPPI-TIME doll-baby is more irresistible than ever, because she now has a soft, natural-feeling vinyl plastic head .. AND .. a lustrous wig of Saran that can be combed, brushed and set .. time after time .. just like any child's. *Yet she still sells at last year's low price.* **$5.98**

Tilt her one way and she says "Mama" .. tilt her the other way and you'll hear an appealing "Papa." Her sparkling glassene go-to-sleep eyes are shadowed with long dark lashes. Her soft, warm vinyl arms, legs and head can be washed. They look and feel amazingly real .. with intricate lifelike details. Plump cotton-stuffed cotton body contains voice. She wears a dainty dress of fine quality ninon with a matching bonnet, and cotton petticoat, panties, imitation leather shoes and rayon socks. She is about 18 inches tall.

49 N 3187—Shipping weight 3 pounds....................................$5.98

Happi-Time "Teen-Ager" with new "rooted" hair

Rooted hair. Each Saran strand implanted into scalp of soft vinyl head like real hair. Easy to wash, comb, curl. Has endless play value.

$9.95 At long last .. a doll for the "little older" girl .. a teen-ager doll made entirely of soft huggable vinyl plastic. Her Saran hair (wash, comb, set it) actually comes through the scalp, looks realistically "rooted" .. is more permanent, can be set as desired. Her fleshlike head, body, arms and legs are so beautifully proportioned, so delicately detailed, so real feeling, she's like a portrait of the real-life girl next door. Her head turns, her arms and legs are jointed, and she's washable from head to toes.

She has large shining go-to-sleep eyes with long lashes. Wears a smart embossed cotton dress with dainty organdy pinafore, panties, plastic vinyl shoes and rayon sox. 21 in. high.

49 N 3367—Shpg. wt. 3 lbs...........$9.95

(A, B, C, D, E, ILLUSTRATED OPPOSITE PAGE)

Layette Baby with Magic Skin, Saran Wig

A She boasts a bigger-than-ever layette, as well as an improved carrying case with plastic handle, yet she *costs less than the 1951 price of $10.89!* Her cuddly soft Magic Skin rubber body, arms and legs feel just like a real baby .. and can be sponged clean, too! **$9.98**

Dolly's Saran wig can be dampened, combed, brushed and set, over and over again. She loves to be fondled and tells you so in her cooing voice. Her beautifully shaped plastic head is nearly unbreakable, and long dark lashes edge bright go-to-sleep glassene eyes that fairly sparkle with mischief. Baby wears a sunsuit, but she's ready for a long stay, as she brings with her a complete layette in a smart pigskin-grained paper carrying case. Her layette includes: organdy dress, bonnet, slip, diaper, shirt, artificial leather shoes, rayon socks, cotton flannel nightgown, wash cloth, powder puffs, safety pins, wooden clothes pins, rayon sacque.

49 N 3665—14-inch doll, layette, case. Shipping weight 4 lbs...........$9.98

Doll with 6 outfits, Saran wig, Rayve Toy Kit.

B *This little Happi-Time charmer has a different outfit for every occasion* .. play, party, etc. .. six of them, to make her the best dressed dolly in the neighborhood. And her hairdo can be arranged to suit the occasion .. and the outfit, too! *Her plastic fiber hair can be combed, dampened, brushed and set .. over and over.* **$8.99**

Her Rayve Kit includes Toy Wave, tonic and shampoo; bobbie pins, curlers and comb. Made of nearly unbreakable plastic, her body is jointed, and her head tilts and turns. Glassene eyes go to sleep.

She wears a skirt and blouse outfit, panties, socks, imitation leather shoes. Her additional wardrobe includes: 4-piece ski suit, trousers with knit anklets, plastic belt, cap, jacket. Evening gown with slip. Shortie coat, hat, pajamas. Cotton play suit, sunglasses, 2 hair nets.

49 N 3381—14-inch doll with 6 outfits. Shpg. wt. 2 lbs...................$8.99

14-in. Latex Skin Babies .. NOW with Vinyl Heads

Finely detailed soft vinyl head

Warm, lifelike Latex rubber skin

Clean her with soap and water

We're convinced these HAPPI-TIME Babies are the best doll values in over 10 years. From top to toe, they feel startlingly real, with soft lifelike vinyl heads and Latex rubber bodies that just beg for hugs. Delicate molded features are most realistic, from the pert little nose to the dainty shell-like ears. Bright, go-to-sleep glassene eyes are accented by silky dark lashes .. a squeeze brings forth a coo of delight. Each wears a charming outfit of lace-trimmed organdy dress and bonnet, with undies, rayon sox, artificial leather shoes. **$3.94** Molded hair

C **Better.** Has Saran wig to comb, brush, set. *Similar quality sold last year for $6.46.*
49 N 3648—Shpg. wt. 2 lbs.....$4.98

D **Good.** With molded hair. *Popularly priced,* so every little girl can own a Happi-Time Doll.
49 N 3636—Shpg. wt. 2 lbs.....$3.94

Our Best Happi-Time Babies have "rooted" hair

E The ultimate in doll realism. NOT just a glued-on wig, but Saran hair that is actually rooted to her scalp! In fact, it comes from inside her soft vinyl head, as realistically as any child's, with each strand securely anchored, so it can be washed, combed and curled.

Her head, arms and legs are of soft, warm lifelike vinyl plastic. Lustrous dark lashes edge her go-to-sleep glassene eyes. Cries softly when you tip her. Cotton-stuffed body is covered with washable Vinyl coated fabric. Wears dainty organdy dress, bonnet, slip, undies, imitation leather shoes, socks. 3 hair curlers.

49 N 3173—18-inch baby doll.
Shpg. wt. 2 lbs. 8 oz........$7.98

79 N 03180—22-inch baby doll.
Shpg. wt. 4 lbs.............$12.95

Beginner's Dolly

She's tiny and perfectly detailed .. just right for the littlest "mother." **$2.79** Washable plastic from head to toe .. and she brings her grooming needs right with her (doll-sized plastic hair brush, comb, mirror, 3 hair curlers, 3 bob pins). Her Saran hair can be combed, brushed and set. Go-to-sleep glassene eyes. Arms and legs jointed, head turns. Wears rayon dress, panties, shoes painted on. 10¾ inches tall.

49 N 3035—Shipping wt. 1 lb....$2.79

A $9⁹⁸

C $4⁹⁸

D $3⁹⁴

BIGGEST VALUES IN

HAPPI·TIME

REG. U.S. ——— PAT. OFF.

DOLLS IN OVER 10 YEARS

E $7⁹⁸
18-inch

B $8⁹⁹
Saran wig to comb,
brush and set

New "rooted" hair
can be washed, set

18-inch Happi-Time "Snoozie"

$5⁷⁹

Our Lullabye Baby now has bright glassene go-to-sleep eyes with dark silky lashes, yet she *costs less than her 1951 price of $5.89!* Soft vinyl plastic head, arms, legs and plump, cotton-covered, cotton-stuffed body. Crying voice. Flannel gown, diaper, blanket, bow. Painted hair.

49 N 3615—Shpg. wt.
2 lbs. 4 oz......$5.79

11½-inch Happi-Time "Snoozie"

Tiny new-born baby, so soft and sweet-looking she inspires a world of tender care. Rubber-skin body, cotton and foam rubber stuffed. Pliable vinyl plastic head; painted eyes. Jointed arms. Press her tummy and she cries. Flannelette wrapper, diaper, fleecy blanket, bow. 11½ in.

49 N 3609—Shipping
weight 14 oz......$2.79

$2⁷⁹

Fully jointed GROWLING Teddy Bear

New Low Price. This roguish-looking fellow actually GROWLS. He'll assume about any pose imaginable . . his arms and legs are fully jointed and his head turns. A faithful companion, he'll go anywhere and everywhere with your youngster . . share his naps and playtime hours. His perky, friendly face has sparkling eyes and a plastic nose that looks almost real enough to twitch. Brown, cotton-back rayon plush coat, soft cotton stuffed . . in fact, he's altogether a most huggable, lovable animal.

Was ~~$3.79~~
$298
13½-inch

49 N 4352—About 13½ in. Shpg. wt. 1 lb. 4 oz. *Was $3.79.* Now only $2.98
49 N 4353—About 18 in. Shpg. wt. 1 lb. 12 oz. *Was $5.79.* Now only 4.89

Realistic, soft vinyl-nose Bear and Panda

Two-tone Honey Bear with soft vinyl plastic nose, so life-like he can almost smell. He will take lots of rough treatment and never complain. His bright eyes are safely anchored. Cotton-back rayon plush coat in two-tone brown. Cotton stuffed. This year all sizes have shaped feet to make them more realistic than ever. Shipping weights: 1 lb.; 1 lb. 3 oz.; and 3 lbs.

$1.98
12-inch

49 N 4347—About 12 inches. $1.98
49 N 4348—About 15 inches. 2.79
49 N 4349—About 19½ inches. 4.75

Panda has squealer voice in tail. A cuddly toy, made to be hugged . . . his soft vinyl plastic nose and big black safely anchored eyes make him completely irresistible. Coat of cotton-back rayon plush has panda markings. Cotton stuffed. The kind of toy that becomes more lovable with wear, a most congenial companion for any small child. This year all sizes have shaped feet. Shipping weights: 1 lb. 4 oz.; and 1 lb. 6 oz.

$2.14
12-inch

49 N 4380—About 12 inches. $2.14
49 N 4381—About 15 inches. 2.90

Miniature Kitty

Fluffy handful of beauty, cuddled up begging for affection. Cotton-back rayon plush, stuffed with soft cotton. Glassene eyes are sewn in, yarn nose, saucy felt tongue, perky whiskers. About 7¼ inches long.

$1.37

49 N 4023—Shpg. wt. 8 oz. . $1.37

STUFFED
Animals
SOFT 'N CUDDLY

Plush Animals, plastic fabric Animals . . for little tots' nap and playtime

[A] **Popular-priced Panda.** Cotton-back rayon plush coat, cotton stuffed. Shiny eyes, plastic nose, yarn mouth, big rayon ribbon. White and black Panda markings. Who could ever resist him? He'll make a wonderful pet for your youngster. 12 inches tall.
$1.87
49 N 4360—Shpg. wt. 1 lb. . . $1.87

[B] **New washable plastic fabric Puppy**— looks eager for a playmate. Plastic covering on cotton-stuffed body. He's well-trained, too . . snap his heels together and he'll sit up. Soft plastic mask face, comical floppy ears, bell on cap. Clean with damp cloth. 10½ in. high.
98c
49 N 4018—Shpg. wt. 8 oz. . . 98c

[C] **New Washable Horse** is dashing, indeed. Coat is contrasting plastic fabric, plain and shirred, for a very realistic look. Painted features. Plastic "saddle," bell at neck. Firmly stuffed with cotton. Clean with damp cloth. 8½ inches high.
$1.57
49 N 4035—Shpg. wt. 8 oz. . . $1.57

[D] **Musical Bear has imported Swiss** music box in his cotton-stuffed middle. Wind key in back, he'll play a lullaby to little sleepy heads. Two-tone cotton-back rayon plush, bright eyes, plastic nose. About 12 inches tall. Shipping weight 1 pound.
$4.78
49 N 4384. . . . . $4.78

[E] **New Vinyl plastic head Kitty.** Soft, flexible head, excellent detail. Expressive, glassene eyes. Two-tone cotton-back rayon plush body, stuffed with cotton. A kitty children will cherish. About 9½ inches high.
$2.79
49 N 4051—Shpg. wt. 12 oz. . $2.79

[F] **New Twisty Poodle** loves to perform . . takes 1001 poses . . he has a wire frame body. Two-tone coat of cotton-back rayon plush. Safely anchored glassene eyes, plastic nose, neck ribbon. Cotton stuffed. 11 in. high.
$2.79
49 N 4050—Shpg. wt. 12 oz. . $2.79

"Saran Hair" was the big doll buzzword in the 1953 Wishbook. Plastic was still a young science in the early Fifties and it was found that it made excellent and inexpensive hair for dolls. Previously, mohair or human hair had been used. Vinyl, another plastic discovery, was used in more dolls too. Vinyl dolls lasted longer, as opposed to latex or rubber dolls which felt realistic but quickly rotted.

Popular Tiny Tears returned in 1953 in 11, 13 and 13 1/2-inch heights with prices ranging from $9.45 to $11.45. Tiny Tears "Cries lustily and also sleeps, drinks her bottle when she's hungry, wets her diaper, blows bubbles... and bathes like a real infant." All this and she was approved by NBC's "Ding Dong School", surely a major advertiser.

Bonny Braids, at 13 1/2-inch tall, was a popular doll of the day and remains a wanted collectible today. With vinyl head and ribboned braids, the doll sold for $7.49.

Interestingly, note that one doll was sold without clothes... ready to dress... and quite a catalog rarity. Doll accessories were becoming big sellers too. A young girl could choose from a variety of doll cases, strollers, clothes and cribs.

"Walt Disney's Own Peter Pan", based on the movie, sold for $4.78. This doll was only a hint of the flood of Disney doll products to come to the Wishbook's pages in future years.

Sears Christmas
Wishbook
1953

So pretty! So realistic!

Lovable Dolls

Your Christmas tot will be proud to "Baby" the Year 'Round

FOR A MERRY CHRISTMAS

A — $4.89
B — $3.39
C — $1.98
D — $4.97

Lovely long Saran "hair" to comb, brush, set.

$3.69 E
14-in.

F — $2.98
G — $1.45
H — $1.69
J — $2.79
K — $2.79

$3.95
$3.79

Molded Hair Babies are Budget-Priced!

A Adorable in a knitted jacket and bonnet of soft wool. Cherubic face of ever-so-soft vinyl. Latex rubber skin one-piece body is cotton stuffed. Soft cooing voice. Big go-to-sleep eyes. Wears an organdy dress, slip, panties, socks, shoes. 49N3631-17-in. Wt. 2 lbs. 4 oz. $4.89

B Pretty 14½ in. baby she'll be proud to own. Her tiny turned-up nose, sweet little mouth are really angelic . . . molded in durable plastic. Alert glassene eyes close in sleep. Head turns. Baby-soft Latex rubber skin is fun to keep clean. . . Cotton, sponge rubber stuffed body. Jointed arms. Soft "coo" voice. So pretty in a lace and embroidery trimmed ninon dress, bonnet, undies, shoes. 49N3621-14½ in. Wt. 2 lbs. . . $3.39

C A Bargain Value. 15 in. tall . . . washable Latex arms, legs. Turning plastic head, go-to-sleep eyes. Soft, cotton-stuffed cloth covered body. Crying voice. Sheer cotton dress, bonnet, undies, rayon socks, artificial leather shoes. 49 N 3109—Wt. 1 lb. 6 oz. . . $1.98

D A 23-inch bundle of charm that your "little mother" will really enjoy. Pretty, plastic head with tinted molded hair. She cries softly. Pug-nose and tiny mouth are really child-like, accented by wonder-wide eyes with lashes that open, close. Latex rubber skin arms, legs. Cotton covered, cotton stuffed body. Wears assorted style lacy ninon dress, bonnet. Undies, socks, shoes. 79 N 03191-23 in. Wt. 3 lbs. $4.97

Playmate to dress

E Ideal doll for church, school or sewing circle Christmas parties. She's a real beauty, with glossy Saran "hair" that can be dampened, brushed, set and combed in so many different ways! Sweet "little girl" face, body molded of sturdy plastic. Fully jointed. Lovely glassene eyes close at naptime. Fun to dress in the clothes you choose. Wears lace trimmed cotton panties, rayon socks, shoes. Weights: 14 in., 1 lb.; 16 in., 1 lb. 8 oz.; 18½ in., 2 pounds.
49 N 3316G—14-in. . $3.69
49 N 3318G—16-in. . . . 4.59
49 N 3322G—18½-in. . . 5.49

NOTICE: If you buy 12 or more you may deduct 10% from the prices shown on E

Cuddly Baby Dolls . . Eager for Tender Care

F Big Sister is 15 inches tall, has go-to-sleep glassene eyes and curly mohair wig. Composition body with movable arms, legs and head. She wears pretty rayon dress, assorted styles; undies, rayon socks, shoes. 49 N 3320—Shpg. wt. 1 lb. 8 oz. $2.98

G Soft Cuddles. Made of squeezable plastic vinylite. Jointed arms, legs. Bright big painted eyes. Easy to wash. Assorted styles. Squeaks. 49 N 3504—9-in. tall. Wt. 1 lb. . . . $1.45

H Drink and Wet Baby . . . Soft vinyl plastic. 11½ inches of lovable doll with unbreakable vinyl plastic skin . . . feels so real and is easy to keep clean. She moves her arms and legs too. Flannelette diaper and bottle. 49 N 3613—Shipping wt. 14 oz. . . . $1.69

J 11½ inch Happi-Time "Snoozie." Tiny soft and sweet new-born baby. Rubber-skin body, cotton and foam rubber stuffed. Pliable vinyl plastic head; painted eyes. Jointed arms. Press her tummy and she cries. Complete with flannelette wrapper, diaper, fleecy blanket. A real bundle of joy. 49 N 3609—Shipping weight 14 oz. $2.79

K Pete and Repete. Cuddly twins just right for littlest mother to hold. 9¼ inches of soft, snuggly babies, with turning heads, painted eyes, Magic Skin rubber bodies. Squeeze them and they cry in baby voice. Soft diapers. Fleecy outer blanket with pretty bow. 49 N 3607—Shipping weight 1 lb. . $2.79

Baby Boy and Girl for Family Fun!

16½ inch brother and sister make your family complete! Both designed with delicately featured baby-soft vinyl heads, pretty molded hair. Thick lashes fringe expressive glassene go-to-sleep eyes. One piece Latex rubber skin bodies are cotton stuffed . . . feel "almost-real." Easy to clean with damp cloth and fun to take care of. Heads turn. Stylishly dressed, socks and artificial leather shoes.
Baby Brother wears cotton twill pants, flannel jacket with Peter Pan collar. 49 N 3687—Wt. 2 lbs. . . . $3.79
Baby Sister wears lace and ribbon trimmed ninon dress, cotton undies. 49 N 3682—Wt. 2 lbs. . $3.95

$9⁹⁵

$7⁹⁸

$7⁹⁸

Hair rooted to scalp

Comb, brush, curl it over and over

HAPPI·TIME BABIES with Rooted DYNEL HAIR

• "Miracle Hair" . . . each strand securely implanted in soft vinyl head. Can be combed, brushed, set over and over. Keeps color, beauty. Won't tangle or mat.

• "Fairy Skin" . . . wonderfully lifelike vinyl plastic heads, arms and legs are baby-soft, fun to caress. Bright baby complexions glow with a natural, healthful vigor.

She's a 26-inch bundle of joy . . . and a sensational doll value. Just 18 inches last year, she's grown 8 inches and increased in cost by just $1.97. Soft allover vinyl skin and lustrous Dynel rooted hair make her a real beauty . . . and her beauty lasts with just a little tender care from "mom." Dark lashes fringe sparkling go-to-sleep eyes. Lovable vinyl body is fun to clean. Cotton stuffed. Head turns; arms jointed. Coo voice. So cute in lacy ninon dress, cotton slip, panties, socks, shoes.

79 N 03694—26 in. tall. Shpg. wt. 6 lbs........$9.95

The cutest rooted hair poodle cut you've ever seen flatters this sweet baby. And she's all set for sleepy-time, too, with an extra cotton-knit sleeper . . . worth $1.98 alone . . . included at no extra cost. Her pretty vinyl face, arms, and legs are carefully detailed, amazingly realistic. Cotton stuffed body is covered in plastic-coated cloth . . . easy to clean with a damp cloth. Big go-to-sleep glassene eyes have long lashes. Cries softly. Bright cotton two-piece romper suit, socks, shoes.

49 N 3689—21 in. tall. Shpg. wt. 3 lbs. 10 oz. Set $7.98

She's three inches taller! From 18 to 21 inches . . . yet not one penny added in price. A beautiful all-vinyl skin baby, with perfect "little girl" features . . . glowing allover complexion that keeps bright with a damp cloth, looks startlingly real. Coos lovingly when cuddled. Heavy lashes accent glassene eyes that close when she sleeps. Carries her own plastic comb, brush, mirror, and curlers to keep her lovely rooted Dynel hair well groomed. Movable arms. Dainty, lacy ninon dress, undies, shoes.

49 N 3630—21 in. tall. Shpg. wt. 3 lbs. 10 oz. . . . $7.98

Molded hair

Rooted hair

$4.69

$5.79

$7.89

$5.95

Adorable Tousle Head

Price Reduced. Her hair is a mop of soft fur . . . so much fun to groom with her own plastic comb, brush, and mirror. Her cotton and foam rubber stuffed body, arms and legs are soft rubber skin, so easy to clean. Coo voice. Pretty features molded in her hard-to-break plastic head. Go-to-sleep eyes. Wears cotton knit shirt, pants. About 16 in. tall.

49 N 3623—Wt. 2 lbs. *Was $4.98*. $4.69

Vinyl head . . Latex body

As big as a baby, as soft as a baby . . . and every bit as lovable. 26 in. tall, and coos when you cuddle her. Soft vinyl head with pert young features . . . lovely molded hair, bright glassene eyes that close. Latex rubber skin covers her arms, legs, and body . . . makes cleaning easy; feels "almost-real." Soft cotton stuffing, extra cuddly. Dressed in a rayon chemise.

79 N 03085—26 in. Wt. 6 lbs. . . . $5.79

Poodle cut "rooted" hair

Beautiful Saran hair curls riotously around her pretty face. Rooted in her vinyl head so it can be combed, brushed, curled time and again. She coos when cuddled. Pert features accented by big thick-lashed glassene eyes that sleep. Cotton stuffed rubber skin body cleans easily with damp cloth. Jointed arms, legs. Wears cotton diaper, plastic booties.

49 N 3663—20 in. Wt. 4 lbs. . . . $7.89

14-inch Miss with Layette

She's stunning when you dress her in a big felt picture hat, and organdy dress. Molded in hard-to-break plastic. Saran hair can be combed, brushed, set. In lace trimmed slip, socks, shoes. Layette includes blouse, skirt, organdy dress, matching bonnet, hat, panties, comb, brush, mirror, curlers.

49 N 3340—Shpg. wt. 2 lbs. 10 oz. Set $5.95

Was $9.95
NOW
$8⁸⁹
27-inch

$6⁸⁷
22-inch

$5⁸⁹
18-inch

Soft vinyl face

Lovable Lifelike Dolls with Saran Hair

- Saran wigs sewn in layers . . . to comb, brush, set
- Hard-to-break plastic heads . . . go-to-sleep eyes
- The biggest doll values we could find anywhere

27-inch life-size Sweetie Pie, now in taffeta dress, an unequaled value last year, now priced even lower! This baby-sized beauty has Saran hair to brush, comb, and set over and over. A delicately featured hard-to-break plastic head that tilts, turns. Mischievous glassene eyes close at naptime; are edged with thick lashes. Arms and legs are soft vinyl plastic; body cotton stuffed. Arms jointed. Crying voice. She wears a pretty rayon dress, matching undies, and real baby shoes usually found only on costly dolls. Thrill your little girl with sister-sized Sweetie Pie, offered for the last time at this extra low purchase price!
79 N 03197—Wt. 6 lbs. . . . *Was $9.95* $8.89

22 inches of ever-lovin' Baby . . . priced lower than any other doll of similar size and quality that we know of! Her Latex rubber skin arms, legs are warm and life-like; sponge clean with a damp cloth. Cuddly cotton covered body is stuffed with soft cotton. Winsome little crying voice. Adorably dressed in a lace-trimmed ninon dress and matching bonnet, cotton slip, rubber panties, rayon socks, artificial leather shoes.
79 N 03192—22 in. tall. Shpg. wt. 3 lbs. $6.87

Her Baby-soft vinyl plastic face and head make this Baby Doll ever so realistic! Delicate real-life features are framed by glossy fiber "hair" to brush, comb, set. Thick lashes edge big go-to-sleep glassene eyes. Latex rubber skin body is fun to clean. Head turns, arms are jointed. Coos when squeezed. Wears dainty ninon dress and bonnet, cotton slip, panties, socks, shoes, plastic curlers. A wonderful Christmas surprise.
49 N 3678—18 in. tall. Shpg. wt. 3 lbs. $5.89

Rayve Toy Permanent Wave Kit

Includes toy shampoo, curling solution and hair tonic. Six soft plastic curlers, bobby pins, plastic comb and mirror on lid of box. Months of busy after-Christmas fun with this grown-up kit.
49 N 3543—Shipping weight 7 ounces 89c

$7⁸⁹
17½-in.

Lovable 17½-in. all-vinyl plastic Baby Doll

Brand new . . . and as winsome as a baby can be! Glowing baby body, head, arms and legs are all-vinyl . . . soft to your touch, easy to wipe clean. Baby features are carefully molded to perfect proportions. Fully jointed body. Wonder-wide Glassene eyes that close. Pretty molded hair. A joy to "mother." Adorable in knitted shirt and panties. Layette includes pastel cotton romper, braid trim, matching sun bonnet, rayon socks, imitation leather shoes.
49 N 3082—17½ in. tall. Shipping weight 3 lbs. $7.89

288 . . SEARS, ROEBUCK AND CO. PCB

Soft vinyl heads

Ⓐ $5.98   Ⓑ $4.98

Permanent Molded hairdos on Vinyl heads . . 2 sizes

- New all-vinyl heads with permanent molded hair that looks "ever-so-real."
- All-Latex rubber skin bodies . . . soft and lifelike, cleans with damp cloth.

These new style vinyl head dolls, with amazingly detailed molded hair, are becoming more and more popular. Parents and tiny "moms" alike like their neat appearance, their fresh, permanent hairdos. Both have go-to-sleep glassene eyes, edged with thick lashes. Coo softly when cuddled. Soft cotton stuffed bodies with "wipe clean" latex skin. Wear perky cotton dresses, richly trimmed, undies, rayon socks and artificial leather shoes. Real little beauties and wonderful playmates for your young 'uns.

Ⓐ 49 N 3652—Popular 22-inch size, wearing colorful waffle pique dress. Wt. 4 lbs. $5.98

Ⓑ 49 N 3624—18-inch size. Lacy cotton dress. Wt. 3 lbs. $4.98

For a Merry Christmas

They cry or walk!

Action Dolls

with hair to comb . . . real-as-life features

- SHEDS BIG TEARS like a real baby
- SHE BLOWS BUBBLES at playtime
- SHE TAKES BATHS in neck-high water

A National Broadcasting Co., Inc. Service and Trademark

$3.79 15-in.
$4.98

Rooted Hair

Cuddly 15-inch Baby with Saran Hair

Gleaming curls of Saran hair frame a charming "tiny tot" face. Hair can be dampened, combed, brushed, set. Plastic head with big go-to-sleep glassene eyes. Soft Latex rubber skin arms, legs . . . cuddly cotton covered body, cotton stuffed. Head turns. Cries. In ninon dress, bonnet, undies, shoes.
49N3232-15-in.tall.Wt.1lb.8oz.$3.79

All-Latex Baby has Rooted Saran Hair

New low price for 17-in. Baby with shiny Saran Hair, rooted in soft vinyl head . . . as realistic as a child's. Thick-lashed glassene eyes that close. Latex rubber skin 1-pc. body, arms, legs, feel "almost-real." Cotton-stuffed . . . feels soft, cuddly. Cries. Picture-pretty in a lace trimmed ninon dress, undies, socks, shoes.
49 N 3650—17-in. Wt. 2 lbs.. $4.98

"Tiny Tears" cries, wets, and blows bubbles

Big wet tears well up in her eyes and roll down her cheeks, and she'll need to be pacified, just as any baby does. Cries lustily . . . and also sleeps, drinks her bottle when she's hungry, wets her diaper, blows bubbles at playtime with her bubble pipe . . . and bathes like a real infant.

$945 Deluxe doll with fur wig

Her turning plastic head is hard to break; bright glassene go-to-sleep eyes are accented by shiny lashes. Body, jointed arms, and legs are made of soft molded rubber. She wears a knit shirt and panties, but brings a layette that includes sheer organdy dress, bonnet, cotton slip, diaper, bootees, soap, wash cloth, sponge, bottle, tiny bubble pipe and Kleenex . . . all her "every-day" needs.

With Molded Hair but larger doll. Layette and all features described above (no robe). In cardboard box. 13½ in. tall. A favorite of the "little moms" everywhere. Shipping weight 3 lbs.
49 N 3031 . . . . $7.45

De luxe (illustrated) 11½ inches tall. Has tousled fur wig to comb, brush, and wash. Robe added in layette. Packed in handy cardboard carrying case. Shipping weight 3 pounds 3 ounces.
49 N 3032 . . . . $9.45

Our finest "tousled fur wig" Tiny Tears is 13-in. Has layette with all the features of the De luxe. Richly gift packaged in sturdy corrugated suitcase for hard play. Plastic handle. Wt. 5 lbs.
49 N 3037 . . . . $11.45

Pony Tail

Rooted Hair

Rooted Saran "Pony Tail"

Lovely 18 inch playmate with Saran hair in popular "Pony Tail" . . . rooted firmly to soft vinyl head. Can be dampened, combed, brushed, set time and again. Delicate features accented by thick-lashed go-to-sleep eyes. Fully jointed plastic body. Wears rich metallic trimmed rayon dress, undies, gold color metallic-effect shoes.

$9.79 18 in. tall

49 N 3363—18-in. tall. Wt. 3 lbs.. $9.79

Fully jointed

Walks with you

Sits by herself

Hair to comb

"Honey-Walker"

As she walks, her lovely head turns with each step. Sits without support. All plastic body is beautifully detailed, eyes close for sleep. Saran wig can be waved and set, like any child's. Smartly costumed in cotton dress, panties, black patent snap shoes, rayon socks. A mighty welcome surprise on Christmas morning!

$9.49 19-in. size

49N3324—14¼ in. tall. Shpg. wt. 2 lbs. $7.49
49N3325—19 in. tall. Shpg. wt. 3 lbs.. 9.49

14-in. Bridesmaid $4.99

14-in. Bride $4.99

Plastic 14 inch Bride and Bridesmaid

Fully jointed, almost unbreakable plastic bodies. Saran wigs you can comb, brush, and curl . . . wear panties, rayon socks, imitation leather shoes. Beautiful go-to-sleep glassene eyes with lashes. Plastic hair curlers are included. Both dolls 14 inches tall. Dressed in authentic wedding attire.

Bridesmaid Doll. A lovely member of the bride's wedding party . . . in pastel rayon taffeta dress with gold color metallic lace.
49N3351-Shpg. wt. 1 lb. 6 oz. $4.99

Bride Doll is radiantly lovely. Her beautiful bridal gown is of white rayon satin and lace. Net veil and artificial flower.
49 N 3338-Shpg. wt. 1 lb. 6 oz. $4.99

Says "Mama" "Papa".. Dynel Wig.. vinyl head

This famous 18 inch HAPPI-TIME doll-baby is more irresistible than ever because she now has a soft natural feeling vinyl plastic head . . . and a lustrous wig of Dynel hair to be combed, brushed, and set . . . time after time . . . just like any child's. Tilt her one way and she says "Mama" . . . tilt her the other way and you'll hear an appealing "Papa." Sparkling glassene go-to-sleep eyes are shadowed with long dark lashes. Soft, warm, vinyl arms, legs, and head can be wiped clean. They look and feel almost real; lifelike details. Plump cotton stuffed cotton body contains voice. She wears a lacy ninon dress and bonnet of fine quality. Cotton slip, diapers, socks, imitation leather shoes complete her outfit.
49 N 3187—18 inches tall. Shipping weight 3 lbs.........................$5.98

Price Cut on 22 inch Happi-Time "Rooted Hair" Baby

The ultimate in doll realism. NOT just a glued-on wig, but Saran hair that is actually rooted to her scalp as realistically as any child's, with each strand securely anchored, so it can be washed, combed and curled.

Her head, arms and legs are of soft, warm lifelike vinyl plastic. Lustrous dark lashes edge her go-to-sleep glassene eyes. Cries softly when you tip her. Cotton-stuffed body is covered with washable Vinyl coated fabric. Wears dainty, lacy organdy dress, bonnet, slip, undies, vinyl shoes, socks. 3 plastic curlers included.

49 N 3174—18-inch Baby.
Shipping weight
2 pounds 8 ounces........$7.98

79 N 03184—22-inch Baby with richer dress at an amazing price reduction!
Shipping wt. 4 lbs. *Was $12.95*......$9.89

Baby features, cuddly all-Latex skins make popular priced Happi-Time Babies "almost-real"!

Our Best: Almost as big as baby sister, and every bit as cute! Same real-life features as the popular Happi-Time baby at right. Washable all-Latex skin feels so lifelike. She has sweet coo voice. Finely molded plastic head is as bright as a button. Lustrous Saran hair to comb, brush, set. Fluffy lace-trimmed, flocked ninon dress, matching bonnet, undies, shoes, curlers.
49 N 3655—19 inches tall. Shipping weight 2 pounds 8 oz. $5.97
79 N 03677—22 inches tall. Shipping weight 3 pounds.... $7.89

Fine Quality: Gleaming Saran hair to set, comb, brush . . . a real Happi-Time quality baby. Tiny little features are carefully molded in her soft vinyl head. Latex rubber skin body is "warm-as-life," cotton and foam rubber stuffed, jointed arms, head turns. Coo voice. Go-to-sleep eyes. Wears lacy organdy dress, bonnet, undies, socks, shoes.
49 N 3648—14 inches tall. Wt. 1 lb. 10 oz.... $4.98

Good: Delicately detailed soft vinyl head has molded hair, sweet baby-like features. All-Latex rubber body, arms jointed, head turns. Easy to clean. Cotton and foam rubber stuffing makes her "oh-so-cuddly." Go-to-sleep glassene eyes, thick lashes. Coos with delight when squeezed. Wears lace-trimmed cotton dress, bonnet, undies, socks, shoes.
49 N 3636—14 in. tall. Shpg. wt. 1 lb. 8 oz. $3.89

21-inch Teen-Ager with "Rooted" Hair!

- Petal-soft vinyl plastic head
- Beautifully molded plastic body
- Rooted Dynel hair to brush, set

Hair rooted in soft vinyl head

Easy to comb and set in curls

She's a real teen-age friend . . . a perfect companion for the "little older" girl. Her "real-life" vinyl plastic face glows with a peaches-and-cream complexion. Thick-lashed glassene eyes close at naptime. Glossy Dynel "hair" is implanted in vinyl head . . . can be combed, brushed and set in curlers over and over. So perfectly proportioned, so delicately detailed, she's a picture of the little girl next door. Jointed arms, legs; movable head. Easy to clean. Wears embossed cotton dress, dainty pinafore, panties, rayon socks, stylish vinyl plastic shoes. Stands 21-inches tall.
49 N 3361—Shpg. wt. 3 lbs . . . $9.95

$9⁹⁵
21-inch

Active Young Happi-Time Walker

- Walks guided by your hand
- Saran braids to comb, set
- Made of hard-to-break plastic

Thick, glossy braids frame a sweet little face and sparkling eyes . . . a playmate your little girl will love at first sight. She'll love her rich Saran hair that can be dampened, set, combed in any style . . . yet stays lovely and manageable. She walks, too, and turns her pretty head coyly. Her hard-to-break plastic body has jointed arms, legs . . perfect "little girl" details. Thick-lashed eyes close in sleep. Wears a sheer ninon dress with flocking, lace trim. Underthings, vinyl plastic shoes.
49 N 3388—16-in. Wt. 2 lbs.$5.98
49 N 3389—19-in. De Luxe. Shipping weight 2 lbs. 6 oz. $7.95

$7⁹⁵
19-inch

Walks, turns head, sits

Hair to comb, set, brush

FOR A MERRY CHRISTMAS

HAPPI-TIME
Personality Dolls
Pert, popular playmates ..
a little girl's delight!

Walks when guided **Comb, curl hair**

New! Baby-Soft Vinyl Head, Saran Wig

Now! Our layette doll has an "almost-real" appearing vinyl plastic head . . . yet costs no more than last year! She's baby-soft all over . . . with cuddly Magic Skin body, arms and legs. Likes to be sponged clean . . . have her Saran "hair" always freshly set and combed. Coos with delight when cuddled. Thick-lashed glassene eyes close when she's tired. Dressed in a sunsuit, she's ready for a long stay . . . with her layette packed in a pigskin-effect fiberboard carrying case. Includes organdy dress, bonnet, slip, diaper, shirt, artificial leather shoes, socks, cotton flannel nightgown, wash cloth, powder puffs, safety pins, clothes pins, rayon sacque.
49 N 3666—14-inch Doll with large layette, case. Shpg. wt. 4 lbs. $9.98

$9⁹⁸
14-in. doll layette, case

Happi-Time Wardrobe Doll Now Also Walks!

Now she can walk! Guided by her mom's hand, she is as smart as any model. With 5 different outfits, she's ready for any occasion. Cotton play dress, formal party dress, shortie coat and hat set, 3-pc. skiing outfit, sunsuit, sunglasses, 2 coat hangers make up her wardrobe. She wears panties, socks and vinyl plastic shoes all ready to be dressed for play, party or beach. Her Saran fiber hair can be dampened, set, combed to suit the occasion. Molded of finely detailed, hard-to-break plastic fully jointed. Head turns when walking, Glassene eyes close at naptime.
49 N 3384—14½-inches tall. Shipping weight 2 lbs. Doll and wardrobe $9.49

$9⁴⁹
Doll, Wardrobe

PIPER LAURIE starring in "The Golden Blade", a Universal production, color by Technicolor, says, "Your little girl will just love this beautiful walking doll."

She walks when guided, turns her head, rolls her lovely big eyes, and cries. Sits alone.

Comb, brush, curl Saran wig. 3 curlers included.

Pretty head turns realistically as she walks.

Press legs or body—nod her head or press arms against body and she'll sob.

Saucy Walker walks, sits, cries, flirts just like her Tiny Mom

$14⁷⁹   22 in. tall

Young mothers adore Saucy Walker. She tilts her head coyly as she walks; rolls her beautiful eyes; has crying voice, too. Even the strictest "play" mother spoils her. Sparkling glassene eyes have thick dark lashes . . . close when it's naptime. She's perfectly shaped of hard-to-break plastic from the tip of her tiny nose to the ends of her realistic little fingers. Glamorous long braids of Saran hair can be shampooed, set over and over. Dressed in embossed waffle weave cotton dress, print apron, underthings, plastic shoes. She's a little dream.

79 N 03391—De Luxe 22-inch Doll (most popular size, illustrated). Shpg. wt. 5 lbs. $14.79

49 N 3364—16-in. Doll. For smaller tots. Shpg. wt. 3 lbs.$9.29

"Magic Skin" Baby Coos . . . as cuddly as little Baby Sister!

$4⁹⁹

She's a real darling . . . with her tiny baby features perfectly formed. Her head is made of kitten-soft vinyl plastic . . . her body of cuddly Magic rubber skin, stuffed with cotton and foam rubber. Baby Coos loves to be sponged clean. Her sparkling go-to-sleep eyes are fringed with long lashes. She loves to be loved, too, and coos when you cuddle her . . . cries and sobs when squeezed too hard. Though she's dressed in just a sunsuit, she comes complete with crisp organdy dress, matching ribbon-tied bonnet, slip, diaper, bootees, 2 safety pins, 3 powder puffs, 6 clothes pins, wash cloth, and soap. She's about 14 in. tall.

49 N 3041—Shipping weight 1 lb. 6 oz. $4.99

Improved! Yet only $11.29

Walks when led

Sits. Jointed arms, legs.

Comb, brush set Saran Wig.

$4.78
21 in. tall
TV favorite

HOWDY DOODY

WALKING Mary Hartline!

Popular Mary Hartline is better than ever! Now she walks, turns her head, sits . . . all at last year's low price! Carefully molded of hard-to-break plastic, with jointed arms, legs. Thick lashes edge go-to-sleep eyes. Dressed in Majorette costume, boots and baton like famous TV star. Saran wig to set, comb. Curlers incl.
49 N 3358—16 in. tall. Wt. 1 lb. 8 oz . . $11.29

Popular Howdy Doody

Young TV watchers everywhere know and love Howdy Doody's comical freckled face. Carefully designed sturdy plastic head resists hard knocks. Lower jaw is hinged, moves like ventriloquist's dummy. Wonder-wide eyes close at naptime. Cotton stuffed body is covered with simulated sewn-on clothing: shirt, frontier pants, felt boots, bandanna, belt.
49 N 3595—About 21 in. Wt. 2 lbs . . . $4.78

Bonnie Braids Walks, Tilts Head

Now pert little Bonnie Braids WALKS into your heart! She walks with you hand in hand, turning her head from side to side. Her body, arms, and legs are molded in nearly unbreakable plastic. Soft life-like vinyl head is beautifully detailed, with molded hair, and two tiny tufts of rooted hair. Wears a cotton dress with colorful peasant-type bolero, lace trimmed half slip, panties. She's about 13½ inches tall.
49 N 3359—Wt. 2 lbs. . . . $7.49

13½ in. tall
ONLY
$7.49

Walks When Led

Walt Disney's Own Peter Pan!

New! Peter Pan . . . designed by Walt Disney. He's an 18-in. bundle of adventure right from Never-Never Land. His soft vinyl head is perfectly detailed, with molded hair, molded beanie and red feather. Cotton stuffed body is completely covered with cotton backed rayon plush. Peter wears his special costume . . . with felt jacket, gold colored sash, sewn-on felt booties. His arms, too, are of vinyl plastic. A bundle of Christmas joy.
49 N 3583—Wt. 1 lb. 8 oz.$4.78

18 in. tall
JUST
$4.78

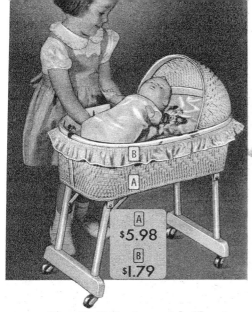

$5.98

A
B

$1.79

New Doll Basket with Hood

A Looks just like baby sister's . . . with firm woven fiber construction that can take lots of active wear. Enameled white with pastel trim. Movable hood keeps sun out of little doll's eyes. Folding legs lock in place . . . on casters. Overall height 26 inches.

79 N 09255—Doll, liner not included. Wt. 7 lbs. . . .$5.98

B 49 N 9253—Pad, Liner for above. Plastic print liner, Tufflex pad, plastic lace ruffle. Shpg. wt. 12 oz. .$1.79

$4.98 Set

New Doll Luggage! 2-pc. set in simulated tweed

Just what every fashionable young doll needs! Attractive brown tweed-effect paper finish is varnished for long wear. Plastic trim is stitched firmly for added smartness, added strength. Plastic handles. Metal hasps, hinges. Lock joint wood frame. Overnight case 7¼x10x 4¾ in. Two-suiter 9x13x5¾ in. For vacations, or stay-at-home storage.

49 N 9238—Shpg. wt. 3 lbs. 4 oz. $4.98

$1.00

$1.98

Traveling Dolls enjoy the comfort, style of this fashionable Luggage

Trim little doll-size suitcase is extra smart . . . fills countless playtime needs. Wood and fiberboard construction will stand up under hard travel, hard play. Colorful striped paper outside, houndstooth inside. Plastic handle. 11x6¾x 3⅝ in. Shpg. wt. 1 lb. 7 oz.

49 N 9230 . . . .$1.00

Doll's Vanity Case is handsomely designed . . . reasonably priced! Fitted with plastic comb, mirror, hairbrush. Durably constructed fiberboard is covered with red imitation alligator paper. Plastic handle. Plated hardware, hasp. Compact 11x8x4 in. deep.

49 N 9215—Wt. 2 lbs. 4 oz.$1.98

$2.89 Large

$4.89 Large

Furniture and Accessories for the well-cared-for doll

Trunks to pack for vacations . . . at-home storage

Tough wood and fiberboard Trunk keeps your little doll's clothes neat and clean and carefully closeted at home . . . or when traveling. Smart canvas-effect striped paper finish is varnished for long life. Lined with houndstooth pattern paper. Drawer in bottom holds accessories. Metal rack and clothes hangers keep dresses neat. Travel stickers on sides show vacation spots. Corners bound in metal for long wear. Metal handle, hasps, hinges. Choice of 2 sizes. Shpg. wts. 5 and 4 lbs.

79 N 09243—18x8¾x8½ inches. . .$2.89
49 N 9234—14x7½x7 inches. 1.98

Metal-over-wood Trunk. Strong, blue-enameled metal over well-built wood construction makes one of the nicest appearing, most durable trunks a little doll could own. Has a metal rack and hangers for her dresses, suits and coats . . . plus a handy drawer for storing accessories and those necessary "extras." Handsome metal binding, corners for added strength. Brass hasp holds trunk securely shut. Travel stickers on outside. Smart houndstooth paper lining inside. Two popular sizes to choose from.

79 N 09231—18x8¾x8½ in. Wt. 8 lbs. $4.89
79 N 09232—15½x8x7½ in. Wt. 7 lbs. 3.98

If you lack ready cash . . build your order to $20 . . use Easy Terms

Metal Walker, Stroller for fresh air outings

$2.19

$1.89

New! Handsome doll walker with basket

Now smart young "moms" can take their favorite doll baby shopping. Handsome metal walker is complete with a wire basket for parcels. 4-inch rubber-tired wheels provide smooth, noiseless travel through the neighborhood. Colored play beads on tray. Blue, pink, ivory enameled finish. 12½ in. long, 8 in. wide.

49 N 8201—Shpg. wt. 4 lbs. 8 oz.$2.19

Gay metal stroller for "airing" your baby

Plenty of fresh air and sunshine keeps a baby doll happy, healthy. Take her for daily trips in this gaily lithographed, all-metal stroller. Adjustable footrest, safety bar, play beads. Blue and ivory enameled with picture trim. 4½-in. wheels. Handle 20 in. from floor . . . *folds down for storing.* Order today.

79 N 08210—Shpg. wt. 4 lbs. . . .$1.89

Special "Extras" for doll care

C 49 N 9249—Plastic covered High Chair Pad. Fits 79 N 09210 chair. Wt. 6 oz. .89c

D 49 N 9250—Quilted Plastic Bumper Pad. Tufflex filled. Fits all cribs listed. Shipping weight 8 ounces. 85c

E 49 N 9254—Quilt, pillow slip, sheet set. 16x26-in. patchwork cotton quilt. 16x 26-in. sheet, pillow slip, 6x8-in. felt pillow, clothespins, drawstring laundry bag. Shipping weight 8 ounces. $1.98

F 49 N 9252—Plastic covered Mattress, Pillow Fits 79 N 09240, 79 N 09244. Shipping weight 12 ounces. $1.29
49N9251—Same as above. Fits 49 N 9201, 79 N 09202, 79 N 09227 beds. Shipping weight 8 ounces. $1.09

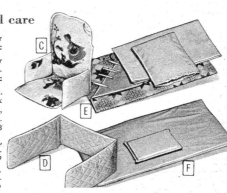

C
D
E
F

Happy Pup on Wheels

Bright-eyed little pup wags his tail vigorously, bell tinkles **$3.79** as he rolls along beside his young master. Cotton-back rayon plush body is cotton stuffed. Colorful plastic leash, collar. On durable steel frame with smooth rolling rubber wheels. 12 in. long.
49 N 4130—Shpg. wt. 2 lbs.........$3.79

Friendly Plush Snowman

New! A snowman so soft and warm he'll be a con- **$2.89** stant naptime friend. Deep cotton-back rayon plush body is gleaming white, cotton stuffed. Black felt eyes, nose, mouth...black plastic buttons. Wears rakish red wool jersey hat and scarf.
49 N 4044—13 in. high. Wt. 1 lb...$2.89

Soft Mohair Kitten

Adorably soft little kitten has bright eyes, securely **$2.89** fastened. Her squeaky voice is a joy to children. Fluffy mohair plush is extra cuddly, stuffed with soft cotton. Realistic whiskers, yarn nose, ribbon bow. 11½ in. tall.
49 N 4015—Shpg. wt. 1 lb.......$2.89

Snowy White Lamb

A snuggly bundle of snow **$1.89** white fluff. Coat is rich, deep cotton-back rayon plush. Soft vinyl plastic face is accented by jet black button eyes, securely anchored. Cotton stuffed. Black hoofs. Ribbon has bell that tinkles. 9½ in. tall.
49 N 4037—Shpg. wt. 1 lb......$1.89

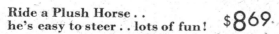

Cat, Mouse Make Music

Mouse perches on kitten's head. To wind Swiss music **$7.69** box, turn Mousie. They keep tots amused. Mouse revolves as music plays. Kitten has soft vinyl face, cotton-back rayon plush body.
49 N 4378—12½ in. Wt. 1 lb. 8 oz. $7.69

12-in. Musical Bear

Perfect sleepytime friend. Imported Swiss music box **$4.79** tinkles a lullaby from his cotton stuffed tummy. Soft cotton-back rayon plush body. Wind key in back. Plastic nose, bright eyes.
49 N 4384—Shpg. wt. 1 lb......$4.79

Ride a Plush Horse..
he's easy to steer.. lots of fun! $869

Happi-Time Plush Horsie is a frisky little stallion . . . loaded with plenty of pep and energy. He'll hold up to 100 pounds with no trouble at all . . . and hold up all day under the rough-and-tumble treatment your hard-riding young cowpokes are bound to give him. He's mounted on strong, rugged steel frame with rubber-tired wheels that roll smoothly and quietly. Steering is extra easy with this bronco. Guide him in any direction . . . to the left, right, or around in circles with the smooth, shaped wooden handle. Never gets tired . . . never gets cross. Handsome indeed, with his beautiful two-tone coat of cotton-back rayon plush, long flowing mane and tail. Bright plastic bridle, harness, reins and saddle are easy to take care of . . . wipe clean and bright with a damp cloth. Sparkling glassene eyes are firmly anchored . . . can take plenty of hard, rough play wear. Stuffed with cotton and excelsior, he'll stay sleek and young-looking for a long time to come. Height from saddle to floor, 14 inches. Measures 19x9¾x21 inches high overall.
79 N 04096—Easy to assemble. Shipping weight 8 pounds................$8.69

Sleepytime Puppy

$2.89 So wonderfully soft and snuggly..he's a perfect naptime companion. Tiny bells nestle in his ears . . . tinkle quietly. Cotton-back ray-on plush is stuffed with marsh-mellow-soft cotton. Sleeping eyes are felt lashed. Felt nose, mouth. Ribbon collar.
49 N 4166—12½ in. Wt. 1 lb. $2.89

Famous Smokey Bear*

New! Smokey...authen-tic fire prevention bear! **$4.79** Made of rayon plush, cot- 17 in. tall ton stuffed. Soft vinyl face. Wears blue twill pants, felt hat, metal Ranger Badge, belt . . . carries plastic shovel. 2 Smokey window stickers, applica-tion for membership in Junior Forest Rangers included. Join and help Smokey prevent fires.
49 N 4390—17 in. high. Wt. 3 lbs.. $4.79
*Copyright: U.S. Dept. of Agriculture.

Animal Favorites

A Little Bear Cub . . . alert, bright-eyed, and ready for play. Rich brown rayon plush coat. Cotton stuffed body. 10½ in. long.
49 N 4327—Shpg. wt. 14 oz......$1.69

B Tiger Lily . . . a lovable, laughable little kitten with thick cotton-back rayon plush body, pert plastic face.
49 N 4342—15 in. long. Wt. 1 lb...$3.79

The highest rated television show of 1954 was CBS's "I Love Lucy" starring Lucille Ball and Desi Arnaz. So it is no surprise that the 1954 Sears Wishbook prominently featured the Ricky Jr. doll, based on Lucy's real life (and TV life) son, Desi Jr. The catalog showed a photo of Lucy and Desi proudly admiring their doll progeny, which was 17-inches tall and priced at $9.97. The little doll came with an embroidered monogram and cool "leather-effect California-Type" sandals. Ricky Jr. is an extremely collectible doll today.

With Western TV shows gaining in popularity, another TV character doll was released in 1954. Annie Oakley was listed as "a rootin' tootin' 'Sweet Sue' cowgirl" dressed in neckerchief and vest, and including hat, gun belt and tiny guns. Eighteen inches tall, she sold for a pricey $11.45.

Miniature dolls, long featured in the Wishbook, were most likely manufactured by the Hollywood Toy Company. These inexpensive dolls, which sold for as little as $1.69, were only 7 1/2-inches tall and were cheaply constructed. The clothes were often stapled right to the doll, taking the fun out of dressing them. Today, these dolls draw little collector interest.

Teddy bears were becoming more popular, as the 1954 Wishbook featured ten bears in various sizes and shapes. Of note is the Famous Smokey Bear which included a membership card in the Junior Forest Rangers. Seventeen inches tall, and priced at $4.79, the bear was authorized by the U.S. Department of Agriculture.

Sears Christmas

Wishbook

1954

NEW! Happi-Time Steel Wagon and Wood Block Set

HAPPI·TIME
REG US   PAT OFF

Best value Wagon and Block Set we've seen. Has 32 blocks! Large steel wagon with solid metal disc wheels and steel axles. Swivel mounted front wheels turn freely; body 13½x7x5¾ in. Plus 14-in. handle. Colorful 1 5/16-in. square wood alphabet picture blocks have grooved top and bottom that interlock snugly.
49 N 4897—Shipping weight 4 pounds .... Set **$1.98**

Terry Cloth Pets
NEW! Cute lamb and pup are *sanitary because they are washable!* Foam rubber stuffed, covered with nubby, tubbable cotton terry cloth. Lamb, 6 in. tall; pup, 7 in. long.
49 N 4021—Wt. 12 oz..... **$1.79**

Cuddle Doll
Snugly cotton-stuffed body covered with cotton-backed rayon plush in assorted pastels. Ribbon bow. Painted plastic mask face. 13 in. tall.
49N3548—Shpg. wt. 12 oz..**$1.79**

New 3-piece Gift Set for Baby
Plastic Birdie on perch "flies" when baby hits his ring—attached to flat surface with strong suction cup. Huggable rubber Teddy Bear, brightly colored. Plakies are plastic discs on metal chain ring.
49 N 4487—Birdie perch, 7 in. high. Wt. 1 lb.3-pc. Set **$1.79**

4-piece All-Rubber Fire Dept. Set
Kiddies can race to the scene of the "fire" with this exciting fire department fleet and it won't matter if they careen across your polished floors or bump into furniture because set is made *entirely of rubber* and flexible vinyl. Includes fire engine and pumper, each 7¾ in. long; fire chief car, 5 in. long; and motorcycle policeman, 4 in. long. Easy-rolling wheels.
49 N 5248—Shipping weight 1 pound 6 ounces **98c**

Stuffed Animals
huggable, lovable pets, perfect naptime pals

ITEMS DESCRIBED BELOW
ARE ILLUSTRATED ON OPPOSITE PAGE ▶

[A] Fully Jointed Growling Teddy Bear. $2.98. 13½-in. size. Pose him in all sorts of life-like positions. Arms, legs are jointed, head turns. He's cotton stuffed for extra softness, has cotton-backed rayon plush coat. Glassene eyes.
49 N 4352—13½ in. tall. Wt. 1 lb. 4 oz..$2.98
49 N 4353—18 in. tall. Wt. 1 lb. 12 oz... 4.89

[C] Honey Bear. $1.98. 12-in. size. Now with shaped feet. Two-tone markings on cotton-backed plush coat—cotton stuffing. Squeaker in tail. Bright glassene eyes are designed to stay in. Soft vinyl plastic snout.
49 N 4312—12 in. tall. Shpg. wt. 1 lb...$1.98
49 N 4354—15 in. tall. Wt. 1 lb. 3 oz.... 2.98

[E] NEW jumbo-size Honey Bear. $4.49. He's almost as big as his little playmate—measures 27 in. tall! Vinyl plastic face; bright, sparkly glassene eyes. Pliable cotton-stuffed body; cotton-backed rayon plush coat that tots love to cuddle close. Shaped forepaws and feet.
79 N 04385—27 in. tall. Wt. 2 lbs...... $4.49

[G] NEW French Poodle. $5.79. Curly cotton-backed rayon plush coat, styled in an authentic "poodle cut." Sparkling rhinestone-trimmed velveteen collar and leash. Has pert velveteen bow on tail; pretty floral bouquet and bow on head. Cotton stuffed. About 13½ in. high.
49 N 4070—Shpg. wt. 1 lb. 12 oz..... $5.79

[J] NEW Black Sheep. $2.79. This roguish pet has a curly, fleecy-soft jet-black coat of cotton-backed rayon plush. His face is made of felt with yarn mouth. Rayon ribbon at neck. Makes a lovable crib or play pen companion for the tots on your gift list.
49 N 4053—12 in. high. Wt. 1 lb. 4 oz... $2.79

[L] Pup on Wheels. $3.79. Bright-eyed pup wags his tail vigorously, bell tinkles as his young master pulls him along. Cotton-backed rayon plush body; cotton stuffed. Bright plastic leash, collar. Strong, durable steel frame with easy-rolling rubber wheels that won't mar floors.
49 N 4130—12 in. long. Wt. 2 lbs...... $3.79

[N] Musical Bear. $4.79. He'll lull your tot to dreamland as a soft lullaby tinkles from imported Swiss music box in his cotton-stuffed tummy. Huggable cotton back rayon plush body. Plastic nose; bright eyes. Ribbon bow at neck. Now has shaped feet.
49 N 4384—12 in. tall. Shpg. wt. 1 lb.... $4.79

[R] Sleepytime Puppy. $2.79. Tiny bells tinkle in his ears. Soft and snuggly, he'll be your tot's inseparable naptime companion. Cotton-backed rayon plush is stuffed with marshmallow-soft cotton. Felt-lashed eyes. Felt nose, mouth.
49 N 4166—14 in. long. Wt. 1 lb....... $2.79

[T] NEW "Ding Dong School" Algy. $4.79. Safe, sanitary Algy is treated with dust seal to help prevent the formation of household dust irritants. Cotton-stuffed, cotton-backed rayon plush body. Eyes move, close. Vinyl face, painted features. Comes in pliofilm bag.
49 N 4351—16 in. long. Wt. 1 lb. 6 oz.. $4.79

[B] Famous Smokey Bear*. $4.79. Authentic fire prevention bear. Cotton-stuffed rayon plush with soft vinyl face. Wears blue twill pants, felt hat, Ranger badge, belt—carries plastic shovel. Membership card Jr. Forest Rangers incl.
49 N 4390—17 in. tall. Shpg. wt. 3 lbs..$4.79
*Copyright: U.S. Dept. of Agriculture

[D] Popular-priced Panda. $1.79. 12-in. size. Authentic panda markings on cuddly cotton-backed rayon plush body. Sparkling glassene eyes stay put. Plastic nose; felt tongue.
49 N 4331—12 in. high. Shpg. wt. 1 lb...$1.79
49 N 4332—15 in. tall. Wt. 1 lb. 4 oz... 2.79
49 N 4333—18 in. tall. Shpg. wt. 2 lbs... 3.79

[F] NEW Zippy Chimp, $6.49. Howdy Doody's pal. Squeeze his arm and he speaks in a chimp-like voice. Vinyl face, ears, hands and shoes. Curly cotton-backed rayon plush body; cotton stuffed. Wears Howdy Doody felt hat; cotton "T" shirt; corduroy coveralls.
49 N 4088—16 in. tall. Shpg. wt. 4 lbs........$6.49

[H] Mary's Little Lamb. $1.39. Downy-soft cotton back rayon plush, that's white as snow. Wears a perky red bow around his neck, with bell to keep him from straying. Cotton-stuffed body, red felt tongue, bright sewed-in button eyes, turned up wool yarn nose.
49 N 4046—6 in. high. Shpg. wt. 8 oz... $1.39

[K] NEW! Roy Rogers "Trigger" Steering Rider Horse. $8.95. Frisky Palomino steers easily in any direction, has authentic Roy Rogers Western saddle made of flexible vinyl plastic. He's mounted on steel frame that holds up to 100 pounds with no trouble at all. Smooth-rolling wheels with rubber tires. Cotton-back rayon plush coat, stuffed with cotton and excelsior. Height from saddle to floor 12 inches. 19x10x21 inches high overall.
79 N 04080—Shpg. wt. 8 lbs.......... $8.95

[M] NEW Pussy Cat. $2.79. Cuddlesome cotton-backed rayon plush body is cotton-stuffed. Felt ears. Bow.
49 N 4017—15 in. high. Wt. 1 lb....... $2.79

[P] Fluffy Miniature Kitty. $1.39. She's irresistible—so sweet and cuddlesome, your tots won't bear to have her out of their sight. Cotton-backed rayon plush with cotton stuffing. Securely attached glassene eyes, tiny yarn nose, felt tongue, perky whiskers.
49 N 4023—7½ in. long. Shpg. wt. 8 oz.. $1.39

[S] NEW! Jungle Babe. $2.98. Sleepy tot is curled up comfortably for a nap, has a spotted leopard coat of cotton-backed rayon plush, cotton-stuffed. Has soft plastic mask face, felt hands. A perfect naptime friend for tots' slumber hours.
49 N 4060—16 in. long. Wt. 1 lb. 6 oz.. $2.98

[V] NEW! Nelle Belle Pony. $6.29. Playful pet has spotted hide, pert vinyl face, ears, hoofs; flowing yarn mane, tail. Rides on felt harness and bridle. Felt saddle stirrups and blanket. Silky-soft cotton-back rayon plush with cotton stuffing.
49 N 4087—14 in. high. Shpg. wt. 3 lbs.. $6.29

A $2.98

GR-R
GR-R

B $4.79

D $1.79

C $1.98

E $4.49

F $6.49

G $5.79

H $1.39

J $2.79

Roy Rogers
Authentically
styled saddle

K $8.95

L $3.79

M $2.79

N $4.79

P $1.39

R $2.79

S $2.98

T $4.79

V $6.29

She walks when guided, turns her head, rolls her big eyes. She cries, sits alone.

Pert little head turns realistically as she walks.

Saran wig to comb, brush, curl. 3 curlers included.

HAPPI-TIME
REG. U. S. PAT. OFF.

She WALKS!
She FLIRTS!
She SITS!
She CRIES!

Yet she's only **$11⁷⁹**
23 in. tall

NEW! Walking Doll, Wardrobe with Deluxe Steel Trunk $14⁹⁵ Entire Set

Same Quality was $14.79! Now 23-in. HAPPI-TIME WALKER has PLUS features . . sells for $3.00 less

Most popular walking doll we've seen, now at an unbelievably low price. Made by one of the finest nationally-famous doll makers. She's a real beauty in her crisp embossed cotton dress. PLUS a lace trimmed cotton gabardine hat and coat. She tilts her little head coyly as she walks; rolls her thick-lashed glassene eyes and closes them at bedtime, has a sweet crying voice. Molded from almost unbreakable plastic. Saran curls can be combed, brushed, set over and over. Complete with undies, vinyl shoes, curlers.

79 N 03399—Deluxe 23-inch Doll. Shpg. wt. 5 lbs. $11.79

49 N 3345—17-inch Doll. Eyes close, *do not roll.* Shpg. wt. 3 lbs. *Same quality was $9.29* $8.75

A seasoned "world traveler" with her luxurious wardrobe in a 9x9x16 inch all-steel trunk. *A value we think is unmatched at this low price!* Hard-to-break plastic. Walks when guided, tilts her tiny head. Saran "hair" to comb, brush, set in curlers. Metallic-effect vest, skirt, sheer cotton blouse, undies, socks and vinyl shoes. Trunk reinforced at corners with steel hinges, snap fasteners. Wardrobe includes lacy rayon and cotton dress, taffeta formal, panty, 2-pc. percale pajamas, housecoat, ribbed fabric coat and hat, extra socks, vinyl shoes, sunglasses, curlers, comb, brush, mirror, hangers.

79 N 03343—16-in. Doll, Deluxe Steel trunk and Wardrobe. Shpg. wt. 6 lbs. . . . Set $14.95

Each strand of hair rooted to her scalp

Baby-soft vinyl head, tiny life like features

Rooted Saran "hair" can be combed, brushed, set in curlers

HAPPI-TIME
REG. U. S. PAT. OFF.

Now with soft Vinyl heads, rooted Hair at last year's low prices

Our Best: She's baby-sister size, with real-as-life rooted Saran hair to comb, brush, set! Cuddly soft all-Latex skin body is cotton stuffed, so much fun to sponge clean. Soft vinyl head. Big glassene eyes close. She has a sweet "coo" voice. Wears a ninon dress with elastic in sleeve, buttons and buttonholes; undies, shoes, socks. 2 curlers only.

$5.97 19-inch

49 N 3661—19-in. Doll. Shpg. wt. 2 lbs. 8 oz. $5.97

79 N 03662—23-in. Doll. Shpg. wt. 5 lbs. $7.89

Fine Quality: Pretty 16-inch Miss with rooted Saran hair, bright floral sprays shining from her curls. Baby-soft vinyl head, perfectly molded features. And she'll love to comb, brush and set her "hair." Soft vinyl arms, legs. Cotton stuffed easy-to-clean vinyl-coated cotton body. Crying voice. Wears rich lace-trimmed cotton dress with buttons and button holes. Lace trimmed undies, vinyl shoes, socks.

$4.98

49 N 3649—16 in. tall. Shpg. wt. 3 lbs. $4.98

Thrift priced Special

Good: Delicately detailed soft vinyl head has molded hair, lovable baby-like features. All-Latex rubber body can be sponged clean from head to toe. Arms jointed, head turns. Cotton and foam rubber stuffing is "oh-so-cuddly." Big sparkling glassene eyes have thick lashes, close. Soft little "coo" voice. So pretty in her frosty lace trimmed ninon dress with matching bonnet, undies, socks and shoes.

$3.79

49 N 3636—14 in. tall. Shpg. wt. 1 lb. 8 oz. $3.79

"Rooted" hair

Comb, brush, set

She walks with you, turns her head, sits

Hair to comb, set

$7.95
21 inches tall

Happi-Time Playmates . . All-vinyl skin, Rooted Saran hair

Teen-ager with pony tail. Now, all baby-soft vinyl plastic. Her Saran hair is pulled back in a pony tail with pert bangs . . "rooted" to her head so it can be combed, brushed, set. So perfectly proportioned, so delicately detailed, she's the picture of the girl next door. Cries softly when cuddled. Thick-lashed go-to-sleep eyes. Jointed arms. Wears dress of printed percale and sheer cotton with brocaded sash, lace trim . . undies and vinyl saddle shoes. Shipping wt. 4 lbs.

$7⁹⁸

49 N 3398—21 inches tall.....................$7.98

Now, with rooted Saran hair and a perky new bonnet . . yet priced so low! A beautiful all-over vinyl skin baby doll with adorable "little girl" features and a glowing complexion that keeps bright with a damp cloth. Looks amazingly real. Coos lovingly when cuddled. Big go-to-sleep eyes. Carries her own plastic comb, brush, mirror and curlers. Movable arms, head. In rich rayon taffeta dress with crisp cotton apron. Sheer bonnet, undies, shoes. Shipping weight 4 pounds.

$7⁹⁸

49 N 3635—21 inches tall.....................$7.98

Active Happi-Time Walker

Now . . last year's 19-inch miss has grown 2 inches . . yet she's not a penny more! Thick, glossy braids frame a sweet young face and sparkling big go-to-sleep eyes . . a playmate your little girl will love. Rich Saran hair can be dampened, combed, set. She walks, too, and turns her pretty head coyly. Her features are beautifully molded in hard-to-break plastic that stays bright with a damp cloth. Wears a sheer cotton and rayon taffeta dress with lace trim. Underthings, vinyl plastic shoes, 2 plastic curlers.

49 N 3356—16 inches tall. Shpg. wt. 2 lbs. *Was $5.98*....$5.69
49 N 3357—21 inches tall. Shpg. wt. 3 lbs.............7.95

$7.95
14 inches tall

BABY SOAP

Special Purchase! Layette Baby with Saran Wig

Petal-soft vinyl head with "tiny tot" features . . "almost-real" Saran hair . . .
20-piece layette is carefully detailed . . complete in sturdy striped cardboard suitcase.

Normally our price would be $9.98. Lovable layette doll has pinchable vinyl plastic head, with gleaming Saran curls you can comb, brush, set over and over again. She's baby-soft all over . . with cuddly Magic Skin body, arms, legs. Loves to be sponged clean. Coos with delight when cuddled. Thick-lashed glassene eyes close at bedtime. She's adorable in her assorted style rayon and lace sunsuit. Her layette includes a sheer cotton dress, bonnet, slip, diaper, shoes and socks, print cotton nightie, washcloth, 3 powder puffs, 2 safety pins, 6 wooden clothes pins and soap.

49 N 3668—14-inch doll, with layette and case. Shipping wt. 3 lbs.............. $7.95

18-inch Happi-Time "Mama-Papa" Doll now has Rooted hair . . at last year's price

Baby-soft vinyl plastic head

Rooted hair to comb, set

Get more for your money! A Christmas value that will ease your budget, please your family!

$5⁹⁸

Rooted Saran curls, assorted style hairdos

Famous 18-inch bundle of joy is even more irresistible than ever before! Besides her glowing baby-soft vinyl head, she has short, curly Saran hair that's ROOTED to stay in, stay lovely (assorted hairdos). Tilt her one way and she calls "mama" . . the other way she calls "papa." Sparkling glassene go-to-sleep eyes with long lashes. Soft, warm vinyl arms, legs and head can be wiped clean. They look and feel almost real. Cotton-stuffed cotton body holds voice. She wears a lacy ninon dress and bonnet, cotton slip, diapers, socks and leather-effect shoes.

49 N 3189—18 inches tall. Shipping weight 3 lbs........................$5.98

Lovable TINY TEARS appears with Miss Frances on DING DONG SCHOOL .. on NBC Television

DING DONG SCHOOL

A National Broadcasting Co., Inc. Service and Trademark

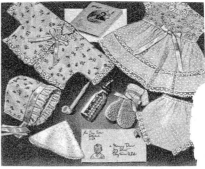

New! Layette for Tiny Tears

A Christmas surprise for "Tiny Tears" and her mom. Layette includes sheer embroidered cotton dress and panties, lacy rayon taffeta jacket and bonnet, diaper, knit bootees, pacifier, bubble pipe and nipple bottle.

$3.59
11½ in.

49 N 3450—For 11½-in. doll. Wt. 1 lb.... $3.59
49 N 3451—For 13½-in. doll. Wt. 1 lb.... 3.77
49 N 3452—For 16-in. doll. Wt. 2 lbs.... 4.49

Handsome, durable leather-effect carrying case

Sheds big tears when sad, like a real little baby

She blows bubbles with her own bubble pipe

She just loves to bathe in neck-high water

"Tiny Tears" cries, wets, blows bubbles like a real baby

$939
11½ in. tall
Fur wig

She's as lovable and lifelike as baby sister! Big wet tears well up in her eyes and roll down her cheeks, to melt the heart of the sternest young mom. She cries lustily, closes her thick-lashed glassene eyes at naptime, drinks her bottle, wets her diaper and blows bubbles .. even comforts herself with her pacifier like any real infant. And she loves to be bathed. Her pretty head is molded of hard-to-break plastic. Jointed body of soft molded rubber. Embossed cotton romper suit, with layette that includes lovely cotton pique dress, panties and bonnet, flannelette nightie, soap, kleenex, 2 clothespins, wash cloth, bubble pipe, nipple bottle, socks, shoes, diaper, sponge, and pacifier. *See sizes below.*

WALKS with you, sits, turns head

Dressed like Annie Oakley of TV fame

"Tiny Tears" with Molded Hair

As pert and pretty as can be, with realistic molded hair. (Not illustrated.) She has all the features described above, except her layette includes tiny knitted bootees instead of shoes and socks .. and the nightie and clothespins are not included. Comes in a colorful cardboard box. A favorite of little mothers everywhere.

13½-inch size
49N3031—Shipping weight 3 pounds... **$7.45**

New 16-inch size
49N3033–Shipping weight 4 pounds... **$9.45**

"Tiny Tears" with Curly Fur Wig

Loves to have her tousled curls combed, brushed, washed. Exactly as described above, (11½-inch size has bootees instead of shoes, socks), she's a favorite with tiny moms everywhere. Ready to go anywhere, in her "ready for hard play" fiber board suitcase. Smart leather-effect finish, with snap lock, sturdy handle. Easy to store.

11½-inch size
49N3032— Wt. 3 lbs. **$9.39**

13½-inch size
49N3037— Wt. 4 lbs. **$11.29**

16-inch size
49N3044— Wt. 6 lbs. **$13.98**

New! TV's Annie Oakley

$11.45
18 in. tall

She's a rootin' tootin' "Sweet Sue" cowgirl! Saran hair is rooted to scalp .. can be combed, brushed, set. Annie walks with you, tilts her head, sits. Go-to-sleep eyes. Hard-to-break plastic body, fully jointed. Wears blouse, neckerchief, vest, skirt, felt boots, hat, and gun belt, with tiny guns.
49 N 3379—18 in. tall. Wt. 2 lbs. 10 oz... $11.45

RICKY, JR. of TV's "I Love Lucy"

Rooted hair to comb, brush

$9.97
17 in. tall

A handsome little lad that will make your tiny mom as proud as mother Lucy! His thick mass of wavy Saran hair is combed in a pompadour to look just like his dad's. It's rooted, too, so it can be combed and brushed again and again. Ricky, Jr. is molded of baby-soft vinyl from his head to his toes .. his plump little body perfectly shaped. Bright glassene eyes are shadowed with thick lashes, close in sleep. Handsomely attired in a crinkle cotton shirt with his own monogram, short pants, and leather-effect "California-Type" sandals. 17 in. tall.
49 N 3071—Wt. 3 lbs..... $9.97

Order regularly and receive your Sears catalogs regularly

New! Active Miss joined at wrists, knees, elbows, shoulders, hips

Jointed arms, elbow, wrist

Jointed legs and knees

Walks with you

She actually sits alone

- Dainty "little girl" features
- She sits like a lady, walks with you
- Shimmering rooted Saran hair

$12.98
18 in. tall

Now a Doll with more play features than ever! A doll that's breathlessly beautiful yet packed with features for fun. Made by Madame Alexander, one of the most outstanding doll manufacturers of all time, she's jointed to sit, kneel, stand, bend her arms just like little sister. She walks, too just by pulling her legs down gently to make them rigid. Saran hair is rooted to her scalp—can be combed, brushed, set with her own plastic comb and curlers; packed in hat box. She's made of almost unbreakable plastic from head to toe. Wears billowy, lacy organdy dress, rayon taffeta slip, step-ins. Mesh hat trimmed with flowers, lace. Patent leather-effect shoes, socks.
49 N 3396—18 inches tall. Shpg. wt. 3 lbs.......... $12.98

Doll Favorites
many at big savings to stretch your Christmas budget!

New! "Posie" can kneel, sit, walk or stand

$14.95

She's the doll of a hundred poses .. and she's more lifelike than any doll you've ever seen! Why? Because Posie is JOINTED AT THE KNEE .. so she can sit like a little lady, she can kneel to say prayers, or sit at your feet while you read a bedtime story. She's everything little mom could want .. yet priced to ease your budget. Perfectly shaped of hard-to-break plastic from her head to her toes. Fully jointed. And, of course, walks with you .. tilting her head coyly and rolling her beautiful eyes. Gorgeous long curls of Saran hair can be dampened, combed, brushed and set over and over again. Dressed in embossed waffle weave cotton dress (assorted styles), undies, and plastic shoes. 3 plastic curlers included.

79 N 03367—De Luxe 24-inch Doll. Shipping weight 5 lbs...................$14.95

Walks when guided; rolls her big eyes
Saran hair to comb, brush, set on curlers
Sits like sister.. knees bend
Jointed knees so she can kneel, sit
Pretty head turns coyly as she walks

New! Now, Beautiful Toni WALKS, too

$9.29

Same quality without walking mechanism was $11.29 and up, last year. Now, she walks, turns her head flirtatiously. Her thick NYLON tresses are treated to stay radiant through shampoos, "permanents". 14½ in. tall. Her hard-to-break plastic body can be sponged clean. Thick-lashed go-to-sleep eyes. She wears an embossed cotton dress with embroidery-trimmed organdy pinafore, attached cotton undies; vinyl shoes. Play Wave Kit contains Toni creme shampoo, harmless play-wave solution, curlers, comb, end-papers. To make play-wave solution refill, mix 1 teaspoon sugar, ⅓ cup water.

14½ inches Tall	16 inches Tall	Deluxe 21 inches Tall
49N3365—Wt. 1 lb. 14 oz.	49N3366—Wt. 2 lbs. 4 oz.	49N3368—Shpg. wt. 4 lbs.
Economy Size..... $9.29	Popular Size..... $11.29	Our Finest....... $16.98

Mary Hartline, Bonnie Braids Walk when led

Big Values . . . Popular "Personality" dolls

$11.29

New! Mary Hartline has ROOTED hair to comb, brush, set. *She walks, turns her head, sits.* Fully jointed hard plastic body, soft vinyl head; eyes close. Wears rayon majorette costume, boots, baton like famous TV star. With curlers to set her platinum hair.
49 N 3362—16 in. tall. Shpg. wt. 2 lbs. $11.29

Was $7.49 $6.99

Save! Winsome Bonnie Braids walks with you, turns her head, sits. Soft vinyl head with 2 tufts of rooted Saran hair, bright bows. Eyes that close. Hard-to-break plastic body; fully jointed. In crisp cotton dress, undies, vinyl shoes.
49 N 3359—13½ in. tall. Shpg. wt. 2 lbs.. $6.99

Was $7.49 $6.89

Save! Betsy McCall, popular doll to sew for. Head of baby-soft vinyl. Hard plastic body; fully jointed. Big glassene eyes close. Saran hair to comb, brush, set. Cotton dress (assorted styles) undies, shoes. Easy-to-sew pattern included.
49 N 3355—14½ in. tall. Shpg. wt. 2 lbs.. $6.89

TV's Howdy Doody

$4.78

A favorite with young TV viewers everywhere! Howdy 21 in. tall Doody's comical freckled face and head is carefully designed of sturdy plastic to resist hard knocks. His lower jaw is hinged, moves like a ventriloquist's dummy. Wonder-wide eyes close at nap time. Cotton-stuffed body is covered with simulated sewn-on plaid shirt, pants, boots, "Howdy Doody" bandanna and belt. Shipping weight 2 lbs.
49 N 3595—21 in. tall.... $4.78

Make-Up Doll at Big Savings

Was $11.29 $6.99
14½ in.

A spectacular Christmas value! Lovely HARRIET HUBBARD AYER Make-up combines 2 favorite "little girl" pastimes. Her face and arms are molded in real-as-life vinyl plastic "Magic Flesh" that can be made up again and again. Saran hair can be combed, brushed, styled. Her "very own" Make-up Kit contains harmless lipstick, rouge, powder, eye shadow, eyebrow pencil, perfume stick, Cleanse-Ayer cream and tissues. Fully jointed plastic body. In cotton dress (assorted styles) undies, shoes.
49N3380—14½ in. Wt. 1 lb. 14 oz. Was $11.29 $6.99
49N3383—16 in. Wt. 2 lbs. 4 oz. Was $12.98.... 8.99

13-inch Babee-Bee has Hat-Box Carrying Case

- She drinks, wets, cries
- Baby-soft vinyl head, tiny features
- Heavily-lashed go-to-sleep eyes
- Rubber body to sponge clean

$8.95

New! She's as winsome as a baby can be, has jointed arms, legs, turning head. Her layette includes a perky wrinkle-free dress and slip, bootees, bib, sturdy steel weighing scales, plastic diaper bag, diaper, powder, soap, nursing bottle and bubble pipe .. all in her very own gay plaid carrying case with 3 metal fasteners, plastic handle made for long hard hours of playtime fun. Babee-Bee's pert little features are delicately molded in baby-soft vinyl. Her wavy molded hair and peaches-'n'-cream complexion can be sponged clean just like baby sister's. Your little mother will love to "mother" Babee-Bee. Whether it's playtime, naptime, bath-time, dinner-time, or travel-time, she's ready. Dressed in undershirt, panties, and a cotton flannel kimono.

79 N 03544—13-in. Doll, Layette and Carrying case. Shipping weight 5 lbs..........Set $8.95

12-inch Cindy Lee, Formula Set—Case

$5.49
Set

She's all set for dinner . . . dressed in her tiny little bib and diaper. And dinner's really fun to fix with Cindy's own miniature formula set. It's just like Mom's . . . four little nursing bottles with rubber nipples in an easy-to-use wire rack; a painted steel pan with cover, measuring cup, plastic measuring spoon, and funnel for mixing the formula; and a bottle cleaner brush. You'll find a teething ring and bubble pipe, too! All contained in a sturdy, leather-effect snap-lock carrying case. Cindy is made of cuddly all-rubber that you can sponge clean over and over. She's fully jointed with big plastic set-in eyes and pretty molded curls .. and she drinks from her bottle, wets her diaper and cries when hugged.

49 N 3513—12-inch Doll, Formula Set and Case. Wt. 4 lbs........$5.

3 FAMOUS 'SUNBABES'
- DRINK from tiny bottles
- WET their diapers
- Completely WASHABLE

Fully jointed

Walks with you

Sits by herself

Hair to comb

Walks when guided— hair can be set

Lovable "Sunbabe" Drinking-Wetting Dolls
Sized to Suit "Play Moms" of Any Age

"BANNISTER BABY"® . . 18 **$8.95** in. tall, inspired by Constance Bannister, famous baby photographer. Molded of all-vinyl, jointed arms, legs. Head turns. Eyes close. Drinks from her bottle, wets diaper, cries, blows bubbles from plastic pipe. Dressed in terry cloth robe, bootees, undies. Shpg. wt. 4 lbs.
49 N 3546............$8.95

New! 13-in. **$3.59** BABEE-BEE with delicately molded vinyl head, big glassene eyes that close. Rubber body is fully jointed. She loves to be sponged clean .. drinks from her bottle (and she wets her diaper, too!) Coos when hugged. Corduroy coat, bootees, diapers, nursing bottle.
49 N 3533—Wt. 2 lbs. $3.59

New! Tiny "SO-WEE" .. just 10 **$1.75** inches tall and made especially for the tiniest of little mothers! Loves to splash in the tub .. drink from her own bottle. Coos lovingly when squeezed. Wonder-wide stationary plastic eyes can't fall or be plucked out. All-rubber from head to toe. In bib, diaper. Bottle.
49 N 3514—Wt. 1 lb. . . .$1.75

Popular "Honey Walker" .. An Effanbee Doll

$7.29
14¼ in. tall

She WALKS with you, tilting her pretty little head from side to side. Or she'll sit demurely all by herself. Her shiny long Saran hair can be combed, brushed, set over and over again. Really a wonderful "go-everywhere," "do anything" friend for your busy little tot. All plastic body is almost unbreakable. Glassene eyes close. So pretty in her rayon taffeta dress, gay straw hat, undies, black patent snap shoes, socks.
49N3326—14¼ in. tall. Wt. 1 lb. 10 oz. $7.29
49N3328—18 in. tall. Wt. 2 lbs. 6 oz.. 9.39

Now! 14-in. Bride Walks .. costs same

$4.99

Same fine quality almost-unbreakable plastic doll that we offered last year . . . but now she can WALK with you! She's radiantly lovely in her gown of rayon satin and lace .. her glowing Saran hair set off with net veil. Her hair can be combed, set on plastic curlers that are included. Fully jointed. Glassene eyes close. Wears undies, vinyl shoes. 14 inches tall. Shpg. wt. 1 lb. 6 oz.
49 N 3336..............$4.99

for a joyous Christmas!
Lovable Playmates
to "mother" the year around

$7.89

Huggable 18-in. all-vinyl Baby Doll

Just as winsome as a baby can be! Glowing baby body, head, arms and legs are all vinyl . . . so soft to your touch, so easy to sponge clean. Beautiful peaches 'n' cream complexion, and pert little features . . . all carefully molded to perfect proportions. Fully jointed body makes her more baby-like than ever. Sparkling glassene eyes are thick lashed, close when she's sleepy. Pretty molded hair. Really a joy for any young mother. Adorable in knitted shirt and panties, just like baby sister wears. Layette includes soft pastel cotton romper with button and braid trim, matching sun bonnet trimmed with a shiny satin ribbon, rayon socks, and imitation leather shoes. A Christmas delight!

49 N 3082—About 18 inches tall. Shipping weight 3 lbs..... $7.89

Lifelike vinyl from head to toe

Popular Soft Dolls . . fun-loving playmates for tiny tots

New! Amazing TALKING doll repeats her favorite nursery rhyme. She's 24 inches [tal]l, with soft vinyl face, big wonder-wide glas[se]ne eyes, and bright yarn bangs. Mechanism in [ba]ck, with crank handle to make her talk. [Co]tton stuffed and ready for fun. Cotton flan-[nel] apron dress, bonnet brim.
[49N]3540—24 in. tall. Wt. 2 lbs......... $3.69

[O]riginal Raggedy Ann, every tot's favorite. [Rig]ht from the storybooks, and cotton stuffed [to mak]e her extra huggable. Dressed in bright [dress], with striped legs, cotton yarn hair, but[tons], painted face. A bundle of fun.
[49N35]30—15 in. tall. Wt. 1 lb........... $2.89

C "Knock-about" teenager, 26 inches tall and ready for the roughest play! Cotton stuffed, washable painted plastic "mask" face; washable vinyl coated arms, legs. Yarn hair. Dressed in sturdy denim slacks, jacket.
79 N 03516—Shipping weight 2 lbs...... $2.79

D Sweet young 15-inch charmer . . . enjoys tiny tot's rough-and-tumble affection. Painted "mask" face. Cotton dress, undies.
49 N 3545—Shipping weight 14 oz......... $1.89

E 11-inch Beauty. Body covered with bright percale. So cute in cotton tie-on apron style dress. Stuffed with cuddly soft cotton.
49 N 3511—Shipping weight 10 oz......... $1.17

$5.98 $3.59 $4.19

Permanent Molded Hairdos on Baby-Soft Vinyl Heads

[He]r pretty hairdo looks so [re]al. A favorite with parents [a]nd tiny moms alike, because [i]t looks so neat, so fresh. Big thick-lashed eyes close at nap-time. Coos softly when cuddled. Easy to wipe clean—Latex rubber skin body is cotton stuffed. Jointed arms. So cute in sheer ninon dress, taffeta overskirt, undies, shoes.
49N3652—22 in. Wt. 4 lbs. $5.98

Adorable baby brother and sister to make your family complete! Both carefully designed with tiny little turned-up noses, pretty smiling mouths, and bright glassene eyes shadowed with thick lashes, that close for bed time. Vinyl heads feel amazingly baby-like. Dewy-fresh complexions and pretty molded curls make them look "almost real." One-piece Latex rubber skin bodies are cotton stuffed, really cuddly. Fun to sponge clean. So cute in their fashionable outfits . . really delightful playmates.

16-inch Baby Brother is in cotton twill pants, flannel jacket.
49 N 3687—Wt. 2 lbs..... $3.59

19-inch big Sister in a perky cotton dress, undies, shoes.
49N3684—Wt. 2 lbs. 8 oz.. $4.19

Dolls You Can Sew For

NOTICE: If you buy 12 or more of either doll below, you may deduct 10% from the prices shown . . ideal for sewing circles, church, school

Saran hair to comb, brush

14-in. $3.59

Molded hair $5.39

Ready to Model the Wardrobe You Fashion

Ideal doll for church, school or sewing circles. A real baby size, with baby-soft latex body that makes her really lovable. Can be sponged clean. Soft vinyl head with pert features, big glassene go-to-sleep eyes, pretty molded hair. Cotton stuffing. Dressed in rayon chemise. Shipping weight 5 pounds.
79N03085-26 in. Was $5.79; $5.39

A little beauty that loves to model. Saran hair to comb, brush, set. "Little girl" features molded in hard plastic. Fully jointed. Wears cotton panties, socks, shoes. Shpg. wts.: 1 lb; 1 lb. 8 oz.; 2 lbs.

49N3316G-14 in.......... $3.59
49N3318G-16 in........... 4.59
49N3322G-18½ in. Was $5.49; 5.22

Miniature Dolls
cuddly, captivating companions for delightful playtime hours

HAPPI-TIME Miniatures: Gems in any collection

They're 7½-inches tall—all made of sturdy, practically-unbreakable plastic, with arms that move, heads that tilt and turn, go-to-sleep glassene eyes with eyelashes. All stand alone, dressed in luxurious finery, beautiful in realistic detail. Shoes are painted on. All except nun and groom have curly mohair wigs. Girl dolls wear panties and crinoline half slips.

As low as $1.69

Radiant Cinderella. She's on her way to the ball. Wears a glittery, star-studded dress with net and gold-color braid. Carries a tiny slipper.
49 N 3118—Wt. 12 oz. $1.77

Handsome Bridegroom. Dressed in formal attire. Realistic molded high hat, striped trousers, "tails" and tie. White vest. Watch chain.
49 N 3102—Wt. 12 oz. $1.69

Beautiful Bride. Traditional white rayon satin gown—net trimmed with glamorous full skirt. Net veil, too. Artificial orange blossom bouquet.
49 N 3101—Wt. 12 oz. $1.77

Nun. Black rayon taffeta habit, soft black veil, snowy white collar and headpiece. Metal crucifix, imported Italian rosary beads.
49 N 3106—Wt. 12 oz. $1.77

New Miss Christmas. She's lavishly gowned in a shimmery rayon satin dress and hooded cape with fur-effect trim.
49 N 3105—Wt. 12 oz. $1.77

Cowgirl. Little Westerner is all set for rodeo-time. Wears fringed imitation leather vest, skirt, ray shirt, felt hat. Tiny gun
49 N 3116—Wt. 12 oz. $1.69

Modern Miniatures

[A] **Mary Hartline.** Wears monogrammed majorette outfit with metallic trim, boots; holds baton. Plastic body; movable head, arms. Mohair wig. Eyes close.
49 N 3007—7½ in. tall. Wt. 8 oz. $1.87 ... $1.87

[B] **Howdy Doody.** Dressed in plaid shirt, neckerchief, jeans, painted on boots. Made of practically-unbreakable plastic—eyes and mouth move.
49 N 3003— 8 in. tall. Wt. 8 oz. 98c

[C] **Annie Oakley.** Wears fringed jacket and skirt, cowboy hat, neckerchief, blouse, boots. Plastic body; movable head, arms. Eyes close. Mohair wig.
49 N 3006—7½ in. tall. Wt. 8 oz. $1.87

Musical Stand

Display your doll on revolving musical stand. 'Round and 'round she goes, to the popular tune of your choice. Swiss music box plays—Wedding March, Happy Birthday, or Anniversary March. Rubber attachment holds doll in position. Plastic 4¼-in. diameter base. Doll not included. State tune. Wt. 8 oz.
49 N 3094 ... $2.29

"Joannie Pigtails" with wardrobe

This pert, pigtailed playmate with wardrobe of custom-made clothes and accessories is sure to win the affections of your little girl. She wears her long, shimmering Saran tresses in two neat braids—her "mama" can comb, brush, dampen and set her hair in a variety of different styles. Lovable toddler is realistically molded of nearly-unbreakable plastic—has perfect "tiny tot" features; big, beautiful go-to-sleep eyes, accented by long curling eyelashes.

You can tell from the sizeable wardrobe she carries that she intends to make a long visit. It contains a pretty cotton frock with ribbon at waist, matching bonnet; pajama set with colorful nursery pattern; molded vinyl shoes. She wears panties. She carries her curlers, comb, brush and mirror. Doll has jointed arms, legs, turning head.
49 N 3049—8 inches tall. Shipping weight 1 lb. 4 oz. $2.79

$2.79

New Latex COLORED Dolls

[D] **13-inch Doll with molded hair.** Has a cuddly Latex body; vinyl plastic head, sparkling glassene eyes. Wears a lace-trimmed cotton dress; pants; so and imitation leather shoes. 13 inches tall.
49 N 3550—Shpg. wt. 1 lb. ...$1

$1.97

13-inch

[E] **16-inch Doll with Saran Hair** that's firm rooted to the scalp of her vinyl plastic he—can be combed, brushed and set. Hugga all-Latex body is cotton stuffed. Wears a sh ninon dress with lace trim, matching bonn eyelet-trimmed organdy pinafore; panties; soc and imitation leather shoes. 16 inches tall.
49 N 3551—Shpg. wt. 1 lb. 12 oz. ...$3.8

New Kewpie Doll

One of the most famous and one of the most popular dolls of all time, now in soft pastel cotton-backed rayon plush with cotton stuffing. Your toddler will carry her everywhere she goes—even to bed. Easy to clean molded vinyl head with painted eyes and mouth. Life-like molded ears and cute Kewpie locks. Measures 12 in. tall.
49 N 3541—Wt. 1 lb. $2.79

$2.79

16-inch Sleepy-head Doll

For naptime hours, no doll will prove a more delightful companion than this snuggly sweetheart—so soft and warm, she just begs to be cuddled. Her impish face wi capture your heart—it just asks for love—an she'll be baby's favorite play and crib companion.

Made of kitten-smooth, cotton-back rayon plush in pastel colors, stuffed with soft, white cotton. Her rosy face is made of easy-to-clean, practically-unbreakable plastic with carefully painted features. Her hair is of smooth cotton yarn ringlets, that curl sweetly about her face. She'll take lots of hard treatment. About 16 inches tall.
49 N 3527—Shipping weight 1 pound ... $2.79

$2.79

Order regularly and receive your Sears catalogs regularly

The Davy Crockett craze hit the country big in 1955 as a result of the Walt Disney TV series starring Fess Parker. The boy's section of the catalog was crammed with the Alamo hero's toys -- from guns to tents to coon-skin caps, of course. So it is no surprise to see the 1955 Sears Wishbook features a 17-inch Davy Crockett doll aimed at young girls (and perhaps, the marketers hoped, at boys too) priced at $2.97.

1955 was a big year for character dolls with many newcomers to the Wishbook's pages. Roy Rogers and Dale Evans dolls, just 8-inches high, were $2.37 each. Rose O'Neill's Kewpie doll ("Ideal for toddlers. Collectors like her, too") was sold for just $1.85 for a 12-inch version. The Original Raggedy Ann ("every tot's favorite") was priced at $2.89.

Other TV or comic strip characters appeared as dolls too. Howdy Doody returned again at $4.78 and Dennis the Menace, a 16-inch charmer, was $2.79.

Related toys targeted to young girls gained in popularity. Doll houses and other domestic supplies such as toy vacuum cleaners, dish sets and miniature kitchens were big sellers. Some of these items, like the toy sewing machines featured in the 1955 catalog, have become hot collectibles in their own right. Finding a toy sewing machine in excellent condition is very difficult today.

Shop the easy, modern way
BY TELEPHONE
for number to call see pages 389-392

Index starts on page 381   Easy Terms on page 385

SEARS 1955
Christmas Book

SEARS, ROEBUCK AND CO., 925 S. Homan Ave., Chicago 7, Ill.

Sears Christmas
Wishbook
1955

A $1.95 12-in.

B $1.95 12 in.

D $2.89

C $2.98

E $2.89

$2.98 16 in.

Washable Jointed Honey Bear Poses All Ways

Like a performing circus bear, this funny fellow makes you giggle with his tricks. Move his jointed arms and legs, make him look like he's walking, marching or somersaulting. Honey Bear loves to play and pose, but when he's dirty he takes a bath like a good boy. He's as healthy a bear as you could meet!

His gold-color cotton-backed rayon plush coat is Sanitized® to inhibit bacterial growth. Cushiony Dryex® filling of shredded foam plastic dries faster than any other filling we know of, resists mildew and odors. He's as handsome as a story-book bear with his stand-up ears and puffy paws. He's sure to delight your tot with his playful poses. Tiny yarn nose, firmly secured glassene eyes. Felt tongue. Jaunty bow.

49 N 4133—16 inches. Shipping weight 1 lb................. $2.98
49 N 4149—19½ inches. Shipping weight 2 lbs................. 4.89

Jungle Babe Captures Snoozy Kiddies

$2.98 16 in.

Lazy little leopard girl looks so cozy tykes can't resist curling up with her. Spotted leopard coat of pettable rayon plush; cotton backed. Dreamy little face of pliable plastic wipes clean. Pink felt-lined stand-up ears, dainty paws. 16 inches of nap-time fun. Order early for Christmas.
49N4060—Wt. 1 lb. 6 oz. $2.98

A Tiny Fluffy Kitty .. A Purr-fect Gift

$1.39

As fluffy and puffy as cotton candy, this miniature kitty makes friends with the tiniest toddler. Only 7½ inches long, easy for tiny hands to pet and carry. Perky whiskers frame her pink pug nose and tongue. Soft-to-stroke white rayon plush; cotton backed. Foamrubber stuffed. Pom-pon eyes.
49N4023—Wt. 8 oz... $1.39

Ideal

A Was $11.29 $9.29 16-in. tall

Saran hair to comb, brush, set on curlers

Walks when guided, rolls her big eyes

B Was $14.95 $13.95

Jointed knees so she can kneel, sit

Famous Toni Walking Doll .. Price cut $2.00

A She walks, turning her head flirtatiously as she goes. And now at new record low prices. Her thick NYLON tresses are treated to stay radiant through shampoos, "permanents." Her hard-to-break plastic body can be sponged clean. Thick lashed go-to-sleep eyes. She wears a pretty cotton dress; half slip and panties both lace trimmed, socks; vinyl plastic shoes. Comes with Play Wave Kit with Toni cream shampoo, harmless play-wave solution, curlers, comb, end-papers. To make play-wave solution refill, mix 1 teaspoon sugar and ⅛ cup water.

16 inches Tall	19 inches Tall	Deluxe 21 inches Tall
49 N 3308—Shpg. wt. 2 lbs.	49 N U3309—Shpg. wt. 3 lbs.	49 N U3310—Shpg. wt. 4 lbs.
Was $11.29........$9.29	Normally $14.29....$12.29	Was $16.98........$14.98

C **Big 23-inch Cuddle-up Baby.** A bundle of charms with soft cotton-stuffed all vinyl skin body and "real as life" toes and fingers. Go-to-sleep eyes. Tiny mouth is open showing 2 baby teeth. Holds a stuffed cotton-backed rayon plush pet. Wears a cotton playsuit under cotton and rayon snowsuit; matching bonnet. Rayon socks, shoes.
49 N U3673—Shpg. wt. 5 lbs.......$12.75

D **Walking Doll you Can Sew for.** Saran hair to comb, brush, set. Features molded in hard plastic. Fully jointed. Wears cotton panties, socks, shoes. Wts. 1 lb., 1 lb. 8 oz., 2 lbs.
49NU3305—14½ in. tall. $3.67
49NU3306—16½ in. tall. 4.67
49NU3307—19 in. tall... 5.37

Reduced! "Posie" .. the doll that kneels, sits, walks or stands

B Look! 24 inch Posie is Reduced! Now with beautiful vinyl "magic" flesh face that feels so real and lifelike rooted Saran hair to set. Posie is the doll of a hundred poses .. and she's more lifelike than any dolly you've seen. Why? Because Posie is *jointed at the knees* .. so she can sit like a little lady, she can kneel to say her prayers, or sit at your feet while you read to her. She's everything a little mom could want .. yet priced to ease your budget. And of course she walks with you .. tilting her head coyly. Hard-to-break plastic body. Glamorous long curls of Saran hair can be dampened, combed, brushed and set over and over again. Dressed in nylon dress; cotton undies, socks; vinyl walking shoes. 3 plastic curlers. Savings priced to fit your Christmas budget, order now!
49 N U3315—Deluxe 24-inch Doll. Shipping weight 5 lbs. Was $14.95...........$13.95

E **Walking Bride Doll Reduced!** Almost unbreakable plastic body; movable vinyl arms, head. Lustrous rayon satin and lace gown, lace veil. Fully rooted Saran wig. Rayon panties, socks; vinyl shoes. 14½ in. tall. Shpg. wt. 2 lbs.
49 N U3320..........$4.87

F **Winsome Bonnie-Braids** walks, turns her head, sits. Soft vinyl head with 2 tufts of rooted Saran hair. Eyes close. Hard-to-break plastic body; fully jointed. In cotton dress, undies, vinyl shoes. 13½ in. tall. Shpg. wt. 2 lbs.
49 N U3359—Was $6.99. $5.99

G **Ballerina.** Head turns as she "dances" on her toes. Does the splits. Plastic body, legs; vinyl head, arms. Eyes close. Saran rooted hair. Tu-tu costume of metallic rayon lamé, net; CAPEZIO style shoes, opera hose. Wt. 3 lbs.
49 N U3317—19 in. tall .. $6.95

C $12.75

D $3.67 14½ inch

E $4.87

G $6.95

F Was $6.99 $5.99

If you buy 12 or more of dolls at left, 49NU3305, 49NU3306 or 49NU3307, you may deduct 10% from each price shown.

c PAGE 275 .. DOLLS

$8.98

$7.98

$4.69

These 3 cuties have textured vinyl skin that feels so real, wipes clean with damp cloth.

Three Popular Dolls with Rooted Hair . . Coo Voices . . Soft Vinyl Skin . . Eyes that Close

Now 23 inches tall—almost as big as a real baby! She's made of skin-soft vinyl plastic from head to toe. Amazingly life-like details—you can almost feel her little fingers clasp your hand. Downy-soft cotton stuffing makes her lovable as can be. Gleaming rooted Saran hair to comb, brush, set with her very own curlers. Jointed arms, turning head. Long-lashed go-to-sleep glassene eyes. Squeeze her, hear her coo. She looks so smart in her organdy dress and bonnet, lace-trimmed cotton slip, panties. Rayon stockings, vinyl shoes.
49 N U3170—Shpg. wt. 4 lbs. $8.98

22-in. Dolly richly dressed in dainty nylon dress and fluffy apron. Amazing "Superflex" legs bend at knees and hips—let her sit, kneel. This modern miss wears her rooted Saran hair in pony tail tied with a big red bow. She's made of skin-soft vinyl plastic from head to toe. Soft cotton stuffing. Jointed arms, turning head, heavy-lashed go-to-sleep glassene eyes. Coos when cuddled. Complete with comb, brush, mirror and curlers to care for her rooted hair. Red nylon dress, white apron. Cotton panties, rayon stockings, vinyl shoes.
49 N U3622—Shpg. wt. 4 lbs. $7.98

15-inch Darling loves her cozy candy-striped cotton flannel "Draft-Dodger" sleeper. Pose her 101 ways! Her "Superflex" arms and legs bend amazingly—she even kneels to pray. Modern as can be, she wears her Saran rooted hair in short poodle-cut style—so much fun to comb, brush, set. Entirely of skin-soft vinyl plastic, has cotton stuffing to make her cuddly. Easy to sponge clean. Coos when cuddled. Long-lashed go-to-sleep Glassene eyes. Attired in jaunty red-striped cotton flannel pajamas with zipper tassled night cap, bootees.
49 N U3132—Shpg. wt. 2 lbs. $4.69

[A] 14-in. Baby Coos dresses smartly on a budget. Such a cuddly doll, such a large wardrobe, at so low a price! Her finely-detailed vinyl plastic head has molded curls, long-lashed go-to-sleep glassene eyes. Cuddly "Magic Skin" rubber body is stuffed with cotton and foam rubber to make her feel oh-so-real. Baby Coos, loves to be sponged clean. Jointed arms, turning head, swing legs. Coos when cuddled. Complete with assorted style lace-trimmed cotton sunsuit, lacy organdy dress, bonnet, cotton slip, diaper, bootees, soap, washcloth, 6 clothespins, 3 powder puffs, safety pins.
49 N U3041—Shipping weight 2 lbs. $4.98

[B] Amazing low price for 14-in. Baby Doll. Cuddly latex rubber body, cotton stuffed. Heavy-lashed go-to-sleep eyes. Cries when squeezed. High-impact plastic head has molded curls, cherry-bright cheeks. She's ready to go "bye-bye" in her ninon dress and bonnet trimmed with embroidery, lace. Cotton slip, panties. Shoes, socks.
49 N 3115—Wt. 1 lb. 4 oz. $1.98

[C] 16-in. Party-going Dolly dressed in stylish pinafore. Delicate features and curls molded in skin-soft vinyl plastic head that turns. Thick-lashed go-to-sleep glassene eyes. Squeeze her, hear her coo sweetly. One-piece latex rubber body is easy to clean. Cotton stuffed and cuddly. Embossed cotton dress, bonnet. Panties, shoes, socks.
49 N U3623—Wt. 2 lbs. . . . $2.98

[D] 17-in. Baby Doll in 18-in. Christening Dress. Pretty little baby is dressed in finery for her big day. Vinyl plastic head with baby features, molded hair, go-to-sleep glassene eyes. Latex rubber body, cotton stuffed. Jointed arms, turning head. White sheer ninon dress, bonnet trimmed with lace, embroidery. Rayon taffeta slip. Bootees, panties.
49 N U3624—Wt. 2 lbs. $4.79

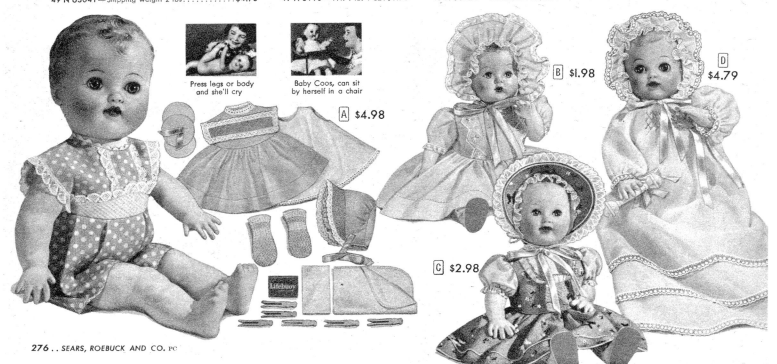

Press legs or body and she'll cry

Baby Coos, can sit by herself in a chair

[A] $4.98

[B] $1.98

[C] $2.98

[D] $4.79

Soft vinyl skin feels so real!

$7.89

$7.49

$7.49

They kneel to "pray"

They play "piggy-back"

They do fancy "dance" steps

Huggable 18-inch all-vinyl Baby Doll

Just as winsome as a baby can be! Glowing baby body, head, arms and legs are all vinyl . . . so soft to your touch, so easy to sponge clean. Beautiful peaches-and-cream complexion and pert little features . . . all carefully molded to perfect proportions. Fully-jointed body makes her more baby-like than ever. Sparkling glassene eyes are thick lashed, close when she's sleepy. Pretty molded hair. Adorable in knitted shirt and panties, just like baby sister wears. Her layette includes a pastel cotton romper with dainty button and braid trim, matching bonnet trimmed with a shimmering rayon satin ribbon, rayon socks, imitation leather shoes. Move her head, arms and legs, pose her in many darling baby positions. Put this bundle of fun under the tree this Christmas, she's sure to steal the heart of your girl.
49 N U3082—18 inches tall. Shipping weight 3 pounds $7.89

Wendy and Billy-Boy bend to 1,001 positions!

See this adorable pair "dance", sit, kneel to pray! They're as nimble and graceful as professional dancers. They're easy to bend to any position and they'll hold it until their young "mother" chooses another stunt for them. See how many different poses you can think of—have fun by the hour! Why, the young lady's braids even stand on end! These agile dolls are made of washable, nearly unbreakable latex foam rubber. A concealed wire makes the wonderful poses possible. Both have twinkly go-to-sleep glassene eyes and molded hair. Pert Wendy wears a plaid rayon taffeta dress, lacy undies, rayon satin ribbons on her braids. Billy wears a cotton shirt and denim trousers. Both wear rayon socks and plastic shoes.
49 N U3590—Wendy Girl Doll. 18 inches tall. Shipping weight 2 pounds $7.49
49 N U3591—Billy-Boy Doll. 18 inches tall. Shipping weight 2 pounds 7.49

A Big Baby Doll at an exceptionally low price. Glossy Saran hair to comb. Latex rubber skin arms, legs. Cotton covered body, cotton stuffed. Plastic head turns. Has crying voice. Glassene go-to-sleep eyes. Wears ninon dress and matching bonnet. Slip, rubber panties, socks, shoes. About 23 inches tall.
49 N U3192—Wt. 3 lbs. . $4.99

B Baby Doll with curls of Saran hair you can comb and set. Plastic head with go-to-sleep glassene eyes. Soft One-piece latex rubber body. Stuffed with cotton to make her cuddly. Head turns. Crying voice. Sheer ninon dress, bonnet. Wears undies, shoes, socks. 15 in. tall. A pretty addition to your tot's doll family.
49 N U3233—Wt. 2 lbs. . $3.29

C A Bright-eyed Young Miss with her molded hair swept back and up; has rayon ribbon bow. Thick-lashed glassene sleeping eyes. Latex rubber skin body, cotton stuffed. Vinyl head moves . . jointed arms. Coos softly. Embossed cotton and rayon parchment taffeta dress, cotton panties, socks, shoes. About 23 in. tall. Same quality was $5.98.
49 N U3650—Wt. 4 lbs. . . . $4.95

Adorable Baby Brother and Sister to complete your doll family. Both carefully designed with tiny little turned-up noses, pretty smiling mouths and bright glassene eyes shadowed with thick lashes that close for bedtime. Vinyl plastic heads feel amazingly baby-like. Dewy-fresh complexions and pretty molded curls make them look almost real. One-piece Latex rubber skin bodies are cotton stuffed, really cuddly. Fun to sponge clean. They coo softly when cuddled.

D Brother. 15½ in. tall. Cotton corduroy pants, flannel shirt, leather-effect shoes.
49 N U3686—Wt. 2 lbs. . $2.87

E Sister. 15½ in. tall. Cotton corduroy and flannel dress. Leather-effect shoes.
49 N U3682-Shpg. wt. 2 lbs. $2.87

D $2.87

E $2.87

A $4.99

B $3.29

C Same quality Was $5.98   Now $4.95

A $1.77   B $1.77   C $1.77   D $1.69   E $1.77

G $2.37   H $2.37

HAPPI-TIME Miniatures gems in any collection

Girls of all ages love to collect these luxuriously dressed, realistic miniature dolls. Dolls A, B, C, D and E are 7½ inches tall—all made of sturdy, practically unbreakable plastic, with arms that move, heads that tilt and turn and go-to-sleep glassene eyes with eyelashes. All stand alone, are dressed in gorgeous finery. Shoes are painted on. All except nun and groom have curly mohair wigs. Girl dolls wear panties and crinoline half slips.

A Radiant Cinderella . . stepping out from fairyland. She's on her way to the ball . . wearing a glittery, star-studded dress with net and gold-color braid trim. Carries a tiny slipper.
49 N 3118—Shpg. wt. 12 oz.$1.77

D Handsome Bridegroom. Wears molded high hat, striped trousers, "tails," tie. White vest; watch chain.
49N3102—Shpg. wt. 12 oz.$1.69

Cowgirl (not shown). Wears fringed imitation leather vest, skirt; rayon shirt, felt hat. Tiny gun.
49 N 3116—Shpg. wt. 12 oz.$1.69

B Realistic Nun. She wears black rayon taffeta habit, soft black veil . . set off by snowy white collar and headpiece. Sweet, angelic face. Metal crucifix; imported Italian rosary beads.
49 N 3106—Shpg. wt. 12 oz.$1.77

E Beautiful Bride. Radiantly lovely in her traditional white rayon satin gown with its glamorous full skirt. Lace trimmed skirt . . net veil, too. She carries an artificial rosebud bouquet to complete a perfect picture.
49 N 3101—Shpg. wt. 12 oz.$1.77

C Miss Christmas. She's as sprightly and gay as the holiday season in her lavish ruby red gown of shimmery rayon satin and hooded cape, all with rich white fur-effect trim and muff.
49 N 3105—Shpg. wt. 12 oz.$1.77

F Revolving "Swiss Music Box" Stand Cut! For dolls A, B, C, D, E, G, H. Turntable holds doll. Plastic 4¼-in. diam. base. Doll not included. Swiss music box plays Wedding March, Happy Birthday or Anniversary Waltz. *State tune. Was $2.29.*
49 N 3094—Shpg. wt. 8 oz..$1.98

F   Was $2.29   Now $1.98

Roy Rogers and Dale Evans. Hard plastic bodies and heads, movable arms, legs, heads. Glassene sleeping eyes. Cowboy hat, boots. 8 in. tall.

G Roy Rogers. Wears plaid cotton shirt, denim pants with imitation leather chaps. Gun holsters with two miniature guns. Has molded hair.
49 N 3054—Shpg. wt. 10 oz......$2.37

H Dale Evans. Wears plaid cotton shirt like Roy's; imitation leather skirt with fringed edges; gun holsters with 2 miniature guns. Mohair wig.
49 N 3055—Shpg. wt. 10 oz......$2.37

DAVY CROCKETT

with frontier style cap. 17 in. tall

$2.97

Davy Crockett Doll. Soft, one-piece latex body, vinyl head. Glassene stationary, set-in eyes. Wears cotton twill frontier outfit. Imitation leather belt, pouch. Molded hair is topped by imitation fur cap.
49 N U3629—Shpg. wt. 2 lbs......$2.97

Petite 8-inch Wardrobe Walking Doll turns her head as she walks, has 4 complete changes of wardrobe. Hard plastic; jointed arms, legs. Sleeping glassene eyes, Saran hair. Wears felt hat, dress; rayon panties, socks; plastic shoes. Layette includes 2-pc. pajamas, blouse with skirt, matching bolero, coat and bonnet. Amazingly low priced!
49 N 3056—Shpg. wt. 10 oz........$2.98

L   M

Joanie Pigtails with Wardrobe. Saran braids to comb, brush and redo. Jointed arms, legs, turning head. Nearly unbreakable plastic. Go-to-sleep eyes. Wardrobe has cotton dress, bonnet; nursery pattern p.j.'s; molded vinyl shoes. Curlers, comb, brush, mirror. Wears pants. 8 in. tall.
49 N 3049—Wt. 1 lb. Was $2.79...$2.39

L Lovable 9-inch "Cuddles" is squeezable vinyl plastic. He has jointed arms, legs; big painted eyes. Squeaks when you hug him. Washable, sanitary. Assorted styles.
49 N 3504—Wt. 1 lb. Was $1.29..$1.00

M Drink and Wet Baby. Soft vinyl plastic. Has jointed arms, legs . . painted eyes. Baby wears flannelette diaper . . holds nursing bottle. Fun for the tiniest tot. 11½ inches tall.
49 N 3613—Shpg. wt. 1 lb.......$1.33

J   K

J Meet Snoozie—a cuddly baby doll little girls just love to care for. She's in her flannelette wrapper, diaper and blanket . . just like real little babies. Soft rubber-skin body so easy to wipe clean, vinyl plastic head that turns. Take good care of her or she'll "cry" in her plaintive little voice when squeezed. Pretty painted eyes. She's 11½ in. long.
49 N 3609—Shpg. wt. 14 oz.... $1.98

K The Campbell Kids—a pair of 9½-in. tall mischievous twins that steal your heart. Their cotton-stuffed latex bodies feel so real, are easy to keep clean, too. Movable vinyl plastic heads with impish features painted on. Their molded hair is topped by white chef's caps. Boy wears red and white suit, white apron, socks. Girl wears red and white dress, white apron, socks.
49 N 3610—Shpg. wt. 1 lb. Pair $2.98

A $1.85
E $1.89
G $1.17
B $4.78
C $2.89
D $2.79
F $2.87
$2.79

Popular soft Dolls . . fun-loving playmates for tiny tots

A Rose O'Neill's original "Kewpie." Soft, rose-tinted vinyl plastic. She's 12 inches of loveable cuddly pudginess. Set-in, glass-like eyes. Her head turns and she smiles sweetly. Dressed in printed cotton playsuit. Easy to wipe clean. Ideal for toddlers. Collectors like her, too.
49 N 3500—Wt. 1 lb. $1.85

B TV's Howdy Doody. His comical freckled face and head is carefully designed of sturdy plastic. Lower jaw hinged; moves like ventriloquist's dummy. Go-to-sleep eyes. Cotton stuffed body; simulated sewn-on plaid shirt, bandana. 21 in. tall.
49 N 3595—Wt. 2 lbs. $4.78

C Original Raggedy Ann, every tot's favorite. Right from the storybooks, and cotton stuffed to make her extra huggable. She's dressed in bright percale, has striped legs, cotton yarn hair, button eyes and a lovable painted face. Sweet little smile wins hearts. 15 in. tall.
49 N 3580—Wt. 1 lb. $2.89

D Dennis the Menace. His antics in the comics have made him famous. Now he's a big 16-inch charmer you can have for your own. He has a vinyl head, latex rubber body, stationary glassene eyes. He wears cotton T-shirt, denim overalls with his name.
49 N 3537—Wt. 1 lb. $2.79

E A Wide-eyed Young Charmer who's just asking to be picked up and loved. She's cotton stuffed to make her ready for "rough-and-tumble" play. Yarn curls; painted face of plastic. Cotton covered body, legs. Cotton dress; matching bonnet. Socks; shoes. 15 in. tall.
49 N 3545—Shpg. wt. 14 oz. . . . $1.89

F Sporty 26-inch College Coed. She's a cheerful looking gal . . ready to burst into a cheer for her school. Cotton stuffed, painted plastic mask face; vinyl coated arms, legs. She wears bright cotton felt skirt and tam, knit cotton sweater. Yarn hair. She looks so smart in her jaunty hat.
49 N U3569—Shpg. wt. 2 lbs. . . $2.87

G A Pretty Young Miss who was made to be cuddled. She's a colorful little beauty with her bright percale-covered body . . her cute cotton tie-on apron-style dress. She's 11 inches of softness and charm . . stuffed with cotton . . her painted face smiling. Just right for the arms of a tiny tot.
49 N 3511—Shpg. wt. 10 oz. . . $1.17

15-inch Sleepy-head Doll

For naptime hours, no dolly will be a more delightful companion than this snuggly sweetheart. Her impish face will capture your heart, and she'll be baby's favorite companion. Made of kitten-soft cotton-back rayon plush in pastel colors, stuffed with soft, white cotton. Her rose face is made of easy-to-clean, practically-unbreakable plastic with carefully painted features. Smooth cotton yarn ringlets frame her face. 15 in. tall.
49 N 3527—Shipping weight 1 lb. $2.79

H K M P S J L N R T

DOLL CLOTHING for all sizes . . De luxe selection for sports, outings, cool days, and parties

H Baby Doll Taffeta Coat and Bonnet. White lacy edging. Fine quality rayon moire taffeta. Shipping weight 8 oz.
49 N 3412—Size 14-15 in $1.59
49 N 3413—Size 16-17 in 1.59
49 N 3414—Size 18-19 in 1.89
49 N 3415—Size 20-21 in 1.89

J Baby Doll Layette. Everything a new "baby" needs. Organdy dress, bonnet. Lawn slip. Imitation leather shoes, rayon stockings. Fits all rubber and vinyl Skin dolls. Shipping weight 14 oz.
49 N 3425—Size 14-15 in $2.19
49 N 3426—Size 16-17 in 2.19
49 N 3427—Size 18-19 in 2.49
49 N 3428—Size 20-21 in 2.49
49 N 3429—Size 22-23 in 2.79

K Snowsuit and Bonnet for Baby Doll. Fine quality cotton fleece. Wool loop trim. Knit cuffs on legs. Tassel tie. Separate belt. Shpg. wt. 8 oz.
49 N 3437—Size 14-15 in $1.69
49 N 3439—Size 16-17 in 1.69
49 N 3444—Size 18-19 in 1.98
49 N 3445—Size 20-21 in 1.98

L Two-piece Baby Pajamas on Hanger. Good quality cotton flannel in assorted kiddie prints. Warm and snuggly for your baby doll on chilly nights. Shipping weight 8 ounces.
49 N 3430—Size 14-15 in 79c
49 N 3431—Size 16-17 in 79c
49 N 3432—Size 18-19 in 89c
49 N 3433—Size 20-21 in 89c

M Bridal outfit for girl doll. Ninon gown, flocked design, lace trim. Floral spray. Lawn slip, net veil. Shpg. wt. 10 oz.
49 N 3420—Size 14-15 in $2.79
49 N 3421—Size 16-17 in 2.79
49 N 3422—Size 18-19 in 2.89
49 N 3423—Size 20-21 in 2.89

N Rich Fur Coat, Hat and Muff Set. Snowy white rabbit fur that dolly can snuggle into on cold days. Shpg. wt. set 12 oz.
49 N 3470—Size 15-16 in $2.79
49 N 3471—Size 17-18 in 2.89
49 N 3472—Size 19-20 in 2.98

P Roller Skating Set for girl doll. Skates on shoes, slacks, bonnet, striped cotton jersey shirt. Shpg. wt. 8 oz.
49 N 3440—Size 14-15 in $1.29
49 N 3442—Size 16-17 in 1.45
49 N 3442—Size 18-19 in 1.45
49 N 3443—Size 20-21 in 1.59

R 3-pc. Evening Gown for Girl Dolls. Pretty rayon taffeta with all-over-net skirt and tinsel trimmed with rosebuds. Tie shoulder straps. Embossed jacket. Rayon panties, lace trim. Shpg. wt. 10 oz.
49 N 3458—Size 14-15 in $1.98
49 N 3459—Size 16-17 in 2.47
49 N 3460—Size 18-19 in 2.59

S Coat and Hat Set specially made for Walking Dolls. Embossed rayon taffeta with metal zipper closing on back of coat. Buttons on front. Shpg. wt. set 10 oz.
49 N 3416—Size 17-18 in $1.79
49 N 3417—Size 22-23 in 1.98

T Dresses for Walking Dolls. Assorted styles, made especially for walking dolls. Full skirts, fancy trims. All with buttons, buttonholes. Shpg. wt. each 10 oz.
49 N 3419—Size 17-18 in $1.19
49 N 3424—Size 22-23 in 1.29

HOW TO ORDER: Doll clothes are sold according to the height of the doll. Measure your doll carefully from head to foot. On your order, state the catalog number of the size nearest the height of your doll. Order several outfits for Christmas.

Clamps to table

Pressure foot

Tension disc

B $1.59

A $6.98
House only

E $1.79

G 89c

F $2.25

C $1.89

$2.98 **D**

$5.79

SEW AND CLEAN FOR YOUR DOLLY

House her handsomely with these homemaker toys

A **NEW 4-room Colonial Doll House.** Beautifully decorated white house has bright red roof, green, black, brown and blue trim. White plastic windows. Sturdy hardboard construction. 2 complete floors. Easy to assemble without tools. 17½x10½x27 in. long.
79 N 01406—Doll House (furniture not included). Shipping weight 11 pounds $6.98

10-pc. Wood Furniture Sets. Choice, each $1.79

Living Room Set. 2 end tables, couch, table, 2 table lamps, floor lamp, coffee table, TV set, chair. Shpg. wt. 1 lb. 49 N 1236.....$1.79	Bedroom Set. 2 single beds, dressing table, cedar chest, night table, 2 lamps, chair, clock and bench. Wt. 1 lb. 49 N 1237....$1.79	Bathroom Set. Tub, toilet, washbowl, 2 towel racks, waste basket, scale, heater, stool, hamper. Shipping weight 1 lb. 49 N 1238....$1.79	Kitchen Set. Stove, sink, refrigerator, table, 4 chairs, bowl and radio. Shipping weight 1 lb. Order for Christmas. 49 N 1239....$1.79

B **Beautiful 21-piece Jewelry and Vanity Chest.** Everything the "little lady" will need for "dress-up," parties. Bracelets, earrings, pendants, rings, etc. with bright realistic gleam and glitter. Includes compacts, lipstick cases, combs and make-believe powder and rouge. All metalized gold and silver colored plastic. 4-drawer cardboard chest 14¼x7x3 inches.
49 N 1293—Shpg. wt. 1 lb. 4 oz. $1.59

C **Friction Vacuum Cleaner with Sparks.** No trouble cleaning house with this working model vacuum. Just push down and forward, listen to the motor hum, watch the sparks fly through transparent lens in motor housing. Actually picks up dust and dirt through suction with aid of revolving brush. Transparent vinyl plastic bag. Handle 23 inches high. Base is 6¾x6½x3⅜ inches high.
49 N 1203—Shipping weight 2 lbs. $1.89

D **Imported Sewing Machine.** Economy-priced . . . imported from West Germany. Sews in chain stitch. Thread tension disc adjusts to fabric thickness. Clamp holds machine firmly to table. Safety guard under needle. Metal smoothly enameled in bright color. 3 needles, thread incl. 8x4½x6½ in. high.
49 N 1277—Shpg. wt. 2 lbs. 6 oz. $2.98

E **Sewing Kit with Doll.** Make a complete wardrobe for 7½-inch plastic doll with movable arms. Simple patterns, easy to use. All materials and accessories to be used with patterns contained in set. Metal scissors, needle, thimble, 4 bobbins of thread, buttons and assorted color rickrack. 11¼x18¼x2½-in. case. Encourages kiddies to learn sewing.
49 N 1235—Shipping weight 2 lbs. $1.79

F **Junior Miss Rhinestone Setter Kit.** Apply beautiful decorations to dolls' wardrobes, and to own clothing, too. Even Mother can make good use of this craft set. Rhinestone setter, rhinestones with separate metal settings, simulated pearl studs, multicolored cup and star sequins, seed beads, bugle beads, needles, thread, felt appliques. Instructions and designs. Fun for young seamstresses.
49 N 1201—Shpg. wt. 1 lb. 4 oz. $2.25

G **Magnetic Paper Doll.** Her name is Magic Mary—and she's a very special paper dolly, too. And she is dressed in an instant, because magnetic attraction makes her clothes cling like magic. Complete with 14 brightly colored dresses to cut out. Doll measures 10 inches tall on sturdy metal base. A thrifty gift.
49 N 1251—Shpg. wt. 1 lb. 89c

Our Finest Imported Toy Sewing Machine

Imported from West Germany. Sews regular machine chain stitch . . . every one even and firm. Thread tension and stitch controls adjust to fabric thickness. Safety guard protects little fingers from pricks, means tiny hands can't get in the way of the needle. Pressure foot keeps material in place while sewing. Child controls speed of the machine with easy-turning handle. Gear-drive and transmission give "big machine" operation—smoother, more even sewing. Made of sturdy steel with brightly enameled finish. Hardwood base. Metal clamp fastens securely to table, keeping machine steady while your little girl sews. Easy-to-insert needle. Complete instructions are easy to follow—your little seamstress will quickly learn to turn out fine dresses for her doll family. Send your order today for Christmas. Overall size 8⅝x4⅝x6¾ in.
49 N 1232—Shipping weight 3 lbs. $5.79

A new doll made a splashy appearance in the 1956 Christmas Wishbook. The Revlon Dolls, manufactured to promote the cosmetics company to young girls who might become future customers, were very popular. The catalog copy describes them best: "Shapely, full-formed young ladies with turning waists that let them bend forward, backward and pose so prettily... made of new "magic touch" plastic that has the smooth, soft, resilient touch of real skin... rooted Saran hair to comb, brush and set... high style dresses, crinolines, high-heeled sandals... they're right from the pages of the fashion magazines!"

In fact, the Revlon Doll clothes were very well made and quite beautiful. Organdy fabrics were the rage and the most prominent dress material. But finding one of these dolls today, complete with its hat and accessories, is extremely difficult. One costumed doll in particular, "Cherries a la Mode", is a rare find.

More Sweet Sue dolls, in outfits such as Bridesmaid, Bride and Sunday Best, appeared in 1956. These dolls are very collectible today.

There were many Happi Time dolls, Sears' house brand, featured this year. Most likely made by the Ideal Toy Company, some are marked as such and some show no manufacturer's mark.

Note the 13-inch Gerber Baby with Feeding Set at $4.79. These dolls, licensed by the baby food maker, had been around long before 1956, but still drew buyer interest. Today they are highly collectible.

SEARS
Christmas
BOOK 1956

SEARS, ROEBUCK AND CO.

Sears Christmas
Wishbook

1956

D		$7.98
B		$12.95 "Cherries a la Mode"
C		$14.95 "Queen of Diamonds"
A		$10.95 "Kissing Pink"
E		$3.95
F		$4.95

Meet the Revlon Dolls! Shapely, full-formed young ladies with turning waists that let them bend forward, backward and pose so prettily . . made of new ''magic touch'' plastic that has the smooth, soft, resilient touch of real skin . . rooted Saran hair to comb, brush and set . . high-style dresses, crinolines, high-heeled sandals . . they're right from the pages of the fashion magazines!

Dolls to cuddle, Dolls to love

[A] ''Kissing Pink'' This little dream is dressed for a date in a smart blue and white striped cotton dress with a crinoline to keep it poofy. A make-believe pearl necklace circles her slender neck. She's 18 inches tall with long legs, a slim turning waist that lets her pose, finely formed fingers. Her ''magic touch'' plastic skin is the most realistic we've felt on any doll—more pliable than most plastics, yet firmer than vinyl. You can comb, brush and set her rooted brunette Saran hair in all the latest styles. Jointed at neck, shoulders and hips. Lashed go-to-sleep eyes. High-heeled sandals, sheer nylon hose, panties.
49 N 3770—Shipping weight 3 pounds. $10.95

[D] 22-inch Vinyl Doll in nylon dress and fluffy apron. Bend her ''Superflex'' legs, see her kneel and sit. Saran hair. Cotton stuffed. Jointed arms; head turns. Lashed go-to-sleep eyes. Coos. Has comb, brush, mirror, curlers, panties, socks, shoes.
49 N 3622—Shipping weight 4 pounds. $7.98

[B] ''Cherries a la Mode'' is ready for church in a flower-bedecked straw hat and a navy blue nylon dress with bright cherry design. Pretend pearl earrings and necklace top off her pretty outfit. She's 18 inches tall with long legs, graceful fingers and a turning waist that lets her bend forward, backward and pose like a model. She's made of ''magic touch'' plastic that feels like real skin. Comb, brush and set her rooted blonde Saran hair in different styles. Jointed at neck, shoulders and hips. Lashed go-to-sleep eyes. High-heeled sandals, sheer nylon hose, crinoline and panties complete her outfit.
49 N 3771—Shipping weight 3 pounds. $12.95

[E] 18-inch Vinyl Doll with lace-trimmed plaid dress, of swishy rayon satin. Molded hair, perky ribbon. One-piece vinyl skin, cotton-stuffed body. Head turns. Go-to-sleep eyes. Coo voice. Cotton half slip, panties, shoes, socks.
49 N 3608—Shpg. wt. 2 lbs. 4 oz. $3.95

[C] The ''Queen of Diamonds'' looks like she just stepped off the cover of a fashion magazine. A white fur stole tops her lavish gown—a beauty with a red cotton velvet bodice and metallic stripes highlighting the bouffant white nylon gauze skirt. The finishing touches: a rhinestone necklace, earrings, ring. She's 18 in. tall with long legs, tapered fingers and a turning waist. Her ''magic touch'' plastic skin has the softness and resiliency of real skin. Her rooted red Saran hair can be combed, brushed, set. Jointed at neck, shoulders and hips. Lashed go-to-sleep eyes. High-heeled sandals, crinoline, hose, panties.
49 N 3772—Shipping weight 3 pounds. $14.95

[F] Big 22-inch Cuddle-Bun now all vinyl at no increase in price! Molded hair, satin ribbon. One-piece cotton-stuffed, vinyl skin body. Head turns. Go-to-sleep eyes. Coos. Chromespun and cotton dress. Panties, socks, shoes.
49 N 3653—Shipping weight 4 pounds. $4.95

Make sure she gets the doll of her dreams, put it on your Easy Terms order. See page 373

A $13.95

B $9.79

C $7.98

D Vas $4.69 $4.39

E $2.89

F $2.89

G $28.79 cash $3.00 down

See her kneel, hear her say her prayers!

Oh, You Beautiful Dolls!

A "Magic Lips" moves her lips as she "talks" and "kisses" you. Press her back, she closes her lips; release pressure and she opens her mouth and coos softly. Comb, brush and set her rooted Saran hair. Finely detailed vinyl head, arms and legs. Vinyl-coated body is cotton stuffed. She wears a lacy nylon dress, rayon half slip, panties, socks and vinyl shoes. 24 inches tall. She comes with a tiny tooth brush for her 3 pretty teeth. Her lashed eyes close for sleep.
79 N 03358—Shipping weight 6 pounds.........$13.95

B New 20-inch Little Miss. A glamorous young lady with a slim, full-formed figure of life-like vinyl. With her "Superflex" legs and jointed shoulders and elbows she can sit, kneel and pose in all sorts of pretty ways. She's dressed for a party in a swishy formal of rayon taffeta, lace and velvet, a crinoline, nylon hose, high-heeled shoes and lace-trimmed panties. Saran pony tail to brush and style. Lashed go-to-sleep eyes.
49 N 3690—Shipping weight 3 pounds 6 ounces....$9.79

C 19-inch "Star of the Ballet." Flexible knees, ankles and jointed waist—she can pose in real ballet positions. Saran hair. Vinyl head, arms. Molded plastic body, legs. Go-to-sleep eyes. Has velvet and net tutu, hose, Ballet slippers, extra street dress, shoes. Practice bar.
49 N 3755—Shpg. wt. 2 lbs. 8 oz................$7.98

D Draft Dodger. Bend her "Superflex" arms and legs, pose her 101 ways ... kneeling, sitting, praying. Rooted Saran hair to comb, brush and set. All vinyl; cotton-stuffed. Lashed go-to-sleep eyes. Coos. Wears striped cotton flannel sleeper and night cap. 15 inches tall.
49 N 3132—Shpg. wt. 2 lbs.....Was $4.69......$4.39

E F Baby Brother and Sister. Vinyl plastic heads, molded hair. Lashed go-to-sleep glassene eyes. One-piece latex bodies; cotton stuffed. Coo voices. 15½ in. tall. Assorted style cotton outfits, shoes. Economically priced.
(E) 49 N 3601—Brother. Shpg. wt. 2 lbs..........$2.89
(F) 49 N 3602—Sister. Shpg. wt. 2 lbs............ 2.89

G New! Meet "Melodie," the doll that walks, talks and sings! She's as much fun as a real live playmate. Just press her magic button, hear her recite rhymes, sing nursery ditties and pray. Take her by the arm and she'll walk along with you. She'll sit on a bench with you, too; her knees and legs are specially jointed so she can kneel, sit and pose in life-like ways. Before she goes to bed, clean her pert vinyl face and comb, brush and set her rooted Saran hair. Then she'll kneel by the bed to say her prayers. "Melodie" is a big girl, 30 inches tall with a sturdy body of hard-to-break plastic. She comes dressed in a fine quality printed organdy dress, lace-trimmed rayon taffeta half-slip, panties, rayon socks and patent leather shoes. A perky straw bonnet tops her curls. 2 batteries, 3 changeable records for Melodie's voice included; easy to operate, nothing to wind. A song sheet for her owner is included so she can sing along with "Melodie."

79 N 03799—Shipping weight 7 pounds.........$28.79

B $18.95
Doll and Accessories

C $9.95
Doll and Bath

A 11½ in. tall with Saran Hair $9.39

Tiny Tears Cries Real Tears, Wets, Blows Bubbles

A She's as lovable and lifelike as baby sister! Big wet tears well up in her eyes and roll down her cheeks. She cries, closes her thick lashed glassene eyes at nap time, drinks her bottle, wets her diaper, blows bubbles . . even comforts herself with her pacifier. And she loves to be bathed in neck high water. Pretty head is molded of hard-to-break plastic. Jointed body of soft molded rubber. Dressed in embossed cotton romper suit. Layette has cotton dress, panties, bonnet, bottle and nipple, Kleenex, diaper, pins, sponge, soap, bubble pipe, washcloth, pacifier and instruction booklet.

Tiny Tears with Saran Hair, Suitcase and big Layette. She loves to have her curls brushed, washed and set. They're firmly rooted in her pretty head. She's a well equipped young lady with layette as described above plus bathrobe. 11½-inch size has bootees—13½ and 16-inch sizes have shoes and socks. She's ready to go in her leatherette-effect fiberboard suitcase with snap lock, plastic handle.

11½-inch size	13½-inch size	16-inch size
49 N 3035	49 N 3036	49 N 3038
Shpg. wt. 3 lbs.	Shpg. wt. 4 lbs.	Shpg. wt. 6 lbs.
$9.39	$11.27	$13.98

Tiny Tears with Molded Hair that looks like real curls. (Not shown). She's pert and pretty as can be— exactly as described above. Keeps little mom busy bathing her, changing diapers, drying tears, playing games. Layette as listed above, plus knit bootees. In colorful display box.

13½-inch size	16-inch size
49 N 3031	49 N 3033
Shpg. wt. 3 lbs.	Shpg. wt. 4 lbs.
$7.45	$9.45

B Our Biggest Tiny Tears now comes with her own Playroom Equipment. 20-inch Tiny Tears plays happily all day in her new 18-inch square plastic playpen. Take her out to change her diaper and she cries real tears. Playpen has quilted pad. She has a pail and shovel to play with. Little moms can't resist her, they make her blow bubbles, bathe her, comfort her with her pacifier. They'll brush, wash and set her pretty rooted Saran hair. Cuddly body of soft molded rubber. Head molded of hard-to-break plastic, in lifelike detail. Glassene go-to-sleep eyes. Cotton romper suit, dress, panties, bonnet; shoes, socks, nipple bottle, Kleenex, diaper, clothes pins, sponge, soap, bubble pipe, cloth, pacifier. Instructions.

79 N 03045L—Shpg. wt. 9 lbs.. . $18.95

C 11½-in. Tiny Tears with Ding Dong School Bath. She cries tears, wets, blows bubbles. 20x 12x29-in. tub holds water, has drain hose with shut-off. Foldaway vinyl dressing table with aluminum legs, shelf, pockets, rubber-tipped legs. Tiny Tears has go-to-sleep glassene eyes, molded hair, hard plastic head, molded rubber body. Layette: nipple bottle, Kleenex, diaper, sponge, soap, bubble pipe, washcloth, bootees, pacifier, instruction booklet. In asst. cotton rompers.

79 N T3087L—Shpg. wt. 7 lbs.. . . $9.95

Layette for 11½-in. Tiny Tears. (Not shown.) Embroidered cotton dress, bonnet, panties, lacy rayon taffeta jacket, diaper, knit bootees, pacifier, bubble pipe, nipple bottle.

49 N 3450—Shpg. wt. 1 lb. $2.79

A $11.95
18-inch

B $13.95
18-inch

C $16.95
22-inch

Sweet Sue Walking Dolls

Fully jointed walking dolls that do almost everything a real little girl can do. Sue bends her knees, kneels to pray, bends her elbows to fold hands, sits; assumes 101 poses. And she'll walk along with her new mama, turning her head as she goes. She has rooted Saran hair to comb, brush, curl and set. Beautifully detailed vinyl arms and gracefully tapered fingers. Delicately tinted features and thick-lashed glassene eyes that close at nap time. Finely molded head, legs, body of break-resistant plastic.

A Sweet Sue is so sweet and demure in her Sunday best. Dainty tucked sheer nylon dress with lace trim and velvet sash. Pastel petticoat with fluffy ruffle. Panties, shoes, socks, flower-trimmed straw hat and bag.

18-inch size	22-inch size
49 N 3705—Shpg. wt. 3 lbs......$11.95	49 N 3706—Shpg. wt. 4 lb. 8 oz....$14.95

B Sweet Sue dressed as a Bridesmaid. A picture of glowing beauty for the wedding in her formal gown of tucked pastel sheer nylon with lace trim. Ruffled petticoat, ribbon sash, panties, shoes, straw bonnet. Corsage.

18-inch size	22-inch size
49 N 3707—Shpg. wt. 3 lbs. 8 oz...$13.95	49 N 3708—Shpg. wt. 4 lb. 8 oz....$16.95

C Sweet Sue the Bride .. a creation of sweet loveliness for her marriage. Exquisite bridal gown of nylon lace and tulle skirt with ruffle. Ruffled rayon satin petticoat, panties, shoes, lace cap, circular veil, corsage.

18-inch size	22-inch size
49 N 3709—Shpg. wt. 3 lbs. 8 oz...$13.95	49 N 3710—Shpg. wt. 4 lbs........$16.95

Toodles, the action doll .. she kneels, drinks, wets

D Toodles the all-jointed vinyl plastic doll now has rooted Saran hair. She's jointed at knees, hips, shoulders, elbows. She's soft and cuddly. Does all the things real babies do—sits, drinks, wets, can hold her toes with her tiny hands. You can comb, brush and set her lustrous hair over and over. he'll even turn her head in any direction and close her eyes at nap time. Her fingers are beautifully detailed and she wears sandals to show off her retty toes. Easy to sponge clean. Wears glazed cotton sunsuit, brings nipple and bottle with her. 21 inches tall.

79 N 03066—Toodles with rooted Saran curls. Shpg. wt. 7 lbs..................$16.95
79 N 03063—Toodles, exactly as above, but with molded hair. Shpg. wt. 6 lbs...... 13.95

*Build your order up to $20 or more and buy on Sears convenient
Easy Payment Plan . . . see page 373 for complete details*

D $16.95
21-inch
with Saran hair

Legs jointed at knees—
see her kneel!

Fully jointed for 101 poses

She loves to touch her toes

Saran hair may be combed, brushed, set

Kneels to say prayers alongside "mamma"

A
$11.49
24 inch

B
$19.45
20-inch

D
$7.95
21-inch

C
$5.49
16-inch

F
$4.98
17-inch

E
$5.69
18-inch

Our Best Happi-Time Dolls

Thick, glossy Saran hair to comb, brush, set.. realistically molded in life-like detail

[G] $9.79

[H] $3.89

[A] Lively Happi-Time Walker with jointed knees, rooted hair and a soft vinyl plastic head. She walks, she sits, she kneels to pray, she has big go-to-sleep eyes and cries too—she's as peppy as her young mother. She can strike almost any pose a little girl thinks of. She seems alive as she toddles through toytown turning her pretty head from side to side, flashing her thick-lashed shiny eyes flirtatiously. She's no trouble at bedtime— as soon as you put her pretty little head on the pillow, her eyes close and she's asleep. You'll love playing beauty shop with her. Her rooted Saran hair seems almost real. It won't fall out and stays lustrous. Brush it, comb it, wave it and set it and she'll look as pretty as a picture. Molded of very strong plastic, she doesn't mind the rough and tumble of the playroom floor. She's all dressed up ready to greet her new mom, and make a good impression. An embossed cotton dress with sewed-in panties, cotton gabardine coat trimmed with rich, thick pile, imitation fur, with hat to match, socks and vinyl plastic shoes.

Deluxe 24-inch Doll.
79 N 03274—Shipping weight 5 lbs..$11.49

17-inch Little Sister.
49 N 3258—Shipping weight 3 lbs...$8.89

[B] Happi-Time Walking Wardrobe Doll with a Big Steel Trunk. Enough clothes in her trunk for a trip around the play world, or a fashion show all on her own. You can see in her walk just how very proud she is as she daintily trips along. Her little head turns from side to side to catch those admiring looks you'll give her. To please her, comb, brush and set her shiny rooted Saran locks in your favorite style. She's very active because her arms and legs are jointed. Tumbles on the floor don't bother her for she's made of very strong plastic. Her eyes close when she sleeps. When she arrives you'll find her wearing a bonny Scotch plaid rayon dress frosted with lace, rayon underskirt and panties, socks, vinyl plastic shoes. Open up her trunk and you'll be thrilled with her fluffy net trimmed rayon taffeta formal with panties, a denim coat and hat, 2-piece cotton pajamas, cotton housecoat, embossed cotton print play dress, comb, brush, mirror, sun glasses, 6 plastic hangers, extra pair of socks and vinyl plastic shoes. All steel trunk with steel reinforced corners, hinges and snap lock.

20-inch Toddler with 3-drawer Trunk.
20¼ x11x11 inches. Shipping weight 14 lbs.
79 N 03722.....................$19.45

16-inch Doll with one-drawer Trunk 16¼ x 9x9 inches. Shipping weight 8 lbs.
49 N 3721.....................$14.95

[C] Rooted Pony-tailed Walking Playmate will be a real "pal" to her new mom. She walks along, turning her head from side to side with the sweetest expression on her cute little face. She's jointed at hips and shoulders so she's always very active. Her long pony tail is made of lustrous rooted Saran and is just as pretty as a real little girl's. You'll brush and comb it and set it in perfect style for all the dolly parties. Her head is of soft, cuddly vinyl plastic and her body of strong hard plastic that wipes clean in a wink. She closes her eyes when she goes to sleep. Dressed in lacy rayon dress (assorted styles), rayon slip and panties, shoes. 2 curlers included.

49 N 3701—16-inch Doll.
Shipping weight 2 lbs.............$5.49

49 N 3702—19-inch Doll.
Shipping weight 2 lbs. 10 oz........$6.98

[D] Adorable Fashion-Plate in her three-piece ensemble. She can sit, kneel, and bend her legs into life-like positions because they are wire-cored with "Superflex". Baby-soft vinyl plastic from head to toe, she's a "pinchy" cuddlesome tyke. She has go-to-sleep eyes and a soft coo voice. Rooted Saran curls to comb, brush and set over and over. Expensive-looking cotton coat with matching bonnet, lacy ninon dress, rayon half slip, panties, socks and molded vinyl plastic shoes.

49 N 3679—17 inch tall. One-piece body.
Shipping weight 3 pounds.........$5.95

49 N 3680—De luxe 21-in. with jointed arms for more poses. Shpg. wt. 5 lbs.....$7.95

[E] Pert Pony Tails, a lovable 18-inch all vinyl plastic bundle of joy at a low price. Her shimmering rooted Saran pony tail accents her delicate little girl features. You can play for hours waving, brushing and combing her hair over and over again. She's a happy little girl, she coos and turns her head to see where her little mom is. Put her to bed and she closes her eyes. She's cuddly all vinyl plastic from head to toes, her body is soft cotton-stuffed. With a damp cloth you can wipe her clean in seconds. Lace-trimmed ninon dress in bon-bon pastels, rayon half slip, panties, socks, shoes. 2 curlers included.

49 N 3239—Shipping weight 2 pounds 8 ounces............................$5.69

[F] Demure Baby Doll looks so pretty in her Sunday best. She's all dressed up to be taken out in her lace-trimmed organdy and embossed-cotton dress with matching bonnet. Her long Saran locks are rooted in: you can comb, brush and set them over and over again in many styles. Cuddle her up close and feel her soft vinyl plastic head and skin—it's almost as soft as a real baby's. Squeeze her and she coos. At bedtime she'll close her thick-lashed, pleading eyes and go to sleep. Cotton lace-trimmed panties and slip, socks, plastic shoes. A lovable companion for any little girl.

49 N 3224—17 inches tall.
Shipping weight 3 pounds.........$4.98

49 N 3246—21 inches tall.
Shipping weight 4 pounds.........$8.49

See our big selection of doll furniture and buggies in this section

Her Highness, the Walking Princess

[G] Her Highness the Princess is an exquisite picture of grace and elegance dressed for the ball in her beautiful gown. Exquisite rayon brocade with sweeping nylon tulle overskirt and a rose garland around the waist draw admiration from all as she proudly walks along turning her head. Lustrous, rooted Saran hair to set, comb, style. Soft vinyl plastic head, hard plastic body. Jointed arms and legs. Go-to-sleep glassene eyes. Half slip, panties, ball slippers. 19 inches tall. Order now.

49 N 3749—Shpg. wt. 4 lbs............$9.79

17-in. Little Sister

[H] A young charmer with rooted poodle-cut hair and big bow. Dressed in lace-trimmed ninon frock, rayon slip, panties. Knit socks, plastic shoes. Comb, brush, set her rooted Saran hair. Coo voice. Latex skin; one-piece cotton-stuffed body. Go-to-sleep eyes.

49 N 3621—Shipping weight 2 lbs...$3.89

Bathe her in neck-high water

Saran hair to wash, brush, set

Dolly cries tears, wets, drinks

New! This dear little dolly looks and feels like a real baby. She cries, sheds real tears, wets her diaper and drinks. She's soft and cuddly vinyl plastic, colored in soft baby pink just as if she were alive. Delicate, detailed features and thick-lashed go-to-sleep glassene eyes make her the most lovable dolly you've ever seen. She's so kissable—from her pert nose to cute little separate toes and fingers. She's dimpled like baby too—in all the same places. You'll love to bathe her, powder and lotion her. Wash, brush and set her rooted Saran curls over and over; it always stays beautiful. Her arms and legs are jointed. Pretty cotton romper suit and matching bonnet. With her she brings a plastic diaper bag with zipper, bottle, comb, brush, mirror, bottle brush, bib, shower cap.

49N3069—13½ in. tall. Wt. 1 lb. 10 oz..$8.35
49N3070—16 in. tall. Wt. 2 lbs. 4 oz....11.45
79N03072—20 in. tall. Wt. 5 lbs.....14.75

Avoid the rush, the commotion of Christmas crowds. Shop the easy, convenient Sears catalog way

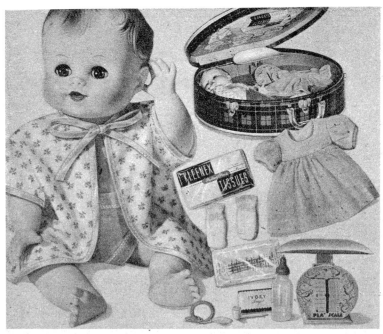

13-inch Babee-Bee with Layette, Carrying Case $9.45

She drinks, wets, cries, blows bubbles. Soft vinyl body; go-to-sleep eyes. She's as winsome as a baby can be, has jointed arms, legs, turning head. Her layette includes dainty ninon dress with lace trim, knit booties, steel weighing scales, soap, plastic nursing bottle, teething ring, bubble pipe, Q-Tips, Kleenex . . all in her own assorted gay colored carrying case with three metal snap fasteners, plastic handle.

Her pert little features are delicately molded in baby-soft vinyl. Her wavy molded hair and peaches-'n'-cream complexion can be sponged clean with a damp cloth. She cries when squeezed, has thick-lashed glassene eyes that close at naptime. Dressed in cotton flannel kimono and panties.

49 N 3719—Shipping weight 5 pounds..$9.45

18-inch "Bannister Baby"® drinks, wets, cries $9.29

As adorable and cute as any baby you've seen . . inspired by Constance Bannister, famous baby photographer. Baby-soft molded vinyl plastic head, delicately tinted in almost unbelievable prettiness. She has such a wide-eyed appealing look in her thick lashed, go-to-sleep, glassene eyes that you can't resist hugging her cuddly soft vinyl body. She drinks, wets, cries, blows bubbles, turns her head and loves a tubbing. Has jointed arms and legs. Wardrobe includes lace-trimmed ninon dress, rayon slip, booties, knit cotton panties, cotton flannelette robe. Comes with polyethylene nursing bottle, plastic bubble pipe.

49 N 3564—Deluxe 18-inch size illustrated.
Shipping weight 4 lbs.............. $9.29

49 N 3712—Popular 12-inch size has cotton slip. Shipping weight 2 lbs......... $5.29

The "Gerber Baby" is a ward of Gerber Products Co., Fremont, Mich.

[A] $2.69

[B] $1.75

13-in. Gerber Baby with Feeding Set $4.79

You'll have so much fun at feeding time with Gerber Baby, 'cause she brings along all her equipment . . 3 polyethylene bottles with wire rack, plastic funnel, spoon, metal cereal bowl and bottle brush. She'll drink and she'll wet. Squeeze her soft molded rubber body and she'll cry. She blows bubbles. Soft vinyl head with go-to-sleep eyes, jointed arms, legs. She's tubbable, has bib, panties, booties, diaper, bubble pipe.
49 N 3718—Shipping weight 2 lbs............. $4.79

18-inch All Vinyl Doll with Saran hair $8.98

She's everything that little mothers dream of in baby dolls. Her head turns and she has jointed arms and legs. She loves to be bathed and have her lustrous rooted Saran baby curls combed, brushed and set. She drinks, wets, cries and blows bubbles. Her head and body are soft, smooth, molded vinyl. Thick-lashed glassene eyes close at naptime. Dressed in cotton panties and cotton flannel baby jacket. Printed cotton flannel jacket and diaper soaker, booties, bubble pipe, polyethylene nipple bottle. A beautiful baby—put her under your Christmas tree.
49 N 3717—Shipping weight 3 pounds.................$8.98

12-in. Betty Bows

[A] Lovable Betty has a bow in her molded hair. Turnable vinyl head, molded rubber body, jointed arms, legs. Drinks, wets, cries, sleeps, blows bubbles, is tubbable. Go-to-sleep eyes. Wears rompers. Bubble pipe, polyethylene bottle. Order yours now.
49 N 3505—Wt. 1 lb. $2.69

10-in. Tiny So-Wee

[B] So-Wee was made especially for the tiniest doll mommies. Loves to splash in the tub, drink from her bottle. Cries when squeezed. Molded entirely from rubber, set-in plastic eyes. Wears cotton diaper. Polyethylene bottle. ●
49 N 3514—Wt.1 lb. $1.75

More dolls than ever before appeared in the pages of the 1957 Sears Christmas Wishbook, but for some reason only one teddy bear was evident... a cute 13-inch Musical Teddy with glassene eyes and Swiss music box built in. More than likely, Sears wanted to fill the catalog's pages with more lucrative dolls.

Sweet Sue returned in 1957, with a Forties look that would soon become dated with the upcoming arrival of Barbie. Another doll, Pony-Tail Teen, looked suspiciously like Lucille Ball's Lucy character from the hit TV show "I Love Lucy".

Revlon dolls, in 18-inch full size or the smaller 10 1/2-inch Little Miss Revlon, were very popular, particularly because of the wide variety of beautiful, well made clothes available. These clothes, and those for Betsy McCall, are highly collectible today. It takes some experience to identify them however, as they were often unmarked. Knowledgeable collectors can tell which are which by the snap design, stitching and other clues.

A 32-inch Jerry Mahoney Doll, a "replica of the famous TV funster" was offered for a pricey $13.87. It had full controls for ventriloquism and came with his own cardboard suitcase.

Finally, Shirley Temple, a doll classic based on the young child star, was offered this year in a 17-inch version. Shirley dolls, made under license by Ideal Toys, had been sold since 1937 and initially were made of composition material. This 1957 version is worth about $300 -- much more if mint and in the original box.

Sears Christmas

Wishbook

1957

Somersaulting Kitten . . Beautiful Lying Tiger

Musical Kitty. Wind her tail, she turns somersaults to tune of Swiss music box. Coat of long white rabbit fur, embroidered nose, glassene eyes, felt ears, perky bow. Cotton stuffed.
49 N 4109—8 inches long.
Shipping weight 1 pound...... **$4.47**

Thrifty Tiger is a big value at this low price. Lovable pet for tots; handsome mascot for teens. Cotton-backed rayon plush. Cotton stuffed. Locked-in glassene eyes. Jaunty bow. 16 inches long.
49 N 4065—Shipping weight
1 pound 6 ounces........... **$1.87**

Hobo Mutt. This happy fellow's merry vinyl face sports a "5 o'clock shadow." His wired legs assume many funny poses. Coat of synthetic chamois fiber and shaggy rayon plush. Wears a polka dot kerchief, eye patch, tail splint and carries a pack. Cotton stuffed. 12 inches long.
49 N 4054—Shipping weight
1 pound 8 ounces.................. **$4.47**

Lifelike Cocker Spaniel. Pull gently on his leash, he waddles along, barking when you squeeze bulb on his leash. Soft lamb fur, natural markings. Droopy ears. Plastic collar, leash. Glassene eyes. Lightly packed cotton stuffing .. put him in 101 poses. 14 inches long.
49 N 4190—Shipping weight
1 pound 10 ounces................ **$5.47**

Ride the Playroom Range on Roy Rogers' Trigger!

Frisky as a real pony, but so easy to steer the tiniest dude can ride him. Trigger steers smoothly in any direction, just like every well-trained cow pony. He rolls quietly on rubber-tired wheels. His steel frame is so strong it supports up to 100 pounds. Palomino color, cotton-backed rayon plush coat with flowing white mane and tail. Stuffed with springy cotton and excelsior. Western-style vinyl plastic saddle is 15 inches from the floor; wipes clean. 19x10x21 inches high.
79 N 04080—Shipping weight 8 pounds............................. **$9.47**

For Tots to Pamper and Pet
Lovable companions with snuggly stuffing

[A] Lion in a Basket. This cute lion cub –sits demurely in his own plastic basket. So lovable, you can't resist him. Soft cotton-backed rayon plush. Locked-in glassene eyes. 8 in. high. Gift packaged.
49 N 4032—Shipping weight 1 lb...... **$1.86**

[B] Hollywood Hound has soulful felt eyes that beg you to love him. Tweak his felt nose, he'll squeak. Crush-resistant, polka-dotted washable cotton-backed rayon plush. Stuffed with non-allergic featherfoam plastic. Red felt tongue. Ribbon bow. 12 inches long.
49 N 4044—Shipping weight 1 lb...... **$2.97**

[C] Coy Kitten. Love her, tub her—her chubby body is filled with washable fast-drying, feather-light Dryex— shredded foam plastic. Cotton-backed rayon plush coat. Hand-painted vinyl face.
49 N 4147—12 in. long. Wt. 1 lb.... **$2.77**

[D] Rin Tin Tin. A handsome pal and guardian for dog-loving tykes. Rich-colored cotton-backed rayon plush, with lifelike all-vinyl head. Soft cotton stuffing. Smart vinyl collar. 16 inches long. Comes complete with Rin Tin Tin membership card.
49 N 4135—Shpg. wt. 2 lbs......... **$3.97**

Stuffed Animals That make Appealing Pets

[E] Musical Teddy Bear. Teddy was so hungry he swallowed a Swiss music box! Wind key in his back—his tubby tummy tinkles gaily to lure tots to dreamland. Cotton-backed rayon plush; cotton stuffed. Glassene eyes. 13 inches high.
49 N 4157—Shipping weight 1 pound.......... **$3.77**

[F] Miniature Kitten. Tykes can't resist curling up at naptime with this sleepy pet. Just the right size for baby to cuddle. Adorable long felt eyelashes. Soft pastel cotton - backed rayon plush; springy cotton stuffing. 6 inches long.
49 N 4001—Shipping weight 8 ounces......... **$1.47**

[G] New! Mighty Mouse! This cheerful "defender of mistreated mice", costumed in rayon satin, Vinyl face. Cotton-backed rayon plush head. Cotton stuffed. Corduroy lined ears.
49 N 4144—15 inches high.
Shpg. wt. 1 lb.......... **$3.57**
49 N 4142—11½ in. size. (Not shown.) Vinyl ears.
Wt. 10 oz............. **$1.67**

[B] $10.97
14-inch

[C] $8.97
14-inch

[A] $11.97
14-inch

[D] $7.46
14-inch

[E] $12.97
14-inch

Sweet Sue Walking Dolls

- Exquisitely dressed beauties walk with you when guided by the hand
- Soft vinyl heads and firm vinyl plastic bodies with creamy bisque finish
- Rooted Saran hair is fun to comb, brush and set in the latest styles
- Turning waists and heads, jointed arms . . lashed glassene eyes that close
- A, B, C have jointed ankles . . wear high heels or flats, "dance" on their toes . . have plastic case with extra shoes, ballet slippers, ballerina leotard

[A] **Bride,** slender, demure and as lovely as a storybook bride. Heavy rayon satin gown with ruffled nylon tulle insert, ruching and rosebud trim. Hooped rayon taffeta petticoat, ruffled cap with veil, earrings, bouquet, panties, hose, high heels. Jointed ankles, "extras" above. 20 and 25-inch size wear rhinestone finger ring.
49 N 3761—14-in. Wt. 1 lb. 10 oz. $11.97   49 N 3762—20-in. Wt. 3 lbs. $14.97
79 N 03763—25-in. Wt. 5 lbs.   Only $2.00 down on Easy Terms . . . . . Cash   19.95

[B] **Sunday Best.** The prettiest dress in the Sunday School class: sheer embroidered nylon with wide sash, matching rayon taffeta slip. Posy-decked hat. Panties, hose, high heels. Jointed ankles, "extras" above.
49 N 3745—14-in. Wt. 1 lb. 10 oz. $10.97
49 N 3746—20-in. Wt. 3 lbs. 13.97

[C] **Collegiate.** Slender sub-teen with sheer nylon blouse, accordion-pleated cotton skirt and full crinoline. Panties, hose, high heels. Jointed ankles plus "extras" above.
49 N 3740—14-in. Wt. 1 lb. 10 oz. $8.97
49 N 3741—20-in. Wt. 3 lbs. 11.97
79 N 03742—25-in. Wt. 5 lbs. 16.95

[D] **Tea Time.** A glamorous grown-up in a high-style rayon satin party dress with two tiers of cotton accordion pleats. Has earrings, strapless bra, panties, hose and high heels.
49 N 3733—14-in. Wt. 1 lb. 10 oz. $7.46
49 N 3734—20-in. Wt. 3 lbs. 9.97

[E] **Romance.** Hooded lamé and rayon satin coat reverses. Tiered nylon gown with lamé bodice, underskirt. Purse, earrings, hooped petticoat, bra, panties, hose and high heels.
49 N 3768—14-in. Wt. 1 lb. 10 oz. $12.97
49 N 3789—20-in. Wears rhinestone ring.
Shpg. wt. 3 lbs. $16.95

They Walk in Beauty

- Feature dolls on these 2 pages (except G) walk when guided by the hand
- They have rooted Saran hair you can comb, brush and set in latest style
- Skin-soft vinyl plastic heads that turn . . pretty delicately molded features
- Pose their jointed arms . . go-to-sleep glassene eyes with realistic lashes
- Check the description of your favorite for extra features

ITEMS DESCRIBED BELOW SHOWN ON FACING PAGE

[A] **Walking Grown-up with Steel Trunk and Big Wardrobe.** Wardrobe includes a cotton gabardine coat and hat, cotton print housecoat, 2-pc. shorty pajamas, polished cotton dress, rayon taffeta formal with panties. Extra hose, pair of high heels, 6 plastic hangers, comb, brush, mirror. Enameled steel trunk is 20x11x11 in. with 3 drawers, plaid paper lining, 2 latches, handle. All vinyl plastic doll walks, turns at waist. Pretty hairdo. Wears a rayon taffeta dress, earrings, pearl-like necklace, panties, hose, high heels. 18 inches tall.
79 N 03724—Shipping weight 13 pounds....................................$17.75

[B] **Walking Ballerina** with jointed ankles, knees and turning waist walks, kneels and poses. Wears nylon tutu with nylon ruffles, metallic-sparked net overskirt, metallic cloth bodice. Panties, hose, Capezio ballet slippers. Pony tail hairdo. Hard plastic body; vinyl arms. Has rayon taffeta dress, panties, leotard, hose, ballet slippers, high heels, ring and imitation pearl necklace. 19 inches.
49 N 3757—Shipping weight 2 pounds 8 ounces.................................$7.97

[C] **The Most Happy Family—Mama, Baby, Sister and Brother.** Mama walks, turning her head from side to side; her knees are jointed so she can kneel, too. Hard plastic body, vinyl arms. 20 in. tall. In linen-look cotton skirt and bolero, hat, lace-trimmed blouse-slip combination, hose, high heels, ring. Children are all vinyl with jointed arms and legs, turning heads, do not walk. 8-in. baby in bunting has molded hair. 10-in. Sister and Brother in outfits to match Mama's. Sister has rooted Saran hair. Brother has painted eyes, molded hair.
79 N 03790—Shipping weight 5 pounds.................................$19.95

[D] **Happi-Time Walking Toddler in Coat and Bonnet** rolls her eyes flirtatiously when you play with her, turns her head from side to side as she walks, kneels to pray and sits on a chair. Jointed legs and knees to form many life-like poses. Hard plastic body; vinyl arms. Cry voice. Cotton gabardine coat and bonnet, embossed cotton dress with sewn-in panties, socks, shoes. 23 inches tall.
79 N 03281—Shipping weight 5 pounds.................................$11.87

[E] **Walking Toddler** turns her head as she walks. Hard plastic body. Cotton corduroy coat and hat, rayon dress, panties, socks, shoes. 17 inches tall.
49 N 3711—Shipping weight 2 pounds.................................$5.37

[F] **Walking Ballerina with Wardrobe.** Walks, kneels and poses like a prima ballerina with her jointed ankles, knees and turning waist. Wears a nylon tutu with tricot ruffles, sequin-sprinkled net overskirt and metallic cloth bodice. Panties, hose, real Capezio ballet slippers. Extra clothing: embossed cotton afternoon dress, rayon taffeta party dress with panties, nylon hose, socks, flatties, pair of high heels. Double-door fiberboard case with dancing rail, hangers.
49 N 3758—Hard plastic body, vinyl arms. 19 inches tall. Shpg. wt. 4 lbs...........$9.27

ITEMS DESCRIBED BELOW SHOWN ON THIS PAGE

[G] **Ballerina** with turning waist and jointed legs sits alone and poses. Pink pony tail. Net tutu; rayon satin bodice. Attached panties, hose, ballet slippers.
49 N 3754—All rigid vinyl plastic. 17 inches tall. Shpg. wt. 1 lb. 8 oz..............$4.77

[H] **Walking Bride.** A sophisticated beauty in her rayon satin gown with its low cut back and lace overlay. All vinyl plastic. Lacy net veil, buckram half slip, lace-trimmed panties, full-length nylon hose, high-heeled shoes, bouquet.
49 N 3727—19 inches tall. Shipping weight 2 pounds...........................$5.87

[J] **Walking Teen-ager** with turning waist poses prettily. Wears corsage, sheer ninon dress with rich trimming. Printed rayon taffeta underdress. All vinyl plastic. Lace-trimmed panties, hose, high heels, 2 curlers. 20 inches tall.
49 N 3765—Shipping weight 2 pounds 4 ounces..............................$7.47

[K] **Low-priced Happi-Time Walking Toddler** with jointed knees. She walks, kneels, sits alone. Pony tail. Hard plastic body. Lace-trimmed cotton dress, sewed-in half slip, lace-trimmed panties, socks, shoes. Cry voice. 23 inches tall.
79 N 03263—Shipping weight 4 pounds.................................$7.74

[L] **Coat, Hat and Muff Set.** Soft white imitation fur. Shipping weight 12 oz.
49 N 3970—Size 15–16 inches.$2.67   49 N 3971—Size 17–18 inches....$2.77
49 N 3972—Size 19–20 inches.................................... 2.97

[M] **Bridal Outfit.** Rich Ninon gown, lawn slip, net veil. Floral spray. Wt. 1 lb.
49 N 3420—Size 14–15 inches.$2.77   49 N 3421—Size 16–17 inches....$2.77
49 N 3422—Size 18–19 inches. 2.87   49 N 3423—Size 20–21 inches.... 2.87

[N] **8-piece Layette for Toddler Walking Dolls.** Cotton and rayon coat, bonnet. Percale dress, panties. Socks, shoes, 2 hangers. Shipping weight 1 lb.
49 N 3489—Size 17–19 inches....$2.97   49 N 3490—Size 23–24 inches....$3.37

[P] **Baby Doll Coat and Bonnet.** Moire rayon taffeta, lacy trim. Shpg. wt. 10 oz.
49 N 3411—Size 12–13 inches.$1.47   49 N 3412—Size 14–15 inches....$1.47
49 N 3413—Size 16–17 inches. 1.52   49 N 3414—Size 18–19 inches. 1.77
49 N 3415—Size 20–21 inches. 1.77

[R] **Sleeper and Robe for Baby Dolls.** Print cotton flannel. Shipping weight 1 lb.
49 N 3403—Size 12–13 inches.$1.17   49 N 3404—Size 14–15 inches....$1.17
49 N 3405—Size 16–17 inches. 1.27   49 N 3406—Size 18–19 inches. 1.57
49 N 3407—Size 20–21 inches. 1.67

NOTE: To order clothing, measure doll from head to foot, order size nearest height of doll

Image labels (in illustration):
[G] $4.77
[H] $5.87
[J] $7.47   [K] $7.74
[L] $2.67 15–16 in.
[M] $2.77 14–15 in.
[N] $2.97 17–19 in.
186 SEARS C   [P] $1.47 12–13 in.   [R] $1.17 12–13 in.

[B] $7.97

[C] $19.95
cash
$2.00 down

[A] $17.75

[D] $11.87

[E] $5.37

[F] $9.27

Oh, You Beautiful Dolls

P $7.67

R $3.97
15 inch

S $7.64
18 inch

V $1.27
14-15 in.

T $7.74

Every one of the glamour girls on these 2 pages has all of these features:
- Shimmering rooted Saran hair that's fun to comb, brush and set again and again
- A turning vinyl plastic head with delicately molded features
- Jointed arms so they are easy to dress and lashed, glassene eyes that close
- Check the description of your favorite doll for other features

ITEMS (A) TO (N) BELOW SHOWN ON FACING PAGE

Happi-Time Glamour Girls, the loveliest we've seen at these low prices

They have all of the features above plus turning waists so they can pose and grown-up figures of skin-soft, "magic-touch" vinyl plastic. Lovely, high-style dresses plus half slips, panties, high heels, nylon hose, earrings, and imitation pearl necklace.

A **Happi-Time Teen-Ager.** Lace-trimmed organdy blouse with puff sleeves, cotton print skirt, hose. Jointed legs, sits alone.
49 N 3781—18 inches tall. Wt. 2 lbs. 6 oz...$ 7.74
49 N 3782—20 inches tall. Shpg. wt. 4 lbs... 11.47
79 N 03783—22 inches tall. Shpg. wt. 5 lbs.. 14.77

B **Happi-Time Walking Deb.** She walks as gracefully as a model to show off her rustling rayon taffeta formal with its net overskirt, decolletage and velvet streamers.
49 N 3784—18 inches tall. Wt. 3 lbs.......$10.97
49 N 3785—20 inches tall. Shpg. wt. 4 lbs... 14.77

Revlon Walking Dolls . . see features of these lovely sophisticates on facing page

C **Snow Pink,** sure to be the most striking girl at the tea dance. Wears a swishy rayon taffeta dress with bouffant net over half skirt and a garden-gay nosegay. Poofy net-trimmed half slip. Order early for Christmas.
49 N 3775—18 inches tall. Shpg. wt. 3 lbs... $10.77
49 N 3776—20 inches tall. Shpg. wt. 4 lbs... 13.77

D **Evening Star,** our most beautifully dressed Revlon doll. Cotton velvet coat with bunny fur trim, rayon taffeta lining. Rayon taffeta dress woven with metallic threads. Belt. Sewed-in half slip. Ring, earrings, necklace.
49 N 3779—18 inches tall. Shpg. wt. 3 lbs... $14.27
49 N 3780—20 inches tall. Shpg. wt. 4 lbs... 17.77

Our Best, most beautiful Clothing for slender, grown-up dolls

E **Long Torso Afternoon Dress.** White and gold color scrolls on crisp "crystal" rayon taffeta. Lined bodice; button back. In assorted pastel colors. Shipping weight 8 oz.
49 N 3446—Size 14-15 inches............ 87c
49 N 3447—Size 18-19 inches............$1.17
49 N 3448—Size 20-21 inches............ 1.37

F **Roman-Striped Jumper with Sheer Lace-Trimmed Nylon Blouse.** Heavy rayon satin jumper. Sewed-in lace-trimmed rayon taffeta half slip. Rosette. Snaps. Panties. Shpg. wt. 1 lb.
49 N 3461—Size 14-15 inches............ $2.37
49 N 3462—Size 18-19 inches............ 2.67
49 N 3463—Size 20-21 inches............ 2.87

G **Ballet Costume.** Nylon net tutu, nosegay. Rayon taffeta bodice; net overlay. Panties, nylon hose, ballet slippers. Wt. 1 lb.
49 N 3464—Size 14-15 inches............$1.67
49 N 3465—Size 18-19 inches............ 2.27
49 N 3466—Size 20-21 inches............ 2.47

H **Hat and Coat.** Smart flared coat with button closures and snug cloche. Cuddly cotton and rayon fleece. Shpg. wt. 1 lb.
49 N 3467—Size 14-15 inches............$2.57
49 N 3468—Size 18-19 inches............ 2.97
49 N 3469—Size 20-21 inches............ 3.27

J **Accessory Outfit.** Girdle, garters, hose, bra. High heels in plastic case. Wt. 12 oz.
49 N 3449—Size 14-15 inches............$1.37
49 N 3451—Size 18-19 inches............ 1.37
49 N 3452—Size 20-21 inches............ 1.37

K **¾-Length Quilted Duster.** Heavy nylon tricot with lace trim. Shpg. wt. 14 oz.
49 N 3488—Size 14-15 inches............$1.37
49 N 3491—Size 18-19 inches............ 1.47
49 N 3492—Size 20-21 inches............ 1.77

L **3-piece Negligee Set.** Romantic negligee, nightgown, panties of sheer pink nylon trimmed with lace, rosettes and ribbons. Flowing, full-cut lines. Shpg. wt. 1 lb.
49 N 3408—Size 14-15 inches............$1.97
49 N 3409—Size 18-19 inches............ 2.67
49 N 3410—Size 20-21 inches............ 2.87

M **Bridal Outfit.** Fitted bodice with flocked nylon overlay, silver color threads. Rayon taffeta skirt with net overskirt, ribbon streamers. Cap, veil, panties. Shpg. wt. 1 lb.
49 N 3484—Size 14-15 inches............$3.27
49 N 3485—Size 18-19 inches............ 3.97
49 N 3486—Size 20-21 inches............ 4.27

TO ORDER CLOTHING: Measure doll from head to foot, order size nearest height of doll.

Shirley Temple, the dimpled curly-top of movie fame is back

N All "magic-touch" vinyl plastic that feels like real skin. Jointed legs, sits alone. Organdy dress, sewn-in half slip, panties, socks, shoes. Fiberboard case with bobby pins, curlers.
49 N 3777—17 inches tall. Shpg. wt. 3 lbs...$10.47   49 N 3778—19 inches tall. Shpg. wt. 3 lbs. 6 oz. $13.47

ITEMS (P) TO (V) BELOW SHOWN ON THIS PAGE

P **Pink Fairy Princess.** Turning waist, jointed elbows, legs let her pose. Pink hair. Net tutu, detachable plastic wings. All vinyl. Underskirt, panties, ballet slippers, wand.
49 N 3737—17½ inches tall. Shpg. wt. 2 lbs.. $7.67

R **Walking Undressed Teen-Ager.** She walks gracefully, turning her head from side to side. Slender hard plastic body, vinyl arms. Rayon satin chemise, hose, high heeled shoes.
49 N 3633—15 inches tall. Wt. 1 lb. 6 oz.....$3.97
49 N 3636—18 inches tall. Wt. 1 lb. 12 oz.... 4.97

S **Pony-tail Teen.** Jointed elbows, flexible wired legs . . sits, kneels, poses. All vinyl. 1-pc. cotton-stuffed body. Cotton dress, half slip, panties, hose, high heels, jewelry.
49 N 3648—18 inches tall. Shpg. wt. 2 lbs... $7.64
49 N 3649—20 inches tall. Shpg. wt. 3 lbs... 9.47

T **New! Meet Margie, our sweet sub-teen.** She's as real looking as your sister with a turning waist and jointed elbows and legs so she can sit alone and pose naturally. Made entirely of vinyl plastic that feels as smooth and soft as real skin. All dressed up for the school party in a flocked ninon dress, slip, panties, socks, shoes and necklace.
49 N 3642—17 in. tall. Shpg. wt. 2 lbs. 4 oz...$7.74

V **Roller Skating Set for regular little Girl dolls.** Shoe-skates, slacks, bonnet, and striped cotton jersey to make your dolly the smartest at the rink. Wt. 8 oz.
49 N 3440—Size 14-15 inches............$1.27
49 N 3441—Size 16-17 inches............ 1.37
49 N 3442—Size 18-19 inches............ 1.47
49 N 3443—Size 20-21 inches............ 1.57

HAPPI·TIME
REG. U.S. PAT. OFF.

Revlon Walking Dolls

- Guide them . . they'll walk
- Painted fingernails, lashed sleeping glassene eyes
- Stylish dresses, nylon hose, earrings, necklace
- Rooted Saran hair to comb, brush and set
- Skin-soft vinyl heads and "magic-touch" vinyl bodies
- Grown-up figures; jointed arms, turning waists

[C] 18-inch $10.77

[A] 18-inch $7.74

[B] 18-inch $10.97

[E] 87c 14–15 in.

[F] $2.37 14–15 in.

[D] $14.27 18-inch

[H] $2.57 14–15 in.

[G] $1.67 14–15 in.

[N] $10.47 17 in.

[J] $1.37 14–15 in.

[K] $1.37 14–15 in.

[L] $1.97 14–15 in.

[M] $3.27 14–15 in.

Stage a Miniature Fashion Show!

Petite fashion plates with high-style clothing

Each of the glamour girls and Nun Doll on these 2 pages has jointed arms ..
turning head .. lashed glassene eyes that close for sleep

(F) $2.97 (G) $2.97 (H) $2.97

$1.74 $1.74 $1.74

[M] $1.57

[P] $1.57

[N] $1.57

ITEMS (A) TO (E) DESCRIBED BELOW ARE SHOWN ON THE FACING PAGE

[A] Walking Grown-Up. Turns her head as she walks, kneels, sits. Jointed knees. Rooted Saran hair. Vinyl plastic head; hard plastic body. Lace chemise, hose, heels. 12 in. tall.

49 N 3498—Doll only. Shpg. wt. 14 oz....... $2.57
49 N 3434—Party Dress. Full skirt with lace overlay, blouse. Rayon taffeta. Shpg. wt. 10 oz.... $1.67
49 N 3479—Ballerina. Nylon net tutu, rayon bodice. Panties, ballet slippers. Shpg. wt. 10 oz.... $1.67
49 N 3487—Rain Outfit. Working plastic umbrella, hooded plastic coat with snaps. Wt. 10 oz..... $1.67
49 N 3438—Afternoon Ensemble. 3 pieces: print skirt, blouse, bolero. Cotton. Shpg. wt. 10 oz.... $1.67

[B] Walking Ballerina. She walks, kneels, turns at the waist and poses. Jointed knees. Rooted Saran hair to comb, brush and set. Vinyl plastic head; hard plastic body. Lastex® rayon tutu, nylon net full length hose, ballet slippers. Head band. 10½ inches tall.

49 N 3607—Shipping weight 12 oz.......... $2.87

[C] New! Little Miss Revlon, shapely grown-up, as pretty as the models in fashion magazines. She has jointed legs and turning waist so she can sit alone and pose like a real fashion model. It's fun to comb, brush, set her rooted Saran hair. Vinyl plastic head and arms. "Magic-touch" body of firm vinyl feels like real skin. Painted fingernails, toenails. Wears earrings, bra, panty girdle, high heels. 10½ inches tall. Order her high-style clothing below.
State pony tail or wind-blown hair style.

49 N 3076—Doll only. Shpg. wt. 1 lb........ $2.82
49 N 3265—2-piece Nightie. Flowered organdy shortie nightie and panties with lace trim. Shpg. wt. 8 oz.. 86c
49 N 3266—Campus Dress. Long torso, polka-dot cotton. Full skirt, loop trim. Shpg. wt. 8 oz...... $1.37
49 N 3267—Pajamas. Puckered cotton top and pants with lace trim, snaps. Shpg. wt. 8 oz.......... $1.37
49 N 3268—Evening Coat. Sweeping, full cut. Fluffy cotton and rayon fleece. Shpg. wt. 8 oz...... $1.77
49 N 3269—Blue Jeans. 3 pieces: fitted denim jeans, striped cotton blouse, sun hat. Shpg. wt. 8 oz... $2.27
49 N 3271—Pedal Pushers. 3 pieces: plaid cotton pants, turtle-neck sweater, sun glasses. Wt. 8 oz... $2.27
49 N 3272—Peasant Outfit. Cotton skirt, blouse; panties, rick-rack trim. Crinoline. Shpg. wt. 8 oz... $2.67
49 N 3273—Formal. Print nylon with posy trim. Sewed-in half slip, hose, headband. Shpg. wt. 8 oz.. $3.77
49 N 3264—Accessory Set. (Not shown). 2 pair hose, 2 pair plastic high heels. Shpg. wt. 8 oz.......... 86c

[D] Betsy McCall, a petite walking model for the most gorgeous outfits you've ever seen. Separate outfits are created by a famous fashion designer, carefully sewn of fine fabrics, beautifully detailed with bright piping, romantic ruffles, lacy trim, snap-fastener, tie or button closings .. the finest couturier touches.

Betsy walks, sits and kneels. She has jointed knees, shiny Saran hair and wears a lacy chemise, rayon socks and vinyl shoes. All hard plastic with a creamy bisque finish. 8 inches tall.

Order her outfits separately from below ... see nine others in our Fall General Catalog!

49 N 3002—Doll only. Shpg. wt. 1 lb........ $2.07
49 N 3083—Coat and Hat. Charcoal gray cotton felt coat. Pink hood, mittens. Shpg. wt. 10 oz.... $1.44
49 N 3084—Schoolgirl. Pin-dot cotton dress, panties, shoes, socks. Shpg. wt. 10 oz................. $1.44
49 N 3086—Playtime. Print skirt. Panties, belt, blouse combo. Rayon taffeta. Shoes, socks. Shpg. wt. 10 oz. $1.44
49 N 3088—Mommy's Helper. Cotton apron, pants. Mop, iron, shoes, socks. Shpg. wt. 10 oz....... $1.44
49 N 3093—Birthday Party. Flocked nylon dress. Picture hat. Petticoat, panties. Shpg. wt. 10 oz..... $1.87
49 N 3095—On The Ice. Plaid cotton skirt, jumper top, jersey shirt, tam, skates. Shpg. wt. 10 oz........ $1.87
49 N 3096—Sweet Dreams. Nylon tricot peignoir, gown; lace trim. Slippers. Shpg. wt. 10 oz...... $2.37
49 N 3098—Sunday Best. Tucked nylon sheer dress, Hat, slip, panties, shoes, socks. Shpg. wt. 10 oz.. $2.37
49 N 3099—Sugar and Spice. Nylon gown with coin dots. Slip, stole, panties, shoes. Shpg. wt. 10 oz.. $2.83

[E] Bride with Trousseau and Trunk. All-vinyl plastic doll with rooted Saran hair to comb, brush and set over and over again. Jointed legs and a turning waist. 10½ inches tall. Lace-trimmed nylon and rayon gown, net veil, bouquet, panties, high heels and earrings.

Trousseau: bra, nylon negligee, cotton sweater and shorts, net-trimmed rayon taffeta party dress, crinoline with net flounce, straw hat. Three plastic hangers. 12x6x6-inch fiberboard trunk, plastic handle, metal snap lock, hinges.
49 N 3290—Complete Outfit. Shpg. wt. 2 lbs.. $7.77
49 N 3277—Bride only. Shpg. wt. 12 oz....... 3.67

*Build your order up to $20 or more
and buy on Sears Easy Terms*

ITEMS (F) TO (W) DESCRIBED BELOW ARE SHOWN ON THIS PAGE

11-inch Walking Dolls. These chubby cuties walk when you guide them by the hand, sit alone and kneel. It's fun to comb, brush and set their rooted hair. Jointed legs and knees. Skin-soft vinyl plastic heads; hard plastic bodies. Completely dressed and ready to play with you in pretty dresses, panties, socks and shoes. 11 inches tall. Shipping weights 1 pound.

[F] 49 N 3125—Tea Party Girl with fancy hairdo. Cotton dress, rick-rack trim............... $2.97
[G] 49 N 3124—School Girl with fancy hairdo. Cotton dress, rick-rack trim............... $2.97
[H] 49 N 3126—Bride. Bobbed hair. Rayon satin gown, net veil, tiny bouquet.............. $2.97

Walking Teen Agers. These slender darlings turn their heads as they walk, kneel and pose like true models. Jointed knees. Dynel hair to comb and brush. The party girl and bride wear assorted style hairdos .. the ballerina wears the popular pony-tail style. All hard plastic. All are completely dressed and ready for fun. 8 inches tall. Shpg. wts. 10 oz.

[J] 49 N 3003—Bride. Rayon satin gown, net veil, panties, hose, tiny bouquet, high heels...... $1.74
[K] 49 N 3056—Ballerina. Net tutu, rayon satin bodice. Panties, ballet slippers........... $1.74
[L] 49 N 3023—Party Girl. Print nylon dress, panties, hose, high heels................. $1.74

Happi-Time Collector Dolls. All stand alone, are dressed in gorgeous finery. Made of practically unbreakable plastic. Mohair wigs. Dresses, half slips, panties. 7½ in. tall. Shpg. wts. 12 oz.

[M] 49 N 3105—Miss Christmas. Maroon rayon satin gown, hooded cape. Fake fur trim........ $1.57
[N] 49 N 3106—Nun. Rayon taffeta habit. Crucifix imported Italian rosary. No hair........... $1.57
[P] 49 N 3101—Bride. Bouffant rayon satin gown; lace trim. Net veil, bouquet............. $1.57
49 N 3102—Bridegroom. (Not shown.) Trousers, tails, high hat. Painted hair.................. $1.47
49 N 3094—Revolving Swiss Music Box. (Not shown.) For 7½-inch dolls. Plastic; 4½-inch base. Turntable revolves playing merry tune. Shpg. wt. 8 oz....... $1.97

[R] **Baby Fluffy.** Rooted Saran hair. Jointed legs, sits alone. All vinyl plastic. 11 in. tall. Panties, socks, shoes. Order clothes separately.
49 N 3565—Doll only. Shpg. wt. 1 lb....... $2.67
[S] 49 N 3566—Cotton Print Play Dress. Rick-rack trim. Panties. Shpg. wt. 8 oz......... 84c
[T] 49 N 3567—Flocked organdy Party Dress. Posy-trimmed bonnet. Slip. Shpg. wt. 8 oz...... $1.67
[V] 49 N 3568—Pinafore-style Cotton Dress. Sewed-on apron. Bonnet, panties. Shpg. wt. 8 oz.... $1.67
[W] 49 N 3569—Ski Outfit. Cotton fleece pants, multi-color jacket with hood. Ski poles, shoes with skis, socks. Shpg. wt. 8 oz.............. $2.67

Party Dress

Ballerina

Rain Outfit

Afternoon Ensemble

A $2.57 Doll only

B $2.87

2-pc. Nightie   Campus Dress   Pajamas   Evening Coat

LITTLE MISS REVLON

Blue Jeans   Pedal Pushers

C Doll only $2.82

Peasant Outfit   Formal

BETSY McCALL

Coat and Hat   Schoolgirl   Playtime

Mommy's Helper   Birthday Party

D $2.07 Doll only

On the Ice   Sweet Dreams   Sunday Best   Sugar and Spice

E Complete Outfit $7.77

[A] $2.77
each
14½-inch

[B] $1.97

[C] $2.87

[D] $3.47

[E] $3.77

LOW-PRICED, COTTON-STUFFED CUDDLE-UPS

[A] **Brother and Sister,** low-priced look-alikes to complete your doll family. Skin-soft vinyl plastic from head to toe, easy to wipe clean. Heads turn, legs are wired so they can sit and kneel. Molded hair. Lashed, go-to-sleep glassene eyes. Coo voices. Assorted cotton outfits. Boy has trousers, jacket. Girl has dress, panties, Both have shoes, socks.

Shipping weight 1 pound 8 ounces.
49 N 3604—14½-inches. Boy...**$2.77**
49 N 3605—14½-inches. Girl... 2.77
Shipping weight 2 lbs. 4 oz.
49 N 3611—19-inches. Boy.....**$3.94**
49 N 3612—19-inches. Girl..... 3.94

[B] **15-inch Cutie.** Petal-smooth vinyl plastic head with delicate features, wipes clean. Head turns; molded hair. One piece latex body, coo voice. Lashed, go-to-sleep glassene eyes. Ninon dress, bonnet. Half slip, panties, shoes, socks.
49 N 3110—Shpg. wt. 1 lb. 4 oz. **$1.97**

[C] **16-inch Baby** dressed in lovely lace-trimmed plaid rayon taffeta dress and bonnet, plus panties, shoes and socks. Vinyl plastic head turns; molded hair. 1-piece latex body. Coo voice. Lashed, sleeping glassene eyes.
49 N 3619—Shpg. wt. 1 lb. 8 oz. **$2.87**

[D] **15-inch Baby** with bobbed rooted Saran hair to comb, brush and set. Vinyl plastic, 1-pc. body and head wipe clean. Head turns. Lashed, go-to-sleep glassene eyes. Coo voice. Ninon cotton dress; half slip, panties, shoes. socks.
49 N 3236—Shpg. wt. 1 lb. 8 oz. **$3.47**

[E] **16-inch Baby** with long curly rooted Saran hair to comb, brush and set. Vinyl plastic head and 1-piece body. Head turns. Lashed, go-to-sleep eyes. Coos. Ninon and cotton dress; half slip, panties, vinyl shoes, socks.
49 N 3631—Shpg. wt. 1 lb. 10 oz. **$3.77**

$13⁸⁷

32-inch Jerry Mahoney Doll

This replica of the famous TV funster has controls just like those found on professional ventriloquists' dummies. You can make Jerry open and close his mouth and move his head realistically in all directions as he pretends to talk. Booklet gives tips on ventriloquism—have loads of fun with Jerry at parties! Wears cotton gabardine suit, bow tie, shoes. Hard plastic head; painted hair, eyes. Fiberboard torso. Cotton-stuffed legs, arms. Vinyl plastic hands.
49 N 3588—Shpg. wt. 4 lbs. $13.87
49 N 3594—24-in. doll similar to above, not shown. Mouth only moves by string. Composition hands. Shpg. wt. 3 lbs. $5.87

[F] $1.86

[J] $3.77

[L] $2.80
15-inch

[G] $1.37

[H] $1.93

[K] $2.80 15-inch

Soft, squeezy companions for the crib crowd . . easy to keep sweet and clean

[F] **16-inch Snuggler** in a pert rayon print dress, bonnet. Panties, socks, shoes. Yarn curls. Cloth covered; cotton stuffed. Painted plastic face wipes clean.
49 N 3551—Shpg. wt. 1 lb. . . . **$1.86**

[G] **14½-inch Cuddly-Wuddly** for tots. Dainty cotton print apron and body. Stuffed with cotton. Yarn ringlets. Painted plastic face.
49 N 3501—Shpg. wt. 10 oz. . . . **$1.37**

[H] **25-inch Patti,** big, flippity-floppity teen-ager with candy-striped skirt to match her hands, feet. Yarn pony tail. Painted plastic face. Cotton stuffed.
49 N 3593—Shpg. wt. 2 lbs. **$1.93**

[J] **13-in. Popeye Comic.** Easy-to-clean vinyl, fully jointed to pose 101 ways. Pinch his face, pipe whistles. Painted features.
49 N 3503—Shpg. wt. 1 lb. 8 oz. **$3.77**

[K] **Original Raggedy Ann,** button-eyed favorite of tots. Yarn hair, merry painted features. Cotton dress, apron and stuffing.
49 N 3580—15-in. Wt. 1 lb. . . .**$2.80**
49 N 3583—20-in. Wt. 1 lb. 8 oz. 3.77

[L] **Original Raggedy Andy,** just like his playmate Raggedy Ann. Bright cotton shirt, trousers, hat.
49 N 3592—15-in. Wt. 1 lb. . . . **$2.80**
49 N 3603—20-in. Wt. 1 lb. 8 oz. 3.77

Variation was the theme in the 1958 Sears Wishbook. Shirley Temple was back in 12-inch, 15-inch and 17-inch dolls. Lots of new clothes to fit her were available too. For $9.97, a fairly high price in 1958, a young girl could get a 12-inch Shirley doll with four outfits and a gift box. Collectors value this set today at $450 and higher depending on condition.

The model-like Revlon Dolls had most of the glamour in 1958. They featured outfits designed by "famous Designers" and wore creations with such sophisticated names as "Queen of Diamonds", "Kissing Pink" and "Fifth Avenue." Miss Revlon could also have clothes ranging from a ballerina outfit to a leopard print "Calypso Lounger." One wonders who the famous designers were.

Betsy McCall was back in 8-inch and 14-inch dolls made by American Character Toys. They were later manufactured by other companies. "Full-figured" Toni dolls were available in a 10 1/2-inch height with plenty of new outfits.

Teddy bears were back in style in 1958, with eight different models shown with prices ranging from $1.89 to $7.98 for a 19-inch growling teddy. Most were probably made by the Knickerbocker Toy Company for Sears. Other plush toys were featured including two Betsy McCall animals, a lamb and a dachshund. For fans of the hugely popular ABC/Walt Disney series "The Mickey Mouse Club", a plush Mickey Mouse was for sale for $3.79... looking suspiciously like a teddy bear with mouse ears!

Sears Christmas
Wishbook
1958

Whimsical Pets for Teens

$5.49 [B]

$4.39 [C]

FLUFFY ANIMALS WITH SWISS MUSIC BOXES

[D] $4.49 with Music Box

[A] $3.79

[E] $4.49

[A] **Musical Teddy Bear.** Cuddly soft, lovable night-and-day companion for tots. Wind the key in his back, his tubby tummy tinkles a gay tune. Cotton-backed rayon plush; cotton stuffed. Locked-in glassene eyes.
49 N 4157—13 inches tall. Shipping weight 1 pound......$3.79

[B] **Musical Bluebird.** A sure sign of happiness. Two-tone cotton-back rayon plush .. blue head and back, yellow breast, underbody. Genuine Swiss music box.
49 N 4023—12 inches tall. Shipping weight 1 lb. 7 oz.....$5.49

[C] **Musical Doggie.** Wags his tail in the friendliest fashion, while music box plays a merry tune. Cotton-backed rayon plush body. Glassene eyes. 10 inches long.
49 N 4019—Shipping weight 1 pound 5 ounces.........$4.39

[D] **Musical Skunk.** When Swiss music box plays, he moves paw up and down "smelling" flower. Cotton-backed rayon plush, vinyl face. Cotton-stuffed. 9 in. tall.
49 N 4025—Shipping weight 1 pound 5 ounces.........$4.49
49 N 4158—No music box or action. Shpg. wt. 1 lb.......2.69

[E] **Musical Pup** has a bee on his nose .. snout twitches, music plays as he tries to shake it off. Cotton-backed rayon plush. Cotton stuffed. 9½ inches tall.
49 N 4024—Shipping weight 1 pound 9 ounces.........$4.49

Favorites with the Teen-age Crowd

[F] **Circus Clown.** He's a laugh a minute with his brightly painted vinyl face and funny clown suit. Livens-up any teen-ager's room. Soft cotton-stuffed body. Order early, avoid the Christmas rush.
49 N 4182—24 inches tall. Shipping weight 2 pounds 2 ounces..................$4.69

[G] **Zippy Chimp** squeaks when you squeeze his arm. Vinyl face, ears, hands. Curly cotton-backed rayon plush; cotton stuffed. Cotton corduroy suit, felt hat. Build your order to $20 or more .. use Sears Easy Terms.
49 N 4088—16 inches tall. Shipping weight 1 pound 12 ounces..................$5.95
49 N 4095—21 inches tall. Shipping weight 3 pounds..........................8.47

[H] **Sailor Seal** is all set for a shore leave in his white felt sailor hat. Painted vinyl face. Cotton-backed rayon plush. 13 inches tall. Cotton stuffed.
49 N 4176—Wt. 2 lbs..$3.79

[J] **Rin Tin Tin.** Like the famous TV dog. Cotton-backed rayon plush. 21 inches long. Shipping weight 1 lb. 12 oz.
49 N 4135..........$3.98

[K] **Professor Poodle's** in a class by himself when it comes to laughs. Cotton-backed rayon plush; cotton stuffed. Wt. 1 lb. 12 oz.
49N4114—20 in. tall.$3.98

[L] **Scribble Pup.** Covered with heavy cotton fabric designed for autographing. 18 in. long. Wt. 1 lb. 14 oz.
49 N 4108......$2.59

[M] **Spareribs.** He's long and lean and nothin' but a hound dog . . . but so cute he's sure to go straight to the heart of any youngster . . . or teenager. Cotton-backed rayon plush. Soft, huggable cotton-stuffed body. Comic vinyl plastic face. 24 inches long. Shpg. wt. 1 lb. 9 oz.
49 N 4175......$4.69

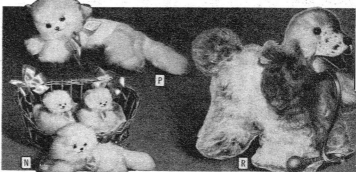

Lovable, lifelike animals with beautiful fur coats

[N] **Mother Cat and 2 cuddly Kittens** in a ribbon-trimmed basket. Grown-ups and teens adore them. All have soft, white rabbit fur coats, with soft cotton-stuffed bodies. Glassene eyes, pink felt ears. Cat is 11½ in. long; kittens 5½ in. long. Wt. 1 lb. 15 oz.
49 N 4008..........$5.89

[P] **Sleepy Cat.** Lifelike and irresistible to all ages . . . a lovable pet. She has a lovely coat of long white rabbit fur, with white plush underbody. Glassene eyes, pink lined plush ears. 18 in. long. Wt. 1 lb. 4 oz.
49 N 4007......$4.47

[R] **Cocker Spaniel.** Pull on his leash, he waddles along, barking when you squeeze bulb on leash. Soft lamb fur, natural markings. Droopy ears. Put him in 101 poses. Cotton stuffing. 14 in. long. Wt. 2 lbs.
49 N 4190......$5.79

418 SEARS

'n' Tots, for Love 'n' Laughter

$1.89 [A]

$1.89 [B]

$3.89 [C]

$5.97 [D]

$5.98 [E]
16-in. size

[A] **Washable Teddy.** Cotton-backed rayon plush. Quick-drying Dryex® foam plastic, cotton filling.
49 N 4102—13½ inches high. Shpg. wt. 1 lb. 3 oz....$1.89

[B] **Washable Panda.** Cotton-backed rayon plush; Cotton and Dryex® foam plastic filling.
49 N 4126—13½ inches high. Shpg. wt. 1 lb. 3 oz...$1.89

[C] **Cuddly Bear.** He's cute as a button .. just begging to be loved. When he's soiled, scrub him with soap and water. Cotton-backed rayon plush .. cotton and Dryex® (shredded foam plastic) stuffing.
49 N 4123—20 inches tall. Shpg. wt. 1 lb. 11 oz.....$3.89

[D] **Big, big Teddy Bear.** Almost "real bear" size, but he's gentle and friendly as a kitten. Lustrous, long pile, cotton-backed rayon plush; soft cotton stuffing. Very light in weight. Pompon nose; red felt tongue. "Shapeable" ears. Rayon neck ribbon.
79 N 04153—29 inches tall. Shipping weight 5 lbs.....$5.97

[E] **Growling Teddy.** Rough play pal growls with mock ferocity when picked up. Jointed arms and legs .. he takes on 1001 poses. Brown mohair plush, cotton backing, foam stuffed, felt paw pads.
49 N 4067—16 inches high. Shpg. wt. 2 lbs. 10 oz. ...$5.98
49 N 4068—19 inches high. Shpg. wt. 3 lbs. 2 oz.....7.98

$3.59
each

BETSY McCALL ANIMALS

Betsy Lamb with "baa" voice. Shaggy white cotton-backed rayon plush; foam stuffing. Plastic locked-in eyes. Pink felt face. 14 inches long.
49 N 4186—Wt. 1 lb. 6 oz...$3.59

Dachshund. A happy hound who's *long* on lovability. Cotton-backed rayon plush. Foam stuffing. Button eyes; squeaker in nose. 22 inches long. Send your order today!
49 N 4187—Shpg. wt. 1 lb. 5 oz..$3.59

[F] [G] [H] [J] [K]

Big Balky Mule and Poochy, the Sleepy Pup

As cute as he is stubborn, with his comical "won't-budge-an-inch" pose. Cotton-backed rayon plush; cotton stuffing. Wears straw hat, rayon ribbon. 17 inches high.
49 N 4179—Wt. 2 lbs. 4 oz....$3.97

Poochy's so sleepy he just can't stay awake. Cotton-backed rayon plush; cotton stuffed. Squeaker in ear. 17 inches long.
49 N 4191—Wt. 2 lbs. 11 oz..$3.39

Soft, huggable companions for tots' naptime or playtime

[F] **Ruff 'n' Reddy,** two comical buddies want to be friends with your tots, too. Ruff, the dog is 16 in. tall; Reddy, the cat, is 11 in. tall. Both have cotton-backed rayon plush bodies; cotton stuffing. Sit naturally. As cute as on TV.
49 N 4018—Wt. 1 lb. 12 oz...$3.98

[G] **Mickey Mouse.** Calling all "Mouseketeers" .. here's Mickey, looking for some fun. Soft pile cotton-backed rayon plush; foam rubber stuffing. Squeak voice. 15 inches tall.
49 N 4195—Wt. 1 lb. 2 oz...$3.79

[H] **Tired Tiger.** He's home from hunting, ready for a nap. "Like real" gold-color rayon plush, black striping. Cotton stuffed.
49 N 4064—22 inches long. Shpg. wt. 2 lbs........$2.98
49 N 4065—16 inches long. Shpg. wt. 1 lb........$1.94

[J] **Floppy Dog.** Big and cuddly. Cotton-back rayon plush; soft cotton stuffing. Locked-in glassene eyes; pompon nose.
49 N 4138—16 inches tall. Shpg. wt. 1 lb. 10 oz..$2.89

[K] **Donald Duck.** Lively and full of mischief as ever .. a long-time favorite with tots everywhere. Lustrous white, yellow and pale blue plush; stuffed with soft foam rubber. Comical molded vinyl face; painted features. Shaped arms, feet and tail. Squeak voice. Rayon ribbon. 13 inches tall. Shpg. wt. 1 lb. 3 oz.
49 N 4194.......$3.79

We All Drink and Wet

[A] $9.69

[B] $7.98

[C] $7.98

[D] $8.97

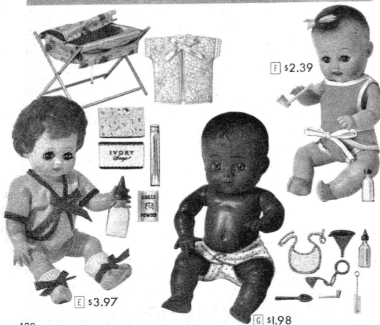

[F] $2.39

[E] $3.97

[G] $1.98

Sweet Baby Faces need a "Little Mother's" Care

[A] **A big, lifelike vinyl Baby** in glider-chair. Molded hair, coo voice. She's 21 in. tall, fully jointed . . drinks and wets, cries tears. Wears sun suit, socks, sandals. Lashed sleeping eyes. Head turns. She has nursing bottle with her. Glider chair has real gliding action, is 18x10x17½ in. high. Aluminum-finish steel frame, embossed plastic fabric covering. Shpg. wt. 8 lbs.
79 N T3288L—Doll and glider....$9.69
79 N 03255—Doll only. Wt. 4 lbs.. 6.49
49 N 9246—Glider only. Wt. 4 lbs. 3.39

[B] **Baby in Basket** ready to go visiting. Wood basket has embossed cotton cover, removable dainty flounce. Taffeta pillow and coverlet. All-vinyl 13-in. baby has jointed arms, legs, turning head with acetate fiber hair, sleeping glassene eyes with lashes. Dressed in cuddly fleece carriage suit with hood. Carries bottle. Basket is 16¾x10x6 inches . . holds this sweet baby comfortably.
49 N 3259—13-inch baby and basket. Shipping weight 3 lbs. 10 oz......$7.98

[C] **Contented Baby in her play pen.** All-vinyl plastic 13½-in. baby doll that drinks and wets. Jointed arms, legs and turning head let you place her in many lifelike poses. Molded hair and lashed sleeping glassene eyes. She wears a 2-piece sun suit and ribbon-tied bootees. She has her own bottle, rattle, powder, clothespins, sponge, soap, swabs, clothesline, washtub, dress, bonnet and robe. Smoothly finished wood playpen is 14x14x10¼ inches and has swivel casters. Has plastic-coated play pen pad, easy to wipe clean. Send your order today.
49 N 3254—Shpg. wt. 5 lbs......$7.98

[D] **13-inch soft vinyl Baby** with her own scale, layette and "hat-box" carrying case. She has jointed arms, legs, turning head. Molded hair, lashed glassene sleeping eyes. She drinks, wets, coos and blows bubbles. Dressed in flannel kimono, panties. Layette includes dainty ninon dress, bootees, soap, bottle, teether, bubble pipe, Q-tips, Kleenex and baby scale. Colorful carrying case of fiberboard with plastic handle . . 15x16x5 inches.
Here is an outfit that will give a little "mother" hours of enjoyment . . has everything baby needs.
49 N 3719—Shpg. wt. 5 lbs......$8.97

Budget-priced Drink-Wet Babies . . . love to be bathed, too

[E] **Big-Value Baby with bathinette and layette.** All vinyl-plastic baby with jointed arms, legs, turning head. Has Saran hair, lashed glassene eyes that close. She loves her bath in the wood-frame bathinette that's 12x8x9½ in. high. Comfortably dressed in a play suit; brings her kimono, bottle and bath accessories with her.
49 N 3233—10½-inch baby with bath and accessories. Shipping weight 1 lb. 10 oz..$3.97

[F] **Lovable 12-inch Baby** with a bow in her pretty molded hair. Vinyl head turns, molded rubber body has jointed arms, legs. She drinks, wets, coos, blows bubbles. Go-to-sleep eyes. Wears rompers. Bubble pipe and her own plastic bottle included. She loves to be sponged clean.
49 N 3505—12-inch Baby. Shipping weight 1 pound........................$2.39

[G] **Sweet little 10-inch Baby** of soft rubber with turning head. Molded hair and set-in plastic eyes. Fully jointed. She drinks and wets; cries when squeezed. With diaper, bottle, bib, bottle brush, etc.
49 N 3516—Colored baby with accessories. Shipping weight 1 pound.........$1.98
49 N 3515—White baby with accessories (not shown). Shipping weight 1 pound... 2.39

We Are So Like Real Babies

[A] Bannister Baby $7.94   [B] Almost Lifesize! $12.98 with Saran hair   [C] Christening Baby $9.79

Big lifelike Babies .. A, B and C Drink and Wet

[A] **Bannister Baby®** .. as adorable as the babies in Constance Bannister's photographs. She drinks from her bottle, wets her diaper, blows bubbles. Wears cotton robe, diaper. Made of skin-soft vinyl plastic .. fun to bathe. Arms and legs are jointed .. turning head with molded hair and lashed, glassene eyes that close. Layette includes ninon dress and rayon slip, bootees, bubble pipe and bottle. 18 in. tall.
49 N 3564—Shpg. wt. 4 lbs...... $7.94

[B] **"My Precious Baby."** Vinyl baby doll 19 inches tall .. about the size of a real baby! She's on a "bearskin" rug of soft rayon fleece .. has jointed arms, legs, elbows, knees; turning head and lashed glassene eyes that close. Like a new baby she wears her birth-bracelet. Birth announcement included. Her layette consists of organdy dress, bonnet, slip, diaper, shoes and socks. Shipping weight each 5 lbs.
49 N 3292—With Saran hair.... $12.98
49 N 3291—With molded hair... 11.79

[C] **Very, very young Baby** in her Christening dress. Molded after a real baby, with every feature as life-like as can be. Vinyl plastic with turning head, jointed arms and legs. Molded hair, lashed glassene eyes that close. She drinks and wets. Wears lace-trimmed organdy dress and bonnet, rayon taffeta slip, diaper and bootees. Rayon-satin-edged blanket, identification bracelet and bottle included. 17 inches tall.
49 N 3278—Shpg. wt. 4 lbs....... $9.79

[D] **17-inch Baby with her playmate.** Does not drink or wet. She's all vinyl, fully jointed arms, legs and turning head. Molded hair and lashed moving eyes. Appealing "coo" voice. Comes to you wearing a cotton flannelette diaper. Her layette includes cotton romper, bonnet, shoes and socks. Her little playmate is the original Rose O'Neill's "Kewpie" doll molded of vinyl, too; just 6 inches tall. Order now to avoid the Christmas rush.
49 N 3177—Shpg. wt. 2 lbs. 14 oz.. $6.97

Baby with "Kewpie" Playmate
[D] All this for $6.97

Layette and clothing for plump little baby dolls

[E] **Baby Sleeper and Robe Set.** Comfy cotton sleeper, pretty flannelette robe. Shpg. wt. 10 oz.
49 N 3403—Size 12 to 13 inches. . $1.17
49 N 3404—Size 14 to 15 inches. . 1.19
49 N 3405—Size 16 to 17 inches. . 1.29
49 N 3406—Size 18 to 19 inches. . 1.59
49 N 3407—Size 20 to 21 inches. . 1.69

[F] **Coat and Bonnet Set.** Pretty lace-edged rayon taffeta for baby's "dress-up" wear. Shipping weight 10 ounces.
49 N 3411—Size 12 to 13 inches. . $1.47
49 N 3412—Size 14 to 15 inches. . 1.49
49 N 3413—Size 16 to 17 inches. . 1.54
49 N 3414—Size 18 to 19 inches. . 1.77
49 N 3415—Size 20 to 21 inches. . 1.79

[G] **Snowsuit and Bonnet.** Cuddly cotton fleece with wool loop trim. Knit cuffs. Belt. Shpg. wt. 8 oz.
49 N 3436—Size 12 to 13 inches. . $1.69
49 N 3437—Size 14 to 15 inches. . 1.72
49 N 3439—Size 16 to 17 inches. . 1.79
49 N 3444—Size 18 to 19 inches. . 1.87
49 N 3445—Size 20 to 21 inches. . 1.98

[H] **Baby Doll Layette.** Lace-trim Nylon dress, bonnet. Cotton slip, socks, shoes. Shpg. wt. 14 oz.
49 N 3418—Size 12 to 13 inches. . $2.19
49 N 3425—Size 14 to 15 inches. . 2.24
49 N 3426—Size 16 to 17 inches. . 2.29
49 N 3427—Size 18 to 19 inches. . 2.49
49 N 3428—Size 20 to 21 inches. . 2.54
49 N 3429—Size 22 to 23 inches. . 2.79

[E] Low as $1.17   [F] Low as $1.47   [G] Low as $1.69   [H] Low as $2.19

Big Baby Dolls and Toddlers

We're light and easy to carry .. fully jointed, too

B
21-inch
$7.79

A 21-inch $9.97

$4.98 C

Ideal's "Cream Puff"

A **Sweet as cream .. light as a puff.** All-vinyl baby with coo voice and rooted Saran hair; lashed moving glassene eyes; jointed arms, legs, turning head. Wears domestic dotted Swiss dress and bonnet. Cotton panties, slip, socks, shoes.
49N3167—19-in. Wt. 3 lbs.$7.97
49N3168—21-in. Wt. 4 lbs. 9.97
79N03169—23-in. Wt. 5 lbs.12.97

B **Baby Doll in coat, hat and dress.** Jointed arms, legs, turning head, rooted Chromspun hair, lashed moving glassene eyes and coo voice. All vinyl. Rayon taffeta dress, cotton pique coat, hat, panties, socks and vinyl shoes .. so well dressed.
49N3158—21-in. Shipping weight 3 pounds 9 ounces.......$7.79
49N3157—16-in. Wt. 2 lbs. 5.97

C **A sweetheart of a baby doll** .. dressed in lace-trimmed ninon dress and bonnet, sewn-in rayon half-slip, knit cotton panties, socks and vinyl shoes. All vinyl with jointed arms, legs, turning head. Rooted Saran hair to comb and brush. Lashed glassene moving eyes.
49 N 3151—16-inch doll. Shpg. wt. 2 lbs. 4 oz.....$4.98

Chubby Toddler, with Steel Trunk

Doll, Wardrobe and Trunk $7.97

Adorable little girl .. 10½ in. tall, of vinyl, with jointed arms and legs .. turning head with rooted bobbed acetate fiber hair and lashed moving eyes. Wears cotton blouse, jumper, lace-trimmed panties, socks and vinyl shoes. *Her wardrobe* includes cotton corduroy coat and bonnet, nylon dress, rayon taffeta camisole slip and a straw bonnet. Dolly has an enameled *steel trunk*, 12 x 6½ x 6½ inches for her clothing. Fiberboard lined, it has latch, plastic handle, tie ribbons, travel stickers, 2 plastic hangers and sliding drawer . . . corners metal reinforced .. metal hinges.
49 N 3231—Doll, Wardrobe, Trunk. Shipping weight 3 lbs. 12 oz.. .$7.97
49 N 3249—Doll and Wardrobe only. Shipping weight. 1 lb....... 4.87
49 N 9299—Steel Trunk only. Shipping weight 3 pounds 4 oz...... 3.49

D **15-in. Snowsuit Baby.** All vinyl with rooted acetate fiber hair, lashed moving eyes, turning head, coo voice. Wears snowsuit.
49 N 3147—Shpg. wt. 1 lb. 10 oz.. .$3.19

E **New-born Infant,** 18 in. long. Vinyl, molded hair, sleeping eyes, turning head, coo voice. Wears diaper. Cotton flannel bunting .. pockets hold extra diaper, knit bootees.
49 N 3128—Shpg. wt. 2 lbs. 4 oz....$4.67

F G **Choice of Girl or Boy.** All vinyl with molded hair, lashed sleeping eyes, turning head, coo voice.
14½-in. dolls. Shpg. wt. ea. 1 lb. 8 oz.
49 N 3142—Girl; 49 N 3141—Boy. $2.87
19-in. dolls. Shpg. wt. ea. 2 lbs. 4 oz.
49 N 3143—Girl; 49 N 3144—Boy. $3.98

H **Snoozie.** Soft vinyl plastic head turns. Coo voice. Molded hair. Cotton stuffed rubber body. 11½ in. tall.
49 N 3609—Shpg. wt. 14 oz.......$1.87

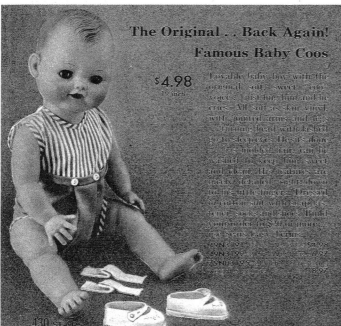

The Original .. Back Again!
Famous Baby Coos

$4.98
16-inch

Lovable baby boy with the original soft, sweet "coo" voice .. first hug him and he cries. All soft as skin vinyl with jointed arms and legs .. turning head with lashed go-to-sleep eyes. He sits down . . . his molded hair can be washed to keep him sweet and clean. His features are nicely detailed, right down to his little fingers. Dressed in cotton suit with snaps, tie, fancy socks and shoes. Build your order to $20 or more . . at Sears Easy Terms.
49N3191.......$4.98
49N3192...Wt. lbs. 6.97
79N03193...lbs. 8.97

15-inch Ballerina
[A] $3.98
(without music box)

[B] 19-inch Ballerina with wardrobe $6.97

[C] 19-inch with wardrobe and built-in Swiss music box $10.98

Dance, Ballerina, Dance,

**[A] Walking Ballerina .. ** All vinyl, jointed arms, legs. Rooted hair in pony tail style. Lashed, moving glassene eyes. Wears net tutu, panties, ballet hose and slippers.

49 N 3204—15-in. Ballerina only. Shpg. wt. 1 lb. 10 oz................$3.98
49 N 3206—19-in. Ballerina, Swiss Music Box inside. Shpg. wt. 2 lbs. 8 oz..$6.97

**[B] 19-in. Walking Ballerina with wardrobe. ** Jointed arms, legs, waist, knees and ankles . . hard plastic body, vinyl arms, soft vinyl turning head. Rooted hair; lashed, moving eyes. Wears tutu, panties, hose, ballet slippers. Includes rayon taffeta dress; high heel shoes, extra slippers, knit leotard, nylon hose.

49 N 3207—Ballerina, Wardrobe. Wt. 3 lbs..$6.97

**[C] 19-in. Walking Ballerina with wardrobe and case. ** Fully jointed . . arms, legs, waist, knees, ankles. Hard plastic with vinyl head, arms. Rooted pony-tail hair; lashed, moving glassene eyes. Wears ballerina costume, hose, ballet slippers, flower-spray. Wardrobe includes: party dress, afternoon dress and hat, two pairs of shoes, anklets, hand bag, necklace, ring. Packed in "double-door" gift case with practice "handrail."

49 N 3208—Outfit as above. Shipping weight 4 pounds..........$8.97
49 N 3209—Same, plus music box in doll. Shpg. wt. 4 lbs. 8 oz....10.98

Shirley Temple and other Big, Beautifully Dressed Dolls

**[D] Shirley Temple. ** "Magic-touch" vinyl plastic. Jointed arms, legs. Rooted hair; lashed, moving eyes. Wears dress, panties, undershirt, socks, shoes. Vinyl pocketbook.

49 N 3693—15-inch. Shpg. wt. 2 lbs..$7.97
49 N 3692—17-inch. Shpg. wt. 3 lbs..,10.77

**[E] 16-inch Walking Doll. ** Hard plastic with soft vinyl arms and head. Rooted hair. Lashed, moving eyes. Head turns as she walks. Wears corded cotton dress, corduroy coat and hat, lace-trimmed panties, socks, shoes.

49 N 3202—Shpg. wt. 2 lbs.........$5.37

**[F] Big 23-inch Walking Toddler. ** Hard plastic body, vinyl head. Jointed arms, legs, knees. Rooted hair. In cotton dress, coat and bonnet, panties, half slip, socks, shoes.

79 N 03247—Shpg. wt. 5 lbs........$9.87
79 N 03248—In dress only. Wt. 4 lbs. 7.89

**[G] Family of 4 vinyl Dolls. ** 18-in. "Mom" has turning waist; all have jointed arms, legs, movable head with moving eyes (except brother with painted eyes). "Mom", daughter have rooted Saran hair; others molded hair.

79 N 03795—Doll family. Wt. 5 lbs. $15.98

[D] Shirley Temple $7.97 15-inch

[E] 16-inch Toddler $5.37

[F] 23-inch Toddler with dress, coat and hat $9.87

same doll in dress only $7.89

[G] Family of four $15.98

Top Fashion Glamour Dolls

by famous Designers

[A] **$9.69**
20-inch

[B] **$17.79**
20-inch

[C] **$13.89**
20-inch

[D] **$12.98**
20-in. Doll with 3-pc. outfit

The six glamorous, grown-up models (A to F) on these 2 pages have lifelike vinyl bodies. Jointed arms, legs, waist and turning head . . so easy to dress and pose naturally. High-style coiffures of rooted Saran hair . . such fun to comb and set. Lashed, moving eyes, painted fingernails. Each one dressed in the height of fashion in exquisite fabrics. Order extra outfits at bottom of these two pages.

Happi-Time Modiste

[A] The most smartly dressed "observer" at the fashion show. Fur-effect plush coat, hat. Metallic thread trims rayon blouse. Pleated cotton skirt. Lace-trimmed panties. High-heel shoes, long hose. Imitation pearl earrings. 20 inches tall.
49 N 3665—Shpg. 4 lbs. . . **$9.69**

[B] **"Queen of Diamonds"** . . luxuriously dressed for the evening in dress with lamé bodice, lined velvet coat and lamé scarf. Lace-trimmed sewn-in slip, panties. Long nylon hose, high-heel shoes. Simulated rhinestone earrings, necklace and ring.
79 N 03678—20-inch. Shpg. wt. 4 lbs. **$17.79**
49 N 3675—18-inch. Shpg. 3 lbs. . . 13.79

Famous *Revlon* Fashion Dolls . . as shown on TV

[C] **"Kissing Pink"** print dress with net and ruffled crinoline . . bodice has imitation rhinestone buttons. Lace-trimmed panties, nylon hose, high-heel shoes. Simulated pearl necklace and earrings.
79 N 03668—20-inch. Shpg. wt. 4 lbs. **$13.89**
49 N 3667—18-inch. Shpg. wt. 3 lbs. . . 9.79
49 N 3666—15-inch. Shpg. wt. 2 lbs. . . 6.97

[D] **"5th Avenue"** . . has jointed knees, other features above. She walks gracefully . . poses as any fashion model. You see her seated in her casual lounging ensemble of cotton blouse, slacks and high-heel shoes . . with earrings and flower-spray. Standing, she wears her jacket of soft cotton fleece.
79 N 03686—20-inch. Shpg. wt. 4 lbs. **$12.98**

Clothing for slender, grown-up Dolls

[K] **Ballerina Costume.** Nylon, layered tutu, bodice, panties, hose, slippers. Wt. 8 oz.
49 N 3464—14-15 inches. . . **$1.79**
49 N 3465—18-19 inches. . . 2.39
49 N 3466—20-21 inches. . . 2.49

[L] **Fleece Coat and Hat** of cotton and rayon . . fully flared coat, beanie hat. Wt. 1 lb.
49 N 3351—14-15 inches. . **$2.45**
49 N 3352—18-19 inches. . 2.98
49 N 3353—20-21 inches. . 3.29

[M] **Leather Coat, Hat.** Rayon taffeta lined, matching beret. Shpg. wt. 1 lb.
49 N 3360—14-15 inches. . **$2.89**
49 N 3361—18-19 inches. . 3.29
49 N 3362—20-21 inches. . 3.59

[N] **Rayon taffeta Sheath Dress.** Brooch, belt. Wt. 8 oz.
49 N 3307—14-15 inches. . . 98c
49 N 3312—18-19 inches. . **$1.19**
49 N 3314—20-21 inches. . . 1.29

[P] **Calypso Lounger.** Handsome 2-piece leopard print taffeta. Ring tie. Wt. 8 oz.
49 N 3317—14-15 inches. . . . 79c
49 N 3319—18-19 inches. . . . 89c
49 N 3321—20-21 inches. . . . 98c

[R] **Knitted Ensemble.** Orlon vestee and skirt. Jacquard-weave jacket. Shpg. wt. 8 oz.
49 N 3324—14-15 inches. . **$1.98**
49 N 3325—18-19 inches. . 2.39
49 N 3326—20-21 inches. . 2.59

[S] **Coat, Hat and Muff.** Soft imitation fur set makes lovely addition to dolly's wardrobe. Rayon lined. Wt. 14 oz.
49 N 3363—14-15 inches. . **$2.29**
49 N 3364—18-19 inches. . 2.59
49 N 3365—20-21 inches. . 2.98

Add dolls' clothing to your order—build your order to $20.00 or more and use Sears convenient Easy Terms

E $13.98 20-inch

F $14.98 20-inch

J $6.69

H $7.69

G $8.69

14-inch Betsy McCall . . Walks

Betsy is a "little Girl" yet so fashion-conscious! She's bisque-finished vinyl plastic with rooted Saran hair and lashed moving eyes. She walks when guided, has jointed arms, legs, waist . . turning head.

G **Betsy in rayon lined checked gingham coat,** gingham dress, beret, rayon socks, shoes, lace-edged panties.
49 N 3663—Betsy with ensemble. Shpg. wt. 2 lbs.........$8.69

H **Betsy in cotton dress** with nylon trimming. Matching panties, straw bonnet, rayon socks, sandals.
49 N 3662—Betsy at playtime. Shpg. wt. 2 lbs...........$7.69

J **Trunk with wardrobe** for 14-in. Betsy. Fiberboard, metal hinges, latch. 15x9½x6 in. Felt jumper dress, blouse, 2-pc. pajamas, bathrobe, panties, straw hat, 2 pairs of shoes, socks. Betsy doll not included.
49 N 3661—Trunk with wardrobe. Shpg. wt. 3 lbs........$6.69

Big Toni Walking Dolls . . . with Toni* Play-Wave Kit

E **American Beauty Doll** in her formal gown of nylon tricot. She has all features described on the opposite page . . and walks, too. Bouffant skirt is fully draped over pink taffeta underskirt. Combination marquisette slip with lace-edged taffeta panties. Long hose, silver-color slippers. Her pin and earrings are simulated rhinestone.
49 N 3773—20-inch doll. Shpg. wt. 3 lbs.......$13.98
49 N 3672—14-inch doll. Shpg. wt. 2 lbs....... 9.98
79 N 03793—25-inch doll. Shpg. wt. 6 lbs...... 17.98

F **Walking Bride** . . radiant in her luxurious gown of nylon lace and net. Billowing skirt over hooped taffeta petticoat. Peaked, decorated bridal cap has fingertip-length nylon tulle veil. Lace-edged taffeta panties, full-length hose. High heel slippers are decorated with simulated rhinestones. Imitation diamond ring and pearl earrings.
79 N 03796—25-inch doll. Shpg. wt. 6 lbs......$19.95
49 N 3786—20-inch doll. Shpg. wt. 4 lbs......... 14.98
49 N 3674—14-inch doll. Shpg. wt. 2 lbs......... 10.98

Toni Kit has comb, brush, curlers, play-wave solution in squeeze bottle applicator

To Fit Dolls from 14 to 21 inches tall

T **Accessory Outfit.** 2-way stretch girdle, bra, nylon hose, garters. Shoes in plastic case. Shpg. wt. 10 oz.
49 N 3449—14 to 15 inches..............$1.39
49 N 3451—18–19 in...$1.39   49 N 3452—20–21 in... 1.39

V **Jumper and Blouse.** Rayon satin jumper, nylon blouse. Sewed-in taffeta half slip. Panties. Wt. 1 lb.
49 N 3461—14 to 15 inches..............$2.39
49 N 3462—18–19 in...$2.69   49 N 3463—20–21 in... 2.89

W **3-pc. Negligee Set.** Negligee, nightgown and panties of sheer nylon, trimmed with lace. Shpg. wt. 1 lb.
49 N 3408—14 to 15 inches..............$1.98
49 N 3410—18–19 in...$2.69   49 N 3410—20–21 in... 2.89

X **Bridal Gown Set.** Ruffled rayon taffeta with nylon net overskirt, cap and veil. Panties. Shpg. wt. 1 lb.
49 N 3484—14 to 15 inches..............$3.29
49 N 3485—18–19 in...$3.98   49 N 3486—20–21 in... 4.39

Y **Chic gown** . . nylon lace over rustling rayon taffeta. Panties. Shpg. wt. 1 lb.
49 N 3366—14 to 15 inches..............$2.89
49 N 3367—18–19 in...$3.29   49 N 3368—20–21 in... 3.39

TO ORDER CLOTHING: Measure doll from head to foot . . order the size nearest height of doll.

T **V** **W** **X** **Y**

We are Fashionable Dolls.. Demure and Pretty

19-inch Doll, Trousseau and Trunk $11.79

Sophisticated Walking Bride. 19-inch doll of vinyl plastic has jointed arms and legs; turning waist and vinyl head. Rooted Saran hair, lashed go-to-sleep glassene eyes. Wears heavy rayon satin bridal gown with lacy net overskirt and overblouse. Net veil, lace-trimmed rayon panties, full length hose, high heels and nosegay. Her trousseau includes rayon taffeta party dress with ruffled half slip; street dress with matching hat and handbag; gaily printed cotton sundress; lace-edged ninon robe; bra and panties; extra pair high heels; pearl-like earrings and necklace. Fibreboard trunk 20½x9½x7 in. high has snap latch, metal hinges.

49 N 3677—19-inch doll, trousseau and trunk. Shipping weight 5 pounds............ $11.79
49 N 3676—15-inch doll, trousseau and trunk. As above, but doll does not have turning waist. Trunk 15½x10½x5 inches. Shipping weight 3 pounds............................ $7.98
49 N 3688—19-inch doll in wedding gown only. Shipping weight 2 pounds............ 5.97
49 N 3687—15-inch doll in gown. No turning waist. Shipping weight 1 lb. 8 oz......... 4.97

18-inch Doll, Wardrobe and Steel Trunk $16.75

Pert Teenager has all-vinyl body, jointed arms and legs; turning waist and soft vinyl head. Rooted Saran pony tail hairdo. Lashed go-to-sleep glassene eyes. Wears full-skirted rayon taffeta dress with gathered waist, scoop neckline, "gardenia" at bodice; half-slip; panties, high heels and nylon hose. Wardrobe: cotton school dress; rayon taffeta housecoat; embossed cotton coat; denim pedal pushers; rayon taffeta formal; extra high heels and nylons; comb, brush, mirror and 6 plastic hangers. Trunk, 9¼x9½x20¼ in. long of enameled steel. Piano-type hinges, 2 snap latches, metal handle. 3 drawers with leather pulls, extra doll clothes hangers.

79 N 03657—Shipping weight 13 pounds.................. Complete set $16.75
49 N 3671—Doll with wardrobe only. No trunk. Shipping weight 2 lbs...... 11.77

Build your order to $20.00 or more and use Sears Convenient Easy Terms

Low-Priced, Fully Jointed Dolls

- Long-lashed bright glassene eyes that go to sleep
- Rooted plastic hair to comb, brush and set
- All have soft vinyl heads and arms. A, B and C have firm vinyl bodies. Nurse (D) has hard plastic body
- A, B, and C have turning waists to pose so prettily

[A] **Grownup walks** when guided by hand; bending knees permit sitting. Wears full cotton skirt with blouse trimmed with gold-color buttons, belt; natural straw hat; net gloves, net half-slip, cotton panties, high heels and nylons. Chromspun hair.
49 N 3794—18-inch doll. Shipping weight 2 pounds............... $7.79

[B] **Teenager** with perky Saran pony tail hairdo. Dressed for a party in a full-skirted pale blue rayon taffeta dress with metallic gold-color stripes, fluffy white nylon trim at neckline; attached half slip; panties; earrings; rosebud corsage; high heels and nylons.
49 N 3656—18-inch doll. Shipping weight 2 pounds............... $5.79

[C] **Undressed Glamor Girl** wants style-conscious "little mother" Wears rayon chemise, full-length nylon hose, high heels. Has flower spray in long curly Saran hair. For clothing see pages 434-435.
49 N 3696—15-inch doll. Shipping weight 1 pound 6 ounces........ $3.59
49 N 3697—18-inch doll. Shipping weight 1 pound 12 ounces....... 4.64
49 N 3698—20-inch doll. Shipping weight 2 pounds............... 5.77

[D] **Walking Nurse with "Baby" in Carriage.** Nurse has rooted acetate fiber hair and wears white cotton uniform with blue trim; cape and cap; knit panties; nylon hose and vinyl shoes. 8-in. vinyl baby has molded hair, jointed arms and legs. Wears rayon fleece snowsuit. Flexible vinyl carriage, 8x4x11½ in. long has movable hood and turning removable wheels.
49 N 3747—14-inch Nurse. Shipping wt. 2 lbs......... Complete set $5.87

We're 10½-in. Miniature Dolls.. All with Wardrobes

10½-in. Doll with Big Wardrobe **$5.79**

10½-in. Bride with Extra Outfits **$4.89**

10½-in. Bride with Trousseau and Trunk **$7.79**

Grown-up Doll of hard plastic with turning soft vinyl head. Fully jointed, turns at waist. Rooted Saran hair; lashed eyes. Wears cotton blouse, rayon taffeta skirt, half-slip, panties, high heels. Wardrobe: cotton housecoat, rayon taffeta party dress, rayon satin ballerina costume, vinyl slippers, bra, panties, "straw" picture hat, simulated pearl earrings, necklace, plastic handbag, nylons. Gift boxed.

49 N 3946—Shipping weight 2 lbs.. $5.79

Lovely bride with full-formed body. All-vinyl plastic doll has jointed arms and lifelike turning head. Rooted chromspun hair; long-lashed moving glassene eyes. Wears puffed-sleeve rayon taffeta wedding gown with metallic sparked net overskirt and lace trim, matching headband has a flowing net veil, high heel shoes, cotton panties. Wardrobe includes lace-trimmed nylon party dress with ribbon, lace-trimmed cotton dress with loop design, 2-piece cotton playsuit has checked top and pair of contrasting slacks. In gift box.

49 N 3944—Shipping weight 1 lb. 6 oz...... $4.89

June Bride assumes many pretty poses because her all-vinyl body has jointed arms, legs; turns at head and waist. Rooted acetate hair. Long-lashed moving glassene eyes. Lace-trimmed wedding gown of rayon taffeta has full nylon overskirt, lacy bodice. Flowered headband, net veil, simulated pearl earrings, panties, high heels, nosegay. Trousseau: iridescent rayon taffeta party dress with nylon collar, rosette; matching "straw" hat; strapless gown has metallic lame-type bodice, a rayon taffeta underskirt topped by metallic sparked nylon; lace-trimmed nylon negligee; rayon ballerina costume, net tutu, vinyl slippers; bra. 4 plastic hangers. Fiberboard trunk, 12½x6½x6½ has hanging bracket for trousseau; sliding cardboard drawer. Snap latch, metal hinges, plastic carrying handle.

49 N 3275—Bride with trousseau and trunk. Shipping weight 2 pounds...... $7.79
49 N 3277—Bride in wedding outfit only. Shipping weight 12 ounces........... 3.79

Just 10% down on orders of $20 or more

I'm Fluffy .. 11 inches tall

[A] **Washable vinyl plastic body!** Rooted Saran hair! Jointed arms and legs. With panties, socks, shoes. Order clothes separately below.

49 N 3565—11-inch doll only. Shpg. wt. 1 lb...... $2.69

Clothing only .. to fit "FLUFFY". Wt. each 8 oz.

[B] 49 N 3381—2-piece Cotton Sleeper. Elasticized waist, enclosed feet, duckling design on front........... 89c

[C] 49 N 3382—Cotton print Dress and Organdy Pinafore. Bow at back. Matching hat and panties.... $2.79

[D] 49 N 3380—Printed Cotton Street Dress. Rickrack and ribbon trim, matching panties.............. 89c

[E] 49 N 3383—Coat, Hat and Muff. Soft pile Rayon plush. Wrist strap on muff; chin strap on hat.......... $2.79

Happi-Time 7½-inch Collector's Miniatures

Beautiful dolls with exquisite features made of practically unbreakable plastic with mohair wigs, jointed arms and head. They all stand alone, dressed in gorgeous finery. Dresses, half slips, panties. 7½ inches tall, lashed glassene eyes that close for sleep. Shipping weight each 12 ounces.

(F) 49N3105—Miss Christmas. Maroon rayon satin gown; hooded cape. Fake fur trim. $1.69

(G) 49N3106—Nun. Rayon taffeta habit. Crucifix, imported Italian Rosary. No hair... 1.69

[H] 49 N 3101—Bride. Bouffant white rayon satin gown has lovely lace trim. Flowing net veil. Beribboned bouquet.................... $1.69

49 N 3102—Bridegroom (not shown). Trousers, tails, high hat. Painted hair...... 1.49

49 N 3094—Revolving Swiss Music Box (not shown). For 7½-inch dolls. Plastic 4½-inch base. Turntable revolves playing merry tune. Shipping weight 12 ounces........... $1.79

We're 10½-inch Miniatures.. Just Right to Dress

Little Miss *Revlon* $2.82 10½-inch Doll only

[A] Shapely grownup, as pretty as the models in fashion magazines. She has jointed legs and turning waist so she can sit alone and pose. It's fun to comb, brush, and set her rooted Saran hair. Vinyl plastic head and arms. "Magic-touch" body of firm vinyl feels like real skin. Painted fingernails, toenails. *Please state pony tail or bobbed hair style.*
49 N 3076—Doll with bra, panty girdle, shoes, earrings. Shpg. wt. 1 lb. $2.82

Clothing for Miss Revlon. High-style, nicely made. Shpg. wt. each 8 oz.
(B) 49 N 3973—2-piece Pajamas. Cotton with lace trim, snap closure 88c
(C) 49 N 3974—Print Dress. Cotton pique with jacket-effect. Snaps 88c
(D) 49 N 3975—Striped Dress. Cotton, full skirt lace-trimmed panties 1.37
(E) 49 N 3979—Toreador Outfit. Cotton blouse, velvet pants, sash, shoes 2.29
   49 N 3264—Accessories (not shown). 2 pair hose, 2 pair high heel shoes 88c
(F) 49 N 3978—Ballerina Outfit. Rayon taffeta trimmed with metallic thread and net. Shoes, and flower spray for hair. Snap closure 1.79
(G) 49 N 3976—Rain Outfit. Water-repellent plastic coat and hood, corduroy lined. Matching handbag and belt. Clear plastic boots 1.37
(H) 49 N 3977—Evening Coat. Full cut. Fluffy cotton and rayon fleece 1.79

Glamorous *Toni* Doll $2.82 10½-inch Doll only

[J] Full-figured vinyl doll with soft, bisque finish. Jointed arms, legs, turning head. Lashed moving eyes. Rooted Saran hair . . you can comb, brush, set it. In fashionable undies, high-heel shoes. For play wave set, see below.
49 N 3912—Shipping weight 1 pound $2.82
49 N 3913—Play Wave Kit (not shown). Includes solution, squeeze bottle, applicator, curlers, comb, brush and make-up cape. Shpg. wt. 8 oz 89c

Clothing for 10½-inch Toni Doll. Exquisite detail. Shpg. wt. each 8 oz.
(K) 49 N 3958—Tea Time. Rayon taffeta dress, straw hat, long hose, shoes $1.87
(L) 49 N 3959—Stewardess. Blue cotton tailored uniform, hat. Hand bag, shoes . . 1.87
(M) 49 N 3960—Coat and Hat. Felt coat, straw hat, kerchief, long hose, shoes . . 2.37
(N) 49 N 3961—High Society. Taffeta bell-shaped harem skirt dress, posy hair-band, long hose, high-heel shoes. High-style for Toni's partying 2.37
(P) 49 N 3962—Bon Soir. Glamorous nylon ensemble: sheer nighty, lace-trimmed negligee, "jewelled" slippers 2.83
(R) 49 N 3963—Suburbanite. Plastic car-coat, corduroy hood, slack suit, shoes . . 2.83
(S) 49 N 3964—Romance. Satin formal dress in the new chemise style. Lined with taffeta. Genuine Ranch Mink stole. Rope of "pearls," long hose, shoes 3.79

I'm SHIRLEY TEMPLE.. 12-inches tall

[V] 12-inch Shirley Temple Doll. All vinyl with jointed arms and legs, turning head, rooted Saran hair and lashed moving eyes. Dressed in rayon taffeta slip, matching panties, socks, patent leather shoes. Hair bow. Wt. 1 lb.
49 N 3938—Doll as described above only $3.77

Buy Shirley's wardrobe below. Shipping weight each 8 oz.
(T) 49 N 3969—Nylon Party Dress. Attached slip, panties. "Straw" hat (2 hat pins), pocketbook. Doll not included. See 49N3938 above . $2.87
(W) 49 N 3965—2-piece cotton pajamas, ribbon for hair . 1.37
(X) 49 N 3968—Pedal Pushers, shirt, belt, sunglasses, ribbon 2.39
(Y) 49 N 3966—Cotton pique dress. Attached slip, panties. Shirley Temple pocketbook. Matching hair ribbon $1.79
(Z) 49 N 3967—Jumper Dress, attached cotton blouse, slip, panties, hair ribbon. Shirley Temple pocketbook $1.79

Complete Outfit . . 12-inch Shirley Temple Doll with 4 outfits in a gift box. Same doll as described at left. Includes: cotton dress with cotton panties, "pearl" necklace; soft fleecy coat, "straw" hat; 2-pc. cotton pajama set; 3-pc. blouse, shorts and skirt ensemble of cotton. All outfits highly styled with careful detailing, snap closures. Buy extra outfits at left.
49 N 3950—Doll outfit. Shipping weight 2 pounds 12 ounces $9.97

I'm BETSY McCALL
..just 8 inches tall
Have your own Betsy now .. dress her 7 different ways

A
Betsy in undies only
$207

B
'Birthday Party' Dress Outfit
$1.87
Order doll (A) separately

**A petite walking model .. sits, kneels, too!
Shiny Saran hair .. lashed, sleeping eyes**

[A] Betsy is of hard plastic with a creamy bisque finish .. has jointed arms, legs, knees, turning head .. so easy to pose and dress. Buy doll and outfits separately here.
Doll only, wearing lacy chemise, socks, vinyl shoes.
49 N 3002—8-inch. Shipping weight 10 ounces.............$2.07

Betsy's wardrobe outfits, created by a famous fashion designer, carefully sewn of fine fabrics. Shpg. wt. each 10 oz.
[B] 49 N 3953—Birthday Party nylon dress. Matching underskirt, panties, socks, shoes, straw bonnet....................$1.87
[C] 49 N 3956—Sunday Best. Pleated nylon pinafore over taffeta dress. Matching panties, knitted hat, bag, socks, shoes......$2.37
[D] 49 N 3957—Sugar and Spice. Nylon flocked skirt with suede yoke. Nylon tricot stole, slip, panties, shoes, flower spray.......$2.83
(E) 49 N 3952—Felt Coat and Beret. Socks, shoes...........1.44
[F] 49 N 3951—Play Time. Cotton dress, matching panties. Cute straw bonnet, socks, shoes.................................$1.44
[G] 49 N 3954—On the Ice. Full flare cotton felt skirt, suede top, skater's hat, sweater, panties, ice skates.................$1.87
(H) 49 N 3955—Sweet Dreams nylon negligee, gown, slippers... 2.37

**Doll and Outfits in play-time
"stage-setting" packages**

Betsy McCall in chemise, socks and shoes with outfits for her varied activities.
[J] **Designer's Studio.** Betsy in artist's smock, beret. Dressmaker's form, 2 precut outfits, fabric, thread, thimble, 5 McCall patterns. Instruction sheet.
49N3910—Doll with outfits. Wt. 1 lb. 3 oz. $4.67
[K] **At the Ranch.** Betsy with blue denims, cotton blouse; riding skirt, blouse, vest, hat, boots, holster, pistol; cotton square-dance dress, panties.
49 N 3911—Doll with outfits. Wt. 1 lb. 6 oz. $5.67
[L] **Day with Betsy.** Doll in chemise, shoes, socks. Has 2-pc. pajamas, housecoat for morning; blouse, velvet skirt, bonnet for afternoon; gown, underskirt, stole, slip, panties, shoes for parties.
49 N 3929—Doll with outfits. Wt. 1 lb. 4 oz. $6.67

BETSY McCALL 8-INCH DOLL IN THREE PACKAGED OUTFITS

[J] **Designer's Studio**
Doll, outfit, accessories $4.67

[K] **At the Ranch**
Doll, 3 outfits $5.67

[L] **A Day with Betsy**
Doll, 3 outfits $6.67

Refrigerator $3.94   Sink $4.47   Stove $3.27   Dish Cabinet $3.94

Modern Kitchen and Store

Reinforced corrugated fiberboard Kitchen Appliances for little housekeepers

Supermarket $2.97

[A] **Right-Size Toy Refrigerator** has separate freezer compartment and shelves in door for more space .. greater play value. Plastic pull handles. Reinforced hinges. Blue and red on white. Little homemakers will love storing "perishables" for later use in preparing meals for the "family." Don't disappoint them, place your order in plenty of time for Christmas.
79 N 01150—18x11x38 in. high. Easy-to-follow assembly directions. Shipping weight 8 pounds...... $3.94

[B] **Right-Size Toy Sink** has lift-out plastic sink tray for easy filling, non-working drain and faucets. Corrugated fiberboard treated with water-repellent coating. 2 doors, 2 roomy shelves.
79 N 01151—19¼x10⅜x26½ in. Easy-to-follow assembly directions. Shipping weight 6 pounds..... $4.47

[C] **Right-Size Toy Stove** has 4 big make-believe burners, red knobs, pull-out drawer, clock timer, oven, oven shelf and look-in plastic oven window for kitchen-like realism. Fiberboard.
79 N 01137—16x11x26½ in. high. Easy-to-follow directions. Shipping weight 5 pounds........... $3.27
79 N 01152—Save $1.20 on matching ensemble of (A), (B), (C) above. Shipping weight 19 pounds. $10.48

[D] **Dish Cabinet** has 3 shelves, cutlery drawer, storage compartment. Blue, red on white.
79 N 01136—16½x11¼x40 in. high. Dishes not incl. Easy-to-follow directions. Shpg. wt. 6 lbs....... $3.94

[E] **Supermarket** with packages, toy money. Red, blue, tan tile effect outside; shelves.
79 N 01138—34x20¼x61 in. high. Easily assembled. Shpg. wt. 8 lbs............................ $2.97

Stewardess Set $4.87   **Diaper Bag Set 92c**   **16-pc. Bath Set $1.95**   **31-pc. Feeding Set $1.84**   **5-drawer Nursery Chest $8.87**

"Miss American Airlines" Set in sky blue "flight-case" with carrying handle. Contains reproductions of AA hat pin, flight wings, stewardess ring, post cards and luggage stickers; flight service tumbler, serving tray and accessories, stewardess diploma; cotton felt hat fits all sizes. Many other flight accessories.
49N1077—Shpg. wt. 4 lbs. $4.87

Pretty vinyl carrying bag holds everything dolly will need while traveling with her new mother. Double-opening bag has two sturdy metal catches and double carrying straps. Accessories include plastic milk bottle, diaper with pin and plastic bib to protect dolly's clothing.
49 N 1391—Wt. 1 lb...92c

Pretty drink and wet doll with sleeping eyes comes with her own pastel polyethylene bath set. Accessories are bassinet, baby bath and diaper pail with cover; cotton flannel doll blanket. Plastic vanity tray has carrying handle .. holds baby's hair comb, rattle, bar of soap and six clothes pins. Wt. 2 lbs. 6 oz.
49 N 1083........... $1.95

Everything a new mother needs to feed her dolly. 5 polyethylene bottles with caps, nipples. Enameled metal sterilizer with cover, plastic bottle rack, tongs. Measuring cup, spoon, funnel. Orange juicer with strainer, feeding dish, spoon, teething cup, rattle. For cleaning up .. bottle brush, soap powder and sponge. Pastel colors. Attractively gift boxed.
49 N 1373—Wt. 1 lb. 11 oz. $1.84

Spacious utility chest with solid wood frame construction and sturdy masonite top. Colorful nursery design print covered with scratch and stain-resistant Mylar® wipes clean in a jiffy. Five drawers ideal for toy or clothes storage. 12x19x28 inches high.
79 N 01395—Shpg. wt. 12 lbs...... $8.87

The big doll news in 1959 was the release of Barbie by the Mattel Toy Company. However, Barbie is conspicuous by her absence in the 1959 Sears Wishbook. The doll that was to revolutionize the toy industry did not appear until the following year's Christmas catalog and then just briefly.

Sears continued to offer the classics. Shirley Temple was available with several new outfits based on her movies which were experiencing newfound popularity due to television. These included Heidi, Rebecca of Sunnybrook Farm, Captain January and Wee Willie Winkie costumes.

Brides and ballerinas were favorites in 1959 and many of the classic dolls were offered in these variations. Little Miss Revlon's bouffant satin and lace traditional dress including tiara, face veil, shoes, stockings and petticoat could be had for $3.77... a high price in those years.

Sears' tall Honey-Mate dolls and the look-a-like Patty Playpal dolls were extremely popular. They were made by the Ideal company and other doll makers such as Uneeda.

Many character dolls debuted this year. Emmet Kelly, Sad Sack, Little Lulu and Popeye were all available. Even American Bandstand host Dick Clark had his own 27" doll ("a fine gift for teen-agers") priced at $7.49. Surprisingly, today Dick Clark still looks about the same as his 1959 doll namesake!

Sears Christmas
Wishbook

1959

For tots 'n teens

1. **Comical Chimp . .** a barrel of fun for all! Wired arms, legs and tail . . pose him in lots of jolly positions. Expressive face has felt nose and lips, plastic button eyes. Extra-rich pile body of rayon plush, long tail. Cotton-stuffed. 25 inches high when seated.
79 N 04330—Wt. 7 lbs..........$9.99

2. **Dancing Doll Playmate.** A friend to any child. Attach elastic on feet to child's shoes and . . WHEEEE, child and doll dance together! Cotton-stuffed red cloth body. Cotton yarn pony tail. Candy-striped percale dress, organdy apron. 40 in. high.
49 N 3530—Shpg. wt. 4 lbs.......$3.27

3. **Whimsical Tiger . .** soft and lovable. Glassene eyes. Black and yellow striped rayon plush, cotton-stuffed.
49 N 4184—13 in. high. Wt. 1 lb....$2.89

4. **Chipper Chipmunk.** Cute vinyl face. Cotton-stuffed rayon plush body has chipmunk coloring. 9 in. tall.
49 N 4343—Shpg. wt. 1 lb........$2.89

5. **Huge Ever-lovin' Hound.** Floppy ears, soulful eyes. Rayon pile plush body. 31 in. long. Cotton-stuffed.
79 N 04334—Shpg. wt. 6 lbs.......$6.49

6. **Cinnamon Bear . .** a real honey! Cuddlesome rayon plush, cotton-stuffed. Shapeable ears. 30 in. tall.
79 N 04338—Shpg. wt. 4 lbs.....$6.49

7. **Cocker Spaniel.** Floppy-eared and adorable. Brown rayon plush, cotton-stuffed. 20 in. tall.
49 N 4168—Wt. 3 lbs. 8 oz.....$6.79

8. **Scribble Pup . .** it's fun to have the whole gang sign him! Cotton covering, stuffing. 18 in. long.
49 N 4108—Wt. 2 lbs........$2.79

9. **Giant Leopard.** Cub size, he looks playful . . wonderfully real. Huggable, cotton-stuffed rayon plush. Glassene eyes. 16½x45 in. long.
79 N 04183—Shpg. wt. 10 lbs...$27.95

10. **Man's Best Friend.** Pose his legs, cock his ears as you fancy. Rayon plush, cotton-filled. 25 in. high.
79 N 04337—Shpg. wt. 7 lbs....$12.98

11. **Poochy, the Sleepy Pup . .** irresistible. Cotton-stuffed rayon plush. Squeaker in ear. 17 in. long.
49 N 4191—Wt. 2 lbs. 11 oz.....$3.39

We're big-as-life *Honey-Mates* ..waiting to play with you

- Each of us has lashed eyes that close realistically for sleep
- Our hard-to-break vinyl bodies are true-to-life proportions
- Pose us . . our heads turn and tilt . . arms and legs are jointed
- Care for our rooted Saran hair as your mommy cares for yours

Candy-sweet 3-year-old $23.75

[1] Little girl-of-your-dreams come true! A pretty, 35-inch tall play-mate with luxurious blonde curls, a sweet, round face. Her dress is peppermint-striped cotton with attached slip. White organdy pinafore with sash and braid trim. Lace-edged panties. Stretch socks, patent leather shoes. Perky ribbon bow in her hair. Buy her size 3-year dresses, slips.
79 N 03374L—Shpg. wt. 8 lbs......$23.75

Chubby 2-year-old $23.85

[2] A little sweetheart . . with soft red ringlet curls. Her chubby little legs are just like those of a two-year-old toddler. She's daintily dressed in nylon organdy with lace trim, matching rayon taffeta slip and panties . . lace-edged. Stretch socks. Patent leather shoes. A lovable little playmate for a lucky little girl. Wears 18-month size and she is 32 inches tall.
79 N 03372L—Shpg. wt. 9 lbs......$23.85

Pert 3-year-old Tot $23.85

[3] So like a real little girl, in her crisp play apron. Soft brunette hair hangs straight . . braid it or tie it with bows! She's 35 inches tall; dress her in size 3 outfits. She comes to you in a white cotton broadcloth dress with attached taffeta slip, matching panties. Blue striped apron with big "crayon" pocket. Stretch socks. Patent leather shoes. Ribbon in her hair.
79 N 03376L—Shpg. wt. 8 lbs......$23.85

Adorable 1-year-old $16.95

[4] 29 inches of bouncing baby. Her blonde hair curls tightly around her baby face. She wears daintiest dotted swiss dress with lace trim . . Rayon slip and panties. Stretch socks, suede shoes. Wears size 12-mo.
79 N 03371—1-yr.-old. Wt. 7 lbs....$16.95

3-month-old baby doll. (Not shown.) Like baby above, but 3-month size . . just 24 inches long. In bootees.
79 N 03370—3-month-old. Wt. 6 lbs.$12.97

Order extra clothing for Honey-Mate Dolls from the regular section of children's clothing in Sears Big Catalog. Use Easy Terms . . see page 294

24-in. Mouth-string Operated **$5.89**

Whimsical Characters we love

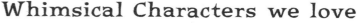

Jerry Mahoney Ventriloquist Dummy

A professional dummy, patterned after the famous TV funster. Now, budding ventriloquists can own a dummy that moves its eyes, mouth and head. All movements separately controlled as on professional dummies. Jerry wears assorted color cotton gabardine suit, white shirt, tie, shoes. Hard plastic head, painted hair. Torso is fiberboard. Legs and arms cotton stuffed. Vinyl hands. In corrugated valise, with instruction booklet.

49 N 3591—32-in. Jerry described above. Shpg. wt. 4 lbs......... $18.98
49 N 3588—32-in. Jerry. Painted, non-moving eyes. Shpg. wt. 4 lbs... 13.89
49 N 3594—24-in. Jerry. Similar to above, but with cotton stuffed body. Mouth moves with string manipulation. Shpg. wt. 3 lbs............... $5.89

[A] **Famous Emmet Kelly** . . the sad-faced clown. Wonderful replica, now all vinyl one-piece body. Emmet stands on his feet, wears sewed-in cotton shirt and clown pants . . felt coat, big tie. Vinyl shoes.
49 N 3850—13½ in. tall. Shpg. wt. 1 lb..... $2.69

[B] **"Poor Pitiful Pearl."** A sad sight in her patched cotton dress, scarf and ragged socks and shoes. See the change in this 13-inch vinyl doll when you put on "rejuvenation" outfit (included). Fully jointed body, go-to-sleep eyes, rooted Saran hair.
49 N 3848—Shipping weight 1 lb. 6 oz..... $4.97

[C] **"Prithilla"**—Cute little tomboy of vinyl. 12½ in. tall, with rooted Saran hair, sleeping eyes. Jointed arms, legs; turning head. In cotton shirt, jeans . . socks, shoes.
49 N 3395—Shipping weight 1 lb. 6 oz...... $3.89

[D] **Sad-Sack.** Vinyl 16-in. doll. One-piece body. Comical GI Joe . . dressed in buck private's cotton uniform, buckle, belt, cap.
49 N 3888—Shipping weight 1 lb. 4 oz...... $3.97

[E] **Rose O'Neil's Kewpie.** Plastic jointed to pose 1,001 ways. Coo voice. Cotton suit.
49 N 3542—13-in. doll. Shpg. wt. 1 lb. 6 oz.. $2.89

DICK CLARK
and
Football Hero
to Autograph

27-in. Dick Clark

[F] Teen-age idol . . as a most alive-looking autograph doll. From vinyl head to stylish shoes he's an exciting autograph item for memorable occasions. Dick wears cotton poplin jacket, pants. Vest, sewed-on shirt with cuffs and cuff links. Cotton stuffed body. A fine gift for teen-agers.
79 N 03570—Shipping weight 4 pounds........ $7.49

Football Hero

[G] Just the thing for autographs of the entire football team . . the cheer leaders . . or your friends in the stands. Big 15-inch doll is cotton-stuffed . . has lots of room on his cloth covered body for names and quips. Ball point pen included.
49 N 3568—Wt. 2 lbs. 4 oz. $4.77

Soft Companions for tiny tots

[H] **Sleepy-head** . . soft and squeezy. A real crib-pal. Washable, cotton-backed rayon plush . . feather-foam stuffed. Vinyl face . . curly yarn hair. 14 inches long.
49 N 3504—With Swiss Music Box that plays a gentle tune. Shipping wt. 1 lb..... $4.79
49 N 3527—Without music box. Wt. 14 oz. 2.69

[J] **Cuddly-Wuddly.** A soft 14½-inch doll for little ones. Cotton stuffed body, painted plastic face, yarn ringlets. Cotton-print apron and fabric body.
49 N 3501—Shipping weight 14 oz..... $1.47

[K] **"Patti"** . . a big, 25-inch flippity-floppity doll with striped cotton skirt and pinafore. Painted plastic face, yarn hair, pony tail style. Cotton-stuffed body.
49 N 3593—Shipping weight 2 lbs..... $1.97

from Favorite Books and Comic Strips

[A] thru [D] **Mickey** .. the 11-inch all-vinyl Boy doll. Molded in fine detail with turning head; jointed arms and legs. Nicely detailed cotton uniforms, molded-on hats. Painted-on features; socks, shoes. Shpg. wt. each 1 lb.
(A) 49 N 3345—Baseball Player.............$2.69
(B) 49 N 3343—Football Player............. 2.69
(C) 49 N 3349—Cub Scout.................. 2.77
(D) 49 N 3344—Sailor..................... 2.69

[E] **Dennis the Menace.** Lovable little prankster .. carefully molded in vinyl. Colorfully dressed in cotton shirt, overalls .. molded vinyl shoes. Clothing removes. Painted features.
49 N 3847—14 in. tall. Shpg. wt. 1 lb. 8 oz.....$3.87

[F] **Little Lulu**—14½-inch fabric doll, cotton-stuffed. Painted face, curly yarn hair. Cotton dress, undergarment. Simulated shoes.
49 N 3843—Shipping weight 14 ounces.......$3.77

[G] **16½-inch Little Lulu** in Western outfit. Cotton felt skirt, cotton shirt, "10-gallon" cowboy hat, boots. Tiny gun in holster to complete the outfit. Soft cotton-stuffed body. Painted face, yarn hair.
49 N 3554—Shipping weight 1 pound.............$5.87

[H] **Popeye** the Sailor Man. Fully-jointed vinyl .. pose him in a hundred-and-one ways! Pinch his face and he whistles through his pipe! A realistic colorful 13-inch reproduction.
49 N 3503—Shipping weight 1 pound 8 ounces $3.77

[J] **Laughing Popeye** .. turn handle at his back and hear him He-He, Ho-Ho, Ha-Ha. This spinach-eating champion is 21 inches tall .. has cotton-stuffed body. His face and muscular arms are vinyl. Costume is of cotton, neatly made like the authentic Popeye clothing. A most hilarious fellow.
49 N 3541—Shipping weight 2 pounds.............$5.77

Raggedy Ann and Andy

[K]-[L] The original button-eyes favorites of tots and adults for many, many years. Soft, cotton-stuffed fabric bodies with yarn hair and merry, painted features. Ann is dressed in cotton dress and apron, Andy in cotton shirt, pants and hat. Clothing removes. Choose from 3 big, floppy sizes!

Size Inches	Catalog Number		Shpg. wt. each	Price each
	(K) Andy	(L) Ann		
15..	49 N 3592..	49 N 3580..	1 lb..........	$2.79
20..	49 N 3603..	49 N 3583..	1 lb. 6 oz....	3.77
32..	79 N 03605..	79 N 03585..	5 lbs........	8.69

Buy Fluffy .. order her clothing separately

I'm Fluffy .. just 11 inches tall

[M] **Vinyl Doll** with rooted Saran hair. Jointed arms and legs, turning head, go-to-sleep eyes. Dressed in lace-trimmed cotton pants, vinyl shoes and socks. Every little girl will love to dress a dolly in the new and different outfits listed below.
49 N 3565—11-inch doll only. Shpg. wt. 1 lb.........$2.69

Clothing for Fluffy. Shipping weight each 8 oz.
[N] 49 N 3381—2-piece Cotton Sleeper..............89c
[P] 49 N 3379—Cotton play outfit, babushka..........89c
[R] 49 N 3384—Polka dot dress of cotton, with felt bolero and hat. Matching panties................$1.89
[S] 49 N 3383—Soft rayon plush Coat, Hat, Muff. Wrist strap on muff; chin strap on hat......................$2.79

Collectors' Happi-Time Miniatures .. just 7½ in. tall

Beautifully-dressed dolls with exquisite features. Dolls of practically unbreakable plastic, with mohair wigs, jointed arms and heads. They all stand alone, dressed in their gorgeous finery ... dresses, half-slips and panties. Lashed, glassene eyes close. Shpg. wt. each 12 oz.

[T] 49 N 3105—**Miss Christmas.** Rayon satin gown, hooded cape, fake fur trim.....$1.69
[V] 49 N 3106—**Nun** in rayon taffeta. Crucifix, imported Italian Rosary. No wig..... 1.69
[W] 49 N 3101—**Beautiful Bride.** Bouffant white rayon satin gown with lovely lace trim. Flowing net veil and beribboned bouquet.............................$1.69
49 N 3102—**Bridegroom** (not shown). Dressed in traditional trousers, tails and high hat. Painted hair. Ideal for wedding parties wtth purchase of Bride above.............$1.59

I roll my eyes,
I have long lashes
I sit so nicely

Toodles Toddler with Hair

She walks with you when you guide her and stands alone. An exquisitely dressed little girl—23 inches tall. She has rooted Saran hair. Wears a lace-trimmed nylon dress with embroidered yoke, sleeves. Dainty tulle ruffles enhance her matching nylon baby hat. Lace trimmed slip, ruffled panties, shoes, socks complete her wardrobe. She has the features described at left, below but does not drink, wet or coo.

Shipping weight 5 pounds.

79 N 03268 . . . . $15.45

Toodles with Molded Hair

Adorable 23-inch Toodles walks with you when guided and is dressed for play in her cotton seersucker romper with embroidered eyelet collar. Matching sunbonnet shades her pretty eyes. Shoes and socks on her toddling little feet complete her outfit. She's all vinyl, jointed and life-like; has rolling, sleeping glassene eyes. She's much too grown-up to drink, wet or cry but loves to be bathed.

Shipping weight 4 pounds.

79 N 03266 . . . . $11.97

I'm Toodles .. Take me
with you wherever you go

Toodles with Kart $17.97

The action baby-doll that feels and poses like a real baby .. jointed arms and legs, head turns. She's vinyl plastic, drinks and wets; bathe her in a tub like a real baby. Coy rolling and sleeping glassene eyes with long curled lashes. See her on TV.

Toodles in her Super Kart. Fun galore with this big 22-in. cuddly baby. Brush and comb her curly rooted Saran hair. Take her with you on shopping trips. 18x13x23½-in. high Super Kart is all steel, wood push handle —use it as a high chair or stroller. Basket at bottom is removable. Toodles dressed in cotton sateen romper, socks and shoes, ribbon in her hair. Has her own bottle, drinks and wets, coos when hugged. Pose her in many ways.
79 N 03265—Toodles in Super Kart. Partially assembled. Wt. 11 lbs. $17.97

Buy the dolly your little girl will love .. use Easy Terms. Page 294 for details

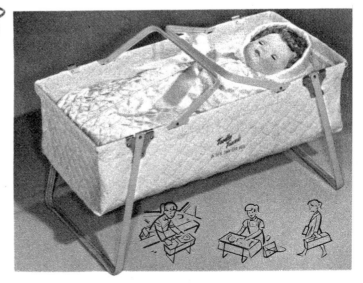

Traveling Infant Toodles in her Car Bed

Soft vinyl 16-inch infant Toodles is a great little traveler. Her quilted car bed has tufted air-filled mattress, sturdy metal frame. Toodles nestles snugly in a glamorous lace-trimmed rayon satin bunting with matching satin bonnet over her rooted curly Saran. hair. Underneath, she wears a cute checked romper and knitted booties. Toodles has pretty, sleeping glassene eyes with lashes .. jointed arms and legs, movable head to pose in all the cute positions of a real little baby. She coo's happily when you squeeze her. See how many ways her car bed can be used in the small views above.
49 N 3263—Infant Toodles in 20-inch Car Bed. Shipping weight 5 lbs. 6 oz. $11.87

Big Baby Dolls Dressed in Attractive Outfits

All three have soft, easy-to-clean vinyl bodies . . lashed sleeping eyes, turning heads. Rooted Saran hair to comb and set. Each is dressed in dainty panties, socks, and vinyl shoes.

[1] **17-inch Baby.** Jointed arms and legs. She drinks and wets, has her own bottle. Lace-trim polished cotton dress and bonnet.
49 N 3174—Shipping weight 2 lbs. **$3.98**

[2] **15-inch Baby.** Cotton stuffed one-piece body. "Coo" voice. Lace-trim cotton dress, sewed-on sheer apron. Knit panties.
49 N 3171—Shipping weight 1 lb. 8 oz. **$2.98**

[3] **19-inch Baby** in cotton coat and bonnet. Older toddler . . she stands alone. Jointed arms and legs. Rayon dress. Knit panties.
49 N 3176—Shipping weight 2 lbs. 8 oz. **$5.97**

17-inch Sub-teen Doll, Travel Wardrobe

Sweet little girl doll . . has trunk, will travel! She's nicely dressed in the latest style polished cotton, with attached net slip . . roses in her rooted Saran hair. Her body is soft vinyl, with jointed arms, legs . . turning head with lashed, sleeping eyes. Trunk 18x9x9 inches, is sturdy fiberboard, with plastic covering and handle, metal latches . . . big drawer, hangers. Wardrobe includes extra cotton dress, robe, coat and bonnet . . accessories for her vacation travel . . 2 pairs of shoes and socks, sun glasses, extra hangers. Add it to your Easy Terms account at Sears . . order now, pay monthly. See page 294 for details.

49 N 3375—Doll, Wardrobe, Trunk. Shpg. wt. 6 lbs. **$12.97**

Doll, Wardrobe and Case

Big 14½-inch Baby Doll with rooted Saran hair to comb, brush, set. All vinyl with turning head, lashed sleeping eyes. Now with jointed arms and legs . . stands alone and sits. Wears glazed cotton dress, panties, socks, shoes. She brings pajamas, ninon nightie, robe, summer dress, coat and hat . . plus brush, comb, mirror, tissues, curlers, extras. All packed in fiberboard carrying case 15¾x5¾x12 in., plastic handle, metal hinges, snap lock.

49 N 3156—Complete outfit. Wt. 5 lbs. **$7.67**

8-inch Drink-wet Baby

Adorable infant . . drinks and wets, has sleeping eyes. All vinyl, jointed body, dressed in panties. Wardrobe of nylon dress with matching bonnet; flocked nylon dress and bonnet; cotton dress, bib; flannel sleeper; sunsuit; diaper bag, diaper, clothespins; blanket; 3 bath sponges; bottle; washcloth; shoes.
49 N 3531—Shipping weight 1 lb. 8 oz. . . **$3.99**

12-inch Baby

Drinks and wets! Vinyl head turns, molded rubber body has jointed arms legs. "Coo" voice. Go-to-sleep eyes. Wears rompers, brings her own bubble pipe and plastic nursing bottle. Pretty bow in her molded hair. Can be sponged clean.
49 N 3505—Shpg. wt. 1 lb. **$2.39**

15-inch Cutie

One-piece cotton-stuffed vinyl skin body, vinyl head. Molded hair, lashed sleeping eyes. Coos when squeezed. In ninon dress, matching bonnet, half-slip, knit panties, socks and shoes. A lot of lovable baby doll, sweetly dressed.
49 N 3112—Wt. 1 lb. 4 oz. **$1.99**

17-inch Baby

Big, soft colored dolly. Cotton-stuffed one-piece vinyl skin body, lashed sleeping eyes, turning head. Coos when squeezed. Rooted Saran hair. Fluffy ninon dress with attached slip . . stylish "bonnet-brim." Knit panties, socks, shoes.
49 N 3507—Wt. 1 lb. 10 oz. **$2.98**

14-inch Baby

Fully jointed vinyl body . . arms, legs, turning head . . stands or sits. In embossed cotton dress with matching bonnet, socks, shoes. Vinyl head has molded hair, lashed sleeping eyes.
49 N 3120—Wt. 1 lb. 4 oz. **$2.98**

I'm Famous *Shirley Temple*

17-inch Shirley as Adventuresome Heidi

Big, dimpled-cheek doll of "Magic-Touch" vinyl plastic. Curly, rooted Saran hair to comb and brush. Lashed moving eyes. Jointed arms and legs. She wears her Swiss mountain outfit styled after her movie-hit "Heidi" costume. Colorful cotton dress with lace and embroidery. Attached slip, matching panties edged with lace. Slippers, socks. Her head turns and she carries a little plastic bag.

49 N 3623—17-inch doll. Shipping weight 3 lbs...... $9.97
49 N 3622—15-inch doll. Shipping weight 2 lbs....... 7.67

$9.97
17 inch

Shirley with Wardrobe

Popular size, 12-inch doll with 4 outfits . . all in pretty gift box. Shirley is all vinyl with jointed arms, legs; turning head, rooted Saran hair and lashed, moving eyes. She's dressed in rayon slip, panties, shoes, socks. Outfit consists of: Tailored trenchcoat, tote bag, visored babushka; Cotton dress . . plastic bag; Sun dress with hat and sun glasses; Party dress with its own slip and imitation pearl necklace. All outfits highly styled, carefully detailed. Buy other outfits at right.

49 N 3986—12-inch Shirley Temple doll with 4 outfits. Shipping wt. 2 lbs. 12 oz..... $9.87

Shirley with separate Outfits

[A] Shirley Temple Doll in rayon taffeta slip, matching panties, socks, shoes. All vinyl, with jointed arms, legs; turning head, rooted Saran hair; lashed moving eyes.
49 N 3938—Doll only. Shipping weight 1 pound........ $3.74

[B] 49 N 3804—"Rebecca" costume. (Doll not included.) Pert cotton flannel shirt, overalls, panty for summer. Wt. 8 oz.... 1.87

[C] 49 N 3805—Knit cotton pajama set for cool nights. With peaked night-cap. Shpg. wt. 8 oz...... 1.37

[D] 49 N 3806—Captain January costume. Snappy sailor suit of cotton, with tie, cap, shoes. Wt. 8 oz..... 2.87

[E] 49 N 3807—Wee Willie Winkie outfit. Pleated skirt, jacket, cap. Socks and shoes. Shpg. wt. 8 oz.......... 2.87

[F] 49 N 3808—Rain outfit. Trim plastic raincoat, rainhat and bag. Shipping weight 8 ounces................. 1.37

Little Miss *Revlon* ..10½-inch grown-up Doll..Outfits

$2.67
10½-inch doll only
[G]

[G] As pretty as a fashion magazine model! This easy-to-dress doll has jointed legs, turning waist . . she can stand alone and pose. Beautiful rooted Saran hair can be combed, brushed and set. Vinyl plastic head and arms. "Magic-touch" vinyl body, feels like real skin. She's nicely groomed with painted fingernails, toenails . . wears shoes, lacy bra, panty-girdle and earrings. Shipping weight 1 pound.
49 N 3076—Pony Tail doll........................ $2.67
49 N 3078—Bobbed Hair doll..................... 2.67
49 N 3817—Revlon GIFT Set. Doll with 4 assorted, different outfits (not shown). Wt. 2 lbs........ 7.57

Clothing for 10½-inch Miss Revlon Dolls. Shpg. wt. each 8 oz.
[H] 49 N 3810—2-piece Pajamas. Floral print cotton with lace....88c
[J] 49 N 3811—Pretty cotton sun dress, panty for summer........ 88c
[K] 49 N 3812—Glamorous knit dress with "pearl" trim at top. Matching knit stole. High style and colorful............................ $1.37
[L] 49 N 3813—Winter ensemble .. Stylish flared velvet coat, set off with muff and head band of fake fur, shoes.................... 2.87
[M] 49 N 3814—Bride's outfit. Bouffant rayon satin and lace in traditional style. Tiara and face veil, shoes, stockings and petticoat...... $3.77
[N] 49 N 3815—Formal elegance. Black lace with rayon taffeta under-skirt. Matching stole and floral headband. Shoes......... $2.87

Prima Ballerinas ..pride of the ballet

[1] **All-vinyl 15-in.** ballerina, jointed arms, legs. Rooted hair to comb and set in pony tail style. Lashed moving eyes. Wears net tutu, panties, ballet shoes. Pretty as a picture .. a real treat for little ballet aspirants. Fun to dress in other outfits, too. See page 492.
49 N 3636—Wt. 1 lb. 2 oz. **$3.98**

[2] **20-inch ballerina-skater.** She walks when guided, poses naturally. Jointed arms, legs, waist, knees and ankles. Soft vinyl arms and turning head. Hard plastic body. Rooted hair, lashed moving eyes. Wears her ice-skating outfit with scarf and skates. Has extra tutu, lace-trim panties, nylon ballet hose and slippers. A beautiful doll with exquisite features.
49 N 3639—Shpg. wt. 2 lbs. 8 oz...**$7.97**

[3] **20-inch walking ballerina** with wardrobe and case. Fully jointed .. arms, legs, waist, knees, ankles. Hard plastic with vinyl head and arms. Rooted hair; lashed moving eyes. Wears ballerina costume, hose, slippers. Wardrobe includes lovely rayon party dress, imitation pearl necklace, high heel shoes. Practice outfit of leotard, ballet slippers; rayon taffeta dress, purse, hat, shoes, socks. All in 20x5½x13-inch cardboard carrying case with metal latch, plastic handle, wood practice bar.
79 N 03642—Shipping weight 5 pounds..........**$9.97**

We're 10½-inch Miniatures .. all with wardrobes to make us lots of fun

Lovely Bride Doll

Pretty as a picture with her rooted "Perma-curl" hair, long-lashed moving eyes. Full-formed all-vinyl body with jointed arms, turning head. She wears white rayon satin and lace gown with net face-veil, panties, shoes .. wears earrings. Her wardrobe includes a cotton sun dress with matching stole and plastic handbag, tiny little mirror and brush, dainty nylon ruffled negligee. In gift box for Christmas giving.
49 N 3846—Outfit. Shpg. wt. 1 lb. 4 oz.........**$4.87**
49 N 3277—Bride in wedding gown only. (Not shown.) Jointed arms, legs..turning waist, head. Shpg. wt. 10 oz..**$3.77**

Santa says .. "Build your order to $20 or more and use Sears Easy Terms .. see page 294 for details"

Nancy Ann with vacation clothes

Nancy Ann has lots of fun, brings clothes for skating and an afternoon in the sun. She is vinyl, full-formed and jointed, with turning waist and head. Pert pony tail hairdo is rooted Saran, can be combed and brushed. Lashed moving eyes. She's dressed in girdle and bra, wears earrings and slippers. Wardrobe includes stylish sun dress, shoes, sun glasses; pretty party dress with slippers; brushed rayon coat and felt hat; 2-pc. pajamas, roller skates, hair curlers, comb and mirror. Her finger and toe nails are painted.

Nancy and her wardrobe come in a gift box, a wonderful present. For additional dresses see Revlon doll dresses on page 292—ideal for Nancy.
49 N 3840—Shipping weight 1 lb. 10 oz.........**$7.87**

Princess with Trunk and Wardrobe

A beautiful fairy princess with the most gorgeous array of clothing. Her all-vinyl body has jointed arms, legs .. turning head. Rooted hair, long-lashed moving eyes. Her gown has rainbow-colored rayon net skirt with gold-color lamé bodice, rayon satin slip. She wears her crown, slippers, and panties.

Her wardrobe includes a rayon velvet dress and rabbit fur-trimmed cape that's truly regal; hoop-skirted dress with hat, pantaloons, slip; dainty nightie with overskirt, bra, bedroom slippers, nylon hose and parasol. 12½x6½x 6½-inch fiberboard trunk has drawer and hangers .. plastic handle, metal catch and hinges.
49 N 3845—Shipping weight 1 lb. 12 oz...............**$7.97**

22-inch Nap-time Gal

Adorable toddler, all ready to snuggle down to sleep. She's all vinyl, with jointed arms, legs. Turning head has the prettiest Saran rooted hair to comb and set. Has her own bottle . . drinks and wets. Wears diaper and shirt under her snuggle-bunny of soft rayon fleece. Note the full length zipper and knit cuffs. Feet of suit have non-skid soles, too.

Carries her own teddy bear and wears her identification bracelet.

49 N 3690—Shipping weight 4 lbs.....$13.97

So Sweet.. So Big.. They look so real

Famous Playtex Dryper Baby

Big as life . . and just as natural. All vinyl, accurately molded to actual size of a 3-month old baby. She drinks, wets, coos. Has rooted Saran hair. Wears undershirt and Dryper (2 packages of drypers included). Baby's head, arms and legs move naturally . . pose in any position. Lashed sleeping eyes. Brings her own bottle, flannel gown, play dress, panties, booties, soap and washcloth.

79 N 03272—23-inch doll. Shipping weight 5 lbs........$15.97
49 N 3271—21-inch doll. Shipping weight 4 lbs...........11.97

Very Young Baby in Christening Dress

Molded to look like a few weeks old infant. Every feature as lifelike as can be. Vinyl plastic with turning head, jointed arms and legs. Molded hair, lashed sleeping eyes. She drinks and wets, too. Wears lace-trimmed organdy dress and bonnet, rayon taffeta slip, diaper. Has her own rayon satin-edged blanket. Identification bracelet, bottle with nipple. Layette includes cotton rompers, dress, bonnet, slip, shoes, socks. Doll 18 in. tall.

79 N 03273—Doll and outfit. Shipping weight 5 lbs......$13.97

Exquisite *Madame Alexander* Dolls

Painstaking care and attention to detail and quality. Madame Alexander dolls bring you the finest in workmanship, exquisite dolls that will be treasured for generations. The finish of the plastic is superb. They have jointed arms and legs. Turning heads, lashed, go-to-sleep eyes, Saran hair to comb, brush and set.

Walt Disney's Sleeping Beauty

[1] No other word but "gorgeous" can describe the costume this golden-haired doll is wearing. Shimmering rayon satin gown has gold-color trim. Gold-color lace cape is full and sweeping. Princess crown of gold-color with rhinestone sets that glitter and glow. The Princess wears full ruffled slip, lace-edged panties. Nylon hose have seams. Golden slippers, shiny ring and necklace. Her beautiful rigid plastic body has soft Vinyl arms . . . her elbows and knees are jointed too. Buy this for your little princess.

79 N 03682—21-inch Princess. Shipping weight 6 lbs......$17.97
79 N 03681—17-inch Princess. Shipping weight 5 lbs.......13.97

MARYBEL the get-well Doll

[2] "Hospitals don't scare me . . 'cause I know just what goes on!" Here's a wonderful way for little girls to get to know about some of life's little unhappinesses . . in a "fun" sort of way. MARYBEL herself is a very lovely doll . . and perfectly healthy too. But play-troubles come with her. She has a cast for make believe broken arm or leg . . Crutches just her size . . red dots and spectacles for measles . . yellow spots for chicken pox! Band-aids and bandages are included for minor scratches. A little girl will love MARYBEL whether sick or well . . and will adore dressing her. She comes in pretty shortie pajamas and slippers; has a ribbon bow in her glossy rooted hair. Body of rigid vinyl, jointed arms, legs and turning waist.

49 N 3670—16-inch doll. Shipping weight 4 lbs. 5 oz...$12.37

[1] $17.97 21-in.

[2] $12.47

"Barbie - The Famous Model" made her first appearance in the Wishbook's pages in 1960. Some experts say retailers were initially reluctant to stock these dolls, made by Mattel, because they were so sexy looking with their thin figures and large busts. In fact, it is quite amazing to see the contrast between Barbie and other dolls surrounding her in the catalog that year. Barbie certainly stood out, despite the tiny space allotted her. But girls rushed to buy Barbie and many other dolls were surely pushed to the back of the shelf.

Barbie was first available with only one option, her hair color -- either blonde or brunette -- which, interestingly, was not even referenced in this debut advertisement. Looking at today's Barbie, her family, friends, accessories and massive wardrobes, it is hard to believe her "career" began so modestly.

The first Barbie was available in a sleek strapless bathing suit. No other doll had ever been this daring! She was priced right at just $2.26. Mint condition examples of the original Barbie have sold for over $5,000!

Two other dolls of note appeared in 1960. Peter Playpal (sold here under the Honey Mate brand) was the handsome brother of Patty Playpal. Although boy dolls are not as collectible as girl dolls, Peter Playpal attracts great collector interest. Initially offered for $24.88, he goes for about $800 today in good condition! Toodles, made by American Character in 25 and 30-inch heights, had eyes that "watch you from any angle... never stray".

Sears Christmas

Wishbook

1960

1 $24.88

2 $21.88

3 $18.88

4 $14.88

Life-size *Honey Mate* Dolls..

- Hard-to-break vinyl bodies with true-to-life proportions
- Heads turn .. arms, legs are jointed .. lashed eyes close

Handsome Brother

1 Big as a 4-year old and just as cute. A 38-in. playmate for boys and girls. His washable rooted Saran hair is cut in popular little boy style. He wears long cotton pants, red Blazer cotton jacket with crest on pocket, cotton shirt, Eton cap, shoes, socks. *$2.50 down on Easy Terms .. see page 294.*
79 N 3378L—Wt. 10 lbs......$24.88

Brown-tressed Heidi

2 Realistic 3-year old now walks with your guidance. Her shining brown rooted Saran hair is swept back in' a smart hairdo. She models a lovely cotton dress, in traditional peasant fashion, slip, panties, shoes and socks. 36 in. tall .. wears size 3 dresses. *$2.50 down.*
79 N 3388L—Wt. 9 lbs. Cash $21.88

Bundled-up Toddler

3 Our most life-like doll! Has detailed fingers and toes .. swivel, as well as turning head, to assume practically any position .. rooted "Perma-curl" plastic hair to brush and set. She wears a fluffy cotton coat, cotton felt hat, cotton skirt, knit blouse, panties, socks, shoes. 36 in. tall .. wears size 3 children's clothes.
79 N 3377L—Wt. 9 lbs...... $18.88

Pert Playtime Gal

4 Dressed for rough and tumble fun in corduroy slacks, cotton blouse, knit sweater, kerchief, panties, rayon socks, shoes. This typical 3-year-old will walk with a little help from you. Keeps young mothers occupied for hours. Her rooted "Perma-curl" hair waves naturally .. fun to wash and set. 36 in. tall.
79 N 3369L–Shpg. wt. 9 lbs. $14.88

Life-size Tiny Tots to cuddle

5 **Infant in her own bye-bye chair.** True-to-life 25-inch baby from her plump legs to her tiny face. Comes in cotton sleeper-sack, diaper, ribbon-trimmed blanket. Has her own bottle, soap, washcloth and booties. Plastic chair has a removable tray with big play beads.
79 N 3294C—Wt. 7 lbs......$18.87
79 N 3229C—Baby with accessories, less bye-bye chair. Wt. 6 lbs. $15.98

6 **Appealing 1-year-old.** 28 inches of bouncing baby .. yet light and easy to carry for tiny mothers. Rooted Saran hair curls around her face. Dressed in sheer nylon outfit with matching slip, panties, shoes, socks. Wears size 12 months.
79 N 3348L—Wt. 9 lbs.... $15.88
79 N 3347C—23-in. 3-month old, like baby above except wears booties. Shpg. wt. 5 lbs.. $12.87

5 $18.87 Doll, Seat

6 $15.88 28-in. doll

Use Sears Easy Terms .. see page 294

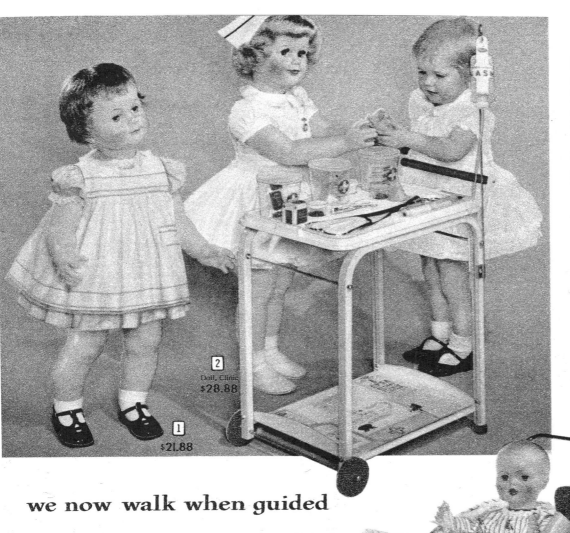

Doll, Clinic
$28.88

[1] $21.88

Chubby 2-year-old

[1] A little sweetheart with the true-to-life proportions of an irresistible two-year-old. Her curly pixie hair-do is treated so that it will always fall naturally into place. She's daintily dressed in cotton pinafore dress with matching slip, stretch socks and toddler-type shoes.

79 N 3354L—32-inch doll.
Shipping weight 8 pounds. *Only $2.50 down on Terms.* Cash $21.88
79 N 3341L—28-inch doll.
Shipping weight 7 lbs..... 18.88

Nurse with clinic

[2] The picture of efficiency in white polished cotton uniform, cap, apron, nylon lingerie, white shoes, socks. Kidd-E-Clinic is all-steel cart (14x21x22 in. high) with wheels, handle. Has over 30 hospital play items as stethoscope, forceps, charts. Shipping weight 18 lbs.

79 N 3394L2—*$3 dn.* Cash $28.88
79 N 3401L—36-inch nurse only. Wt. 9 lbs. *$2.50 down.* Cash $23.75
79 N 3402L—Kidd-E-Clinic only. Shipping weight 9 lbs...... $8.95

we now walk when guided

- Our big-as-life vinyl bodies have jointed arms, legs, movable head
- We have lashed sleeping eyes . . rooted plastic hair to wash, set

Big Sister actually walks beside carriage as you push it along!

Of course, she'll even walk alone with you . . when you leave the buggy and baby at home. She has those features described above, too. Baby Sis, however, hasn't had time to grow much hair . . hers is molded plastic. Big Sis is 35 inches tall in her pretty cotton bolero dress, cotton blouse, rayon panties, socks and shoes . . and she loves having her hair groomed. Baby is 25 inches tall, wears cotton flannel sleeper-sack, diaper (which she wets if watered) and has matching blanket.

Carriage is of vinyl plastic with steel frame and folding hood. Freight (rail or truck) or express.
79 N 3342N—3-piece set. Shipping weight 30 lbs....$37.99

Sister Dolls, Buggy
$37⁹⁹
cash
$4.00 down

Beautifully styled extra Outfits for big or small Toddler Dolls

[3] 5-piece Sports Ensemble. Includes print cotton cord skirt with loop trim, polished cotton blouse with cord collar, matching panties, vest and hat.

49 N 3440—16 to 17 inches. Shpg. wt. 7 oz........$2.47
49 N 3441—20 to 21 inches. Shpg. wt. 9 oz......... 2.67
49 N 3442—30 to 32 inches. Shpg. wt. 14 oz....... 2.97
49 N 3443—34 to 36 inches. Shpg. wt. 15 oz....... 3.77

[4] Sweater and Skirt Set. Soft rayon fleece sweater, tam. Multi-color knit trim. Cotton felt skirt.

49 N 3453—16 to 17 inches. Shpg. wt. 6 oz........$1.47
49 N 3454—20 to 21 inches. Shpg. wt. 8 oz......... 1.87
49 N 3455—30 to 32 inches. Shpg. wt. 13 oz........ 2.87
49 N 3456—34 to 36 inches. Shpg. wt. 1 lb......... 3.19

[5] Cold Weather Outfit. Plaid print cotton cord coat with fine edging on collars and cuffs . . buttons snugly. Matching cord hat with ribbon ties.

49 N 3475—16 to 17 inches. Shpg. wt. 7 oz........$1.97
49 N 3476—20 to 21 inches. Shpg. wt. 9 oz........ 2.17
49 N 3477—30 to 32 inches. Shpg. wt. 12 oz....... 2.97
49 N 3478—34 to 36 inches. Shpg. wt. 13 oz....... 3.29

Toodles ..the Doll with peek-a-boo eyes

Her eyes watch you from any angle . . never stray

We walk with you when guided

[1] Toodles goes for a Sunday stroll in her gay cotton dress, crisp white pinafore and saucy sailor hat. She wears patent Mary Jane slippers, socks, panties. Toodles is lifelike in every detail with jointed arms and legs; turning head; toddling feet. She "walks" with her play mommy's help, sits and stands. Her glassene eyes open and close, "follow" her little mother everywhere. Lifelike vinyl with rooted Saran hair to brush, long curled eyelashes. You be the judge . . she will win the beauty contest.

79 N 3310C—25-inch doll. Shpg. wt. 5 lbs. .$14.98
79 N 3311L—30-inch doll. Shpg. wt. 7 lbs.. 16.98

[2] Toodles, the belle of the birthday party in a lovely Grecian dress exquisitely fashioned of permanently pleated embroidered nylon sheer. Sewn-in lace-edged taffeta slip has a billowing net ruffle and lace-edged panties. To complete her costume, she has a ribbon for her hair; imitation pearls 'round her neck; rayon satin slippers. Toodles has all the wonderful features described above and "walks" with her mommy to the party!

79 N 3308C—25-inch doll. Shpg. wt. 5 lbs. .$13.88
79 N 3309L—30-inch doll. Shpg. wt. 7 lbs. 15.88

[3] Toodles dressed for the pajama party in an exotic cotton and rayon quilted mandarin robe sparked with "gold-color dust". Embroidered robe has ruffle trim and two patch pockets. Underneath, Toodles wears embroidered cotton pajamas and matching slippers with gay pompons. Next morning, Toodles changes to her extra dress of cotton pique with lace trim with its matching panties, shoes and socks. Toodles has the same exciting features described in (1): walks, sits, stands, and has pretty peek-a-boo eyes!

79 N 3315C—25-inch doll. Shpg. wt. 5 lbs. .$15.98
79 N 3316L—30-inch doll. Shpg. wt. 7 lbs. 18.98

[2] $13.88
25-inch

[1] $14.98
25-inch

[3] $15.98
25 inch

[4] $14.77
25-inch

[5] $11.77
25-inch

We both will say "Mama" to you

[4] Peek-a-boo-eye Baby Toodles plays in the snow in her cozy cotton and rayon flannel snowsuit. Knit-edged pompom hat, mittens, big scarf, booties keep her toasty warm. She wears a cotton romper underneath, carries her bottle. Too young to walk . . she still drinks, wets, has a waterproof "Mama" voice. Wash her molded vinyl body, comb, set her rooted Saran hair. At bedtime her eyes close. Her arms, legs are jointed; her head moves.

79 N 3187C—25-inch doll. Shpg. wt. 5 lbs. .$14.77
79 N 3189L—30-inch doll. Shpg. wt. 7 lbs.. 17.88

[5] Baby Toodles stays at home in her embossed cotton romper topped by a full-length all-around embossed cotton pinafore. Her outfit is just like the ones real little sisters wear! Toodles is very proud of her adorable topknot hairdo and shows it off with a pert hairbow. She wears soft-soled rayon satin shoes and socks. Feed her from the bottle she carries and change her wet diaper. She has the same wonderful features as Baby Toodles (4) above.

79 N 3186C—25-inch doll. Shpg. wt. 5 lbs. .$11.77
79 N 3188L—30-inch doll. Shpg. wt. 7 lbs. 14.88

Other Toodles dolls, see page 366

Marybel the get-well Doll $10.98

The perfect doll for little girls who like to play hospital. Marybel has a cast for make believe broken arms or legs; crutches just her size; red dots and spectacles for measles; even yellow spots for chicken pox. Band-aids and bandages are included for minor scratches. Remove her pretend diseases and bandages and Marybel gets well right away! She wears pretty shortie pajamas, slippers, a ribbon bow in her distinctly styled rooted wig of Saran. Exquisitely fashioned with rigid vinyl body; jointed arms and legs; turning waist and head; lashed, go-to-sleep eyes. Marybel has all the superb details which always characterize Madame Alexander dolls.

49 N 3670—16-inch doll. Shpg. wt. 3 lbs. 12 oz. . .$10.98

Madame Alexander Dolls

Famous Little Women $8.67 each

Louisa May Alcott's "Little Women" come to life! Plastic bodies with jointed arms and legs. Saran hair wigs are styled of the period. Turning heads; lashed, go-to-sleep eyes. Each doll wears little black suede slippers, white nylon socks. 12 in. high. Shpg. wt. each, 1 lb. 6 oz.

[1] 49 N 3649—Amy, lovely in a cotton dress with ruffled floral pinafore, and pantalets $8.67

[2] 49 N 3651—Beth, shy and angelic, wears a polished cotton dress, lace-trimmed pantalets $8.67

[3] 49 N 3653—Meg, sensible Meg wears a lace-trimmed organdy pinafore, cotton dress, pantalets $8.67

[4] 49 N 3658—Jo, the tomboy wears a pin-dot cotton dress, red cotton pinafore, pantalets $8.67

Granny Sleep Set

Cotton flannel nightgown, 2 pc. pajamas with elastic waist and ankles. Moppet cap keeps dolly warm. Shpg. wt. 14 oz.

49 N 3416—14 to 15 inches $1.97
49 N 3417—18 to 19 inches. 2.59
49 N 3419—20 to 21 inches. 2.69

Beautiful extra Clothing for slender grown-up dolls 14 to 21 in.; Toddlers 18 to 35 in.

[5] **Ballerina.** Nylon tutu, panties, nylon hose, slippers. Wt. 14 oz.
49 N 3464—14 to 15 inches $1.79
49 N 3465—18 to 19 inches 2.39
49 N 3466—20 to 21 inches 2.49

[6] **Formal Gown.** Lovely nylon net and taffeta. Panties. Wt. 14 oz.
49 N 3420—14 to 15 inches $2.57
49 N 3421—18 to 19 inches 2.77
49 N 3422—20 to 21 inches 2.97

[7] **Bridal Outfit.** White rayon taffeta and nylon net gown. Bridal veil, petticoat and panties. Shpg. wt. 14 oz.
49 N 3484—14 to 15 inches $2.97
49 N 3485—18 to 19 inches 3.57
49 N 3486—20 to 21 inches 3.87

[8] **Jumper Dress.** Iridescent rayon taffeta jumper, attached slip. Rayon taffeta blouse, panties. Shpg. wt. 14 oz.
49 N 3430—14 to 15 inches $1.97
49 N 3431—18 to 19 inches 2.47
49 N 3432—20 to 21 inches 2.67

[9] **Accessory Outfit.** 2-way stretch girdle, bra, nylon hose, garters. Shoes, plastic case. Shpg. wt. 8 oz.
49 N 3449—14 to 15 inches $1.39
49 N 3451—18 to 19 inches 1.39
49 N 3452—20 to 21 inches 1.39

[10] **Coat, hat, muff** of Orlon® Dynel imitation fur. Rayon lined. Wt. 14 oz.
49 N 3363—14 to 15 inches $2.29
49 N 3364—18 to 19 inches 2.67
49 N 3365—20 to 21 inches 2.98

[11] **Coat and Matching Hat.** Cotton and rayon fleece. Flared coat. Wt. 14 oz.
49 N 3351—14 to 15 inches $2.57
49 N 3352—18 to 19 inches 2.98
49 N 3353—20 to 21 inches 3.29

For Toddler Dolls

[12] **Artificial Leather** coat, belt, beret, and purse. Rayon lined. Wt. 1 lb.
49 N 3458—18 to 21 inches $2.49
49 N 3459—30 to 32 inches 2.98
49 N 3460—34 to 36 inches 3.98

[13] **Big Set.** Purse, shoes, socks, slippers, panties, leotard, hair net. Wt. 1 lb.
49 N 3467—18 to 19 inches $2.29
49 N 3468—20 to 21 inches 2.49
49 N 3469—30 to 32 inches 3.49
49 N 3470—35 to 36 inches 3.79

$3.44

Ballerina with wardrobe
$7.77

Pretty Prima Ballerinas

15-inch vinyl ballerina, has jointed arms, legs. Rooted hair to comb and set. Lashed moving eyes. Wears net tutu, panties, ballet shoes, flowers in her hair . . . pretty as a picture. Fun to dress in other outfits, too. See page 362.

49 N 3625—Shipping wt. 1 lb. 3 oz. $3.44

20-inch Walking Ballerina with Wardrobe. Full jointed arms, legs, knees and ankles. All vinyl; plastic legs. Rooted hair, lashed moving eyes. Wears ballerina costume, hose, slippers. Wardrobe has rayon party dress, high heels, hose, leotard, ballet slippers, cotton dress, panties, jacket.
49 N 3635—Shpg. wt. 2 lbs. 6 oz. $7.77

20-inch Walking Ballerina-Skater. (Not shown.) Has features described above. Wears ice-skating outfit, scarf, skates. Has stage tutu, panties, ballet hose, slippers.
49 N 3639—Wt. 2 lbs. 6 oz. *Was* $7.97 . .$6.87

20-inch Bride, Trousseau, Trunk $10.67

Pretty as a picture in her bridal gown of heavy rayon satin becomingly trimmed with net and lace. Fingertip veil accents her rooted Saran hair and lovely lashed sleeping eyes. Fashioned of sturdy vinyl with jointed arms and legs, turning head. She wears lace panties, dainty slippers. Trousseau includes one rayon taffeta party dress; one cotton afternoon dress; a one-piece slack outfit; simulated pearl necklace; plastic hat; sheer housecoat; fur-look rayon jacket; crinoline; long nylon hose; shoes, purse. Sturdy fiberboard trunk with metal hinges and latch, plastic handle, hangers.
79 N 3683C—20-inch Doll; 20½-inch Trunk; Wt. 6 lbs. .$10.67
49 N 3673—15-inch Doll. 15¼-inch Trunk. Wt. 4 lbs. . . 7.77

Every Little Girl Wants a *Costume Doll*

15 inch
$4.57

$6.98

$4.77

$9.98

Miss Revlon

Glamour doll of all vinyl. Jointed arms, legs, turning waist, head. Rooted Saran hair and moving eyes. Painted toes and fingernails. Wears undies and shoes. Order her wardrobe on page 362.
49N3694–15 in. Wt. 2 lbs.$4.57
49N3695–18 in. Wt. 2 lbs. 4.87
49N3699–20 in. Wt. 3 lbs. 5.97

Girl Scout Dolls

15 inches tall and all vinyl; rooted Saran hair; sleeping eyes; freckles. Jointed arms, legs, turning head. Wears official green cotton uniform, neckerchief, beret, pants, socks and shoes. Shipping weight 1 lb. 10 oz.
49 N 3648—Girl Scout $6.98
49 N 3645—Brownie Scout in official uniform (not shown) $6.98

Walking Toddler

Sweet 15-inch toddler walks along when guided by her play mommy. She has vinyl jointed arms and legs, turning pretty head. Plastic body. Beautiful, lashed, glassene eyes open and close. Wash, comb, set her rooted, Dutch Bob style Saran hair. She wears a lovely lace-trimmed organdy dress, panties, shoes and socks.
49 N 3626—Shpg. wt. 1 lb. 8 oz. .$4.77

Pony-tailed Teenager with Wardrobe

20-inch vinyl doll has lashed, go-to-sleep green eyes, rooted carrot-red hair and a sweet adorable face with a cute turned up nose. Her jointed arms, legs, and head move. Wears cotton slacks under an artist's smock; shoes, socks. Wardrobe includes rayon party dress; cotton skirt and blouse; cotton and cotton-flannel combination sport jacket; leotards; panties trimmed with lace; vinyl hat with daisy trim; sunglasses, shoes. All in a 21x10x7-inch cardboard carrying case with metal hinges and latch, plastic handle.
79 N 3684C—Shipping weight 5 pounds $9.98

15-in. Doll . . trunk full of clothes

An adorable vinyl toddler with jointed arms, legs, turning head . . . lashed go-to-sleep eyes and rooted acetate hair that's washable. Dressed in rayon taffeta dress, panties, socks and vinyl shoes . . and a complete wardrobe including coat, street dress, hat, pajamas, nightgown, housecoat, 3-piece vanity set, tissues, curlers, set of luggage, all packed in 16-in. fiberboard trunk with metal hinges, plastic handle.
49 N 3139—Doll, trunk, clothes. Wt. 4 lbs. 9 oz. $6.88

$6⁸⁸

Big-as-life Toddler

All dressed up for a party in dainty cotton organdy dress, with attached slip and panties. Her rooted Saran hair is swept into a ponytail, but you comb and set it any way you like. Appealing lashed eyes open and close. Hard-to-break vinyl body has jointed arms, legs, turning head. Wears socks and shoes.
79 N 3302C—31-in. doll. Wt. 6 lbs $8.99
79 N 3301C—28-in. doll. Shpg. wt. 4 lbs. 6.99

$8⁹⁹
31-in.

17-inch Doll, Big Wardrobe, Trunk

Our best . . has trunk, will travel! Soft vinyl doll is dressed for visiting in lace trimmed polished cotton dress, undies, socks and shoes. Rooted Saran hair, jointed arms, legs, turning head with lashed, sleeping eyes. Her vacation wardrobe features cotton dress, robe, coat and bonnet, 2 pairs of shoes and socks and sun glasses. Sturdy, reinforced fiberboard trunk (18x9x9 inches) has big drawer, extra hangers, metal hinges and latches, plastic handle.
49 N 3338—Doll, wardrobe, trunk. Shpg. wt. 6 lbs...$12.97

$12⁹⁷

"Barbie," the famous model and her latest fashions

[1] An exciting new doll with fashion appeal for girls of all ages! So grown-up and life-like, she almost breathes. Flesh-toned vinyl plastic body has movable arms, legs and head making her easy to dress . . she poses on her plastic stand! Rooted Saran hair can be set and brushed to suit her outfit. Wears striped jersey swimsuit, sun glasses, earrings and shoes. From Japan.
49 N 3701—"Barbie" doll 11½ inches tall. Shpg. wt. 1 lb. $2.26

Wardrobe for "Barbie" doll. From Japan. Shipping weight each 4 oz.
[A] 49 N 3702—Cotton sailcloth sundress, wedge-heeled white sandals 77c
[B] 49 N 3704—Glamorous party dress with velvet top, white rayon satin skirt and gold color belt. Matching gold color bag, stylish black shoes $1.13
[C] 49 N 3705—Zippered sheath dress of polished cotton, matching shoes . . . 1.13
[D] 49 N 3706—Dressy gold color brocade outfit. Accessories include imitation "pearl" jewelry, tricot gloves, velvet purse and shoes 1.57
[E] 49 N 3707—Casual ensemble. Cardigan and slip-on sweater set, cotton flannel skirt, shoes. Also tiny knitting bowl, needles, yarn, scissors 2.27

Collectors' Miniature Dolls

Exquisitely dressed Happi-time miniatures (just 7½ inches tall). Practically unbreakable plastic with jointed arms, heads, lustrous mohair wigs, open and shut lashed eyes. They all stand alone to model their gorgeous finery. Shipping weight each 14 oz.

[2] 49 N 3165—New Majorette. Rayon-satin costume, rick-rack trim, crinoline slip. Baton $1.59
[3] 49 N 3106—Nun dressed in black rayon taffeta. Crucifix, imported Italian rosary. No wig 1.69
[4] 49 N 3101—Beautiful Bride. Rayon satin gown, flowing net veil and beribboned bouquet 1.69
49 N 3102—Bridegroom (not shown). Wears traditional trousers, tails and high hat. Painted hair . . 1.59

Cuddly Teddy Bears
. . ready to love

[1] **Baby Bear** . . a cute and fuzzy naptime, playtime pal. Easy to wash with soap and water. Short pile, beige rayon plush . . soft cotton and Dryex® stuffing. Locked-in eyes.
49 N 4123—20 in. tall. Shpg. wt. 1 lb. 11 oz. **$3.77**

[2] **Smokey Bear** . . a playtime forest ranger with his plastic badge, hat and shovel. Tan short pile rayon plush and blue denim stuffed with Dryex® foam and cotton. Locked-in button eyes.
49 N 4346—14 in. tall. Shpg. wt. 1 lb. 3 oz. **$2.77**

[3] **Teddy Bear.** Jointed hind legs let him sit naturally. Soft, short pile rayon plush body is cotton stuffed. Red cotton felt tongue, sewed in button eyes, cotton felt eye patches, paw pads. Complete with gay rayon neck ribbon. 19 in. tall.
49 N 4192—Shipping weight 2 lbs. 8 oz. **$4.33**

[4] **Crouching Bear** strikes an appealing pose. Fine, long pile rayon plush is white tipped with dark brown. Cotton filled. Button eyes, vinyl nose, mouth, cotton felt claws. Red ribbon.
49 N 4347—18 inches long. Wt. 2 lbs. 12 oz. **$5.88**

Washable Teddy and Panda. When soiled, just scrub with soap and water . . they dry quickly. Soft, short pile rayon over Dryex® foam plastic and cotton stuffing. 13½ inches tall.
(5) 49 N 4102—Teddy. Shpg. wt. 1 lb. 3 oz. . **$1.88**
(6) 49 N 4126—Panda. Shpg. wt. 1 lb. 3 oz. . . 1.88

Send no money, pay later on Sears Charge Plan . . see pages 295 and 296

[7] **Bugs Bunny** hops out of the comics into any child's heart. He sports a Bugs Bunny button, rayon bow tie. Gray and white short pile rayon plush body, molded vinyl face. Wired ears you can shape yourself . . long floppy legs. 29 in. tall over-all. Cotton filled. Wt. 1 lb. 12 oz.
49 N 4097 . . . **$3.44**

[8] **Frisky Pony** . . big enough to ride! Tiny dudes will love his soft palomino coat of rayon plush, his tot-size, plastic sheeting seat. Supports 100 pounds! Cotton, excelsior stuffing. Has steering handle, sturdy rubber tires. Seat height 15 inches. Shipping weight 8 lbs.
79 N 4349C—15½x8x21 inches high **$8.88**

Quick Draw McGraw and his friends . . straight from your TV screen. All are Featherfoam® filled with soft rayon plush bodies and comic vinyl faces. Accessories (hats, ties, collars, jackets, etc.) are of soft cotton felt.

[9] **Quick Draw McGraw** . . in his cotton neckerchief, cowboy hat and simulated plastic gun and holster.
49 N 4350—19 inches tall Shpg. wt. 1 lb. 14 oz. . . . **$3.77**
79 N 4351C—28 inches tall Shpg. wt. 5 lbs. **$7.44**

[10] **Blabber** looks so funny in his small-size hat.
49 N 4354—17 inches tall Shpg. wt. 1 lb. 12 oz. . . . **$3.77**

[11] **Snooper** holds onto his plastic magnifying glass.
79 N 4355C—21 inches tall Shpg. wt. 3 lbs. **$5.99**

[12] **Ba-Ba-Looey** . . Quick Draw's sidekick has South-of-the-Border accent.
49 N 4352—15 inches tall Shpg. wt. 1 lb. 8 oz. **$2.95**
79 N 4353C—21 inches tall Shpg. wt. 3 lbs. **$4.44**

[13] **Augie Doggie** . . funny face, cotton felt ears.
49 N 4356—12 inches high Shpg. wt. 1 lb. 5 oz. **$2.95**

[14] **Doggie Daddy** . . with his cotton yarn tuft of hair, floppy cotton felt ears.
49 N 4357—18 inches tall Shpg. wt. 2 lbs. 6 oz. . . . **$4.44**

Although Barbie was catching on elsewhere it was hard to recognize the trend in the 1961 Sears Wishbook. The doll still received minimal ad space. It is interesting to note that the price for the standard Barbie had been reduced to $1.97. Several new outfits were added including a rayon satin gown known as "Enchanted Evening", a ballet dress and even a terry bathrobe... which Barbie made look quite glamorous!

Other dolls took the spotlight in 1961. Betsy Wetsy, available in 13, 17 and 23-inch heights, drank, wet, cooed and "cried real tears." Made of rubber, she came dressed in a romper outfit and included a layette and tub. Miss Ideal, made by Ideal Toys, of course, came in 25 and 30-inch versions and allowed girls to play "beauty shop." Her rooted nylon hair was "so real you can shampoo it, set it, in many different styles." Prices went as high as $19.99.

Betsy McCall and Shirley Temple were still popular and even more outfits were offered for them. A Pollyanna doll, based on the hit Disney movie of the year, was available in three sizes: 10 1/2, 17 and 32-inch heights. The doll, rushed to the marketplace, had little resemblance to young Hayley Mills who starred in the film.

The power of television was making itself felt in the Wishbook's pages. One ad display was headlined "Famous TV Dolls of 1961" and pitched Thumbelina and Hedda Get Bedda, both heavily advertised on children's programs of the time.

1961 CHRISTMAS BOOK

Sears Christmas

Wishbook

1961

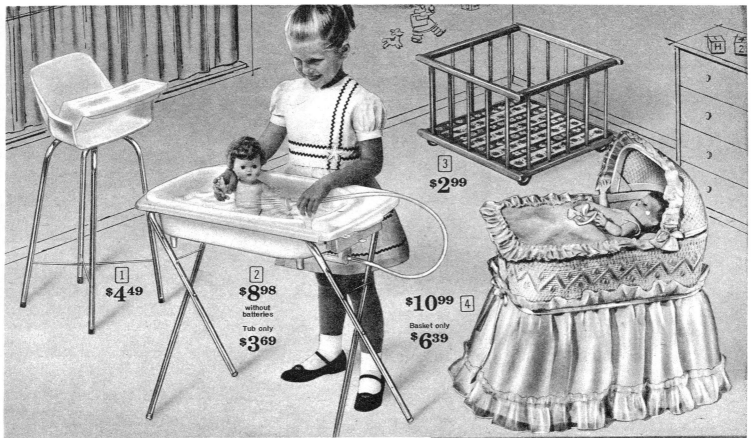

[1] 4^{49}

[2] 8^{98}
without batteries

Tub only
3^{69}

[3] 2^{99}

10^{99} [4]

Basket only
6^{39}

Have a Real Dolly Nursery

Almost baby-size! Extra sturdy and realistic .. with features sure to please little mothers

[1] **Convertible High Chair** becomes a car seat. Big enough for dolls up to 30 in. tall. Shaped plastic seat set securely on brass-finish metal stand. Plastic tray holds play dishes (not incl.). Vinyl leg tips.
79 N 9252C—Shpg. wt. 3 lbs..........$4.49

[2] **Battery operated Spra Bath.** Give doll a shampoo and shower with a real spray attachment. Has battery-driven motor. Water recirculates .. no need for faucet attachment. Molded polyethylene tub won't rust or leak. Brass-finish metal stand. Removable sling. Tub: 26x14x5 in. (No doll.) Uses 3 "D" batteries, order below.
79 N 9289CM—Shipping weight 7 lbs...$8.98
79 N 4662M—"D" batteries. Wt. 8 oz..2 for 39c

Tub only. As above, but no spray device.
79 N 9294C—Shipping weight 3 lbs $3.69

[3] **Playpen** has swivel casters so even the littlest girl can move it easily. Put 'baby' here to play. Sturdy wood construction. Heavy decorated hardboard bottom. 17x16x12 in. high. Partly assembled.
79 N 9297C—Shpg. wt. 5 lbs...........$2.99

[4] **Deluxe Bassinette** .. so pretty for dolly's naptime. Dainty organdy skirt with nylon embroidery-trimmed ruffle; pillow and mattress have matching coverlet. White enameled, woven fiber basket. Folding, lock-in-place legs with rolling casters. Lightweight. Movable, detachable hood. Basket is 23x12x26 in. high. (No doll.)
79 N 9329C—Shpg. wt. 8 lbs........$10.99

Fiber Doll Basket has movable hood, casters. Legs fold, lock in place. Pastel trim.
79 N 9255C—23x12x26 in. Wt. 6 lbs....$6.39

3^{98}

9^{98}

Swing-Car Seat Duo

Lift the seat off swing .. it has wire hooks for use as a car seat. Sturdy steel frame; silver-color finish. Flower print on white vinyl seat. Plastic (no-mar) tips on legs. 16x15x 28 in. high. Folds compactly.
79 N 9307C—Wt. 4 lbs .. $3.98

Bunk Bed Ensemble

Stack the two 15x26 in. hardwood beds .. you have a 27 in. high double decker! White finish. White accessories: padded mattresses, ruffled pillows. Matching ladder and side rails. Easy to assemble.
79 N 9295C—Wt. 14 lbs..$9.98

Comfy Carry-All 1^{79}

Use this handy set in your doll carriage or crib. When you go visiting, it serves as a car bed and diaper-bag. Clear vinyl pocket holds soap, washcloth, doll bottle and clothespins. Vinyl cotton filled mattress; 11x20-in. rich looking satin cover and pillow.
49 N 9263—Shpg. wt. 15 oz.........$1.79

Comfy Carry Basket 3^{98}

Carry dolly and her things in this wood basket with luxurious satin pillow, coverlet. Pink vinyl lining, mattress. Nylon skirt, taffeta underskirt. Sheet, pillowcase, blanket in hidden compartment. Vinyl pocket holds washcloth, soap, bottle, clothespins.
49 N 9243—15x10x6 in. Wt. 2 lbs. 4 oz.$3.98

Colonial Cradle

5^{98}

Rock dolly to sleep in this big cradle. Sturdily built to last the 'babyhood' of several dollies, it's made of hardwood with fine maple finish. Well turned corner posts, dowel sides, rails. 19-inch steam-bent rockers. 6½-in. head panel. Colonial print fabric covers the softly tufted mattress and pillow. Size: 26x14x18 in. high. Partly assembled.
79 N 9247C—Wt. 9 lbs..$5.98

"Betsy Wetsy"

drinks, wets, coos
and
cries real tears

Betsy Wetsy with layette . . low as $5⁷⁷ with molded hair

Betsy Wetsy with tub and layette $7⁹⁸ 13-inch size

Betsy in romper dress $8⁸⁸

Famous Betsy has the most precious baby face ever to win an adoring little girl's heart. Look at those big, moving, innocent eyes. Large tears well up in them and roll down her cheeks. Vinyl plastic body has a skin-soft touch. Arms, legs are jointed, head turns. Rooted Saran hair is baby styled.

[1] **Now Betsy adds a new thrill to mother's care.** She comes with bubble bath. And she loves to be bathed in her tub full of water, bursting with fragrant bubbles. Dressed in romper. Layette includes: assorted style cotton dress and bonnet; diaper; 2 safety pins; 3 powder puffs; bottle and nipple; soap; washcloth; tissues; 6 clothes pins; booties. Molded plastic tub in size to fit each doll, along with package of 12-oz. bubble bath.

49 N 3167—13-inch doll, layette and tub. Wt. 3 lbs.........$7.98
49 N 3168—17-inch doll, layette and tub. Wt. 4 lbs......... 11.88
79 N 3169C—23-inch doll, layette and tub. Her tub has bracket to fit across standard size bath tub. Shpg. wt. 6 lbs..........$14.97

[2] **Betsy with rooted Saran hair.** Wears panties to match dress. Layette has two-tone cotton dress, bonnet; 3 powder puffs; soap; washcloth; bottle, tissues; 6 clothes pins and booties.

49 N 3130—13-inch doll, layette. Shpg. wt. 2 lbs.............$6.77
49 N 3131—17-inch doll, layette. Shpg. wt. 3 lbs............. 9.66

[3] **Betsy with molded hair.** Otherwise the same as (2) above.

49 N 3128—13-inch doll, layette. Shpg. wt. 2 lbs........$5.77
49 N 3129—17-inch doll, layette. Shpg. wt. 3 lbs............. 7.88

[4] **Betsy is 23 inches tall.** She's as pretty as a beauty contest winner. Lifelike detail and skin tone. Her doting young mother can dampen, brush and set her rooted Saran hair. She's ready for feeding time with her own bottle. Fully jointed to assume lifelike positions. Drinks, wets and has sleeping eyes. Dressed for play in adorable romper outfit. A dainty bow ties her shining hair. Booties fancied with bows.

79 N 3190C—23-inch doll. Shipping weight 4 lbs............$8.88

"Happi-Time" Doll in playpen with layette

$9⁸⁸

Drinks, wets and cries tears. This 18-inch baby is a little dream with distinct fingers and toes. Long lashes frame her sleeping eyes. And when she cries, big tears roll down her cheeks. Soft vinyl body has jointed arms and legs, turning head. Comes to her playmate in diapers and quilted nylon tricot robe.

Accessories include: dress; hat; panties; diaper; 2-pc. knit suit; soap; sponge; bottle. 17x18-inch playpen has nylon net over metal frame.

79 N 3110C—Wt. 7 lbs........$9.88

FAMOUS TV DOLLS OF 1961

Hedda so sick

Hedda go sleep

Hedda is bedda

THUMBELINA cuddly and soft .. even wriggles like a new born baby $13.88

20-inch infant that's almost alive! Note her darling baby face. A precious armful of softness that's light as a feather to hold. Wind key in back .. and see how slowly and realistically her body moves just like a real baby's. She can hold her tiny toes in her hand .. her thumb to her mouth. Cloth body, vinyl head with rooted saran hair, vinyl limbs, wears knit baby outfit.
49 N 3288—Cuddly Thumbelina. Shipping weight 5 pounds..............$13.88

HEDDA GET BEDDA $6.88
This doll has three intriguing faces

21 inches tall. Hedda holds new excitement for your little girl. Imagine, she has three faces .. "poor sick Hedda," "sleepy Hedda" and "Happy, all Bedda Hedda." All you do is turn pompon on top of nightcap and presto—Hedda changes her expression. All vinyl and washable. Dressed in embossed cotton pajamas, vinyl nightcap .. even carries her own play thermometer.
49 N 3533—21-inch doll. Shipping weight 3 pounds 8 ounces............$6.88

CARTOON CHARACTERS

[1] **Dennis the Menace.** This lovable prankster is 14 inches tall .. molded in vinyl and has painted features. See how gay he looks in his striped cotton shirt and overalls (removable). Socks, molded vinyl shoes.
49 N 3847—Wt. 1 lb. 8 oz..$2.98

[2] **Little Lulu**—14½ inches tall, steps out of your favorite comic strip with big black eyes and black cotton yarn curls. Soft fabric doll, cotton stuffed. Painted face. Cotton dress, undergarment. Simulated shoes.
49 N 3843—Wt. 14 oz.....$4.19

[3] **Popeye the Sailor Man.** Jointed vinyl .. pose him many ways. Pinch his face and he whistles through pipe. Watch him flex his muscles. Authentically painted face and molded on sailor suit. 13 in. tall.
49 N 3503—Wt. 1 lb. 3 oz.$3.87

[4] **13-inch Kewpie** coos softly when you pinch her arm. Sits, tilts her head, moves arms and legs .. assumes many poses. Wears cotton playsuit, socks, shoes. Has jointed vinyl body, head; painted features.
49 N 3542—Wt. 1 lb. 6 oz.$2.87

322 SEARS PCB

FAMOUS SHIRLEY

Doll with wardrobe $7.99

[5] A 12-inch darling with dimpled cheeks, sleeping eyes and a shiny bow in rooted Saran hair. Unbreakable vinyl, jointed arms, legs and turning head. Wears outfit that goes nicely under dresses. Included are raincoat with knitted collar; hat; pocketbook; party dress and simulated pearl necklace; school dress and sunglasses; 2-pc. lounging outfit. Wt. 2 lbs. 12 oz.
49 N 3986—Costumes may vary slightly........$7.99

12-in. doll; outfits $3.47 doll only

[6] Doll dressed in pretty chemise, socks, shoes.
49 N 3938—Doll only. Shpg. wt. 1 lb.......$3.47
Separate Outfits. May vary slightly. Doll not incl.
[A] 49 N 3853—2-piece pedal pusher, print cotton shirt with pique trim and straw hat. Wt. 8 oz....$1.77
[B] 49 N 3854—Party dress of flocked nylon. Attached petticoat, panties and purse. Wt. 8 oz....$2.17
[C] 49 N 3851—2-piece outfit in cotton. Wt. 8 oz..89c
[D] 49 N 3856—3-piece cardigan suit. Pleated skirt. Panties, purse, hat, shoes and stockings. Wt. 8 oz.$2.97
[E] 49 N 3855—Cotton felt coat, matching beret with tassel, medallion and purse. Wt. 8 oz.........$2.17
[F] 49 N 3852—2-piece pajamas in cotton flannelette with perky night cap. Wt. 8 oz................$1.27

25-in. doll $17⁹⁹ **25-in. doll $16⁹⁹**

Play "beauty shop" ..
MISS IDEAL
has rooted nylon hair that's so
real you can shampoo it, set it,
in many different styles

Upswept hairdo

Popular pony tail

Beauty kit with comb, curlers, waving lotion

Fully jointed .. she can even balance on one foot

Doll of molded plastic and shaped like a grammar school girl. So delicately tinted and precisely defined, she almost comes alive. Her large, smiling eyes are twinkled with thick lashes, open and close. Jointed arms, hips, ankles. Has moving waist. Takes lots of lifelike poses. Carries beauty kit fitted with comb, curlers and waving lotion.

Miss Ideal in Town and Country Out-fit. Long, curly bob with French bangs for versatile styling. Yellow and white checked sleeveless cotton dress teamed with black velvet. Floaty skirt with tiny bows. Velvet and lace trim top, velvet belt. Rayon velvet jacket. "Straw" hat. Sewn in petticoat, has net ruffle. Lace trim panties. Vinyl shoes.
79 N 3669C–25-in. doll. Wt. 5 lbs. $17.99
79 N 3671C–30-in. doll. Wt. 7 lbs.   19.99

Miss Ideal in Campus Outfit. Long flowing hair easily pulled back into a long pony tail. Pink dress has puff sleeves. Red trim and bouquet set-off deep midriff. Top overlaid with sheer embroidery has squared neckline. Attached petticoat circles in gathers, net ruffle over hem. Lace-edged panties, vinyl slippers.
79 N 3667C–25-in. doll. Wt. 5 lbs. $16.99
79 N 3668C–30-in. doll. Wt. 7 lbs.   17.88

Miss Ideal in Capri-styled Outfit (at right). Wears hair braided in long pig-tails with wispy curls fringing her pretty face. Gold-colored cotton smock top is gathered in billowy folds from rounded neckline yoke, snaps in back for easy dressing. Capri pants have flirty slash at side of leg. Carries sun-glasses. Wears vinyl shoes.
79 N 3663C–25 in. doll. Wt. 5 lbs. $15.88
79 N 3666C–30 in. doll. Wt. 7 lbs.   16.99

25-in. doll in Capri Outfit
$15⁸⁸

TEMPLE DOLLS

15-in. dolls in beloved story book costumes

Dimple-cheeked Shirley is fashioned of unbreakable vinyl. Has jointed arms and legs. Curly, rooted Saran hair to wash, comb and brush. Closing eyes with long lashes.

1. **Pretty as a picture** in her red cotton party dress. Gaily strung in rows of ric-rac. Attached lacy petticoat. Lace-edged panties. Socks, vinyl shoes, hat.
49 N 3312—Doll and outfit. Shpg. wt. 2 lbs. $6.33

2. **Shirley in her Swiss Mountain Outfit** styled after her movie hit "Heidi." Colorful cotton dress trimmed in lace and embroidery. Lacy undies. Socks, vinyl slippers.
49 N 3628—15-in. doll, outfit. Wt. 2 lbs. *Was $6.77.* $5.97
49 N 3629—17-in. doll, outfit. Wt. 2 lbs. 8 oz. *Was $8.88.* 7.99

3. **Shirley plays Cinderella** in beautiful nylon dress. With shiny speckled top and has beaded tiara on her head. Attached rayon taffeta petticoat. Lacy panties. White socks, vinyl slippers.
49 N 3317—Doll and outfit. Shpg. wt. 2 lbs. $8.99

4. **Shirley in blue and white cotton Bo Peep costume.** Printed panniers at sides. Bright red apron. Attached slip has lace and net ruffle. Pantaloons ruffled at ankles. Red straw hat ties becomingly. White socks and shoes.
49 N 3314—Doll and outfit. Shpg. wt. 2 lbs. $7.99

1 $6³³   **2 $5⁹⁷** 15-in.   **3 $8⁹⁹**   **4 $7⁹⁹**

We've got loads of Clothes . .
and we're such fun to dress up

25-inch Stunning, slender model

$7⁸⁸ doll and accessories   **$1⁹⁷** Cotton dress   **$3⁹⁷** Velvet outfit

[1] She's gorgeous! She's new! She's shaped like a real-life teenager. Molded of vinyl plastic with jointed arms, legs. Sleeping eyes are glamorized with long lashes . . just like a movie star's. Rooted Saran hair in flattering page boy . . can be washed, curled and set to suit her separate outfits.

Wears knit cotton bathing suit, coolie-styled straw hat, sun glasses, high heel slippers. Accessories include plastic bag with stockings and panties. Also, necklace, earrings.

79 N 3691C—With accessories. Shpg. wt. 3 lbs. $7.88

(2)   49 N 3562—Cotton dress, smartly striped. Wt. 10 oz.. . 1.97

(3)   49 N 3563—Long sheath in shimmering black rayon velvet with luxurious make-believe fur stole. Shpg. wt. 1 lb. $3.97

FLUFFY 11-in. sweetie

$2⁵⁷

[4] Pretty vinyl doll has rooted Saran hair to comb and set. Jointed arms and legs, turning head, go-to-sleep eyes. Wears undies with lace, socks, vinyl shoes.
49 N 3565—Doll only. Wt. 12 oz.. . . . $2.57

Clothing for Fluffy. Shpg. wt. ea. 4 oz.
(5)   49 N 3383—Coat, hat and muff.. . . . $2.17
(6)   49 N 3410—Checked cotton dress and pants, felt hat with check trim.. .$1.79
(7)   49 N 3409—Cotton dress with Bermuda shorts attached, Babushka. 97c
(8)   49 N 3381—2-pc. cotton sleeper. . .78c

POLLYANNA of movie fame

$7⁹⁸ 10½-in. doll, wardrobe

[9] 10½-in. doll has cute pug nose. Vinyl with jointed arms, legs; turning head, sleeping eyes. Curly rooted acetate hair. Crisp checked gingham dress stands out over crinoline petticoat, pantaloons. Straw hat, vinyl shoes. Included: rayon taffeta and velvet gown, velvet bolero; cotton dress with organdy pinafore; cotton camisole; cotton skirt, white middy blouse; hangers, nylon snood. Fiberboard trunk. Wt. 2 lbs.
49 N 3450—10½-in. doll, wardrobe and trunk. . . . $7.98

[10]   **Larger size Pollyanna**—Doll only.
79 N 3391C—32-in. doll. Shpg. wt. 6 lbs.. . . . . . $14.88
49 N 3601—17-in. doll. Shpg. wt. 2 lbs. 7.88

16-in. Drink-wet Baby $3⁸⁸

Cuddly, baby-faced doll. Vinyl with jointed arms and legs; sleeping eyes; sprayed hair. Wears cotton fleece robe with hood, diaper, knit bootees. Comes with lace-prettied dress of printed cotton, diaper to match for dress-up time. Layette includes: cotton flannel blanket with ribbon, terry towel, sponge, soap, 3 powder puffs, plastic nursing bottle.

49 N 3146—Colored doll and layette. Wt. 2 lbs.. . $3.88
49 N 3145—White doll and layette. Wt. 2 lbs. 3.88

She coos $1⁸³

10-inch baby drinks and wets. All vinyl with jointed arms, legs and turning head. Lashed go-to-sleep eyes. Wears diaper and carries her own nursing bottle.

49 N 3161—White doll Shpg. wt. 12 oz.. . . . $1.83
49 N 3173—Colored doll Shpg. wt. 12 oz. $1.83

Mickey $2⁶⁶ each

11-inch vinyl All-American boy is tubbable. Jointed arms, legs and turning head. Painted features. Removable cotton uniforms, molded hats.

(11)   49 N 3344—Sailor
(12)   49 N 3343—Football player
(13)   49 N 3345—Baseball player
49 N 3318—Boxer. With robe and gloves. (Not shown.)
Shpg. wt. ea. 1 lb.. . Each $2.66

Saran Wigs give dolly a "new" look

Low as **$1¹³**

You'll be amazed at how a new wig dresses up a favorite doll. Can be dampened, combed and set again. Glue, instructions included. *State color* blonde or brunette. Wt. each 8 oz.

How to order: Wig size is number of inches around doll's head. For fractional inch measurement, order next size larger.

Cat. No.	Size	Price	Cat. No.	Size	Price
49 N 3520	8	$1.13	49 N 3523	12	$1.77
49 N 3519	9	1.29	49 N 3525	13	2.07
49 N 3521	10	1.37	49 N 3526	14	2.17
49 N 3522	11	1.59	49 N 3529	15	2.57
			49 N 3539	16	2.87

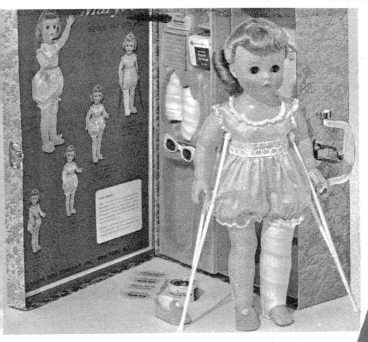

Do you like me?
Let's go to the park
May I wear my new dress?

CHATTERBOX . .

24-inch toddler
that loves to talk

$17 88

Her voice is natural, she speaks distinctly. Push button and she talks—lay her down, she stops. Here are some of the play plans she discusses with mommy. "Who is coming to our tea party?," "I hope we have cookies," and many more. Voice box is electronically operated on 2 "C" batteries, included.

Silky lashes sweep her closing eyes. Bows glisten in her rooted Saran hair. She's beautifully detailed of hard plastic, has soft vinyl head. Her pique dress has front pleats, lacy-edged collar, puff sleeves. She wears white socks and baby shoes. Instructions included.

Shipping weight 5 pounds.
79 N 3696C $17.88

MARYBEL the get-well doll $11 48

16-inch doll in search of a little nurse. She has a cast to heal make-believe broken arms or legs; crutches just her size; black glasses to wear when she's dotted with red measles; yellow spots for chicken pox. Bandaids and bandages for minor scratches. When little nurse removes her pretend diseases and bandages Marybel gets well right away.

She's exquisitely fashioned with rigid plastic body and is realistically tinted. Has jointed arms, legs. Turning waist and vinyl head. Her long-lashed eyes go to sleep and her glorious rooted Saran hair is distinctively styled. Note her pretty shortie pajamas and slippers. Marybel has the fine workmanship so characteristic of all Madame Alexander dolls.
49 N 3670—Doll, accessories packed in trunk. Shpg. wt. 3 lbs. 8 oz..$11.48

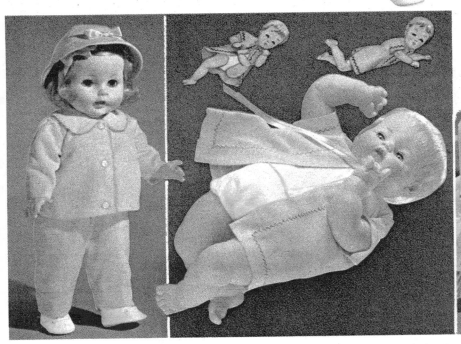

CAROLINE $8 98

14-inch doll with the cutest expression you've ever seen. Molded of hard plastic with jointed arms, legs. Note her chubby, dimpled hands. Soft vinyl head turns. Rooted Saran hair is curled and bow-tied. Lashed eyes close at nap time. She's ready for play in corded cotton jacket, slacks and brimmed hat. Underneath is a cotton romper. White socks, oxfords complete her outfit.
49 N 3676—Shpg. wt. 2 lbs. $8.98

CUDDLY INFANT $11 98

Lovable 23-inch baby. We call her "kitten" because she's so soft, chubby, dimpled and huggable. Her precious face will steal any little girl's longing heart. Beautiful closing eyes have thick, sweeping lashes. Rooted Saran hair is fine . . daintily frames her face in wispy baby style.

Made of soft vinyl filled with Kapok. Featherlight to hold. So limp she flops into many poses . . can even put her finger in her mouth. Comes to her mommy's arms in shirt and diaper . . and an adorable nylon tricot wrapper with stitched trim and streaming bow. Exquisitely made and detailed like all Madame Alexander dolls.
49 N 3276—Shipping weight 4 lbs. 8 oz $11.98

LITTLE WOMEN $8 98 each

Louisa May Alcott's storybook heroines come to life 12 inches high. Your little girl has read about them, loved them and admired them. See what beautiful faces they have. Lashed eyes go to sleep. Saran hair is set in styles of the period.

Plastic bodies have jointed arms, legs . . . turning heads. Each doll wears wide-sweeping dress, pantalets, underskirt, nylon socks, "suede" slippers. Clothes are well made of fine fabrics.
(1) 49 N 3649—Pretty Amy, cotton dress, lace edged pinafore.
(2) 49 N 3653—Sensible Meg wears white organdy pinafore.
(3) 49 N 3658—Tomboy Jo, pin-dot dress, red pinafore.
49 N 3651—Angelic Beth (not shown) dressed in solid polished cotton dress, contrasting trim; (no pinafore).
Shipping weight 1 pound 8 ounces . . . . Each $8.98

"Charge It" if you wish . . see pages 218A, 218B for information

Best-dressed Dolls in town .. and their latest

HAPPI-TIME Doll

10½-in. . . looks like teen $7⁵⁷

A delight to dress, to pose . . she stands alone! Big glassene eyes are fringed in long, thick lashes. Beautifully molded head and arms of vinyl plastic. Turning waist. Jointed vinyl legs. She's glamorous right down to her painted fingernails and toenails. Rooted Saran hair to wash and set. Wears bra, girdle, high heel shoes and earrings. Her wardrobe is a little mother's joy. Includes rain outfit, afternoon dress, evening gown, crinoline, nylon stockings, high heel shoes, pocket book, sun glasses, imitation pearl necklace, 3 hangers. (Outfits may vary slightly.)

49 N 3817—Doll and wardrobe. Wt. 1 lb. 4 oz..$7.57

BETSY McCALL

8-in. . . walks, sits, kneels $1⁷²

[1] *See her on TV!* Hard plastic, creamy bisque finish. Jointed body, moving eyes. Chemise, socks, shoes.
49 N 3002—Betsy McCall doll. Saran hair. Wt. 8 oz..$1.72

Outfits. May vary slightly from illust. Wt. each 6 oz.

[A] 49 N 3849—Checked gingham dress. Matching coat lined in red. Black beret. Shoes, socks...............$1.79

[B] 49 N 3824—White rayon satin wedding dress. Veil, bouquet, panties, half-slip under dress, slippers.....$1.97

[C] 49 N 3828—Strapless evening gown in sheer nylon. Matching slip, panties. "Straw" hat. Shoes.......$1.97

[D] 49 N 3857—Cotton jumper over striped romper. Shiny brass button. Shoes and socks...............$1.29

[E] 49 N 3858—Cotton velvet skirt. Taffeta blouse and panties combination. Shoes, socks.................$1.14

[F] 49 N 3844—White quilted robe with sash over two-piece cotton pajamas. Slippers........................89c

TODDLER with layette and trunk
$7⁷⁹

Charming, wide-eyed and 13 inches tall. Rooted plastic hair . . Dutch-style hair-do. Vinyl plastic body. Turning head, moving arms, legs . . and eyes. Dressed in print cotton, sewed on organdy apron, knit stretch leotard, white shoes. Wardrobe; flocked nylon dress etched in lace, attached rayon taffeta slip. "Straw" hat, taffeta robe, 2 plastic hangers. Blue linen-effect fiber trunk (14x8½x7½-in.). White binding has gold-color spreckling. Plastic handle, brass color metal hardware.
49 N 3032—Doll, wardrobe; trunk. Wt. 4 lbs.....$7.79
49 N 3039—Doll and wardrobe. Shpg. wt. 1 lb.....4.79

8-in. drink-wet baby is fully jointed too .. has layette $3⁹⁹

Lovable infant is everything a little mother dreams of in baby dolls. She drinks, wets . . loves to be bathed and dressed . . closes her pretty eyes at nap time. All-vinyl body is completely jointed, nicely detailed. Layette includes one cotton, one rayon dress; matching bonnets; cotton dress and bib; cotton sleeper; sun-suit; diaper; clothespins; 3 sponges; bottle; washcloth; shoes. Outfits may vary slightly.
49 N 3531—Shipping weight 1 lb. 8 oz........$3.99

Tiny Baby Dolls love to be posed $2³⁷ 3 dolls

Soft 8-inch dolls. So lightweight a baby can hug them. Just a flip of the hand and presto you have a new pose. Gay trimmings for mantle, tree, little girl's room. Surprise stocking stuffers. Vinyl face, painted features, has blond bangs. Vinyl hands. Cuddled in cotton flannel bunting with hood. Assorted pastel baby colors. Shpg. wt. 7 oz.
49 N 3202—3 dolls.................$2.37

Look, I have six cut-out costumes $2⁹⁷

Glamorous Collette is copied from a French idea. She's plastic, 9½ inches tall, has a beautiful painted face and looks like a model. Comes to your little girl with an exciting wardrobe. It's fun to cut costumes from a master piece of crease-resistant cloth and easily fitted to doll. No sewing, just cut at neck and arms and slip over doll's head. From Hong Kong. Shpg. wt. 12 oz.
49 N 3834—Doll with costumes.......$2.97

"Charge it" . . see page 218A

high-fashion wardrobes

A B C D E F

BARBIE, teen-age model and her fabulous wardrobe $1.97 Doll only

☐1☐ She's beautiful! So lifelike she almost breathes. Flesh-toned vinyl plastic body is full jointed. Poses on removable wire frame stand. Rooted acetate hair. Wears striped jersey swimsuit, sun glasses, earrings, shoes.
49 N 3701—Doll 11½-in. tall. From Japan. Wt. 10 oz...$1.97

☐A☐ Wardrobe for Barbie doll. From Japan. Shpg. wt. each 6 oz.
49 N 3702—Sailcloth sundress, white wedge sandals.....76c

☐B☐ 49 N 3706—Dressy gold color brocade outfit. Imitation pearl jewelry, tricot gloves, velvet purse, shoes.....$1.66

☐C☐ 49 N 3704—Party dress. Velvet top, white satin skirt, gold color belt. Gold color bag. Black shoes...........$1.32

☐D☐ 49 N 3734—Terry robe and slippers. Bath towel, washcloth, shower cap, bath brush, bath soap, powder puff...$1.66

☐E☐ 49 N 3735—Complete ballet set. Black cotton practice leotard and tights. Sparkling performance Tutu and tiara, ballet shoes and shoe bag. Ballet program...........$2.37

☐F☐ 49 N 3737—Rayon satin gown. Necklace and drop earrings, high-heel shoes, long gloves, simulated fur stole.....$2.66

20-IN. BRIDE
Comes with all-occasion trousseau and trunk
$10.77

Here comes the bride—out of your little girl's dreams into her loving heart. Radiant in heavy rayon satin gown drifted with net and lace. Finger-tip veil frames rooted Saran hair. Moving eyes have long lashes. She's made of sturdy vinyl plastic with jointed arms, legs, turning head. Wears rayon panties, high heel shoes—all ready to be dressed for the wedding.

Trousseau: rayon taffeta formal with matching stole; print cotton afternoon dress, 2-piece slack outfit, simulated pearl necklace, crinoline; dress coat trimmed in leopard cloth print, matching hat; nylon hose; high heel shoes and pocketbook .. all packed in lightweight fiberboard trunk.
79 N 3686C—20-inch doll, 20½-inch trunk, clothing. Wt. 6 lbs..........$10.77
49 N 3607—15-inch doll, 15½-inch trunk, clothing. Wt. 4 lbs............ 7.95

16-inch Doll .. trunk full of clothes $6.99

A lovable bundle of charm with a bright baby face. Rooted acetate hair with bow. Her lashed eyes close in sleep. Jointed plastic body, soft vinyl head. Wears flowering polished cotton with organdy apron. Knit panties, rayon socks, vinyl shoes.

Wardrobe includes striped polished cotton housecoat; nylon nightgown; 2-piece flowered cotton flannel pajamas; striped cotton dress with trim; cotton coat; straw hat. Accessories: 3-piece vinyl luggage set, Kleenex, comb, brush, mirror, 3 curlers .. all packed in 16¾-inch fiberboard trunk with metal hinges, plastic handle.
49 N 3144—Doll, trunk, clothes. Shpg. wt. 4 lbs. 9 oz...............$6.99

BALLERINA
Walks too .. has wardrobe $9.77 Doll and Wardrobe

20-inch star of the ballet! New feather hair style gives her a French appearance. Jointed with movable head, waist, arms, hips, knees, ankles. Dances on toes, can be posed in most ballerina positions. Walks when play mother guides her. Vinyl with plastic legs. Wears Tutu over knit stretch tights, ballerina slippers.

Fashions include flower-strewn cotton sundress; long formal sheath in rayon taffeta with lame evening jacket; 3-piece assorted design cotton play suit; crinoline; sheer nightgown; panties; plastic handbag; high heel shoes; nylon hose; molded plastic hat; flats and socks; 4 plastic hangers.
49 N 3685—Doll, wardrobe. Wt. 3 lbs.....$9.77
49 N 3608—Doll only. Wt. 1 lb. 10 oz.....5.97

"i want a pal

[1] **Jumbo Bear** is 28 inches tall, yet lightweight and easy to carry. He has shaped arms and feet—sits naturally. Cocoa and honey-colored rayon plush. Cotton filled.
79 N 4139L—Wt. 5 lbs........$5.94

[2] **Bugs Bunny** hops right out of the comics to play with you. Gray and white rayon plush body. Cotton filled. Long floppy legs, molded vinyl face. You can shape his wired ears. Colorful bow tie. Cotton filled.
49 N 4097—29 in. tall over-all.
Shpg. wt. 1 lb. 12 oz........$3.44

[3] **Corky** . . the friendly pup with droopy, yarn lashes and red plastic tongue. Brown rayon plush; white chest, paw pads. Cotton filled.
79 N 4004C—20 inches tall.
Shpg. wt. 4 lbs.............$6.44

[4] **Cry-Baby Bear.** Please choose him for a friend—he's so sad and lonely. Cocoa and gold color rayon plush, cotton stuffed. Vinyl face.
49 N 4114—16 inches tall.
Shpg. wt. 3 lbs. 3 oz........$3.69

[5] **Begging Bear.** Has real cotton felt paw-pads with make-believe claws. This huggable cub is cocoa brown rayon plush with white snout and chest, stubby tail. Cotton stuffed.
49N4103—14½ in. tall (seated).
Shpg. wt. 2 lbs. 6 oz........$4.33

[6] **Smokey Bear** . . famous forest ranger with plastic badge, hat and shovel. Clad in blue cotton denim, he's made of tan rayon plush. Dryex® foam plastic and cotton filled.
49 N 4346—14 inches tall.
Shpg. wt. 1 lb. 3 oz........$2.87

[7] **Washable Panda** dries quickly after you scrub him. Rayon plush; Dryex® foam plastic and cotton filled.
49 N 4126—13½ inches tall.
Shpg. wt. 1 lb. 3 oz........$1.99

[8] **Cuddle Bear** is tan rayon plush stuffed with Dryex® foam plastic and cotton. Shaped arms and feet.
49 N 4079—18 inches tall.
Shpg. wt. 1 lb. 8 oz........$2.99

[9] **Washable Teddy.** Just scrub with soap and water. Rayon plush; Dryex® foam plastic and cotton filled. Tan and brown.
49 N 4102—13½ inches tall.
Shipping weight 1 lb. 3 oz....$1.88

Your T. V. Favorites

(10)-(11) Rayon plush filled with Featherfoam®, foam plastic, cotton. Vinyl faces Cotton felt accessories.

[10] **Ba-Ba-Looey** sports a south-of-the-border sombrero, kerchief.
49 N 4352—15 inches tall.
Shpg. wt. 1 lb. 8 oz.........$2.66
79 N 4353C—21 inches tall.
Shpg. wt. 3 lbs.............. 4.49

[11] **Quick Draw McGraw** in western style cotton kerchief and cowboy hat. Has plastic gun and holster.
49 N 4350—19 inches tall.
Shpg. wt. ea. 1 lb. 14 oz.....$3.33

[12] **Hush Puppy** is soft, gray rayon plush. Vest of red cotton felt. Shaped arms, legs. Cotton stuffed.
49 N 4093—About 10 in. tall.
Shpg. wt. 1 lb.............$2.69

[13] **Lamb Chop** has white rayon plush and cotton corduroy body; vinyl head . . painted-on eyelashes. Cotton felt hands. Cotton stuffed.
49 N 4090—10 inches tall.
Shpg. wt. 1 lb..............$2.69

[14] **Charlie Horse** is all dressed up in straw-type hat, denim kerchief. His suspenders, horse shoes and hoofs are cotton felt. Cotton stuffed.
49 N 4096—12 inches tall.
Shpg. wt. 1 lb..............$2.69

Chatty Cathy and Chatty Baby ("We talk, we laugh, we cry") debuted in the 1962 Wishbook. These dolls were extremely popular, in large part because of the heavy television advertising which accompanied them. When you pulled her Magic Ring, Chatty Cathy said 11 different phrases including, "I'm hungry" and "Will you play with me?" When found today, the voice mechanisms in these dolls are almost always broken but they can be repaired.

Barbie was still a year away from making her big splash in the Sears Christmas Wishbook. Her ad space in 1962 was basically the same as the previous year.

The Effanbee Doll Company was highlighted with several dolls including the 15-inch Girl Scout and Brownie dolls priced at $5.98. These are extremely collectible dolls today.

Other dolls of note in 1962 include the Angela Cartwright Doll, based on the young actress who was then starring as "Linda" on the popular Danny Thomas Show. Dressed in a checked cotton pinafore dress and 15-inches in height, the doll was originally priced at $3.98.

On the teddy bear pages, "Jumbo Bear" at 28-inches wore a rayon ribbon bow and sold for $5.99. Two different panda bear styles were offered as well as a 14-inch Smokey Bear.

Sears Christmas

Wishbook

1962

Girls of all ages love the enchantment this BOUDOIR DOLL lends their room

26-inch glamorous doll is dressed in a full-length rayon satin gown with tulle overskirt that sweeps way out when she's seated on your bed or dresser. Wears high heels. Arrange her rooted acetate hair. Cotton fabric body stuffed with cotton. Plastic head, arms, legs sewn to body. Painted features.
79 N 3043C—Shipping weight 3 pounds.........$5.98

$5.98

She sits, tilts her head; moves her arms and legs

20-in. Kewpie Doll. Pinch her soft vinyl arm, hear her coo. Her jointed body poses 101 different ways. Vinyl head has painted features; molded plastic body, legs allow her to stand alone. Cotton dress, panties, patent leather shoes, rayon socks.
49 N 3538—Shpg. wt. 2 lbs. 4 oz. $5.98

13-in. Doll (small views). Wears cotton sunsuit, socks and shoes.
49 N 3542—Shpg. wt. 1 lb. 2 oz..$2.77

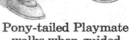
Lullabye Baby

$4.79

[2]

$5.98

3 Tiny Babies on Pillows are great stocking stuffers

Set of 3 soft, 8-inch dolls love to show off their many poses .. they change positions with just a flip of the hand. So lightweight a baby can hug them. Their cute vinyl faces have painted features. Their hands are also made of vinyl. Cuddled in cotton flannel bunting in assorted pastel colors. Imported from Japan.
Shipping weight 7 ounces.
49 N 3262...............Set $2.49

Doll wriggles like a new born baby while Swiss music box plays

12-inch infant almost seems alive! Wind the key in back .. imported music box inside her body plays Brahms' Lullaby. See how realistically her body moves—just like a real baby's. She can hold her tiny toes in her hand, her thumb in her mouth. Her clenched fists and toes are beautifully detailed. Made from vinyl plastic, her arms and legs are jointed, her head turns and has "go-to-sleep" eyes. You can comb her rooted Saran pixie style hairdo. She wears an adorable cotton sleeper.
49 N 3268—Shipping weight 1 pound.........$4.79

Pony-tailed Playmate walks when guided

[2] 19-inch vinyl doll has go-to-sleep eyes and a cute, turned-up nose. Arrange her pretty plastic hair in all the latest styles. Her arms, legs and head jointed to move easily. She walks when you guide her with your hand. Green cotton blouse and print slacks; shoes and socks. Her extra party outfit is an embroidered cotton pique dress, rayon panties.
49 N 3688—Shpg. wt. 2 lbs. $5.98

Angela Cartwright .. TV and Movie Star

[3] 15-inch Angela's sure to please. Her look-alike plays "Linda" on the Danny Thomas show. Plastic doll is jointed, her eyes go to sleep. Has rooted acetate hair in long pony tail. White nylon pinafore tops checked cotton dress. Panties, shoes, socks.
49 N 3362—Wt. 1 lb. 8 oz..$3.98

[3]

$3.98

Slender Doll .. Outfits for 14 to 21-in. dolls

[1] Vinyl Doll. Saran hair, sleepy eyes, undies, shoes. Fun to sew for or dress with gowns shown.
49 N 3660—15-in. Wt. 1 lb.. $3.98
49 N 3661—18-in. Wt. 2 lbs. 4.98
49 N 3662-20-in. Wt. 2 lbs. 8 oz. 5.98
Extra clothes. Wt. each 14 oz.

[A] Ballerina. Nylon tutu, panties, nylon hose, slippers.
49 N 3464—14 to 15 in.....$1.79
49 N 3465—18 to 19 in..... 2.39
49 N 3466—20 to 21 in..... 2.69

[B] Nylon Bridal Dress. Sash, veil, panties, nylon hose, slippers and shoes.
49 N 3481—14 to 15 in.....$2.98
49 N 3482—18 to 19 in..... 3.59
49 N 3483—20 to 21 in..... 3.89

[C] Accessories: girdle, garters, bra, hose, shoes, plastic case.
49 N 3449—14 to 15 in.....$1.59
49 N 3451—18 to 19 in..... 1.79
49 N 3452—20 to 21 in..... 1.98

[D] Negligee and Gown in sheer pink nylon; lace trim. Shoes.
49 N 3495—14 to 15 in.....$1.98
49 N 3496—18 to 19 in..... 2.59
49 N 3497—20 to 21 in..... 2.89

404 SEARS 2 PCB

Belle Telle
whiles away happy hours chatting on her talking telephone

I LOVE YOU VERY MUCH
DO YOU LOVE ME TOO?
MAY WE HAVE A PARTY?
HOW OLD ARE YOU?

$12.98

Belle Telle's hand is sculptured to hold receiver, other objects. She loves to talk on her plastic phone with realistic dial. Mommy removes receiver, pushes magic button. Hear her say: "My name is Belle Telle," "Please play with me," "Please tell me a story." She uses 11 sentences, repeats herself too! Phone has concealed record player with record. Operates on one flashlight battery (order below). 18-in. plastic toddler is jointed. Her vinyl head has go-to-sleep eyes, rooted acetate hair. Wears cotton dress, panties. Socks, shoes.
49 N 3640—Wt. 3 lbs. 8 oz.... $12.98

"D" Batteries. Shpg. wt. each 4 oz.
49 N 4660......Each 16c; 4 for 60c

Swinging Basket; Sister Dolls

Imagine, a basket that swings, a cuddly infant and darling toddler to thrill your little girl. 14-inch infant has painted features, rooted plastic hair. Printed cotton pajamas. Muslin body, stuffed with kapok, is light weight to hold. Her 18-inch toddler sister has big, bright eyes that close to sleep.

Vinyl and rigid plastic with moving arms, legs and head. Rooted plastic hair is accented with a bow. Her lace-trimmed pajamas match baby sister's. She wears sandals. Her splint basket swings on a wood frame and is lined with dotted cotton batiste with nylon lace. Size overall 17x15x11 inches. Shpg. wt. 7 lbs.
79 N 3248L......................... $17.98

FAMOUS EFFANBEE DOLLS

Girls love Dolls in Sailor Costumes
$9.79

Stands 18 inches high. A beauty that delights in showing off her fashionable costume. Cotton dress is spruced-up in nautical print. Solid color coat has dashing sailor collar and bow tie. She wears a winsome "sailor hat," panties, socks, shoes. Her moving eyes are long-lashed, like a movie star's. Rooted Saran hair to shampoo, comb, set. Vinyl and rigid plastic fully jointed. Shipping wt. 2 lbs. 6 oz.
49 N 3361.......... $9.79

15-inch Scout Dolls

They all have adorable faces with a cute turned up nose and rosy cheeks. Go-to-sleep eyes and richly curled, rooted Saran hair to comb, brush and set. Their bodies are rigid plastic with vinyl plastic moving arms, legs and turning head. They wear official cotton uniforms, panties, socks and shoes.

[1] With Blue Bird Uniform. White blouse, blue skirt and beanie. Red vest.
49 N 3770—Shipping weight 1 lb. 6 oz.... $5.98
With Campfire Girl Uniform. (Not shown). White blouse, blue skirt, beanie, red tie.
49 N 3771—Shipping weight 1 lb. 6 oz.... $5.98
[2] With Girl Scout Uniform. Green dress and beret, belt, yellow tie.
49 N 3648—Shipping weight 1 lb. 6 oz.... $5.98
With Brownie Scout Uniform. (Not shown). Brown color, belt, beanie, orange tie.
49 N 3645—Shipping weight 1 lb. 6 oz.... $5.98

$5.98 each

Fluffy, 11-inch sweetie $2.67

[3] Fluffy is a cute little charmer to dress. All vinyl plastic . . jointed arms, legs; head turns. Has go-to-sleep eyes, rooted Saran hair, rayon panties, socks and shoes.
49 N 3565—Doll only. Shpg. wt. 11 oz.....$2.67
Clothing for Fluffy. Shpg. wt. each, 4 oz.
(A) 49 N 3383—Coat, muff and hat of cotton-backed rayon plush that looks like fur. Each has smooth, red rayon lining............$1.99
(B) 49 N 3360—Cotton dress, panties, hat.. 1.79
(C) 49 N 3359—Cotton apron-dress, panties 1.37
(D) 49 N 3381—2-piece knit cotton sleeper....82c

Precious Drink and Wet Babies

10-inch cuties with sweet baby faces to win your little girl's heart. Adorable lashed eyes close to sleep. Rooted plastic hair to wash, brush and set. Each carries its own bottle. All vinyl and fully jointed.
[4] Baby wears cotton dress, ribbon trim. Bloomers, shoes and socks.
49 N 3265—Shipping weight 14 ounces.....$3.39
[5] Baby wears print and solid color cotton dress, panties, socks and shoes.
49 N 3266—Shipping weight 14 ounces.....$3.39

$3.39 each

11-inch Mickey $2.79 each

The All-American boy. His painted features give him a saucy look little folks adore. All vinyl with jointed arms, legs; turning head. Removable cotton uniforms. Molded hats.
(6) 49 N 3344—Sailor
(7) 49 N 3343—Football player
(8) 49 N 3345—Baseball player
Shipping wt. each 11 oz.....Each $2.79

Musical Cradle Doll ✓

**Wind the Swiss music box ..
Cradle swings to lullaby music** **$15⁹⁸**

19-inch vinyl doll lulled to sleep in her musical cradle, shuts
her thickly-lashed eyes just like a real baby. She looks appeal-
ingly pretty .. her rooted plastic hair is done in a wispy baby
style, adorned with a big rayon satin bow. Her chubby arms and
legs are jointed.

Doll comes dressed for naptime in a braid-trimmed nightie
of cotton broadcloth. Keeping her warm is a lace-trimmed
quilted rayon satin coverlet and pillow. Her plastic nursing
bottle is tied to her hand. She drinks and wets. Cradle of woven
fibers has vinyl liner, swings on decal-trimmed wooden frame.
25x14x18 in. high over-all. Swiss music box plays rock-a-bye-
tune. Basket has movable hood and plastic beads.
79 N 3250L—Shipping weight 9 pounds...................$15.98

**Cuddly Baby has her own basket ..
Drinks from self-refilling bottle** **$9⁹⁸**

22-inch infant is all bundled up in her blanket of rayon and cotton
fleece and snug baby clothes. She wears cotton diapers and rayon
sacque. Her woven splint basket has smooth vinyl liner, trimmed
with rayon taffeta and net. It's fun to "feed" her, too. Raise the
pretend, Carnation nursing bottle to her mouth .. see the milk
"disappear" (no liquid escapes). Turn it upright—bottle refills like
magic.

Doll's soft cotton body is Kapok and foam filled. She has
clenched fists, true-to-life toes and rooted, pixie-styled plastic hair.
She even shuts her eyes when she's sleepy. Arms and legs are sewed
on, giving her greater flexibility. Arms, legs and head are skin-
toned vinyl.
79 N 3251C—Shipping weight 6 pounds.......................$9.98

[1] **$2⁹⁵**　　[3] **$4⁹⁷**

[2] **$3⁸⁹**　　[4] **$4⁹⁷**

Even at these low prices, Sears has fully jointed dolls .. each with thickly lashed, go-
to-sleep eyes, and a plastic rooted, "poodle" hairdo that's so much fun to wash and
set. All these dolls come dressed in lovely infants' wear designed for easy dressing

[1] **15-inch Toddler** has a
lightweight, plastic body
that wipes clean easily. She
drinks and wets, carries her
own plastic bottle. Lace-
trimmed dress is colorful
cotton. Knit panties, rayon
socks, slip-on vinyl shoes.
49 N 3014—Wt. 1 lb. $2.95

[2] **18-inch drink-and-
wet baby** has a light-
weight, wipe-clean body
of molded plastic. She
brings her own bottle and
hopes you will feed her.
Cotton print dress with
lace, sewed in rayon slip.
Wears knit panties, rayon
socks and vinyl shoes.
49 N 3036—Wt. 2 lbs. $3.89

[3] **19-inch drink-and-
wet baby** is made
of easy-to-clean sturdy
plastic. Bottle included.
Cotton pique dress,
lace-trimmed rayon
coat and bonnet. Knit
panties, socks, vinyl
shoes. All dressed for
travel. Shpg. wt. 2 lbs.
49 N 3261.......$4.97

[4] **20-inch, drink-and-
wet baby** of bath-
able, life-like plastic
brings her own bottle.
Embroidery and lace
trims her nylon dress
with attached petti-
coat, bonnet. Cotton
panties, socks and
shoes. Wt. 2 lbs. 8 oz.
49 N 3052.......$4.97

**Soft-cuddly Baby Doll with
her own car bed and layette
to go traveling with you**

$5⁹⁷

14-inch baby has a huggable, cotton-stuffed
cloth body with vinyl arms and legs, sewn-on
to move many ways. Comb the rooted plastic
hair fringing her life-like face. She comes in
a print cotton romper, but you can show her
off in the pretty cotton print dress with matching bonnet or dress her for bed in her cotton
flannel diaper and kimono. To keep her warm
.. knit booties and a cotton flannel receiving
blanket. Her portable car bed makes it easy
to take her visiting. It is plastic on a sturdy
metal frame. About 15x7x4 inches.
49 N 3258—Shipping weight 3 lbs......$5.97

WE TALK
WE CRY
WE LAUGH

Now a Doll that actually cries .. just like a real baby $15⁸⁹ *without battery*

21-inch baby cries long and hard when you press the magic button. Feed her .. she gurgles, stops crying and milk mysteriously 'disappears' from her Carnation milk "bottle." No liquid escapes bottle. It refills like magic for next feeding. Her vinyl body has jointed chubby arms and legs—with dimpled hands and toes. She has wispy, rooted plastic hair and thickly lashed, go-to-sleep eyes. Dressed in white cotton shirt and diaper with an elegant nylon tricot sacque. Cry voice operates on one "D" battery (not included, order below).

49 N 3253—Shipping weight 5 pounds....................$15.89

"D" Batteries.
49 N 4660—Shipping weight each 4 ounces....Each 16c; 4 for 60c

Chatty Cathy® $11⁷⁷   Chatty Baby® $8⁶⁶

Doll playmates that really talk! Just pull the magic ring .. they say 11 different phrases at random. Real personalities. Each has movable vinyl head, arms and legs .. sturdy plastic body. Go-to-sleep eyes. Rooted plastic hair. Sorry, no choice of hair color.

20 inches tall .. this doll says "I'm hungry," asks "Will you play with me?" 9 more things. Wears cotton dress with tie-on-apron (assorted styles). Undies, socks and shoes.
49 N 3303—Wt. 3 lbs.........$11.77

18 inches tall .. gives lovable baby-talk. Makes you want to hug her. Dressed in removable pinafore over one-piece dress with panties, red-and-white slipper-socks. Shpg. wt. 3 lbs.
49 N 3330—White Chatty Baby.............$8.66
49 N 3358—Colored Chatty Baby............ ·8.66

$4⁹⁹

Cuddly Baby with rooted hair

20-inch baby cries for her mommy. She's soft to hug since her cotton body is also stuffed with cotton. Vinyl arms and legs are sewn on, letting her pose in a life-like baby way. You can comb her rooted Saran hair and she closes her eyes to sleep. Doll wears cotton shirt, diaper, printed cotton kimono, knit booties.

Cuddly White Doll. Shpg. wt. 2 lbs. 8 oz.
49 N 3254.................................$4.99
Cuddly Colored Doll. Shpg. wt. 2 lbs. 8 oz.
49 N 3257.................................$4.99

She drinks and wets; coos when squeezed
$1⁸⁷

10-inch baby of vinyl has movable arms, legs, and head. Go-to-sleep eyes. She wears a diaper and carries her own nursing bottle.
49 N 3173—Colored doll. Shpg. wt. 12 oz...$1.87

49 N 3161—White doll. Shpg. wt. 12 oz...$1.87

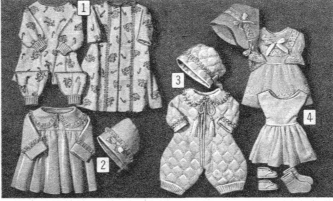

Clothing for Baby Dolls .. Sizes 12 to 25 inches

Keep 'em prettily dressed all year 'round. Smartly styled, nicely detailed. Well made of fine fabrics. Shipping weight each 10 ounces.

[1] **Baby Sleeper, Robe Set.** Cotton sleeper, cotton flannelette robe.
49 N 3403—Sizes 12 to 13 in...$1.19
49 N 3405—Sizes 16 to 17 in... 1.39
49 N 3406—Sizes 18 to 19 in... 1.59
49 N 3407—Sizes 20 to 21 in... 1.79
49 N 3423—Sizes 24 to 25 in... 2.39

[2] **Coat, bonnet** .. cotton cordana or rayon with contrasting collar (assorted styles). Pretty trim.
49 N 3490—Sizes 12 to 13 in...$1.49
49 N 3491—Sizes 16 to 17 in... 1.59
49 N 3492—Sizes 18 to 19 in... 1.69
49 N 3493—Sizes 20 to 21 in... 1.92
49 N 3494—Sizes 24 to 25 in... 2.47

[3] **Snowsuit, bonnet** of rayon quilting. Trimmed collar, sleeves, bonnet. Zipper closure. Tassel tie.
49 N 3461—Sizes 12 to 13 in...$1.79
49 N 3462—Sizes 16 to 17 in... 1.89
49 N 3463—Sizes 18 to 19 in... 1.98
49 N 3471—Sizes 20 to 21 in... 2.19
49 N 3472—Sizes 24 to 25 in... 2.59

[4] **Doll Layette.** Nylon dress, bonnet with pretty, ruffled trim. Cotton slip, socks and shoes.
49 N 3418—Sizes 12 to 13 in...$2.19
49 N 3425—Sizes 14 to 15 in... 2.29
49 N 3426—Sizes 16 to 17 in... 2.39
49 N 3427—Sizes 18 to 19 in... 2.49
49 N 3428—Sizes 20 to 21 in... 2.59
49 N 3429—Sizes 22 to 23 in... 2.98

"New-born" Layette

All the things a little mother needs! Hooded, quilted, rayon and cotton bunting. Two-piece, cable-stitch, cotton-knit sweater set. There's also a belted romper of polished cotton. Diaper, shoes and socks. With nursing bottle, pacifier and rattle. Will keep her busy for hours.

49 N 3566—Size 17 to 19 in. Shpg. wt. 1 lb.........$3.49

49 N 3567—Size 20 to 21 in. Shpg. wt. 1 lb.........$3.79

49 N 3568—Size 24 to 25 in. Shpg. wt. 1 lb.........$4.79

Saran Wigs give dolly that 'new' look   As low as $1¹⁹

You'll be amazed how much a new wig can dress up a favorite doll. Try all the new hair styles—just dampen; then comb and set 'hair.' Glue, instructions incl. Colors 1(blonde), 2(brunette). *State color number.* Shpg. wt. 7 oz.

How to order: Wig size is number of inches around doll's head. With fraction, order next size larger.

Cat. No.	Size	Price	Cat. No.	Size	Price
49 N 3520H	8	$1.19	49 N 3523H	12	$1.89
49 N 3519H	9	1.39	49 N 3525H	13	2.27
49 N 3521H	10	1.49	49 N 3526H	14	2.37
49 N 3522H	11	1.69	49 N 3529H	15	2.77
....			49 N 3539H	16	2.97

28-inch Plush Teddy Bear
$5.99

Jumbo bear is just waiting for a young companion's hugs and attention. He will sit naturally by himself on bed or floor . . but he likes to be carried. Made of fine quality cocoa and honey-colored rayon plush with shaped arms and feet. Filled with lightweight cotton. Glassene eyes, cotton felt nose, red cotton felt tongue and wears a rayon ribbon bow.

79 N 4139L—Shipping weight 5 pounds........$5.99

Only **$2**⁹⁹ each

Only **$1**⁹⁹ each

---

[1] Bulldog with wired front legs to preserve natural stance. Gray and white rayon plush; cotton filled. Wears snug cotton sweater. Glassene eyes, cotton felt tongue. 14 in. tall. Shpg. wt. 2 lbs.
49 N 4199......$2.99

[2] Smokey Bear the famous forest ranger. He's made of rayon plush with blue cotton denim pants. Filled with foam plastic and cotton. Plastic hat, badge, shovel. 14 in. tall. Shpg. wt. 1 lb. 4 oz.
49 N 4346......$2.99

[3] Cuddle Bear . . a big 19-in. armful. Honey-colored rayon plush body. Cotton filled, soft, huggable. Cotton felt tongue and paw pads. Round plastic eyes and nose. Shipping weight 2 pounds.
49 N 4314......$2.99

[4] Cuddle Panda . . 19 inches tall. Black and white rayon plush with cotton felt eye patches, tongue and paw pads. Plastic eyes and nose. Cotton filled, soft, huggable. Shipping weight 2 pounds.
49 N 4303......$2.99

[5] Puppy . . appealing cuddle toy has a coat colored like butter and ginger. Cotton-filled rayon plush. Shapeable ears, pompon nose, anchored plastic eyes. 10 inches long. Shpg. wt. 10 oz.
49 N 4164......$1.99

[6] Skunk . . holds posies. Made of black and white rayon plush, his soft body's cotton filled. Shapeable tail, rolling eyes and pompon nose add winsome charm. 8½ in. tall. Shipping wt. 10 oz.
49 N 4161......$1.99

[7] Baby Bear. Surface washable . . scrub him with soap and water. Tan and brown rayon plush body filled with foam plastic and cotton. Vinyl nose, plastic eyes. 13½ inches tall. Shpg. wt. 1 lb. 3 oz.
49 N 4102......$1.99

[8] Baby Panda is surface washable . . dries quickly. Black and white rayon plush; foam plastic and cotton filled. Vinyl nose, plastic eyes, cotton felt eye patches. 13½ inches tall. Shpg. wt. 1 lb. 3 oz.
49 N 4126......$1.99

"What's up, Doc?"

"You called?"

MATTEL'S
Cecil and Bugs Bunny . .
Pull the ring and they TALK

Cecil (the Seasick Sea Serpent) is 38 in. long, 18 in. tall. He says 11 comical phrases at random. Fluffy green rayon plush, cotton felt trim. Cotton filled. Rolling plastic eyes. No batteries needed. Shpg. wt. 3 lbs.
49 N 4168.........$8.66

Bugs Bunny wisecracks ten different sayings. Carrot-clutching cutup stands 26½ inches tall. Cotton filled; rayon plush. Vinyl face and hands. No batteries needed. Shipping wt. 3 lbs. 4 oz.
49 N 4181.......$7.99

Lovable Floppy Bunny

[9] From the briar patch. Stands 25 inches tall. His body is made of soft gray and white rayon plush and is cotton filled. Has shapeable ears. He holds a carrot in one of his vinyl hands. He wears a mischievous grin on his comic vinyl face. Neck bow, cotton tail.
49 N 4182—Wt. 1 lb. 12 oz......$3.99

MATTEL'S
Cecil and his disguise kit

[10] Cecil the bandit, Super Cecil, Cecil as a pirate, even Cecil as a lion . . what fun youngsters will have outfitting the Seasick Sea Serpent in any of 18 or more disguises. He's 24 inches long, made of soft green rayon plush. Cotton filled. He sits by himself, can be shaped in various positions. Shipping weight 1 lb. 12 oz.
49 N 4121................Kit $4.27

The Barbie explosion hit the Christmas Wishbook big in 1963. The headline read, "Sears puts at your fingertips more of what America's children want most: Barbie and her friends with 4 pages of wardrobes and accessories." The buying public had made the shapely doll a huge success and now there were costumes and accessories galore. Barbie now had bedroom suites, sports cars, authorized carrying cases and more. She even had a beau, Ken, and a best friend named Midge.

She also had competition. Sears aggressively marketed Ideal's Tammy, a teen-ager not as busty or thin as Barbie, along with her Mom, Dad and siblings Pepper and Ted. Tammy was a wholesome family girl... not a flighty high-fashion model! But the public spoke again and Tammy never came near Barbie's popularity.

Collector values of Barbies of this period have soared. The "bubble cut" hair-do Barbies are not quite as pricey as the ponytail style, but sell today for $125-$300 if mint in the original box. Midge sells today for $75-$200 depending upon condition.

Poor Betsy McCall, once the queen of the catalog's doll pages, was now almost lost in the mix despite six new outfits. This would be her last Wishbook appearance.

A cute all-mohair teddy bear debuted in 1963 ("fully jointed with a very fine pile that wears longer".) The 20-inch bear sold for $8.88. Several other new teddies were added to the catalogs pages.

Sears Christmas

Wishbook

1963

This is Tammy's Delightful

See Tammy on preceding page

Dad $2⁷⁶

Basic Dad doll. Stands 13 in. tall. Dressed in slacks, sport shirt and shoes. Plastic.
49 N 3926—Wt. 8 oz...$2.76

Mom $2⁶⁴

Basic Mom doll. Stands 12 in. tall. Dressed in cotton shift dress and shoes. Plastic.
49 N 3928—Wt. 9 oz...$2.64

Sister Pepper $1⁸⁷

Basic Pepper doll. Stands 9 in. tall. Dressed in playsuit, with shoes. Plastic.
49 N 3930—Wt. 6 oz...$1.87

Brother Ted $2²⁹

Basic Ted doll. Stands 13 in. tall, like Dad. Wears shorts, shirt and shoes. Plastic.
49 N 3921—Wt. 7 oz...$2.29

Family

Sears puts at your fingertips
more of what America's children want most

Outfits for Mom and Dad

1 Mom's Party Dress has long, trim lines . . looks so fashionable and sophisticated on Mother's mature figure. On big dates, Tammy likes to wear it, too . . fits her perfectly. Evening wrap is just what Mother wants for parties . . use it with other outfits. Doll not included.
49 N 3929—Wt. 6 oz...$1.64

2 Dad's Suit is neatly tailored . . just right for Sundays or special occasions. And the most convenient thing . . all Dad's clothes fit Ted, too. To make the outfit complete, Dad also comes with dress shirt and striped tie to accent suit. Wears shoes. Outfit only. Doll not included.
49 N 3927—Wt. 6 oz...$2.44

For Tammy's brother Ted

3 Blazer and Slack Outfit adds to Ted's sporty, casual appearance. Looks as good on Dad as on Ted. Doll not included.
49 N 3925—Shipping weight 6 oz......$2.77

4 Car Coat and Cap just right for breezy afternoons. Ted likes to wear them when he goes riding in his sports car.
49 N 3924—Shipping weight 6 oz......$1.69

5 Shirt and Slack Set smartly tailored . . ideal for an afternoon of golf.
49 N 3922—Shipping weight 6 oz......$1.69

For Tammy's sister Pepper

6 Pepper's Party Dress smartly styled in velveteen and nylon. Doll not included.
49 N 3935—Shipping weight 3 oz......$1.64

7 School Dress with matching panties.
49 N 3932—Shipping weight 3 oz......99c

8 Petticoat and Panties.
49 N 3936—Shipping weight 3 oz......88c

9 Coat and Hat with fuzzy collar.
49 N 3934—Shipping weight 3 oz......$1.69

10 Slack and Sweater Set.
49 N 3931—Shipping weight 3 oz....1.27

Matching Striped Nightwear

All are cotton, flannel . . with slippers.
Pajamas for Pepper.
49 N 3939—Shipping wt. 3 oz.....99c
Pajamas for Ted or his Father.
49 N 3940—Shipping wt. 6 oz....$1.27
Nightgown for Tammy, Mother.
49 N 3937—Shipping wt. 6 oz....1.19

Tammy's Bed Set

Set up a sleeping area just for Tammy. Plastic vanity with bench (not shown). Her bed has wood base and is skirted in peppermint stripes . . velvet headboard, pillow.
49 N 9359—Shpg. wt. 1 lb. 8 oz..$2.97

Tammy's Sports Car

Designed with bucket seats to fit Tammy comfortably. Bright-colored plastic with whitewalls. Even holds brother Ted and other 11½–12-in. dolls. Pennant on front fender. Dolls not included.
49 N 9355—Shpg. wt. 2 lbs. 8 oz..$3.97

Tammy loves to travel

11 13-in. plastic case has compartment for Tammy, clothing rack, 6 hangers, accessory drawer. Shiny finish.
49 N 9332—Shpg. wt. 1 lb. 8 oz...$1.77

Her family travels, too

12 All in one . . a compartment for each doll in Tammy's family, plus a removable bed and pillows. 2 racks in wardrobe, 12 hangers, 3 drawers.
49 N 9354—Shpg. wt. 4 lbs. 1 oz..$4.66

Sears puts at your fingertips more of what America's children want most

Barbie *Ken* *Midge* FASHION QUEEN *Barbie*

BARBIE AND HER FRIENDS WITH
4 PAGES OF WARDROBES AND ACCESSORIES

$1⁹² $2²⁹ $1⁹² $3⁹⁶

My three differently styled Saran wigs can be changed to wear with various outfits

These famous Dolls by MATTEL come dressed for a day at the beach

Barbie . . smart, chic, fashion-wise. Stands 11½ inches tall; has movable legs, arms and head for easy dressing. Rooted Saran hair. Shpg. wt. 12 oz.
49N3701—Bubble-cut hair style . $1.92
49N3805—Ponytail hair style . . 1.92

Ken . . Barbie's boyfriend, and a teenager's ideal. Stands 12½-inches tall. Realistically molded hair. Movable arms, legs and head. Shpg. wt. 12 oz.
49 N 3731 . . . . $2.29

Midge . . Barbie's best friend and she's exactly the same size, so she fits perfectly in Barbie's clothes. Jointed for easy dressing. Rooted hair. Shpg. wt. 12 oz.
49 N 3806 . . . . $1.92

Fashion Queen Barbie . . the new 11½-inch Barbie doll that lets you change her hair style and color. Complete with 3 high-fashion wigs . . Bubble-cut, Page boy and Side-part flip styles. Special wig stand included.
49 N 3819—Shpg. wt. 12 oz.. . . . . . . $3.96

Barbie, Ken, Midge are plastic and include stands. Dolls and their clothing on these 4 pages are made by fine artisans in Japan

Barbie and *Ken* the most popular twosome in doll town now have coordinated outfits

1   49 N 3820—Barbie: Bride's Dream. Shipping weight 8 oz... $2.29
    49 N 3821—Ken: Tuxedo. Shipping weight 8 oz............ 3.44

2   49 N 3823—Barbie: Red Flare. Shipping weight 8 oz........ 1.99
    49 N 3822—Ken: Saturday Date. Shipping weight 8 oz...... 3.19

3   49 N 3825—Barbie: Tennis Anyone. Shipping weight 8 oz.... 2.33
    49 N 3826—Ken: Time for Tennis. Shipping weight 8 oz...... 2.33

4   49 N 3829—Barbie: Ski Queen. Shipping weight 4 oz........ 2.66
    49 N 3830—Ken: Ski Champion. Shipping weight 8 oz...... 2.66

5   49 N 3833—Barbie: Masquerade. Shipping weight 8 oz......$1.64
    49 N 3837—Ken: Masquerade. Shipping weight 8 oz........ 1.64

6   49 N 3840—Barbie: Icebreaker. Shipping weight 8 oz....... 2.34
    49 N 3838—Ken: Fun on Ice. Shipping weight 8 oz.......... 2.34

7   49 N 3842—Barbie: Graduation. Shipping weight 8 oz....... 1.19
    49 N 3841—Ken: Graduation. Shipping weight 8 oz......... 1.19

8   49 N 3846—Barbie: Registered Nurse. Shipping weight 4 oz.. 2.27
    49 N 3845—Ken: Doctor. Shipping weight 8 oz............. 2.27

Give a Mix 'N Match Outfit from Barbie's fashion bar

Packages of attractive clothes and accessories with their own delicate hangers. Designed and color coordinated to blend with other fashions in Barbie's wardrobe. Sorry, no choice of color or style.

9   Dress with accessories.
   49 N 3862—Shipping wt. 2 oz....97c

10   Shoes, gloves, sunglasses, jewelry.
   49 N 3864—Shipping wt. 2 oz...89c

11   Lingerie with slippers and mirror.
   49 N 3868—Shipping wt. 2 oz...89c

12   Two-piece pajama set.
   49 N 3867—Shipping wt. 1 oz....97c

13   Jacket with matching hat.
   49 N 3870—Shipping wt. 2 oz...89c

14   Blouse.
   49 N 3866—Shipping wt. 1 oz....77c

15   Skirt with accessories.
   49 N 3869—Shipping wt. 1 oz....77c

16   Slacks with accessories.
   49 N 3863—Shipping wt. 2 oz...77c

More fashions for special occasions

17   Barbie Baby Sits. Apron, clock, snacks. Jointed baby doll . . diapers, basket, bottles. Dress not incl.
   49 N 3848—Wt. 8 oz..$2.27

18   Ballerina. Leotard plus silver color, white tutu. Tiara, shoes, bag.
   49 N 3735—Wt. 8 oz. $2.39

19   Winter Holiday. Warm in hooded shirt, gloves. Tote bag holds shoes.
   49 N 3859—Wt. 8 oz..$2.89

20   Rain Coat. With hat, umbrella and boots.
   49 N 3850—Wt. 8 oz..$1.84

21   American Airlines Stewardess. Outfit, hat, shoes. Carries hand and tote bag.
   49 N 3860—Wt. 8 oz..$2.89

All dolls on page not included

FORMAL WEAR for New Year's Eve and fancy Balls

[1] Where is she going? What will she wear? Pick from this complete selection of evening wear to suit any occasion. Includes matching accessories as shown. Dolls not included.

(1) 49 N 3705—Sophisticated Lady. Full, collared coat, gown. Shipping wt. 8 oz. $3.19
(2) 49 N 3707—Solo in Spotlight. Tight-fitting sheath, flounce. Shipping. wt. 8 oz. 2.44
(3) 49 N 3723—Party Date. Strapless cocktail dress, wide belt. Shipping wt. 4 oz. . . . 1.27
(4) 49 N 3709—Senior Prom. Strapless gown with tulle overskirt. Shipping wt. 8 oz. . . 2.17
(5) 49 N 3708—Dinner at Eight. One-piece hostess capri pants, coat. Wt. 8 oz. 1.97
(6) 49 N 3719—Enchanted Evening. Stole. Gathered swirl sheath. Shpg. wt. 8 oz. 3.22

So that all 3 dolls can share them...
Clothes fit *Barbie, Midge* and

CASUALS for day-long good looks

Any time of the day, any season, Barbie's flare for fashion gets admiring glances everywhere. Accessories shown are included. Dolls not included.

7 Knitting Pretty. Matching skirt, sweaters.
49 N 3730—Shipping weight 4 oz $2.17

8 Garden Party. Print dress with eyelet, ruffles.
49 N 3784—Shipping weight 4 oz $1.64

9 Movie Date. Candy stripe, organdy overskirt.
49 N 3779—Shipping weight 4 oz $1.22

10 Fancy Free. Two-toned cotton with ricrac.
49 N 3774—Shipping weight 4 oz $1.22

11 Busy Morning. Suntop dress, hat.
49 N 3775—Shipping weight 4 oz $1.96

12 Mood for Music. Capri slacks, cardigan.
49 N 3785—Shipping weight 4 oz $2.39

13 After Five. Organdy dress with collar, hat.
49 N 3776—Shipping weight 4 oz $1.64

14 Swinging Easy. Full skirted, cummerbund.
49 N 3778—Shipping weight 4 oz $1.64

15 Sheath Sensation. Fitted with large pockets.
49 N 3781—Shipping weight 4 oz $1.22

16 Friday Nite Date. Jumper, blouse-slip.
49 N 3783—Shipping weight 4 oz $2.11

Ultra-elegant DRESS UPS

For Barbie and Midge, good taste means dressing "just right" for the particular occasion. For such occasions, their wardrobe includes these:

(1) **Career Girl.** In the office, 2-piece tweed suit. Sleeveless pull-over.
    49 N 3787—Shipping weight 8 ounces.............$1.99
(2) 49 N 3797—**Golden Elegance.** Trimmed with "fur." Wt. 8 oz. 3.19
(3) 49 N 3796—**Theater Date.** Satin coordinate. Shpg. wt. 4 oz.. 1.94
(4) 49 N 3795—**Sorority Meeting.** Sweater, sheath. Wt. 4 oz. 1.96
(5) 49 N 3794—**Orange Blossom.** As bridesmaid. Shpg. wt. 4 oz. 1.96

Dolls not included on this page

1

Fashion Queen Barbie

Lovely, frothy LINGERIE

6 Nighty Negligee Set. Full-length gown, grecian bodice. Pleated peignoir. Dog included.
49N3798-Wt. 8 oz.$2.27

7 Sweet Dreams. Embroidered Baby Doll pajamas. Clock, diary.
49N3802-Wt. 4 oz..99c

8 Floral Petticoat. Springtime fresh pattern.. matching bra, panties. Mirror, brush.
49N3803-Wt. 4 oz..99c

Barbie Patterns
(they fit Midge, too)

Sew your own Barbie fashions with 12 specially designed Advance patterns. Each of the 12 patterns are different. All are printed on tissue. Simply pin the tissue to your fabric and cut it out. You're ready to sew a new dress for Barbie. Step-by-step instructions are easy to follow, plus a "Barbie Sewing Book" included.

49 N 3804—Shpg. wt. 2 oz..97c

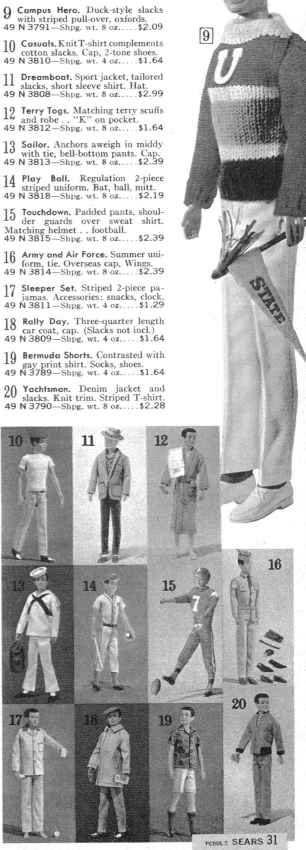

Ken has an outfit for every occasion

Ken's smartly-tailored wardrobe fits perfectly. Accessories, as shown.

9 Campus Hero. Duck-style slacks with striped pull-over, oxfords.
49 N 3791—Shpg. wt. 8 oz.....$2.09

10 Casuals. Knit T-shirt complements cotton slacks. Cap, 2-tone shoes.
49 N 3810—Shpg. wt. 8 oz.....$1.64

11 Dreamboat. Sport jacket, tailored slacks, short sleeve shirt. Hat.
49 N 3808—Shpg. wt. 8 oz.....$2.99

12 Terry Togs. Matching terry scuffs and robe .. "K" on pocket.
49 N 3812—Shpg. wt. 8 oz.....$1.64

13 Sailor. Anchors aweigh in middy with tie, bell-bottom pants. Cap.
49 N 3813—Shpg. wt. 8 oz.....$2.39

14 Play Ball. Regulation 2-piece striped uniform. Bat, ball, mitt.
49 N 3818—Shpg. wt. 8 oz.....$2.19

15 Touchdown. Padded pants, shoulder guards over sweat shirt. Matching helmet .. football.
49 N 3815—Shpg. wt. 8 oz.....$2.39

16 Army and Air Force. Summer uniform, tie. Overseas cap, Wings.
49 N 3814—Shpg. wt. 8 oz.....$2.39

17 Sleeper Set. Striped 2-piece pajamas. Accessories: snacks, clock.
49 N 3811—Shpg. wt. 4 oz.....$1.29

18 Rally Day. Three-quarter length car coat, cap. (Slacks not incl.)
49 N 3809—Shpg. wt. 4 oz.....$1.64

19 Bermuda Shorts. Contrasted with gay print shirt. Socks, shoes.
49 N 3789—Shpg. wt. 4 oz.....$1.64

20 Yachtsman. Denim jacket and slacks. Knit trim. Striped T-shirt.
49 N 3790—Shpg. wt. 8 oz.....$2.28

Pert Betsy McCall
Walks, sits, kneels . . has 5 outfits

1 8-inch plastic doll dressed in chemise, socks and shoes. Saran hair. Moving eyes.
49 N 3002—Shipping weight 8 ounces. $1.67
Extra Outfits below

2 **Bon Voyage** . . cotton corduroy skirt, matching jacket. Print blouse. Shoes and socks. Toy hatbox.
49 N 3883—Shipping weight 4 ounces. $1.79

3 **Party** . . dress, panties, straw hat, shoes, socks.
49 N 3955—Shipping weight 4 ounces. $1.79

4 **TV Time** . . jumper, toreador pants, plastic TV set.
49 N 3954—Shipping weight 4 ounces. $1.37

5 **Winter Weekend** . . ski outfit with skis and poles.
49 N 3953—Shipping weight 4 ounces. $1.79

6 **Patio Party** . . perfect hostess outfit. Tea set, tray.
49 N 3956—Shipping weight 4 ounces. $1.79

Cuddly Li'l Dear has 4 outfits

7 This chubby, lovable doll is a wee bundle of joy . . 8 in. long with soft cloth body; arms and legs of skin-like vinyl plastic. Vinyl head has sleeping eyes, rooted Saran hair. Dressed in robe of easy-care cotton.
49 N 3949—Shipping weight 7 oz. $2.87
Extra Outfits . . Doll not included

8 **Lace-trimmed topper set** . . perfect for playtime.
49 N 3950—Shipping weight 2 oz. $1.49

9 **Pajamas** . . of light blue jersey for sweet dreams.
49 N 3952—Shipping weight 2 oz. $1.49

10 **Embroidered dress,** lace trimmed . . fit for a queen.
49 N 3951—Shpg. wt. 2 oz. $2.87

Bride, trunk, 3-pc. outfit
$4.99

11½-inch bride with embroidered bridal gown plus 3 complete changes: robe, party dress and sport outfit. Jointed plastic. Trunk has plastic handle.
Shpg. wt. 2 lbs. 8 oz.
49 N 3873. . . . . $4.99

Teenage Doll, trunk, outfit
$4.99

12-in. doll with rooted hair. Plastic. Wears shoes, multicolor print dress. 4 extra outfits: sport outfit, street dress, afternoon dress, playsuit. With trunk. Wt. 2 lbs. 8 oz.
49 N 3874. . . . . $4.99

Ben Casey and Nurse
$4.37

12-in. Ben has stethoscope, intern's outfit. 11½-in. nurse wears dress, cap, cape. Plastic. Movable arms, legs, head. Each can wear clothes of like-size dolls.
Shpg. wt. 1 lb. 4 oz.
49 N 3957. . . . $4.37

Debbie Drake does exercises
$2.84

11½-inch plastic doll assumes almost any pose. She's fully jointed, amazingly flexible. Has leotard, just like the real Debbie. Can wear clothes of like-size doll. Wt. 12 oz.
49 N 3958. . . . . $2.84

11½-inch tall Fashion Dolls

Doll only ## 88c

Extra outfits 88c each

Tall slim model has pretty, painted features framed by shining, rooted Saran hair. Plastic, movable vinyl head, arms. Arriving in cotton-knit swim suit, heels, she looks lovely in outfits to order below.

11 **White doll.**
49 N 3962—Wt. 7 oz. 88c

12 **Colored doll.**
49 N 3963—Wt. 7 oz. 88c

Extra outfits for doll above

13 **Tutu and ballet slippers.**
49 N 3959—Wt. 3 oz. 88c

14 **Sports jacket, slacks.**
49 N 3961—Wt. 3 oz. 88c

15 **Sports jacket, pleated skirt.**
49 N 3960—Wt. 3 oz. 88c

Barbie 4-poster Bed
$2⁸⁴

White high-impact plastic with molded vinyl mattress, pillow and under-bed chest with sliding drawer. Spread and canopy are ruffled pink plastic. 7x12x13 inches. Easily assembled.
49 N 9248—Shpg. wt. 1 lb. 6 oz. . .$2.84

Bedding for 4-poster above
4-pc. set $1⁹⁹

Add to Barbie's comfort with fitted bottom sheet, top sheet, pillow case and soft blanket. Cotton.
49 N 9358—Shpg. wt. 3 oz. . . . . .Set $1.99

[2] $3²⁷

[1] $4⁹³

[3] $2⁶⁴

For *Barbie's* Room
(*Midge would love them, too*)

1 Queen-size Bed is white high-impact plastic with gold-color trim, tufted fabric head and footboards. Comes complete with matching spread and bolster. Secret drawer under bed hides "valuables." Measures 18x12x10 inches high overall.
Shipping weight 2 pounds.
49 N 9357 . . . .$4.93

2 Wardrobe is white high-impact plastic with a full door mirror, shoe rack, hat rack, three sliding drawers, six plastic hangers. Matches vanity, 4-poster bed at left and queen-size bed above. Will hold all her clothes neatly. 7x4x14 in. high.
Shipping weight 2 pounds.
49 N 9321 . . . .$3.27

3 Vanity is graceful French Provincial style in white high-impact plastic, trimmed with gold color. Mirror, telephone, Ken's framed picture, tissue holder, stool with pile seat, matching rug. Table measures 7x4x13 inches high overall.
Shipping weight 1 pound.
49 N 9326 . . . .$2.64

A Wardrobe for Ken
$3⁴⁷

Keep his clothes wrinkle-free. High-impact plastic. Has door mirror, shoe rack, hat rack, accessory tray, 6 sliding drawers, hangers. 7x4x14 inches high.
49 N 9356—Shipping wt. 2 lbs. . . .$3.47

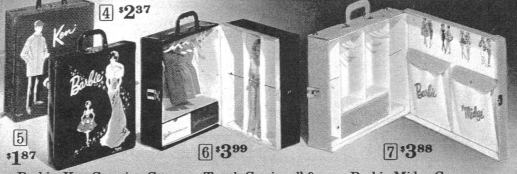

[4] $2³⁷

[5] $1⁸⁷

[6] $3⁹⁹

[7] $3⁸⁸

Barbie, Ken Carrying Cases

4 Ken's Case is washable vinyl, assorted colors. Brass fittings, hangers, double drawers. 11x4x13 inches high.
49 N 9328—Shpg. wt. 2 lbs. 2 oz. $2.37

5 Matching Barbie Case. 10x3x12 in.
49 N 9309—Wt. 1 lb. 8 oz. $1.87

Trunk Carries all 3

6 Holds Barbie, Midge, Ken—and their clothes. Electronically sealed vinyl; aluminum frame. 10x7x13 in. high. Doll, clothing not incl.
49N9331—Wt.3lbs.5oz.$3.99

Barbie-Midge Case

7 Tote both dolls on trips. Vacuum formed section even holds their wardrobe and accessories. Electronically sealed. Screen printed vinyl. 18x4x14 inches high.
49 N 9330—Wt. 3 lbs. 13 oz. $3.88

[8]

[9]

Watch us whiz down the road

New! Hot Rod for Barbie and Ken $4⁷⁷

8 Big drag-race rear wheels, bucket seats, roll bar. Plastic. Turquoise; fuchsia trim, ivory interior. 7¾x18 inches long.
49 N 1460—Shipping weight 2 pounds 12 ounces. $4.77

Snappy Sports Car for Barbie $3⁷⁷

9 Midge and Ken can go riding. Peach plastic body with chrome-color fittings, clear windshield, aqua bucket seats. Free-wheeling rubber-like tires on steel axle. 7½x18 in. long.
49 N 1405—Shipping weight 2 pounds 10 ounces. $3.77

Dolls not included.

Sears wonderful world of
TEDDY BEARS
Sizes from 10 to 29 inches tall

Delightful characters in rayon plush

1 Baby Bear . . a happy traveling companion for any youngster. Plastic eyes, vinyl nose, eyes, mouth. Just right for hugging . . 13½ in. tall. Brown, tan. Foam-plastic, cotton fill.
49 N 4102—Shipping wt. 1 lb. 3 oz..... $1.99

2 Begging Bear has outstretched felt paws; simulated claws. Pompon nose, button eyes. 10 in. Brown, white. Foam-plastic, cotton filled.
49 N 4077—Shipping weight 1 lb....... $2.99

3 Smokey Bear looks alert for fires. Wears uniform pants of blue cotton denim. Plastic hat, badge and shovel. 14 in. tall. Brown and tan. Foam plastic and cotton filled.
49 N 4346—Shipping wt. 1 lb. 4 oz..... $2.79

4 Sleepy Cuddle Bear closes his eyes when put to bed . . has huggable floppy body. Cocoa with brown eyes. 17 in. Cotton filled.
49 N 4081—Shipping wt. 1 lb. 6 oz..... $3.99

5 Cuddle Bear is traditionally the most popular Teddy around. His rayon plush body has shaped arms and legs. Cotton felt nose and mouth . . plastic eyes. 18 inches tall. Beige. Foam plastic, cotton filled.
49 N 4091—Shipping wt. 1 lb. 3 oz..... $2.99

6 Honey Bear has a lustrous, short pile plush body that's a pleasure to hug. Gold color is detailed with cotton felt tongue, paw pads, round plastic eyes and nose. 19 inches tall. Lightweight cotton filled body.
49 N 4314—Shipping weight 2 lbs..... $2.99

7 Seated Bear closes his big blue eyes to sleep . . sits up in a begging position. Highly styled body has extra long pile of lustrous white. Pompon nose . . plastic eyes. Soft blue trim. 19 in. tall. Cotton filled.
49 N 4106—Shipping weight 3 lbs..... $5.89

All Mohair Bear
. . fully jointed with very fine pile that wears longer

8 A full 20 inch brown bear to treasure for years. Closely loomed, thick pile won't crush, or mat. Head stuffed with cotton and excelsior for shape retention. Cotton filled body. Hand-embroidered nose, mouth. Imported glass eyes.
49 N 4192—Shipping wt. 2 lbs. 8 oz.... $8.88

Jumbo 29-inch Bear
Easy to carry because he only weighs 3½ lbs.

$4⁹⁴

So realistic it's like having a baby cub to play with. Yet, he's lightweight . . can be taken along everywhere. His furry body seems life-like, too . . made of cocoa and honey-colored rayon plush. Sits up naturally wherever he's placed . . has shaped arms and legs, glassene eyes. 29 inches tall. Cotton filled. Wears rayon satin bow.
79 N 4189C—Shipping weight 5 pounds........ $4.94

Fully Jointed Bears
50% Mohair and 50% Rayon

18 in. tall. Movable arms, legs . . even the head turns. Beige with simulated claws on paw pads. Hand-embroidered nose, sewn-in glass eyes. Cotton, foam plastic fill. Wt. 2 lbs.
49 N 4123....... $6.89

13 in. Mohair blend pile won't crush or mat. Movable head, jointed legs. Simulated claws, embroidered nose, glass eyes sewn in. Beige. Foam-plastic, cotton filled. Wt. 1 lb. 3 oz.
49 N 4142....... $3.99

Betsy Wetsy was still popular in the 1964 Sears Wishbook, but she would soon fall to Barbie's popularity. Tiny Thumbelina by Ideal was a hit largely due to effective television commercials aimed at girls. The doll was offered in several variations. The 14-inch Thumbelina at $8.88 drinks a bottle and cries, another 14-inch model for $6.29 has lifelike movements ("Such a lazy baby") and the 20-inch doll at $9.99 cries <u>and</u> wiggles.

A deluge of new Barbies and accessories came this year. "Miss" Barbie, who had bending knees and blinking eyes, came with three wigs, a lawn swing and potted plant for $4.99. If found today this set is worth $800-$1,000!

Barbie had page after page of new clothes too. Outfits ranged from a pajama party set for $1.17 to an ice-skating set for $2.39 to a natural mink jacket (real mink!) at $9.99... but luckily that price included the 10% Federal Tax on furs. Today, these clothes are very valuable especially if found in excellent condition. For those who could not afford Barbie's officially licensed designs, many knock-offs appeared as well as a $1.00 envelope of Barbie patterns to make your own clothes.

The nod for the most politically incorrect doll must go to Spank Me, who "cries real tears." Made especially for Sears, when the doll is spanked on it's bottom (conveniently marked "here") "she'll fuss like a real baby." The doll must have sold fairly well as it appeared in subsequent catalogs.

Sears Christmas
Wishbook

1964

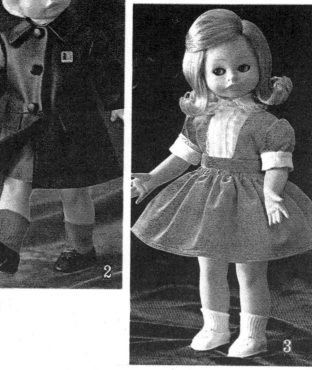

3 delightful kitty dolls with wash-and-comb hair . . wistful faces sculptured by famous Italian craftsmen . . long-lashed go-to-sleep eyes. All are 15 inches tall, made of vinyl. They wear vinyl shoes, full pettislips, knit panties and socks.

Long ponytail, plaid outfit

1 Chic blue-eyed Miss with swingy blonde hair wears a blue knit cardigan. Plaid trim on sweater matches pleated wool plaid skirt. White socks. Shipping weight 1 lb. 8 oz.
49 N 3516.....$7.98

Bubble-cut hair, black vinyl coat

2 Platinum-hued hair contrasts smartly with leatherette easy-snap-close coat, pert hat. Doll wears red cotton dress, socks. Shpg. wt. 1 lb. 8 oz.
49 N 3515...$11.98

Flip-up hair, velveteen dress

3 Cranberry-pink party dress of cotton velveteen complements doll's chestnut hair. Lace-edged collar, cuffs, dress front. Shipping weight 1 lb. 8 oz.
49 N 3369.....$7.98

Kitty
the Bonomi Fashion Doll from Italy

iC italocremona

Outfits for every occasion . . made in Italy for your Bonomi Doll

4 Resort Set. Chic clam-digger cotton pants. Print jacket and hat.
49 N 3375—Wt. 4 oz......$2.98

5 Foul-weather Set. Plastic rain cape. Slacks, knit shirt.
49 N 3379—Wt. 5 oz......$3.98

6 Plaid Dress. Fringed scarf tie and roomy hem-placed pockets.
49 N 3374—Wt. 4 oz.....$3.98

7 Sweater Set. Knit cardigan. Perky pleated skirt. Cotton.
49 N 3377—Wt. 4 oz.....$2.98

8 Wool Coat Set. Warm lined coat. Chin-tie hat. Rayon print dress.
49 N 3382—Wt. 5 oz......$5.98

9 Nylon Ball Gown. Lacy white overlay caught in scallops.
49 N 3386—Wt. 5 oz......$5.98

10 Beach Set. 1-piece play suit. Hooded terry jacket. Cotton.
49 N 3376—Wt. 4 oz......$2.98

11 Lace-trimmed Pajama. So feminine for leisure hours. Cotton.
49 N 3384—Wt. 4 oz......$2.49

Doll not included with outfits

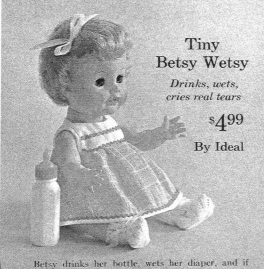

Tiny Betsy Wetsy

Drinks, wets, cries real tears

$4⁹⁹

By Ideal

Betsy drinks her bottle, wets her diaper, and if you gently press her tummy, she cries real tears. Her eyes open and close. Washable, rooted Saran hair that feels soft and real . . jointed arms and legs. Vinyl body. About 12 inches tall.
49 N 3125—Shipping wt. 1 lb. 12 oz......$4.99

Little Dew Drop Tears $4⁹⁹

Help dolly drink her bottle—then hold her forward and she'll cry real tears. She wets, too. All vinyl, fully jointed head with sleeping eyes. Soft, rooted hair. Wardrobe trunk includes coat, hat, print dress and hangers. About 12 inches tall.
49 N 3127—Shipping wt. 2 lbs. 4 oz.... $4.99

Bubble Bath Baby $3⁹⁹

This baby really takes to water . . drinks and wets, too. She has her own bathinette, with bubble bath, soap, clothespins . . even a plastic duck to "play" with. Dressed in diaper and terry cloth bath outfit. She has a change of clothes, too. Rooted hair. Vinyl. About 12 inches high.
49 N 3128—Shipping wt. 2 lbs........$3.99

WA-A-A-A

Spank Me
I cry real tears
$5⁹⁹

This is Sears very own baby, and she's very special. Just turn her over and spank where it says "here" . . she'll fuss like a real baby. Feed her from bottle. Soft, rooted hair . . sleeping eyes . . soft, chubby arms and legs. Vinyl. Dressed in red play outfit. About 20 inches high.
Shipping weight 2 lbs. 13 oz.
49 N 3126...............$5.99

Pat her back gently after her bottle . . she'll burp like a real baby

Mattel's Baby Pattaburp

$6⁶⁶

She's beautiful—and so real. Feed her, place her on your shoulder, pat her on the back . . and she burps. And she can burp again, too. Put her down for her nap, and she'll close her eyes and go to sleep. Rooted hair. Soft body. Dressed in a fluffy pink jacket trimmed with lace and ribbons, pink panties and terry cloth booties. Comes with her own special baby bottle . . and the milk disappears when you feed her. It magically refills itself. Baby Pattaburp is a cuddly 16 inches high.
49 N 3119—Shpg. wt. 2 lbs. 4 oz. $6.66

Little One in Musical Cradle

$6⁹⁹

13-inch drink and wet baby doll snuggles in her cradle. Fully jointed . . rooted hair. Cradle lined and trimmed. Baby wears 2-pc. flannel sleeper. Wood cradle about 17 in. long.
Shpg. wt. 4 lbs. 12 oz.
49 N 3020C.....$6.99

Tearful Tiny Thumbelina

Tiny Thumbelina

Such a lazy baby . . she moves and stretches as if she just woke up

$6²⁹

She's 14 inches long. Just wind disc in back and she makes lifelike movements. Vinyl head, arms and legs. Cotton body. Rooted Saran hair can be washed, set and combed.

Baby wears lovely pink lace-trimmed cotton organdy dress, cotton slip, diaper and booties.

49 N 3211—Shipping weight 1 lb. 8 oz.........$6.29

Extra Outfits for Tiny Thumbelinas

1 Creeper Set. What little mother could resist Tiny in this cunning cover-all set, bootees. Three clothes-pins for washday use. Doll not included.
49 N 3242—Shipping weight 6 ounces.........$2.19

2 Pajama Set. For sleepy-time hours. Hot water bottle, cotton terrycloth animal for play. Doll not included.
49 N 3046—Shipping weight 6 ounces.........$1.94

3 Pram Suit. To keep baby warm . . 2-piece suit with attached hood, bootees, 2 hangers. Doll not included.
49 N 3244—Shipping weight 7 ounces.........$3.27

My eyes open and close when I move . . $8⁸⁸
After my bottle, I shed real tears

14 inches tall. So lifelike, so cuddly, so perfect for a little girl. This wistful baby comes dressed in a blue stripe outfit with a pink bib. Your little miss will have hours of fun as she cares for this lifelike doll. She drinks from a bottle. When her stomach is pressed, look at her eyes fill up with real tears.

Wind her up and she moves and stretches like a real baby. Rock her in your arms and watch her open and close her eyes.

Cute baby's face, vinyl head, arms and legs, cloth body. Fully rooted hair. Wears all of Tiny Thumbelina's clothes.
49 N 3121—Wt. 1 lb. 10 oz.......$8.88

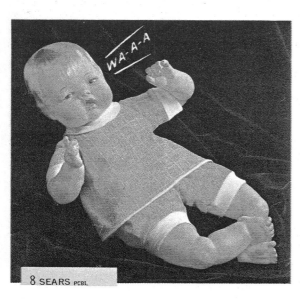

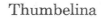

Thumbelina
She wriggles and cries until Mommy picks her up
$9⁹⁹

About 20 inches long. Just wind the key in her back and lifelike Thumbelina will wriggle *and* cry like a real baby. Pick her up to cuddle and she'll stop crying instantly.

Dressed in an adorable knit outfit. Vinyl head, arms and legs. Cloth body filled with plastic foam. Little girls love to wash and comb her rooted Saran hair.

Shipping weight 4 pounds.
49 N 3213...........$9.99

Thumbelina Carry-all $2⁹⁷

Plastic with calf-finish tote for any 14-inch doll. Carry Tiny Thumbelina and her clothes to your playmate's house. Heart-print lining. Clothes rack and 5 plastic hangers; accessory drawer. 14x4x 14 in. high. Shipping weight 2 lbs. 11 oz.
49 N 9208.....$2.97

Rock-a-bye Cradle $2⁹⁷

Picture Tiny Thumbelina nestled in this pink and white rocking crib . . snugly, soft and cozy . . all ready to be rocked off to sleep. Soft pad. Rocking crib is perfectly decorated with Tiny Thumbelina hearts. Plastic 19x10x14 in. high over-all. Shipping weight 3 lbs.
79 N 9209C.......$2.97

Her wigs make this Barbie a Fashion Queen

$3.96

Change her hair style to go with her costumes . . bubble-cut, page boy, and side-part flip. The secret: 3 high fashion Saran wigs. Wig stand included. All Barbie clothes fit Fashion Queen Barbie.
49 N 3819—Wt. 12 oz. . . .$3.96

Mattel's famous Dolls dressed for the beach

1 **Barbie** . . stands 11½ in. tall; has movable legs, arms, and head for easy dressing. Rooted Saran hair. Shpg. wt. 12 oz.
49 N 3701—Bubble-cut. $1.92
49 N 3805—Ponytail. . . 1.92

2 **Ken** . . Barbie's boyfriend, and a teenager's ideal. Stands 12 inches tall. Realistically molded hair. Movable arms, legs, and head for easy dressing.
49 N 3731—Wt. 12 oz. . . $2.29

3 **Midge** . . Barbie's best friend. And she's exactly the same size, so she fits perfectly in Barbie's clothes. Jointed for easy dressing. Rooted hair.
49 N 3806—Wt. 12 oz. . . $1.92

4 **Allan** . . he's a buddy for Ken, a boyfriend for Midge. He's exactly the same size as Ken, so he fits in all of Ken's smartly tailored clothes.
49 N 3716—Wt. 12 oz. . . $2.29

"Miss Barbie"

SHE RUNS

SHE DANCES

SHE BENDS

So lively . . her knees bend, her eyes close
Miss Barbie with 3 Wigs, Lawn Swing and Planter $4.99

Miss Barbie's shapely lifelike legs actually bend at the knees . . and the joints that allow this movement are completely invisible. She can pose like she's running, cheerleading, modeling . . and can even cross her legs when she sits. 11½ inches tall. Saran wigs. Wig stand. Plastic swing, planter. Swing unassembled.
49 N 3704—Shipping weight 1 pound 14 ounces $4.99

Barbie and friends are plastic; with wire stands. They and clothing are made in Japan. Costumes sold separately on pages 23 and 24.

Ken and Barbie on Campus

Dress up for a special date

1 Campus Queen. Satin gown with a bouffant overskirt. Loving cup, roses, long gloves, jewelry and shoes. Shpg. wt. 5 oz.
49 N 3728....$2.97

2 Special Date. Handsome suit with shirt, tie, shoes and socks. Shpg. wt. 5 oz.
49 N 3738....$2.97

Barbie's clothes also fit Midge, Fashion Queen and Miss Barbie. Ken's fit Allan. Dolls not included.

3 A Friday Nite Date: Corduroy jumper, blouse, accessories.
49 N 3783—Shpg. wt. 5 oz. $1.99

4 Campus Corduroys. Jacket, slacks. (Shirt not incl.).
49 N 3739—Shpg. wt. 3 oz. $1.92

5 Victory Dance. Ken looks great in blazer, slacks and vest.
49 N 3732—Shpg. wt. 5 oz. $2.83

6 Garden Tea Party. Cool dress, white gloves and shoes.
49 N 3784—Shpg. wt. 4 oz. $1.64

7 Masquerade. Have a party .. and dress Barbie for a gay time.
49 N 3833—Shpg. wt. 5 oz. $1.69

8 Masquerade. Ken is hard to recognize in mask, costume.
49 N 3837—Shpg. wt. 5 oz. $1.69

9 Graduation. Allan is so distinguished in cap and gown.
49 N 3841—Shpg. wt. 5 oz. $1.24

10 Graduation. Barbie's in tasseled cap, gown. Diploma.
49 N 3842—Shpg. wt. 4 oz. $1.24

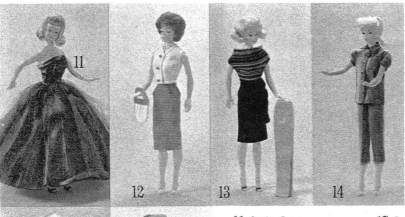

11 Senior Prom.
49 N 3709—Wt. 5 oz. $2.17

12 Crisp 'N Cool.
49 N 3748—Wt. 3 oz. 1.27

13 Knit Separates. Skirt, blouse, slacks, shoes, scarf.
49 N 3727—Wt. 4 oz. $1.22

14 Pajama Party. Pajamas.
49 N 3867—Wt. 3 oz. $1.17

15 Stormy Weather. Raincoat, hat, umbrella, boots.
49 N 3850—Wt. 5 oz. $1.87

16 Knitting Pretty. Pink sweater set, skirt, shoes. Needles, yarns, scissors.
49 N 3730—Wt. 4 oz. $2.27

17 Fountain Boy. Jacket, cap. Tray, sodas, spoons, napkins, (Pants not incl.).
49 N 3726—Wt. 3 oz.. $1.54

18 Sleeper Set.
49 N 3811—Wt. 3 oz. 1.29

19 Fraternity Meeting. White short sleeved shirt, brown slacks, cardigan sweater.
49 N 3749—Wt. 3 oz.. $1.97

20 Campus Hero. Pullover sweater. White duck slacks.
49 N 3791—Wt. 5 oz.. $2.19

21 Terry Togs. Robe, scuffs and accessories.
49 N 3812—Wt. 5 oz.. $1.64

Ken and Barbie Outdoors

1 **Barbie in Hawaii.** Exotic 2-piece swimsuit, grass skirt, lei.
49 N 3284–Shpg. wt. 3 oz.**$1.19**

2 **Ken in Hawaii** . . goes native to tune of his uke. Straw hat, lei.
49 N 3285–Shpg. wt. 3 oz.**$1.19**

3 **Ski Queen.** Barbie at fashion heights in realistic ski outfit.
49 N 3829–Shpg. wt. 5 oz.**$2.66**

4 **Ski Champion.** Ken takes to the slopes completely outfitted.
49 N 3830–Shpg. wt. 6 oz.**$2.66**

5 **Time for Tennis.** Ken's set to go in sweater, shorts, shirt.
49 N 3826–Shpg. wt. 5 oz.**$2.33**

6 **Tennis, anyone?** Barbie's a match in tennis dress, sweater.
49 N 3825–Shpg. wt. 5 oz.**$2.33**

7 **Fun on Ice.** Ken glides along in argyle sweater, slacks, muffler.
49 N 3838–Shpg. wt. 6 oz.**$2.39**

8 **Icebreaker.** Barbie skates in leotard, skirt, jacket, tights.
49 N 3840–Shpg. wt. 5 oz.**$2.39**

9 **Speedboat.** It's a real dream-boat. Now Barbie and Ken (or any other twosome) can go for an honest-to-goodness boat ride. Floats in water or moves smoothly over floors on free-rolling wheels. Plastic, chrome-plated trim. Bucket seats, steering wheel, windshield. About 20 inches long, 8 inches wide and 6½ inches high.
49 N 9314–Wt. 2 lbs. 9 oz.**$4.97**

10 **Barbie Skin Diver.** 2-piece orange and lime swimsuit, sweatshirt, mask and fins.
49 N 3760–Shpg. wt. 3 oz.**$1.44**

11 **Skin Diver.** Striped trunks, sweatshirt, mask, fins, snorkle.
49 N 3772–Shpg. wt. 3 oz.**$1.44**

12 **The Yachtsman.** Ken in denims, jacket, tee shirt, shoes.
49 N 3790–Shpg. wt. 6 oz.**$2.37**

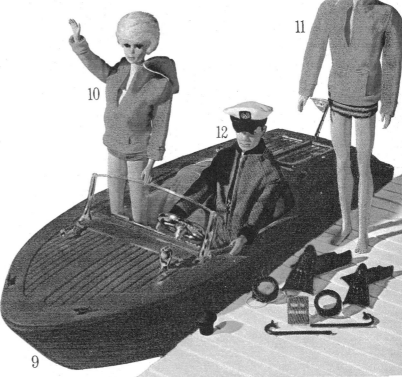

13 **Barbie's Little Theatre** has 4 backdrops, 7 scripts, props and tickets. 32x22x19 in. high. Chipboard. Unassembled.
79 N 9307L—Wt. 9 lbs....**$4.93**

14 **King Arthur.** Armed for battle.
49 N 3286—Wt. 8 oz..**$3.29**

15 **Guinevere.** Elegant in velvet.
49 N 3287—Wt. 7 oz..**$3.29**

16 **Cinderella.** Before *and* after.
49N 3289—Wt. 7 oz. Set **$3.19**

17 **Red Riding Hood.** Wolf mask.
49 N 3288—Wt. 8 oz..**$3.17**

18 **Play Ball.** Uniform, bat, glove.
49 N 3818—Wt. 5 oz..**$1.99**

19 **Roller Skate Date.** No slacks.
49 N 3293—Wt. 4 oz..**$1.22**

20 **Touchdown.** Football outfit.
49 N 3815—Wt. 6 oz..**$2.19**

21 **Casuals.** Tee shirt, slacks, cap.
49 N 3810—Wt. 4 oz..**$1.64**

22 **Country Clubbin'.** Jacket, slacks. Shirt not included.
49 N 3290—Wt. 3 oz......**$1.97**

23 **Rally Day.** Car coat, cap only.
49 N 3809—Wt. 4 oz..**$1.64**

Barbie Sports Plane seats 2 dolls (not incl.). Includes retractable landing gear, turning propeller. 27x27x12 in. Plastic.
79 N 9315C—Shpg. wt. 5 lbs....**$5.66**

Dolls on this page are not included

Barbie's dressed up

1 **It's Cold Outside.** Coat and hat . .
Color may vary on this item.
49 N 3729—Shpg. wt. 5 oz......$1.33

2 **Red Flare.** Velveteen coat, hat, purse.
49 N 3823—Shpg. wt. 6 oz....$1.99

3 **Career Girl.** Tweed suit, hat, gloves.
49 N 3787—Shpg. wt. 5 oz...$2.33

4 **Sheath Sensation.** Sheath, hat, gloves.
49 N 3781—Shpg. wt. 4 oz....$1.27

5 **After Five.** Collared dress, hat.
49 N 3776—Shpg. wt. 5 oz.... 1.67

6 **Fancy Free.** Cotton dress with rickrack.
49 N 3774—Shpg. wt. 3 oz....$1.22

7 **Lunch Date.** Print dress with overskirt.
49 N 3299—Shpg. wt. 4 oz...$1.24

8 **Suburban Shopper.** Dress, purse.
49 N 3775—Shpg. wt. 5 oz...$1.96

9 **Satin Separates.** Skirt, jacket, hat.
49 N 3297—Shpg. wt. 3 oz....$1.47

10 **Theater Date.** Satin coordinates.
49 N 3796—Shpg. wt. 4 oz.... 1.58

Dolls not included on this page.

11 **Dr. Ken on duty.**
49 N 3845—Wt. 5 oz.$2.27

12 **Registered Nurse Barbie.**
49 N 3846—Wt. 5 oz.$2.35

13 **Candy Striper Volunteer.**
49 N 3759—Wt. 6 oz.$1.97

14 **Airline Stewardess.**
49 N 3860—Wt. 5 oz.$2.89

15 **Airline Captain.**
49 N 3758—Wt. 5 oz.$2.89

16 **Ballerina Barbie.**
49 N 3735—Wt. 8 oz.$2.39

17 **Barbie Baby-sits.** Apron, clock, snacks. Jointed baby doll . . diapers, bottles, basket. Dress not included.
49 N 3848—Wt. 6 oz. $1.97

18 **Army and Air Force.**
49 N 3814—Wt. 5 oz.$2.19

19 **Sailor.**
49 N 3813—Wt. 5 oz.$2.39

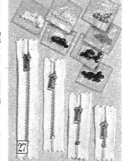
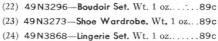

20 **Dog 'N Duds.** Plush dog for Barbie with accessories and food bowl. Shipping weight set 5 oz.
49 N 3725.......$2.37

21 **Barbie's Wig Wardrobe.** Three differently styled Saran wigs with wigstand. Shpg. wt. 5 oz.
49 N 3969.......$2.64

(22) 49N3296—Boudoir Set. Wt. 1 oz......89c

(23) 49N3273—Shoe Wardrobe. Wt. 1 oz..89c

(24) 49N3868—Lingerie Set. Wt. 1 oz......89c

(25) 49N3295—Purse, Shoe Sets. Wt. 1 oz..89c

26 **Barbie Patterns.** 12 fashion designs . . sewing guide.
49 N 3804—Shpg. wt. 1 oz...$1.00

27 **Sewing Accessories Set.**
49 N 3294—Shpg. wt. 1 oz..89c

Barbie loves elegance

Ken, in tuxedo, is
her constant companion

1 **Midnight Blue.** Gown, satin lined cape.
49 N 3754—Shipping wt. 8 oz.... $3.44

2 **Ken's Tuxedo.** Satin-faced lapels.
49 N 3821—Shipping wt. 7 oz.... 3.44

3 **Golden Evening.** 2-pc. knit, belt, bracelet.
49 N 3724—Shipping wt. 5 oz.... $1.67

4 **Solo in Spotlight.** Flounced sheath, "mike."
49 N 3707—Shipping wt. 5 oz.... $2.39

5 **Sophisticated Lady.** Velvet coat, gown.
49 N 3705—Shipping wt. 8 oz.... $3.37

6 **Dinner at Eight.** Hostess pants, coat.
49 N 3708—Shipping wt. 5 oz.... $1.94

7 **Black Magic.** Sheath, tulle cape, gloves.
49 N 3757—Shipping wt. 5 oz.... $1.66

8 **Silken Flame.** Strapless dress, belt, purse.
49 N 3737—Shipping wt. 3 oz.... $1.27

9 **Natural Mink Jacket** made of natural mink
sections. Price includes 10% Fed. Tax.
49 N 3755E—Shipping wt. 4 oz...... $9.99

10 **Evening Splendor.** Brocade ensemble; hat.
49 N 3797—Shipping wt. 5 oz.... $2.97

11 **Orange Blossom.** White eyelet over sheath.
49 N 3794—Shipping wt. 5 oz.... $1.96

12 **Bride's Dream.** Traditional satin, chiffon.
49 N 3820—Shipping wt. 5 oz.... $2.57

13 **Slack Set.** Slacks and blouse of satin.
49 N 3298—Shipping wt. 4 oz.... $1.47

14 **Nighty, Negligee.** Pleated peignoir, gown.
49 N 3798—Shipping wt. 5 oz.... $2.33

Dolls not included on this page.
Prices for outfits only.

Barbie's New Dream House

Living room, bedroom, kitchen and patio

Barbie can live like a princess. Rearrange the floor plan daily. Maximum floor area 44x42 in. Living room-bedroom has bed, night stand, sofa, chairs, tables, lamps, TV, rug, clothes hangers. Chaise on patio. Kitchen with built-in units. Furniture unassembled. Sturdy chipboard. Folds to 21x10x15 in. high. Dolls, clothing not included.
79 N 9304C—Shipping weight 10 pounds................$4.99

$4⁹⁹

Complete with mannequin showcase window   **$4⁴⁷**

Barbie's Fashion Salon

Tastefully designed with curtained stage, alcove for hanging clothes, built-in cabinets, dressing room entrance, even a mannequin with movable arms. Salon furnished with 3-way mirror, arm chairs, coffee table, display case, hat rack. 38x24x17 in. high. Folds for storage; plastic handle. Chipboard, unassembled. Dolls, clothing not included.
79 N 9306L—Shipping weight 10 pounds................$4.47

Plastic sets of Doll Furniture for Barbie snap together

Each set includes indoor or outdoor backdrops *plus* some of the following: telephone, radio, TV, magazines, pictures, games, tumblers, tray

4-in-1 Gift Set **$4⁶⁶**   **Individual Sets** **99c** to **$1⁴⁷**

Gift set: convertible sofa-bed, tables, chair, ottoman, chaise lounge, lawn swing, planter, accessories. Made up of 4 sets below. Indoor, outdoor backdrops.
49 N 9376—Shipping weight 2 pounds................Set $4.66

1 Convertible sofa-bed, foam cushions; coffee table, simulated tile top.
49 N 9323—Shpg. wt. 12 oz. Set $1.44

2 Two-position reclining-back chair, ottoman, end table (match sofa-bed).
49 N 9324—Shpg. wt. 8 oz. .. Set $1.22

3 Chaise lounge, matching side table.
49 N 9327—Shpg. wt. 5 oz. Set 99c

4 Lawn swing. Planter with "plant."
49N9360—Shpg. wt. 10 oz.. Set $1.47

Wishnik Trolls were the mini-fad of 1965 and they were extremely popular for a short time. Girls could carry them in their pockets since they were only 2 1/2-inches high. Just 65¢ in their day, today's collectors value these little good luck charms and they can be pricey. Sears even offered its exclusive "prehistoric model home" for your trolls... a homey little place for $2.99.

Little Miss Echo debuted this year. The 30-inch doll could repeat things back to its owner with a hidden tape recorder built inside. At $14.99 it was the most expensive doll offered in this year's Wishbook, and that price was exclusive of batteries. No wonder, as the doll required two "D" cells and a 9-volt battery!

Character dolls based on hit TV shows and movies were big sellers in 1965. Mary Poppins, Cinderella, Patty Duke and Samantha (based on the "Bewitched" television series) were all available. These dolls are highly collectible today.

Mattel looked to expand its Barbie empire with new additions to the family. Little sister Skipper entered the scene and became an instant hit. The Wishbook featured lots of clothes for the young girl as well as a classroom playset made exclusively for Sears by Mattel. Note the matching outfits for Barbie and Skipper. These sets generate huge collector interest today.

In the teddy bear department, choices were limited in 1965. Honey Bear was offered for $2.99 and stood 19-inches tall. This teddy had big felt eyelashes that made him stand out.

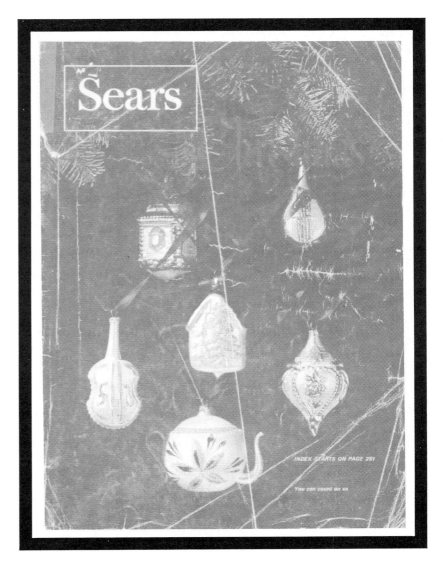

Sears Christmas
Wishbook

1965

*Talk to me . .
sing to me . .
I'll repeat
everything
you say*

Little Miss Echo

$14⁹⁹
without batteries

I'm 30 inches tall

What a wonderful doll. She has a magnetic tape recorder built in. She's plastic, has jointed arms and legs, and rooted hair. Order 2 "D" batteries, one 9-volt battery. Shipping weight 8 lbs.
79 N 3665CM . . . $14.99

"D" Battery. Wt. ea. 4 oz.
79 N 4660 . . . . . Each 16c
4 for 60c

9-volt Battery. Wt. ea. 4 oz.
79 N 6417M . . . . . ea. 35c

You can order toys on pages 441 through 673 until Sept. 1, 1966

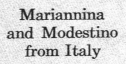

Mariannina and Modestino from Italy
$7⁹⁹ each

15-inch twins have rooted hair, go-to-sleep blue eyes. Plastic. Wt. ea. 2 lbs. 8 oz.

Mariannina. Pigtailed and pretty in plaid dress, shoes, wears a gay smile.
49 N 3483 . . . . $7.99

Modestino. Cute, kissable in his jeans, carries a 4-leaf clover for luck.
49 N 3482 . . . . $7.99

Mama's Baby wears a lacy christening dress and hat

1 Sweet baby doll dressed with the lace and ribbons all little mothers adore. 20 inches long with cotton stuffed body, vinyl limbs and head, sleeping eyes, rooted hair. Wears dress, hat and slip. Has real-baby cry, too.
49 N 3055—Wt. 2 lbs. 12 oz. . $4.99

1 $4⁹⁹

Pretty Baby Doll is Lovable Dressed in polka dots

2 A doll girls love to hug, because her body is soft cloth. Arms, legs and head are vinyl, she has rooted pixie hair, go-to-sleep eyes. In knit booties, pretty dress with matching ruffled bonnet, she's 13 inches tall.
49 N 3058—Shpg. wt. 1 lb. 4 oz. $2.99

2 $2⁹⁹

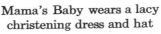

I'm Singin' Chatty . . won't you sing along with me?
$9⁷⁷

Mattel's 17-inch sweet-voiced doll is just waiting for you to pull the Chatty® ring so she can sing for you. You never know what she'll sing next . . it might be "Rock-a-bye Baby" or "London Bridge," or another nursery favorite. Sings many songs. Plastic.
49 N 3518—Wt. 2 lbs. 8 oz. . . . $9.77

Dee-Dee
Cut 'n Button Doll by Mattel

You make her fashion wardrobe without sewing $7⁶⁶

Cut out   Button together

Dee-Dee's a cutie, 15 inches tall, in a lovely party dress. She comes with 4 Cut 'n button outfits so simple to make . . and so much fun for her to wear. Simply cut out the clothes on the lines, button them together . . Dee Dee has a new outfit. Plastic. With instructions.
49 N 3519—Wt. 1 lb. 9 oz. $7.66

Smiling Baby Boy
$12⁹⁸

From Italy an adorable baby with face designed by Bonomi, top name in Italian doll craft. Pale blonde hair is rooted, go-to-sleep eyes have long lashes. In vinyl, fully jointed, 17 inches tall. Wears fleece coat, knit suit, kid booties. Wt. 1 lb. 14 oz.
49 N 3147 . . . . $12.98

Wishnik Troll 65c

What's a Troll? It's 2½ inches of plastic doll with big buggy eyes and a wild mop of hair you rub for luck. It's a toy, a good luck charm, it's fun!
49 N 3664—Shpg. wt. 2 oz...... 65c

Troll Dress-up Set
$1.67

A Bikini and a tutu . . hat and jewelry, and clothes for a well-dressed lady Troll. Shipping weight 3 oz.
49 N 3672...... $1.67

Career Dress-ups
$1.67

Troll can be doctor, lawyer or Indian chief. Set of 3 outfits for Trolls. Shpg. wt. 3 oz.
49 N 3680...... $1.67

Housewife Set
$1.67

Cookbook and curlers, negligee, princess phone . . all the things a good Troll housewife needs. Shpg. wt. 3 oz.
49 N 3681...... $1.67

Every Troll needs a home of his own and only Sears has this one!

Prehistoric model home furnished in true Troll decor $2.99

Our Troll house of vinyl plastic has a weathered tree exterior complete with potted plants and a name over the door. The cozy interior has every comfort a 2½-inch Troll could want . . including a fake marble bath. There's a blazing fireplace with cooking pot, a comfy bed, a big tub chair and hassock, a dining table and chairs. We've even added "animal skin" rugs for a homey touch. All furnishings are vacuum formed. House locks closed, has carrying handle. 12x6x9 in. high. Completely assembled. Doll not included.
49 N 9352—Shipping weight 1 lb. 8 oz......................... $2.99

Save this catalog . . . you can order toys from this book, pages 441 to 673, from now until Sept. 1, 1966

Bride-and-Groom Trolls. She wears a white lace dress, has a veil and flowers . . he's in white tie, tails and a top hat. Romantic pair. 2½ in. tall.
49N3669–Shpg. wt. 5 oz. Set $2.77

Doctor-and-Nurse Trolls . . neat and efficient. He wears a white jacket, a stethoscope. She has blue uniform, hypodermic needle. 2½ in. tall.
49N3671–Shpg. wt. 5 oz. Set $2.77

Sportnik Set has 4 Outfits and Troll Doll
Set $3.77

Golf anyone? Or maybe a football game? Our Sportnik Troll is equipped for both . . has a sporty beret, golf clubs, his own football. He has an outfit for fishing (complete with fish), and one for baseball, too. With accessories.
Shipping weight 10 oz.
49 N 3673 . . . . $3.77

It's a great life in this miniature Troll Village

Includes 12 Trolls . . sold only at Sears $3.99

Set up a Troll land all your own . . on a table, on the floor, anywhere. Let your imagination run riot as you plan activities for 12 Trolls (1½-in. tall) and their 9 animals. See what you get: mountains, houses, furniture, trees, a cart, a sign for "Wild Horses Canyon" and many more delightful pieces, in sturdy plastic. From Hong Kong.
49 N 9389—Shipping weight 1 lb. 4 oz..... $3.99

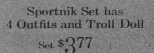

Skipper's Schoolroom

Made exclusively For Sears by Mattel $4.97

School can be fun with Barbie as teacher and Skooter, Skipper and Ricky as pupils. Lifelike chipboard schoolroom contains desks, chairs, learning aids . . and a blackboard wall you can write on. Outside, there's a playground with slide and gym equipment . . plus a lunch patio. 47½x10½x13 in. Folds into carrying case. Dolls not included.
79 N 9343C—Shipping weight 6 pounds....................$4.97

Almost 4 feet long when open

Skipper Wheel Set
$4.97

Gift set includes a scooter, skate board, skates, yo-yo. Two costumes, sunglasses, hat, shoes. Shpg. wt. 1 lb.
49 N 3717....$4.97

1 Student Teacher Barbie. Dress, globe, book, glasses. Wt. 4 oz.
49 N 3348........$1.27

2 School Girl. Wt. 4 oz.
49 N 3349.....$2.44

3 School Days. Wt. 4 oz.
49 N 3276.....$1.94

4 Ricky's Sunday Suit. Blazer, slacks, shoes. Shirt not incl. Wt. 4 oz.
49 N 3350........$1.66

5 Land and Sea. Pedal pushers, jacket, hat, shoes. Wt. 4 oz.
49 N 3354........$1.97

6 Fun Time. Capris, jacket, 2 blouses, shoes and croquet set. Wt. 4 oz.
49 N 3355........$2.47

7 Little Leaguer Ricky. Jeans, shirt, cap, mitt, ball, high socks, sneakers. Wt. 4 oz.
49 N 3356........$1.66

Outfits on this page (except 1, 4 and 7) fit Skipper, Skooter, Cricket—all 9-inch dolls.

Skipper and her pals dress up for parties

8 Town Togs. Jaunty jumper, coat, blouse, hat, hose, shoes.
49 N 3357—Wt. 5 oz...$2.16

9 Red Sensation. Vivid dress, hat, gloves, shoes, socks.
49 N 3282—Wt. 4 oz...$1.24

10 Silk 'n' Fancy. Two-tone full-skirted dress, headband, shoes and socks.
49 N 3281—Wt. 4 oz...$1.27

11 Happy Birthday. Dress, hat, gloves, petticoat, gift—and a yummy pretend cake.
49 N 3358—Wt. 5 oz...$2.47

12 Party Pink. Pouffy dress .. aflutter with ribbons.
49 N 3359—Wt. 2 oz.....99c

NOTE: Dolls not included with outfits on this page.
Clothes are made in Japan. PCBL **SEARS 659**

Matchables for dress-alike sisters

Blue Cotton Candy. Bulky knit sweaters, matching slacks, knit dickeys, shoes. Shpg. wt. each 5 oz.

Outfit for Barbie
49 N 3323 .... $2.67

Outfit for Skipper
49 N 3322 .... 1.67

Dog 'N Duds. Adorable plush dog for Barbie and Skipper to walk. Comes with dress-up outfits, sunglasses, collar, leash, bone, bowl and other items shown below. Shpg. wt. 5 oz.
49 N 3725 .... Set $2.44

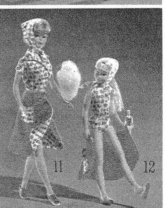

Barbie and Skipper . . fashion look-alikes

1 Bride's Dream. Traditional satin with chiffon overskirt.
49 N 3820–Shpg. wt. 5 oz. . $2.47

2 Flower Girl. Dress with white lacy overskirt.
49 N 3279–Shpg. wt. 2 oz. . $1.44

3 Aboard Ship. Dress, camera, travel folders, poster, book.
49 N 3319–Shpg. wt. 5 oz. . $1.99

4 Ship Ahoy. Skirt, top, jacket, camera, folders, sailboat.
49 N 3311–Shpg. wt. 4 oz. . $1.99

5 Sunny Pastels. Striped shift with matching purse.
49 N 3328–Shpg. wt. 3 oz. . $1.19

6 Fun 'N Games. Sport dress plus mallet, ball, stake.
49 N 3329–Shpg. wt. 4 oz. . $1.19

7 Red Flare. Velveteen flared coat, hat and purse.
49 N 3823–Shpg. wt. 6 oz. . $2.44

8 Dress Coat. Similar to Barbie's but in fitted style.
49 N 3277–Shpg. wt. 4 oz. . $1.97

9 Stormy Weather. Belted trench coat, hat, umbrella, boots.
49 N 3850–Shpg. wt. 5 oz. . $1.99

10 Rain or Shine. Just like Barbie's . . visor on hat.
49 N 3324–Shpg. wt. 4 oz. . $1.64

11 Fun at the Fair. Wrap-around skirt, blouse, kerchief, candy.
49 N 3332–Shpg. wt. 5 oz. . $1.66

12 Day at the Fair. Pocket in skirt holds tiny Barbie doll.
49 N 3330–Shpg. wt. 3 oz. . $1.24

13 Ballerina Barbie.
49 N 3735–Wt. 5 oz. . $2.47

14 Ballet Class.
49 N 3278–Wt. 4 oz. . $1.99

15 Skating Fun.
49 N 3275–Wt. 4 oz. . $1.69

16 Skater's Waltz.
49 N 3840–Wt. 5 oz. . $1.99

17 Lovely Lingerie.
49 N 3868–Wt. 1 oz. . . 94c

18 Under-Pretties.
49 N 3283–Wt. 2 oz. . . 94c

19 Dancing Doll Outfit.
49 N 3333–Wt. 5 oz. . $1.69

20 Me-N-My-Doll.
49 N 3336–Wt. 3 oz. . $1.69

PCBKM
AEDSLG

Now Raggedy Ann and Andy dance along with you to tune of their own music

$9⁹⁹ each

Imagine dancing along with one of these lovable 39-inch dolls. Bands on their feet attach to child's shoes . . imported music box plays a gay nursery tune.

Both dolls have colorful red wigs and locked-in eyes.

Raggedy Ann. Multi-color print dress, white apron.
79N3662C–Shpg. wt. 5 lbs.$9.99

Raggedy Andy. Blue cotton pants, red-and-white checked shirt, cap.
79N3663C–Shpg. wt. 5 lbs.$9.99

RAGGEDY ANN and ANDY

15-inch musical $4⁷⁷ each	15-inch non-musical $2⁹⁴ each	20-inch non-musical $4⁷⁷ each

15-inch Musical Raggedy Ann. This charming rag doll favorite will make sleeptime more welcome and playtime more fun . . just wind up the imported music box and it plays a soft tinkling lullaby to the pleasure of all. She's dressed in a colorful flowered cotton dress topped with a sparkling white apron.
49 N 3629—Shpg. wt. 1 lb......$4.77

15-inch Raggedy Ann. No music box.
49 N 3580—Shpg. wt. 13 oz.....$2.94

20-inch Raggedy Ann. No music box.
49 N 3583—Shpg. wt. 1 lb. 4 oz..$4.77

15-inch Musical Raggedy Andy. The lovable twin to Raggedy Ann. He, too, has an imported music box to delight a boy or girl. He's wearing bright blue cotton trousers with snappy white buttons, gay red and white checked shirt and blue ribbon bow tie. A jaunty blue-and-white sailor cap perches on his head.
49 N 3630—Shipping weight 1 lb..$4.77

15-inch Raggedy Andy. No music box.
49 N 3592—Shpg. wt. 13 oz......$2.94

20-inch Raggedy Andy. No music box.
49 N 3603—Shpg. wt. 1 lb. 4 oz...$4.77

Dancing Dolly $3¹⁷

A 39-inch doll that dances along. Bands on feet attach to child's shoes . . floppy body moves as she moves. Lightweight fabric body, cotton stuffed, yarn hair. Shipping wt. 3 lbs. 8 oz.
49 N 3530........$3.17

Gingham Girl $2⁹⁴

A pert little miss in colorful gingham and ruffles. She has bright yellow yarn braids and sweet painted face. Cotton filled. 18 inches long. Shipping weight 1 pound 8 ounces.
49 N 3635.....$2.94

Crazy Crib $2⁹⁴

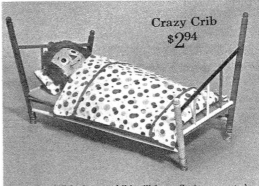

A fun doll bed your child will love. Spring mounted legs give it a gleeful bounce. Native white birch. With pillow, cover. Holds dolls up to 18 in. No doll.
49 N 9223—Shipping weight 1 pound 8 oz. . $2.94

So soft, because of his deep pile "fur"
So big, he stands a full 19 inches tall

Honey Bear $2⁹⁹

From his fluffy round ears to his black felt nose he's a fine furry fellow. Plump, two-tone body of lustrous high-pile rayon plush. Low-pile plush snout and paws. Brown eyes are safety locked-in under black felt lashes. Cotton filled. A crib pet for tots . . decoration for a teen's bed.
Shipping weight 2 pounds.
49 N 4133 . . . . $2.99

Zippy squeaks like real chimp

$5⁸⁹

And he looks just like one, too. Curly rayon plush body is cotton filled. Mischievous face, big ears, hands and shoes are sturdy vinyl that whisks clean with a damp cloth. Dressed for playtime in jaunty hat, shirt and overalls. Lovable chimp stands 16 inches tall.
Shipping weight 1 pound 12 ounces.
49 N 4088 . . . . $5.89

Grooming brush keeps them neat

$3⁶⁹ each

Two perky, winsome pets with luxurious, long rayon plush pile. Each is 11 in. tall . . comes with own grooming brush. Colorful satin collars and bows add a dress-up air. Shpg. wt. each 1 lb.
Sitting Kitten. Pink.
49 N 4143 . . . . $3.69
Sitting Pup. Yellow.
49 N 4140 . . . . $3.69

Fluffy the cat has real fur $3⁹⁴

Stroke her . . she has real white fur . . a thick, soft coat that's smooth and silky. A wonderful bed decoration for tots, teenagers. 18 in. long. Cotton stuffed.
49 N 4007—Wt. 1 lb. 4 oz $3.94

Fur Cat with Kittens . . all in a basket $5⁶⁹

The 12-inch mother cat and her two 5-inch kittens are snuggled together in a decorated gold-color reed basket. All of soft, white fur with cotton stuffing.
49 N 4362—Shpg. wt. 2 lbs $5.69

Siamese Kitten

$2⁸⁴

1 A cuddly beige kitten of soft Creslan® acrylic. She has the delicate seal point markings on her ears and nose. Cotton-and-foam plastic filled. Washable. 15 inches high. Shipping weight 12 ounces.
49 N 4132 . . . . $2.84

Fuzzy the Dog has long-fiber trim

$3⁵⁹

2 Bright-eyed cocoa-colored cuddle pup made of soft rayon plush with acrylic fiber trim on ears, muzzle and feet. Cotton-and-foam plastic filled. About 12½ inches high. Shipping weight 1 pound 2 ounces.
49 N 4137 . . . . $3.59

4 little pets as cute as can be

$1⁹⁹ each

Delightful companions of fine quality rayon plush. Plastic eyes and ribbon bows. Bears have soft vinyl muzzles. Cotton-and-foam plastic stuffed . . so soft and squeezy.

3 Kitten. Gray and white. 12 in. tall.
49 N 4139—Shpg. wt. 12 oz $1.99
4 Puppy. Yellow and white. 11 in. tall.
49 N 4138—Shpg. wt. 12 oz $1.99
5 Baby Bear. Brown. 13½ in. tall.
49 N 4102—Wt. 1 lb. 3 oz $1.99
6 Baby Panda. Black and white. 13½ in.
49 N 4126—Wt. 1 lb. 3 oz $1.99

Magilla Gorilla and Pals

$1⁹⁴ each

Here's that rollicking gang of TV fame . . lots of fun to play with. They're accurately reproduced in short-pile rayon plush with colorful felt trim and accessories. Start a collection of these funny characters. Firm cotton filling for shape retention. About 12 inches high.
(7) 49 N 4135—Magilla Gorilla
(8) 49 N 4136—Ricochet Rabbit
(9) 49 N 4074—Droop-a-Long
(10) 49 N 4075—Punkin Puss
(11) 49 N 4076—Mushmouse
Shpg. wt. ea. 10 oz . . . Each $1.94

The Beatles invasion and the influence of London's Carnaby Street fashions were in full force by the time the 1966 Sears Christmas Wishbook reached American households.

So it is not surprising to see the "mod" trend highly merchandised in the catalog this year. Chipper, Vandina and Stephanie were 15 and 16-inch dolls that were "pert and pretty... the spirit of today in swinging new fashions... long, long hair." From their op-art hats and mini-skirts to their vinyl coats and go-go boots, these dolls were on the cutting edge!

These hip clothes reached to Barbie's family too. Francie, Barbie's "Mod'ern" cousin, had a full line of trendy clothes ranging in price from $1.67 to $2.69. Wild colors, vinyl materials and fake furs filled Francie's closet. For $1.67 Francie could wear Go Granny Go, a long granny dress replete with shoes and a record player to listen to Herman's Hermits, no doubt. There was even a Ken A-Go-Go with black "Beatle" wig, striped outfit, guitar and microphone. Look out Ringo!

A new doll franchise, Kiddles by Mattel, debuted in the Wishbook. These mini-dolls were about 3-inches high and lots of accessories were offered, some exclusive to Sears. Today there are many Kiddles collectors looking for these original items.

Classic looking teddy bears made their way back into the Wishbook's pages. Two Baby Buddies, one a baby bear and another a baby panda, had vinyl muzzles and were priced at $1.99 each.

Sears Christmas
Wishbook
1966

MODS

Pert and pretty . . the spirit
of today in swinging new
fashions . . long, long hair

Chipper and her wardrobe
$9⁹⁹

1 Dressed for all the important
teen doings. Long blonde hair . .
rooted. Plastic body, soft vinyl head,
arms. Moving eyes. 15 in. tall. "Wet
look" outfit: black vinyl raincoat,
hat . . piped in white. White fishnet
hose, go-go boots, dress, panties.
Sport outfit: Orange bell-bottom hip
hugger pants. Polka-dot blouse.
Matching kerchief, slippers. Dress:
Floral knee-knocker skirt, hot pink
bodice, panties. Fishnet stockings,
floral print slippers.
49 N 3420—Wt. 1 lb. 2 oz. . . . $9.99

Vandina in flowered "total look" outfit
$8⁹⁹

2 Whimsical and quaint flowers on
her top and leotard set the style.
Her jumper is A-line. Luxuriously
long rooted blonde hair to wear in
a pig tail or hanging loose. Expressive closing eyes, finely detailed face
and hands. Jointed vinyl. She's 16
in. tall. From Italy.
49 N 3421—Wt. 1 lb. 10 oz. . . $8.99

Stephanie knows checks and waif-knits are "in"
$9⁹⁹

3 Almost op-art black and white
checks . . sharp and chic . . especially so over beautifully knit po'
boy sweater. Matching visor hat.
Long, swinging blonde hair that's
rooted. Pretty eyes open and shut.
White knee socks. Vinyl. She's 16
inches tall. From France.
49 N 3422—Wt. 1 lb. 14 oz. . . $9.99

Every doll family needs a Baby Boy

Smiling Tot $12⁹⁸

4 An adorable baby with face
designed by Bonomi, top
name in Italian doll craft. Pale
blonde hair is rooted, go-to-sleep
eyes have long lashes. Vinyl,
fully jointed. Shaggy coat, blue
knit suit, kid booties. 17 in. tall.
49 N 3147—Wt. 2 lbs. . $12.98

Impish Lad $15⁹⁸

5 Charming baby boy stays
snugly warm in his beautifully knit jacket. It's white and
double breasted. White knit hat
has puffy pompon trim. Underneath, a light blue leotard. Shiny
blonde hair, eyes that open and
close. Jointed vinyl. 20 inches
tall. From Italy.
49N3065—Wt. 3 lbs.2oz.$15.98

Tiny Kissy kisses you to return your love
$7⁹⁴

6 Squeeze her hands to-
gether . . she puckers
up to give you a sweet
kiss. A doll you'll love.
Pretty shift with ric-rac
trim, rocking horse ap-
pliqué. Shiny hair, win-
some eyes that close.
Vinyl, 16 in. tall. Buy it
the easy way . . order by
phone.
Shpg. wt. 1 lb. 10 oz.
49 N 3009 . . . . . $7.94

SAVE THIS CATALOG
You can order toys on pages 467
to 638 from now until Aug. 1, 1967

PCBMKG Sears 619

New! Barbie® and Francie® Color Magic Designer Set

$4⁹⁹

Drop Color Magic crystals in water. As soon as they dissolve, dab harmless solution to specially-treated fabric. Watch color change instantly! Get three sew-free costumes and one ready-to-wear costume, molded dress form, bowl, 2 sponge dabbers. Also flocking, glitter and floral pattern adhesives for decorating dresses. Make new solutions with vinegar or baking soda.
49 N 3703—Wt. 1 lb. 12 oz....$4.99

New! Barbie COLOR MAGIC

Change her hair and swimsuit colors . . instantly

. . over and over again.
Non-toxic, no mess
. . color crystals
do the trick!

From this: ←→ to this!

From this: ←→ to this!

Watch her hair and her clothes change!

Set with Barbie $5⁹⁹

Have a different-looking Barbie almost every day! She's the only doll that changes hair *and* wardrobe color back and forth, over and over again! Set includes bendable Barbie in swimsuit, 3-piece ensemble, hair-styling kit, instruction book, Color Magic crystals, sponge dabbers. Make new solutions with vinegar or baking soda. Shipping weight 1 lb. 10 oz.
49 N 3702.........$5.99

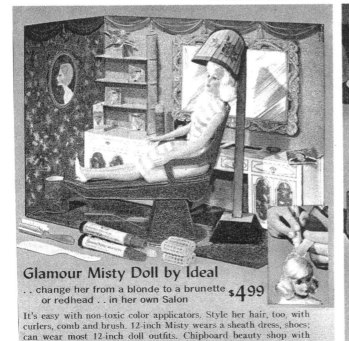

Glamour Misty Doll by Ideal

. . change her from a blonde to a brunette or redhead . . in her own Salon $4⁹⁹

It's easy with non-toxic color applicators. Style her hair, too, with curlers, comb and brush. 12-inch Misty wears a sheath dress, shoes; can wear most 12-inch doll outfits. Chipboard beauty shop with chair, dryer, counter, sink and other items. Unassembled. Shop 11 in. high. Use your phone if you want to order it the easiest way of all. Shipping weight 3 pounds 4 ounces.
49 N 3882...................$4.99

Color 'n Curl

$7 88 without batteries

Doll head with 4 specially-treated wigs change colors. Dryer (order 2 "D" batteries, page 482), rollers, comb, brush, activator solution, spray, wig stand. Wt. 2 lbs. 13 oz.
49 N 3817....$7.88

Barbie and her Friends

Hidden-joint legs bend in 3 positions

Now Barbie, Ken and Midge seem more life-like than ever! Bendable legs have invisible knee joints to make them look like they're running, walking, dancing or even crossing their legs. Dressed in bright beachwear. Barbie and Midge are 11½ inches tall with rooted Saran hair that's easy to comb and brush. Ken is 12½ inches tall with molded hair. Of sturdy vinyl; heads, arms, legs move. Dolls, clothing from Japan.
(1) 49 N 3340—Barbie. Wt. 12 oz....$2.97
(2) 49 N 3343—Ken. Wt. 13 oz......2.97
(3) 49 N 3341—Midge. Wt. 12 oz....2.97

Barbie's Shoe Wardrobe 97ᶜ

Vinyl shoes to match Barbie's clothes. Dressy, casual styles.
49 N 3273—Wt. 1 oz.....97c

Barbie's Wig Wardrobe $2⁸⁸

Three differently styled Saran wigs. Molded head fits on Barbie. Wig stand.
49 N 3969—Shpg. wt. 5 oz......$2.88

Meet **francie**..
Barbie's Mod'ern Cousin

She has bendable legs, realistic rooted shoulder-length hair .. even long eyelashes and her own eyelash brush!

Mix 'n match any way you want

Francie Gift Set $5.99

Francie with her attractive girlish figure, looks marvelous in the vivid colors of her "mod" wardrobe. Sears exclusive set features 11¼-in. doll with bendable arms and legs wearing a one-piece checked swimsuit. Clothing includes slacks, two tops, skirt, shoes.
49 N 3938—Shpg. wt. 1 lb. 5 oz... Set $5.99
Francie Doll only.
49 N 3402—Shipping weight 11 oz... $2.97
NOTE: Francie can wear Barbie's clothes!

Doll only
$2.97

Francie has the perfect slim, teen figure for her swinging "MOD" OUTFITS

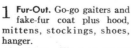

Swinging Outfits

10 Style Setter. Your Francie will look great in these bright coordinates. She can wear the multi-colored floral shift and matching hose in nylon tricot .. then outdoors she'll add her rich blue velveteen cape and hood with decorative front. Matching blue heels, hanger. Doll not incl.
Shipping weight 4 oz.
49 N 3950......$2.77

11 Ken a-Go-Go. Your Ken is ready for fun in a black "Beatle" wig; guitar and microphone. Outfit includes brightly striped shirt with red sleeves and collar. Gold-color twill slacks, red socks; white tennis shoes. Doll not incl.
Shipping weight 4 oz.
49 N 3699......$2.57

1 Fur-Out. Go-go gaiters and fake-fur coat plus hood, mittens, stockings, shoes, hanger.
49 N 3941—Wt. 4 oz. $2.69

2 Gad-abouts. Sweater, skirt, hose. Hat, sunglasses.
49 N 3942—Wt. 3 oz. $1.67

3 Go Granny, Go. Long shift, flats. Phono, record.
49 N 3944—Wt. 4 oz. $1.74

4 It's a Date. Hi-waisted dress, textured hose. Shoes.
49 N 3943—Wt. 4 oz. $1.69

5 Polka Dots 'n Raindrops. Plastic coat with zip pockets, kerchief. Boots.
49 N 3945—Wt. 3 oz. $1.77

6 Leather Limelight. Mix and match the floral tricot blouse, skirt, boots with vinyl capris, skirt, hood, flats.
49 N 3946—Wt. 4 oz. $2.69

7 Clam Diggers. Vinyl jacket, hat. Knit top, stretch pants, shoes, sunglasses.
49 N 3948—Wt. 5 oz. $2.44

8 First Formal. Long gown, ruffled cape. Gloves, shoes.
49 N 3949—Wt. 5 oz. $2.39

9 Dance Party. Dress, hat. Slip, hose, shoes. Records, player, parfait, spoon, napkin.
49 N 3947—Wt. 5 oz. $2.37

NOTE: Dolls not included with clothing above.

Sports Car $2.87

Plastic body with sparkling chrome-color fittings, clear windshield and bucket seats. Rubber-like tires, steel axle. 7½x18 in. No doll incl. Wt. 2 lbs. 1 oz.
49 N 9320......$2.87

KIDDLE CITY

The original home of all the Kiddles.. made exclusively for Sears by Mattel

A self-contained Kiddle kaboodle of 3-dimensional homes, parks, playground, with Lola, Florence, Babe and Bunson Burnie . . all the play excitement of Liddle Kiddleland, plus a tote for visiting

5-piece gift set $17⁹⁹

Kiddle City only $9⁸⁸

Open vinyl case to waken Kiddles for hours of sliding, riding, working and rollicking good times. Close it and carry it like a suitcase. Set consists of 4 Kiddles and case that's a big 22x14x8 in. high so there's room for more Kiddles.

5-pc. Gift Set. Wt. 6 lbs.
79 N 3683 . . . . $17.99
Kiddle City only. Wt. 4 lbs.
79 N 9339C $9.88

Separate Kiddles

These Kiddles are 3 to 3½ inches tall with fully bendable vinyl torsos, brushes, combs, rooted hair.
Shipping wt. each 5 oz.

1 Lola Liddle. Comes with own floating sailboat.
49 N 3686 . . . . $2.27

2 Florence Niddle. Wheels baby in buggy.
49 N 3687 . . . . $2.27

3 Babe Biddle in her car.
49 N 3688 . . . . . $2.27

4 Bunson Burnie. With plastic fire engine.
49 N 3690 . . . . $2.27

Kiddles Gift Set $4⁹⁷

When they dine, Greta Griddle shares her 3-piece dinette set and her dishes with Howard "Biff" Boodle. So "Biff" always lets Greta use his wagon and sandbox as the two play together in this Kiddles set. Vinyl. 3 to 3½ in. figures.
49 N 3684—Shpg. wt. 1 lb. . . . . Set $4.97

Only at Sears

Beat-A-Diddle $2²⁷

A swingin' little singer all dressed for the stage and ready to entertain you. This 3-in. high Kiddle even brings her own microphone and guitar. Rooted hair can be combed and brushed. Vinyl. Like everything else in Sears books, it's so easy to order by phone.
49 N 3685—Shpg. wt. 5 oz. $2.27

Liddle Diddle $2²⁷

Littlest Kiddle of all . . just 2¾ in. tall. Bendable. Vinyl. Sides of crib slide up and down.
49 N 3691—Shpg. wt. 5 oz. $2.27

Kiddle Klub House $2⁹⁹

Compact vinyl Klub House furnished and decorated inside and out. 12x9x6 inches so many Kiddles can meet here. Wt. 1 lb. 7 oz.
49 N 9338 . . $2.99

LASSIE

Big shaggy pal for the child who wants a play-dog of his very own

$7⁸⁹

Re-live beloved Lassie's brave TV adventures. This play-pet seems almost alive. Realistic detailing, fine craftsmanship. About 21 in. long . . dependable, always friendly. Brown and white . . shaggy long-pile plush acrylic body . . flocked vinyl head.
79 N 4187C—Shipping weight 4 pounds.......................$7.89

Zippy squeaks like a live chimp set for fun

$5⁸⁹

Champ chimp is dressed for play . . red corduroy pants, jaunty red-and-white felt hat. Shoes, hands, face, ears are wipe-clean vinyl. Hand-painted face. Body of curly black rayon plush, cotton filled. 16 in. tall. Buy it the easy way—order by phone. Wt. 2 lbs.
49 N 4088....$5.89

Honey Bear . . 19 inches tall . . soft extra-deep plush

$3¹⁹

1 Cute black-felt nose and eyelashes, big brown locked-in eyes make this cuddly fellow an appealing crib pal for tots, bed decoration for teens. Rayon plush. Cotton filled.
49 N 4133—Shpg. wt. 2 lbs...$3.19

Baby Buddies . . 13½ in. tall . . neatly clipped plush

$1⁹⁹ each

Shiny plastic eyes, soft vinyl muzzle. Fine rayon plush. Stuffed with cotton, foam plastic . . so soft and squeezy.

2 Baby Bear. Delightfully brown.
49 N 4102—Wt. 1 lb. 3 oz..$1.99

3 Baby Panda. Perky black, white.
49 N 4126—Wt. 1 lb. 3 oz..$1.99

4 $7⁹⁴   **5** $4⁸⁹

Muppets . . a dog and a frog with mouths that move, bodies of cuddly soft plush

4 Rowlf Dog. Lovable little canine . . floppy ears, funny eyes, a big nose, and an even bigger grin. Stuffed to roly-poly size with cotton, polyurethane. 19 in. tall. Brown.
49 N 4011—Shipping weight 1 lb. 12 oz...........$7.94

5 Kermit Frog. Green is the color of this fanciful frog . . and he sports a bright red rayon plush turtle-neck sweater. Stuffed with cotton, polyurethane. Workable arms. 20 in. tall.
49 N 4020—Shipping weight 1 lb. 2 oz............$4.89

ANIMAL TALK

Just pull the CHATTY-RING® and these talkative toys speak up. They're cute, cuddly . . need no batteries

6 Bugs Bunny. Famous rabbit-rascal is 24 in. tall from his pink ears to his fur-look toes. Vinyl face. Rayon plush. Cotton stuffed. Gray, white.
49 N 4122—Wt. 2 lbs. 2 oz.$7.69

7 Tom and Jerry. A tricky pair. 19-in. stuffed corduroy cat, vinyl face; detachable vinyl mouse.
49 N 4186—Wt. 2 lbs. 2 oz.$7.69

8 Larry the Lion. Honey-colored "king of the jungle" moves his mouth as he growls 11 phrases. Rayon plush over molded foam. He's gentle as a lamb.
49 N 4095—Wt. 4 lbs..$11.99

9 Bernie Bernard. Moves mouth, yodels, says many things. Has pink-lined stay-put ears. Vinyl muzzle, collar. Rayon plush. 13 inch. Wt. 3 lbs.
49 N 4185.........$11.99

10 Biff Bear. Moves mouth, says 11 "bearish" things. Colorful on-off sweater. Vinyl head. Stuffed rayon plush body. 14 in. tall.
49 N 4099—Shipping weight 3 lbs...................$9.99

Dolls seemed to go back to babyhood in the 1967 Christmas Wishbook pages. There were lots of new dolls to compete with Barbie, yet none of them could or would ever beat her in sales and excitement.

Mattel's Baby Walk'N See and Baby Step were the new techno-dolls available at a pricey $11.99 and $16.99. With eyes that looked around as they walked, the dolls were each 18-inches high.

Singin' Chatty Cathy, a new 17-inch version of the popular doll, could sing such classics as "Farmer in the Dell" or "Row, Row, Row Your Boat" with a quick pull of her Magic Ring. She could be had for $9.99.

Mod fashions continued to be popular and lots of dolls had mini-skirts and go-go boots as standard equipment.

Space travel was in the news and on TV. Such hit shows as "Star Trek", "Lost in Space" and "The Jetsons" pulled huge audiences of all ages. So it is no wonder Sears debuted Mini-Martians, little 4 1/2-inch aliens to compete with Kiddles. Professor Pook, Marti, Mini and the gang from Carnaby Comet zoomed around outer space in jet cars and space scooters. However, the concept never made it to the next Wishbook.

Sears Christmas
Wishbook
1967

"Look-around" eyes move when she walks

MATTEL'S BABY STEP

ONLY AT SEARS MATTEL'S NEW BABY WALK'N SEE

The li'l' darling who walks by herself
What fun! She roller skates, too

Sold only at Sears **$11⁹⁹** without batteries

Babystep takes each little step carefully all by herself. Just by turning her hidden switch, you'll send her walking or skating—balloon in hand—all the way across the room. Plastic, 18 in. tall with rooted, synthetic hair. Non-scuff roller skates are included. Uses 2 "D" batteries, order 1 pkg. at bottom of page.
49 N 3019—Shipping wt. 3 lbs. 10 oz.. $11.99

3-outfit Wardrobe for Babystep and Baby Walk'n See

$2⁹⁹ Set

Darling little outfits in this set include pajamas, sunsuit, party dress, comb, mirror. Shipping wt. 8 oz.
49 N 3074. Set $2.99

Dolls that walk along with you hand-in-hand

WALKING DOLLS

She walks all by herself and roller skates, too

Without batteries **$16⁹⁹**

Baby Walk 'n' See is a fast stepping toddler whose measured steps begin with just a turn of her hidden switch. Her "look-around" eyes seem to really see as they move up, down and from side to side as she walks. A perky bow tops her curly blonde rooted hair. Plastic, 18 in. high. Dressed in pinafore-type white peek-a-boo eyelet dress with bright pink lining. Balloon not incl. Uses 2 "D" batteries. Order 1 pkg. below.
49 N 3037—Shipping weight 3 lbs. 10 oz.... $16.99
49 N 4660—"D" Batteries. (2) Wt. 8 oz. Pkg. 36c

26-inch Walker $6⁷⁹

Take her hand and lead your sweet little friend for a walk. Lovely, bright-eyed Annette has rooted, silky-soft blonde hair. Her eyes open and close. "Mod" outfit with harlequin-textured mod stockings and Mary-jane shoes. Plastic jointed body.
79N3254C—Wt. 3 lbs.$6.79

19-inch Walker $4⁹⁹

This sloe-eyed beauty will walk with you as you hold her hand. Lustrous, thick black hair is rooted. Plum and fuschia jacket, matching slacks. Thickly lashed eyes open and close. Vinyl head, plastic, full-jointed body.
Shpg. wt. 1 lb. 10 oz.
49 N 3253 .... $4.99

16-inch Walker $3⁹⁹

This fair-haired toddler needs someone to walk with her. Her eyes open and close. She wears the latest 'A' line shift. Vinyl head with silky-soft long rooted hair that you'll love to 'set' for her. Jointed arms and legs; plastic body.
Shipping weight 1 lb. 6 oz.
49 N 3187 ....$3.99

Your fashionable friend, Carol is 16 inches tall . . fully jointed

$4⁷⁹

1 Perky doll in colorful green and yellow pinafore. Her open-and-close eyes have long and curly eyelashes. Rooted hair. Vinyl body.
49 N 3255—Shipping weight 1 pound 14 ounces..............$4.79

Fashionable Outfits for Carol $1⁶⁹ to $1⁹⁹

2 Yellow cotton suedette coat with orange wool trim. Matching hat. Wt. 5 oz.
49 N 3256 . . . $1.69

3 A-line dress of orange cotton suedette with pleated trim. Shpg. wt. 5 oz.
49 N 3258 . . . . $1.69

4 Mandarin lounging pajamas. Chic white quilted top over black velvet pants. Wt. 5 oz.
49 N 3257 . . . $1.99

NOTE: Doll, shoes, socks not included with outfits above.

Cute baby face

16-inch toddler $6⁹⁹

This darling baby-faced toddler has creamy-smooth complexion, go-to-sleep eyes and a dimple in her chin. Outfitted in a white nylon party dress over baby pink lace-trimmed taffeta slip and panties. She has rooted blonde hair topped with a pink bow. Fully jointed vinyl.
49 N 3259—Wt. 1 lb. 6 oz..$6.99

Mattel's Singin' Chatty "Sing along with me."

17-inch Vocalist $9⁹⁹

Pull the Chatty-Ring® and hear the sweetest voice ever sing your favorite songs. You'll never know which song will be next . . it might be "Farmer in the Dell" or "Row, Row, Row Your Boat" or another happy song. Plastic, fully jointed body with rooted hair, moving eyes.
49 N 3518—Wt. 3 lbs $9.99

Christina

An 18-inch Italian Doll with real-look eyelashes

5 Beautifully detailed with silver blonde rooted hair and pale blue open-and-close eyes. Geometric print dress, matching headband. Patent-look shoes. Fully jointed vinyl body. (Pennant not included).
49 N 3461—Wt. 2 lbs..... $7.99

Outfits for Christina

6 Textured woven suit with double-breasted jacket, covered buttons. Skirt has attached white blouse. Mesh hose, scarf. Hanger.
49 N 3463—Wt. 6 oz...... $3.99

7 Textured jacket, fully lined . . knit collar, patch pockets. Plaid cuffed slacks; red socks. Hanger.
49 N 3462—Wt. 6 oz..... $3.99

8 Double-breasted "mod" coat . . vinyl, full lining, covered buttons and matching "mod" boots. Hanger.
49 N 3464—Wt. 6 oz..... $4.99

9 Silver-colored lamé mini-dress . . fully lined . . with matching hip-belt and zippered vinyl boots. Hanger.
49 N 3465—Wt. 5 oz..... $4.99

Note: Doll and pennant not included with outfits, (6) thru (9)

$7⁹⁹

mini-martians

From up above the sky so high came the MINI-MARTIANS "pinky" high

Professor Pook   Marti   Mini

Bonnie   Meri   Teenie

Mini-Martians $1.49 each

Futuristic sprites a mere 4½ inches tall. They'll take you to their world above where make-believe is so much fun. Made of soft vinyl, their arms and head move. Comb and wash their rooted hair. Remove boots for barefoot space walks. Dressed in supersonic styles. From Japan. Collect all 6 and have your own Mini-Martian community.

49N3246—**Prof. Pook.** Painted glasses. Wt. 3 oz. . $1.49
49N3247—**Marti.** Space lad. Shpg. wt. 3 oz. . . . 1.49
49N3248—**Mini.** In silver-color cape. Wt. 3 oz. . . 1.49
49N3249—**Bonnie.** In lunar sarong. Wt. 3 oz. . . . 1.49
49N3250—**Meri.** In solar shift. Shpg. wt. 3 oz. . . 1.49
49N3251—**Teenie.** In cosmic tent dress. Wt. 3 oz. . 1.49

$2.99

Jet Car for jaunts from star to star

Two Mini-Martians can take a trip in this round car. Clear plastic dome top lets them see everything along the way. Made of molded plastic . . 7½ in. long. Travels on three wheels. Mini-Martians not included.
49 N 9208 – Shipping weight 1 pound $2.99

Offered nowhere in the universe but at Sears

Martian Star House
$3.99

Far beyond earth's bustling pace Mini-Martians dwell at ease

Zooming around in "outer space", Mini-Martians live and play. Nestled among the stars and comets . . a home so streamlined, all their own. Brightly colored outside and in. Space car parks on terrace platform.

Two elevated bunks for sleeping. Video scanner to check on pals. All furnishings vacuum formed. Vinyl house closes for visits to "other planets" . . 15½x5x9 in.
49 N 9203 – Shpg. wt. 2 lbs. 14 oz. .$3.99

Mini-Martians not included with Star House

"Carnaby Comet" Clothes for Mini-Martians

Two outfits in each space-age set.

1 Star Time Togs. For all the Mini-Martian girls. Bright colored stripes . . one tent dress and hostess pajamas.
49 N 3296–Shpg. wt. 3 oz. . . Set 98c

2 Zoom Suits. Just the thing when the girls take the scooter for a spin. Each dress has matching helmet.
49 N 3297–Shpg. wt. 3 oz. . . Set 98c

3 Stellar Shifts. Just meant for special parties. Gold-color dress has gold-color headband. Blue dress has star trimmed headpiece.
49 N 3298–Shpg. wt. 3 oz. . . Set 98c

4 Lunar Leisure Wear. For lounging, games of star tag. Yellow, red jumper, headband. Blue, white jumper.
49 N 3299–Shpg. wt. 3 oz. . . Set 98c

5 Galaxy Garb. For Marti or Professor Pook. Full cape for cold weather, short jacket and helmet for scooter rides.
49 N 3292–Shpg. wt. 3 oz. . . Set 98c

6 Jet Jumpers. Professor Pook wears them, Marti can too. Silver-color is ever so dashing for Martian parties.
49 N 3293–Shpg. wt. 3 oz. . . Set 98c

Dolls not included with above outfit sets

Sporty Space Scooter for errands on the run

$1.99

One Mini-Martian drives this scooter for trips to a "meteor grocery" or "lunar laundromat". It's great for just buzzing around in, too. Made of molded plastic, about 8 inches long. Runs on 3 wheels. Has clear plastic windshield. Mini-Martian not included with space scooter. So easy to buy when you just use the phone.
49 N 9247 – Wt. 12 oz. . . .$1.99

When a little girl is growing up
a doll to love can mean so much
a doll to hug and share a dream...

And when the girl is all grown up
she has a treasure rare
a host of happy memories
that girl and doll have shared.

Baby Cuddles..

Just meant to be held
in coat soft as pussy willow . . snuggle her tight

1 Eyes bright with wonder, cheeks kissed by sun . . she
loves going anywhere with you in raspberry rayon
fleece coat . . matching bonnet, muff trimmed in white
rayon fleece. Under coat she wears dainty crepe dress,
panties . . lace trimmed. Satin shoes, socks. 18-in. kapok
filled body fits right in your arms. Soft vinyl legs, arms,
head. Comb her glossy rooted hair. Eyes close at end of day.
49 N 3092—Shipping weight 2 lbs. 6 oz.........$9.99

2 Party Dress. For special outings. Crisp white organdy
with rows of lace, ribbon bow. Lacy pink slip, panties.
49 N 3095—Shipping weight 11 ounces......$3.99

3 Sleepytime Outfit. Print flannelette pajamas. Cotton
fleeced white robe with flannelette binding.
49 N 3093—Shipping weight 1 lb. 4 oz.........$3.99

4 Pretty Playsuit. Scalloped velveteen top with white
cotton collar, sleeves. Long white jersey tights.
49 N 3094—Shipping weight 10 ounces.......$3.99

NOTE: *Doll, hair ribbons, shoes and socks not included
with outfits (2), (3), (4).*

"I SAY MAMA"

tee-hee
tee-hee
tee-hee

Stick on a funny face, press her hands together . . GIGGLES laughs and laughs and so will you

Only at Sears . .
GIGGLES
with Funny Kit
$9.99

This little moppet will tickle you silly. She cocks her head, rolls her bright blue eyes, giggles, giggles and giggles. With funny kit she's a real ham wearing kookie sun glasses, nose, eyebrows and smiles made of adhesive felt. Elfin face framed by long blonde hair to wash and comb. 18-inch vinyl body. She wears bright mod knit and sandals.
49 N 3140—Shipping wt. 3 lbs. 4 oz......$9.99

Baby Precious

Snuggles against your shoulder . . tilt her slightly, hear her say Mama

$4.99

1 So cuddly you'll just want to hold her always. She has a soft shredded foam body and vinyl legs, arms and head. Her bright blue eyes really close and her rooted hair is caught with a bow. She wears a perky pink poplin dress with embossed velveteen pinafore and knit booties. She's 17 in. tall.
49 N 3101—Shipping weight 2 pounds 1 ounce..$4.99

2 **Dreamy Bunting.** Taffeta jacket . . lace trimmed. Blanket.
49 N 3107—Shipping weight 8 ounces........$1.97

3 **Pajamas.** Two-piece flannel . . print top, solid bottoms.
49 N 3102—Shipping weight 6 ounces........$1.97

4 **Party Dress.** So frilly . . yellow nylon trimmed with lace.
49 N 3103—Shipping weight 6 ounces........$1.97
Doll not included with outfits (2), (3), (4)

Oh so pretty baby says Mama and Papa
$7.99

"MAMA" "PAPA"

5 Straight from the stork's bundle . . this sweet cherub. Tilt her forward then backward to say Mama then Papa. Rooted hair. Soft body filled with shredded foam . . chubby arms, legs. Go-to-sleep eyes. 20 in. tall. Pleated nylon and polished cotton christening dress . . pillow. Panties, booties.
79N3079C-Shpg.wt.4lbs.$7.99

SNUGGLEBUN
and her $9.99
PLAYALL 6

Baby Snugglebun . . a darling doll. Pick her up, she says "Mama". You can comb her rooted hair . . eyes open and close. 15 in. tall, fully jointed plastic. She wears gay striped dress. Her Playall 6 can be a swing, playpen, stroller, highchair, rocker, car seat. Colorful plastic. 13x13x16 in. Unassembled.
79 N 3059C—Shipping weight 7 pounds . . .$9.99

Playtime and Sleeptime Clothes for 10 to 21-inch Dolls

6 Dollies often need new clothes . . like this 3-outfit set for dress and playtime. Dress, coat and bonnet plus 2-pc. playsuit. Dress all your dolls alike for fun.

49 N 3472–For 10-11 in. Wt. 11 oz.	$3.99
49 N 3473–For 12-13 in. Wt. 12 oz.	3.99
49 N 3474–For 14-15 in. Wt. 13 oz.	3.99
49 N 3475–For 16-17 in. Wt. 15 oz.	4.99
49 N 3476–For 18-19 in. Wt. 1 lb.	4.99
49 N 3477–20-21 in. Wt. 1 lb. 1 oz.	4.99

7 Soft, snuggle clothes for dolly's naps or creeping. 3-outfit set includes coverall and bonnet, three-piece sacque, two-piece bunting outfit.

49 N 3478–For 10-11 in. Wt. 11 oz.	$3.99
49 N 3479–For 12-13 in. Wt. 12 oz.	3.99
49 N 3480–For 14-15 in. Wt. 13 oz.	3.99
49 N 3481–For 16-17 in. Wt. 15 oz.	4.99
49 N 3484–For 18-19 in. Wt. 1 lb.	4.99
49 N 3485–20-21 in. Wt. 1 lb. 1 oz.	4.99

Only at Sears . . Mattel's "Baby's Hungry" with Feed and Carry Case plus 9-piece Wardrobe

Her mouth moves . . she chews "food" or sucks on her bottle. And her eyes look all around

$15⁸⁸
without batteries

Baby's really hungry. Put spoon in her mouth, then withdraw it . . she actually chews. Give her a "magic" bottle . . milk disappears as she nurses. Give her feeding bottle . . she drinks, then wets.

She's 17 inches . . jointed vinyl with rooted hair. A polka dot clear plastic bib wipes clean when she dribbles. Plus a frilly cap, diaper and booties.

Vinyl carry case opens to a feeding chair with tray, sun awning and plastic accessory pouch. Dish has pretend carrots, peas, soup. For other outings, dress Baby's Hungry in cotton dress, poplin coat and bonnet or flannel sleeper. Hanger, rattle, bracelet, 2 cookies, too. Uses 2 "D" batteries, order 1 package below.
49 N 3568—Shipping weight 5 lbs. 2 oz. . . . . Set $15.88

"D" Batteries. Package of 2.
49 N 4660—Wt. 8 oz. Pkg. 36c

Baby's Hungry only. Uses 2 "D" batteries, order package above.
49 N 3315—Wt. 3 lbs. 10 oz. $10.97

Feed and Carry Case only.
49 N 9318—Wt. 1 lb. 8 oz. . $4.99

9-piece Wardrobe Set only.
49 N 3471—Wt. 8 oz. Set $2.99

$10⁹⁷
without batteries

SPLISH-SPLASH

TUBSY'S in her bath . . she slaps the water with both her hands and turns her head from side to side

No baby loves a bath more than Tubsy. Fill her vinyl tub with water, bubble bath, too . . when it reaches her tummy she'll start to splash. Take her out . . in diaper and terrycloth robe, she's ready for a nap. Eyes close. Rooted hair you can wash and comb. Tubsy is 18 in. tall, vinyl. Two "D" batteries (order 79 N 4660 below) tucked safe and dry within her body make her splash.
79 N 3318C—Shpg. wt. 6 lbs. $10.97

"D" Batteries. Package of 2.
79 N 4660—Shpg. wt. 8 oz. . . . . . . Pkg. 36c

CRAWLING BABY . . into everything, when she stops she calls "Mama"

1 In terrycloth creeper set and cap. Crawling Baby looks so real. Flick tiny switch, she crawls forward, stops when she reaches an obstacle and says "Mama." Then starts again. 16-in. metal and plastic body, soft vinyl head and arms. Order two "D" batteries, below.
49 N 3312—Shipping weight 2 lbs. . . . $5.88

"D" Batteries. Package of 2.
49 N 4660—Shpg. wt. 8 oz. . . . . Pkg. 36c

Just like a real baby . . TINY THUMBELINA squirms and stretches on her back or tummy

2 Just wind the key in her back, her soft cloth body moves like a baby learning to crawl. So cuddly . . vinyl arms, legs, head. Rooted hair. Tiny Thumbelina wears a dear pink crepe dress, booties. She's bound to bring out the mommy in every little girl. 14 in. tall.
49 N 3088—Shpg. wt. 1 lb. 14 oz. $7.99

1 **$5⁸⁸**
without batteries

BABY DOLLS that do things

$7⁹⁹
2

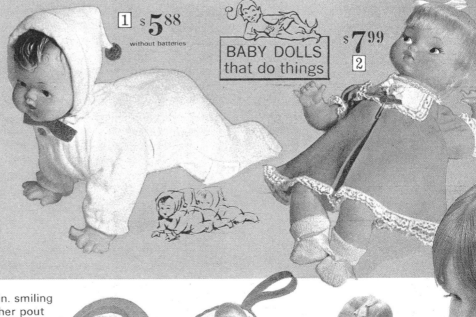

Mattel's New Baby Cheerful Tearful 6-in. smiling imp . . but press her tummy and see her pout

Only at Sears **$4⁹⁹**
in case with nightie

Such a cutie . . smiles with glee. But just press her tummy, vinyl palm-size personality frowns, makes crying noise as real tear trickles down her cheek. Drinks from her bottle, wets. Rooted hair. Wears pink cotton dress, pants, booties. Fits right in oval carry case with frilly nightie.
49 N 3309—Doll in case. Shpg. wt. 1 lb. 4 oz. $4.99
49 N 3308—Doll only. Shpg. wt. 12 oz. 2.99

Lil Sweetie

steals your heart away.
Feels so REAL..
looks so REAL..
even drinks and
wets like a
REAL BABY

$9⁹⁹

This lovable, realistic-looking infant drinks from her own little bottle. Then she'll wet her didy. Lil Sweetie is all soft vinyl and fully jointed. Her soft, blonde baby hair is rooted, can be brushed or combed. She comes in a long christening gown with lace and embroidered rosettes. Sweater, cap and booties are hand-crocheted. Pillow trimmed with embroidery, organdy ruffle. 18 in. tall.
49 N 3160—Wt. 2 lbs. 10 oz.$9.99

Three different outfits

1 **Bunting Outfit.** Take Lil Sweetie for an outing in this warm blanket, jacket and cap. All are trimmed with lovely satin binding.
49 N 3287—Shpg. wt. 12 oz. .$3.99

2 **Robe.** Made of soft printed flannelette to keep Lil Sweetie warm after her daily nap.
49 N 3286—Shpg. wt. 10 oz.$1.99

3 **Bath Towel.** White terry cloth. Has its own hood to keep Lil Sweetie warm after a bath. Shell stitch trim.
49 N 3285—Shpg. wt. 10 oz.$1.19

NOTE: Doll not included with outfits.

Barbie still drew most of the attention in the 1968 Sears Wishbook, targeted primarily to teens and pre-teens. However, lots of other dolls were purchased for much younger girls and baby dolls ruled that arena.

Baby Precious, a simple doll at 17-inches tall, was available as a Black or Caucasian infant for $4.99. This proved that battery-operated, transistorized models were not always necessary to please a child.

Dy-Dee Baby came wrapped in soft bunting and bows. She drank, wet and cooed. You could even get the Dy-Dee Bunting Twins for $9.99.

Other baby dolls debuting in 1968 included Dearest One ("more like a newborn baby than any of our other drink 'n wet dolls"), Little Lost Baby, a 22-inch doll that changed expressions from happy to sad at the flip of a hidden switch, and Randi Reader who could talk for a full seven minutes and knew 15 rhymes. Her eyes moved as she read from her own book.

All-time favorite Betsy Wetsy returned, this time in 11 1/2-inch and 17-inch sizes, along with accessories including tub, crib and tote bag.

Sears Christmas
Wishbook
1968

BABY PRECIOUS

A winsome heart-stealer just waiting to be cuddled

(1 and 2) So soft and caressable. Vinyl legs, arms and head. Her rooted hair is caught with a bright bow. Bright eyes really close. She stands 17 inches tall. Shipping weight 2 pounds 2 ounces.

1 All dressed up in a perky checked play-dress with lace-trimmed pinafore and booties.
49 N 30216......$4.99

2 She wears a gossamer-sheer nylon dress with ribbon and lace trim. Comes with cozy, warm booties.
49 N 30215.......$4.99

Either Doll
$4.99

BABY DOLLS

Enchanting outfits for Baby Precious

3 Soft, cozy 3-piece bunting set. Lace-trimmed sacque, panties, and jacket with hood. Shipping wt. 12 oz.
49 N 30217.... $2.19

4 Luxurious fleece coat with lace-trimmed collar and bonnet. Shipping wt. 10 oz.
49 N 30218.... $2.19
NOTE: Dolls not included.

⑤ $8.99

Newborn Pixie says "Mama" and "Papa"

5 New arrival has white rooted hair that's swirled into a top curl. Tilt her and she'll call out for mama and papa. Soft body . . chubby vinyl arms and legs. 20 inches tall. Wears a long, frilly pleated christening dress. Pillow, panties, booties.
79 N 30219C—Shpg. wt. 3 lbs......$8.99

Baby rests in a quilted sleeping bag that opens into a blanket

6 She cries out softly to be cradled in your arms. Soft, blonde rooted hair; vinyl body, arms and legs filled with virgin kapok. Go-to-sleep eyes. 16 inches tall. Wears white pajamas and carries her own teddy bear. Unzip the quilted sleeping bag for a coverlet.
49 N 30213—Shpg. wt. 2 lbs. 10 oz...$8.99

"WAAA" ⑥ $8.99

Playtime and sleepytime sets for 10 to 21-inch dolls

For Playtime
Perky 2-pc. playsuit; dress and coat with bonnets.
49 N 30224—For 10–11 in. dolls. Wt. 11 oz..$3.99
49 N 30225—For 12–13 in. dolls. Wt. 12 oz.... 3.99
49 N 30226—For 14–15 in. dolls. Wt. 13 oz.... 3.99
49 N 30227—For 16–17 in. dolls. Wt. 15 oz.... 4.99
49 N 30228—For 18–19 in. dolls. Wt. 1 lb.... 4.99
49 N 30229—For 20–21 in. dolls. Wt. 1 lb. 1 oz. 4.99

For Sleepytime
Snuggly pajamas; lace-trimmed playsuit and diaper set with matching bonnets.
49 N 30231—For 10–11 in. Wt. 11 oz.$3.99
49 N 30232—For 12–13 in. Wt. 12 oz. 3.99
49 N 30233—For 14–15 in. Wt. 13 oz. 3.99
49 N 30234—For 16–17 in. Wt. 15 oz. 4.99
49 N 30235—For 18–19 in. Wt. 1 lb.. 4.99
49 N 30236—For 20–21 in. Wt. 1 lb. 1 oz. 4.99

Vinyl-covered Trunk

Keeps doll and her clothes in place

Sturdy wood frame, plastic handle. Hangers included. 16x9x8 inches. 1 drawer.
49 N 92047—Wt. 4 lbs. 8 oz.....$4.99

Same as above but 2 drawers, 20x10x9 in.
79 N 92048C—Shpg. wt. 6 lbs.... $5.99

1 $5.99

Miss Peep coos when you hug her

1 She makes baby cooing sounds when you press her body and arms. 16½ in. tall, made of soft vinyl with real-looking molded hair. You can even take her in the tub with you. Dressed in kimono, diaper and booties all trimmed with pink satin bows. There's even a fluffy blanket to wrap her in.
49 N 30238—Wt. 2 lbs. 3 oz. $5.99

Laugh along with Baby Giggles

3 This curlyhead just chuckles with glee when you move her left arm up and down. She moves her head from side to side, rolls her eyes and giggles merrily. All vinyl with rooted saran curls. Wears a sporty play outfit with matching panties and vinyl sandals. 15 inches tall.
Shipping weight 2 lbs. 14 oz.
49 N 3024 . . . . $8.97

2 $9.99

Darling Baby Boy with a take-me-home smile

2 A little boy for your doll family . . a brother to love and care for. Has pale blonde rooted hair and long-lashed, go-to-sleep eyes. Jointed vinyl body, 17 in. tall. Two baby teeth show through his grin. Wears a 2-piece suit and soft kid booties. Imported from Italy.
Shipping weight 2 pounds.
49 N 30109 . . . . $9.99

Cuddly charmer drinks and wets like a real baby

4 She looks so sweet in her lace-trimmed percale dress you'll want to take her everywhere. Bright eyes peep out from under her frilly bonnet, and close when you tilt her. Rooted hair. Vinyl body, completely washable and fully jointed. 12 in. tall. She carries a polyethylene nursing bottle.
49 N 30239—Wt. 1 lb. 4 oz. $2.99

3 $8.97 $2.99 4

TEE-HEE TEE-HEE

Susan loves drinking her bottle while she rides in her stroller

$5.99 set

Susan is a drink and wet doll who likes to go for a stroll . . and you'll love taking her. You can push her in a sturdy molded plastic stroller . . has a row of colorful play beads. Wears a knit outfit with matching cap. Curly rooted hair, open and close eyes. Soft, jointed vinyl body, 16 inches tall. She's carrying her bottle, waiting to be fed.
49 N 3110—Shipping weight 3 lbs. Set $5.99

DY-DEE BABY

A bundle of softness that coos with delight when you snuggle her . . drinks and wets, too

$5.99

Enchanting Dy-Dee Baby is wrapped in a cozy, soft bunting and sacque. Bunting and hood are trimmed daintily with pink shell stitching. Her sparkling blue eyes look up at you lovingly. She has a fully jointed, all vinyl body with molded light brown hair. Drinks from her own bottle. 14 inches tall, just the right size to cuddle.
49 N 30237—Shipping weight 1 lb. 5 oz. $5.99

"COO" "COO"

AND INTRODUCING the adorable Dy-Dee Bunting Twins

This darling pair drink, wet, and coo. Bunting bag has shell-stitch trim. Matching jackets and hoods over flannel robes and diapers. 14 in. tall, fully jointed all vinyl. Molded hair. Bottles included.
49 N 30199—Shpg. wt. 2 lbs. 8 oz. $9.99

Washable
DRINK 'N WET DOLLS

Pose her as you please

③ 17-inch high Betsy with accessories **$10⁹⁹**

Betsy Wetsy

④ Tote Bag **$1⁹⁹**

⑤ 11½-inch high Betsy with layette **$8⁹⁹**

$8⁹⁷

Dearest One .. so cuddly soft and flexible,
she's more like a newborn baby than
any of our other drink 'n wet dolls

Fine, carefully-detailed features make her so realistic and lovable .. made of skin-soft vinyl from head to toe. Dearest One drinks from her own little bottle, then wets her diaper like a real baby. You can comb her baby-fine rooted hair. When she sleeps her eyes close. Dressed in cotton piqué topper trimmed with lace and embroidery, stretch rhumba leotards and matching bonnet. 19 inches tall.
49 N 30185—Shipping weight 2 pounds 10 ounces.................$8.97

③ 17-inch Betsy. Dressed in her "polka dot and posy" sleeping gown, she's waiting to be rocked to sleep in her plastic cradle. Made of soft vinyl with movable arms and legs. Drinks, wets and cries real tears. Her rooted hair can be washed, combed, brushed.
  Comes complete with polka dot blanket, bottle, pacifier and bubble pipe that really works.
79 N 30249C—Wt. 7 lbs. $10.99

④ Tote Bag. Vinyl. Use as lunch bag too. 9x4¾x7 in. high.
49 N 92049—Wt. 1 lb.....$1.99

⑤ 11½-inch Betsy. Dressed in shower cap and diaper, Betsy plays in plastic shoofly waiting for bath in her plastic tub. She has soap, wash cloth and a bubble pipe to play with that really works.
  Made of soft vinyl with movable arms and legs. She drinks from her bottle, wets her diaper and cries too. Just like a real baby she has her own "polka dot and posy" layette .. includes receiving blanket, flannel saque, kimono, bib, vinyl panties, rattle, pacifier and comb to style her rooted hair.
49 N 30248—Wt. 3 lbs. . $8.99

Randi Reader talks for a full 7 minutes
Have fun reading and learning nursery rhymes with her

① Randi, books and chair **$15⁸⁸** without batteries

1 Dressed like a schoolgirl, she sits in her upholstered vinyl chair and recites 15 full-length rhymes. Her eyes move as she "reads" from her book .. and you follow in yours. Move Randi's arms to any other position and she starts 15 long conversations. 19½ in. tall, strong plastic. Starts by slight push on back—uses 2 "D" batteries, order pkg. below.
79 N 30246C2—Shipping weight 6 pounds.......$15.88
49 N 4660—"D" Batteries. Pkg. of 2. Wt. 8 oz... Pkg. 38

8-pc. Wardrobe for Randi Reader

2 Consists of dress, playtop with skirt and matching pants. Comb, mirror, hangers. Shipping wt. 7 oz.
49 N 30245 . . . $2.99

$11⁸⁸ without battery

Little Lost Baby

Huggable, 22-inch doll changes expressions by moving a concealed switch on the back of her neck

Head rotates from sleeping expression to crying and she cries an authentic baby-cry. Flick the switch again and her head turns to show a laughing face, complete with cooing and babbling. Vinyl face, hands, stuffed cloth body. In unremovable snowsuit with hood. Takes 1 "C" battery, order pkg. below.
79N30207C-Wt. 4 lbs. $11.88

"C" Batteries. Package of 2.
49N4665-Wt. 4 oz. Pkg. 38c

cries real tears
Even her head moves side to side

9 17-inch tall Tiny Tears
$10⁹⁹

8 12-inch tall Tiny Tears
$8⁴⁹

Tiny Tears Boutique

. . There's just the right size Tiny Tears for every little mother. Each one is looking for someone to feed her, change her diaper and wipe her eyes when she cries real tears

6 9-inch tall Betsy Wetsy with accessories
$4⁹⁹

7 9-inch tall Tiny Tears
$6⁴⁹

7 **9-inch Tiny Tears.** She's the littlest, but every delicate detail makes her as lovely as can be. Made of satin-soft, washable vinyl . . even wash and comb her rooted hair.

She comes dressed in a tiny ruffled sunsuit. Layette includes receiving blanket, pillow, organdy dress, sun bonnet, diaper, ruffled panties, sponge, pacifier, bottle, bubble pipe.
49 N 30251—Wt. 1 lb. 3 oz...$6.49

8 **12-inch Tiny Tears.** A most exquisite doll. Dressed like an angel in her flowing gown of domestic dotted swiss and gently wrapped in a lovely receiving blanket that matches dress.

Only the finest workmanship is used for Tiny Tears and her outfit . . she's made of lovely, satin-soft vinyl that's completely washable. You can even wash and comb her rooted hair.
49 N 30252—Wt. 1 lb. 6 oz...$8.49

9 **17-inch Tiny Tears.** Fishnet leotards add just the right touch of "mod look" to her fashionable double knit coat, dress and hat ensemble. Each tiny, precise stitch of this outfit shows the quality of workmanship that went into the making of this doll.

Made of satin-soft vinyl, she's completely washable from head to toe . . you can even wash and comb her hair.
49 N 30253—Wt. 2 lbs. 6 oz... $10.99

6 **9-inch Betsy.** She's pixie size and cute as a button. Like her bigger sisters, she drinks, wets and cries real tears. Made of huggable, soft vinyl—give her a bath in her tub. You can wash, comb and brush her rooted hair.

She's dressed in a blue polka dot playsuit. Plastic tub, high chair, play pen. Feeding set consists of bottle, dish, spoon, pacifier and bubble pipe that works.
Shipping wt. 1 lb. 4 oz.
49 N 30247........$4.99

Bathtub Baby has her own tub, drinks and wets too

Bathtub Baby delights in taking a bath. Completely washable, very soft vinyl from head to toe. Rooted hair. She has her own plastic tub, soap, hooded bath towel and sponge.

Give her her bottle and she drinks . . then wets her diaper like a real baby.

Wardrobe includes gay checked dress, sunsuit, and cotton flannel robe. 20 in. tall.
Shipping weight 4 pounds.
79 N 30254C........$7.99

$7⁹⁹ set

Baby Posie
Lives in her nursery carry case

Only at Sears
$4⁹⁹

This 9-inch tall doll has a soft vinyl body that's completely posable, washable. Rooted hair. Dressed in flower shift and matching panties. Plastic playpen, bathtub, shower cap. Vinyl carry case has 2 drawers; 15x6x12 in. high when closed.
49 N 30271—Shipping weight 4 pounds 2 ounces.......$4.99

Tubsy
Splashes in her bath or hits at her jingling toy when you place it above her stomach

$12⁹⁹ without batteries

Playtime Tubsy's realistic arm action works magnetically from 2 "D" batteries (order below). Place her on her stomach or side and she sleeps.

Convert plastic bathtub to bassinet by adding plastic top, cotton skirt. Tubsy's 18 in. tall, plastic with rooted hair. Comes with kimona, diaper.
79 N 30174C—Shipping weight 6 pounds...$12.99

"D" Batteries. Package of two.
49 N 4660—Shipping weight 8 oz.....Package 38c

Flowers "bloom" for fun with the

PETAL PEOPLE

Pull stem down, petals open to reveal
a spritely 2½-inch cutie that you
can lift out, bend and pose . .
when playtime is over, put her back,
push stem up and petals close

Rosy Rose

Daffi Dill

Sunny Flower

Polly Poppy

Dizzy Daisy

It's play time

It's sleep time

Tiny Tulip

A Sears Exclusive

$1.99 Each

Any 2 for $3.80

Petal People. A garden full of mischievous little pixies to play with. 2½-inch dolls have fully bendable, wired vinyl bodies with rooted hair to brush and comb. Plastic flower and pot 12 inches tall.
49 N 30126—Tiny Tulip   49 N 30127—Rosy Rose
49 N 30128—Polly Poppy   49 N 30129—Sunny Flower
49 N 3013—Daffi Dill   49 N 30131—Dizzy Daisy
Shipping weight each 8 ounces. . . . . . . Each $1.99; Any 2 for $3.80

Flower Shoppe. Gaily colored vinyl carry and show case. 12¾x5x15¼ in. high. Slots on shelf house 3 Petal People (not included). Tote strap.
79 N 92055C—Shipping weight 2 lbs. $4.99

Flower Shoppe with Tiny Tulip, Daffi Dill and Sunny Flower.
79 N 30287C4—Shipping weight 4 lbs. . . . . .Set 9.99

Flower Shoppe with Rosy Rose, Polly Poppy and Dizzy Daisy.
79 N 30288C4—Shipping weight 4 lbs. . . . . .Set 9.99

Show off your Petal People in their own FLOWER SHOPPE

Shoppe only
$4.99

Shoppe with 3 Petal People
$9.99 set

Mattel, flush with revenue from Barbie, released three new talking dolls in the 1969 Christmas Wishbook. Baby Sing-a-Long, who knows the first line of ten favorite songs, let her owners finish the rest of the melody. Teachy Keen at $9.99, was designed to show "good grooming and coordination" to little girls. Baby Drowsy, in both white and black models, always looks tired and it's sleepy little voice repeats 11 bedtime phrases like "I go to sleep now. Nite, nite."

Mrs. Beasley, based on the doll featured in the television series "Family Affair" caught on big. It certainly helped to have the doll seen weekly on network TV! 22-inches high and originally priced at $10.99, this doll is highly collectible but difficult to find today. Collectors can expect to pay $125-$150 for one in good shape.

In Barbie's world there was lots of news. Ken, Stacy, Christie and Barbie were bendable now letting them take on great poses. Thanks to Mattel's Magic Ring, they could talk too. Each doll said six phrases like "Let's go shopping with Barbie!"

Barbie and Ken went "California Formal" to the prom. For $17.99 Barbie came complete with a sashed, flower-trimmed dress and big yellow earrings. Ken, always the fashion trendsetter, wore a yellow Nehru jacket with ascot tie and brocade vest.

Mattel also released Buzzy Bear, a talking teddy who said ten different phrases with a pull of his Magic Ring. Priced at $8.99, Buzzy came in style with a "mod" tie and velvety eyelashes.

Sears Christmas
Wishbook

1969

"Oh where, oh where has my little dog gone"

"Please buckle my shoe"

Baby Sing-a-Song

Teachy Keen

She actually teaches little girls good grooming and coordination

$9⁹⁹

This clever little doll will ask you to button her coat, tie her shoes, comb her hair and use all the other accessories she brings with her. Knows 11 phrases in all—just pull her talking ring. She's 16 inches tall, with a cloth body, arms, legs and blue painted eyes, blonde rooted hair on her vinyl head.
49 C 3097—Shipping weight 2 lbs. 8 oz.......$9.99

"I go sleep now—night, night"

"Mommy, kiss me good night"

Just pull her talking ring. Because she can sing so cheerful. Then you'll sing along and hum the song, and what a good time you'll have.

Separately if or as. **$9⁹⁹**

Such a cutie-pie . . . she'll make you smile and want to sing right along with her. She knows the first line of 10 of your favorite songs and sings them in a cute, childish voice when you pull her ring. She's 16½ inches tall, vinyl, and dressed in a cheery cotton outfit with eyelet trim, plastic shoes. Bright blue eyes; blonde rooted hair.
Shipping wt. 2 lbs. 4 oz.
49 C 30622.........$9.99

6-piece Wardrobe Set for Baby Sing-a-Song

$2⁹⁹ set

Includes 2-piece pajamas made of snuggly cotton flannelette, 1 polished cotton sunsuit, 1 polished cotton dress with rosebud trim, mirror and comb.
Shipping weight 9 oz.
49 C 30687......Set $2.99

Baby Drowsy

With half-closed eyes and a sleepy little voice she repeats 11 bedtime phrases

Each **$6⁴⁹**

What a tired baby she is—all set for bed in her snug flannel sleeper with lace trim. But she doesn't want to stop talking. Just pull her talking ring. Looks so cuddly and feels that way, too, because she has a soft cloth body, arms, legs and a soft vinyl head with rooted hair. 15¾ inches tall. So easy to buy when you just use the phone.

1 49 C 3164—Shpg. wt. 2 lbs.....$6.49   2 49 C 30272—Shpg. wt. 2 lbs.....$6.49

"That's a real rootin', tootin' trick"

Bozo the Clown

An 18-inch tall rascal who says 11 silly phrases to keep you laughing —sold only at Sears

$7⁹⁹

Here he is—big feet and all—the most lovable, laughable clown around. And what a show-off! Just pull his talking ring and he'll be happy to entertain you. He's 18 inches tall, stuffed with cotton, and has bright, floppy yarn hair on his painted vinyl head.

49 C 3675—Shipping weight 2 pounds..........$7.99

"It would be such fun to play jump rope, don't you think?"

TV's Mrs. Beasley

Such a nice friend to have! She's 22 inches tall and says 11 different phrases

$10⁹⁹

Mrs. Beasley just loves little girls, and they love everything about her—the nice things she says when you pull her talking ring, her soft cloth body dressed in its removable polka dot apron, her kind vinyl face with its big painted eyes and "granny-style" glasses, and her rooted hair you can comb. 22 inches tall.

79 C 3579C—Shipping weight 4 pounds........$10.99

23 SKIDDOO

Here are the Roaring 20's Girls!

Each 11½ inches tall and as cute as can be. They look like real "flappers".. sound like them, too

"Can you dance the Charleston?"

$4⁹⁹

Flo

"Oooh, Boop boopy-doo"

Flossie

17-inch tall Crissy has hair that "grows" from a short flip to a floor length cascade

4-piece Gift Set $12.99

1 Crissy with the wide, wide go-to-sleep eyes and thick, shiny hair. She's a dream of a beauty queen. Press her tummy to make her hair grow . . turn the knob on her back to make it short again. Hair is rooted, so you can comb, brush, and set it. Vinyl Crissy wears a lace party dress, panties, shoes. Her formal-length organza gown is trimmed with marabou feathers. Hair-styling booklet, comb included.
49 C 30748—Shpg. wt. 1 lb. 12 oz. Set $12.99

2 Pajamas, quilted robe with lace trim.
49 C 30752—Shpg. wt. 5 oz. $3.99

3 Hooded cape with fur-look trim, pompons.
49 C 30751—Shpg. wt. 5 oz. $3.99
Note: Dolls not included with outfits.

4 Hair Care Kit. Incl. all setting, styling needs.
49 C 30749—Shipping weight 6 oz. $1.99

MINIATURE DOLLS

4-inch tall Pee Wee and Baby Pee Wee $4.99

Two wee vinyl tots with go-everywhere wardrobes of 3 extra outfits for each. They travel in their own plastic steamer trunk with dresser, hangers. Or fit in your pocket. 4 inches tall with 1-piece body, turning head, rooted hair you can comb. Baby Pee Wee drinks 'n wets, too.
49 C 30742—Shpg. wt. 14 oz. Set $4.99

5-inch tall Tiny Teen with trunk and clothes $4.99

The tiniest teen in town is a real fashion plate. Likes to change clothes so often that she travels with her own plastic steamer trunk with dresser and 6 outfits, hangers. 5 inches tall; rooted hair; long eyelashes; vinyl body you can bend and pose. Comes dressed in a lovely bridal gown and veil.
49 C 30741—Shpg. wt. 1 lb. . . Set $4.99

2½-inch PETAL PEOPLE

Petals open—these cuties lift out, bend and pose

Petals close—to keep them safe the whole night through

Each $1.99

Each vinyl pixie has rooted hair; "lives" in a 12-in. tall plastic flower and pot.
(5) 49C30127—Rosy Rose
(6) 49C3013—Daffi Dill
(7) 49C30129-SunnyFlower
(8) 49C30131-Dizzy Daisy
(9) 49C30128-Polly Poppy
(10) 49C30126-Tiny Tulip
Wt. ea. 10 oz. Each $1.99

5 Rosy Rose
6 Daffi Dill
7 Sunny Flower
8 Dizzy Daisy
9 Polly Poppy
10 Tiny Tulip

Chubby little Nana, our Italian baby

She looks so real, so adorable . . 6 inches tall

11 You'll fall in love with her rosy cheeks, dimpled hands, little legs with their creases of baby fat. Vinyl; rooted hair.
49 C 30755—Wt. 8 oz. $2.49

12 Knit slacks, jacket, hat.
49 C 30765—Wt. 5 oz. $1.99

13 Knit slacks, hooded cape.
49 C 30766—Wt. 5 oz. $1.99

13 Doll not included with outfits

14 Canopy Bed. Frame, mattress, canopy and spread.
49 C 30767—Wt. 12 oz. $2.99

Complete Set. Includes doll, 2 extra outfits, canopy bed.
49 C 30759—Wt. 1 lb. 14 oz. $8.99

Ones ..waists twist 'n turn
..legs bend and pose

STACEY ..
She's simply "fab" in her London-look party ensemble

7-piece Gift Set **$6.99**

6 Stacey's all set to have a "super" time in her new dress with its bright satin bodice and metallic shag skirt. A wide satin band defines the low waistline. Satin coat has flattering puff sleeves and a rhinestone flower snap closing. Shoes, hose, hanger included. 11½-inch vinyl Stacey has rooted hair; wears a psychedelic-print knit swimsuit. Phone ordering's a quick and easy way to buy her.
49 C 30444—Shpg. wt. 1 lb. . . . . Set $6.99

SKIPPER ..
Wow! What a "cool" outfit

6-piece Gift Set **$5.49**

7 Skipper really looks "groovy" in this knit pantdress and leather-look coat with its pretend "fur" collar and cuffs. Shoes, hanger included. Skipper is all vinyl, 9¼ inches tall, and has rooted hair. She wears a vibrant cotton playsuit.
49 C 30463—Shpg. wt. 1 lb. . . . . Set $5.49

8 Cotton pantdress can be worn alone or topped by pinafore. Bonnet, shoes.
49 C 30466—Shipping weight 5 oz. . . $1.99

9 Skipper only. Dressed in playsuit.
49 C 3419—Shipping weight 11 oz. $3.49

Pants 'n Pinafore Outfit

Skipper with playsuit **$3.49**

Each **$2.99**

Sleek Sportster
10 A teenage dream of a car for all 11½-inch fashion dolls. Plastic body has steel axles, bucket seats, clearview windshield, and chrome-color grill, headlights, hubcaps. White-wall tires. About 8x18 inches long.
49 C 9320—Shpg. wt. 2 lbs. $2.99

Mad, Mod Sand Buggy
11 It's the rage! Great-looking and rugged. Perfectly-sized for slim 11½-inch dolls. Bright plastic body has steel axles, chrome-color grill and lights, windshield that raises and lowers. Heavy-duty whitewall tires. 9x20 inches long. Doll not included.
49 C 30683—Wt. 2 lbs. 10 oz. . . . $2.99

Barbie and Friends .. *they talk, they bend, they pose*

"Why don't we all go to the movies?" ☐1

"Would you like to have a fashion show?" ☐2

"Let's go shopping with Barbie" ☐3

"What shall I wear to the prom?" ☐4

Ken, Stacey, Christie, and Barbie AT THE BEACH
$4.99 each

(1 thru 4) Each doll says 6 full-length teen phrases .. just pull the talking ring. All vinyl; 11½ inches tall.
(1) 49 C 30373—Talking Ken. Shpg. wt. 10 oz......$4.99
(2) 49 C 30014—Talking Stacey. Shpg. wt. 10 oz.... 4.99
(3) 49 C 30072—Talking Christie. Shpg. wt. 10 oz.... 4.99
(4) 49 C 30015—Talking Barbie. Shpg. wt. 10 oz...... 4.99

8 new Fashion Outfits

Extra Hangers

Take them along .. Barbie and Stacey love to go traveling in their

SLEEP 'N KEEP CASE
Romantic Victorian bedroom stores dolls, clothes, accessories

Only at Sears
$5.99

Barbie and Stacey have a brand new bedroom—and isn't it pretty! Twin beds have filigree headboards, vinyl spreads that match draped canopy. Colorful wall decorations. Washable vinyl case fitted with 2 doll compartments, hanger bar, 2-door storage shelf. Plastic handle, metal snap-lock. 17x3x13 in. Dolls, accessories not included.
49 C 30471—Shipping weight 1 pound 10 ounces.................$5.99

5 Town Turtle. Snazzy blazer, bell-bottoms, pullover. Shoes.
49 C 30377—Shipping weight 8 ounces............$2.99

6 Firelights. Brocade evening jumpsuit. Silver-color slippers.
49 C 30385—Shipping weight 7 ounces............$1.99

7 Winter Wow. 2-pc. costume with belt. Hood, long boots.
49 C 30389—Shipping weight 8 ounces............$2.99

8 Winter Wedding. Brocade gown, headpiece. Shoes, bouquet.
49 C 30362—Shipping weight 9 ounces............$3.49

9 Dream-Ins. Sheer peignoir. matching shorty gown. Slippers.
49 C 30686—Shipping weight 8 ounces............$1.99

10 Hooray for Leather. Jersey top, leatherette skirt. Shoes.
49 C 30382—Shipping weight 6 ounces............$1.49

11 Silver Polish. Jumpsuit has see-thru midriff. Coat. Shoes.
49 C 30685—Shipping weight 7 ounces............$3.49

12 Breakfast at 7. Pajamas, robe with matching lining. Shoes.
49 C 30375—Shipping weight 8 ounces............$2.99

Extra Hangers. Pkg. of 18 plastic hangers with filigree design.
49 C 30681—Shipping weight 3 ounces............Pkg. 99c

NOTE: Dolls not included with outfits.

and now they're dressed in the most smashing outfits ever!

"What are you doing next weekend?"

"Stacey and I are having tea"

"Would you like to be an actress?"

"I have a date tonight"

Julia with jumpsuit $7.99

Barbie and Ken go Formal

In California-inspired Outfits **$17.99** 16-piece gift set

What a handsome couple—just full of things to say when you pull their talking rings. Barbie's ready for the prom in her long, tiered gown with its sashed, flower-trimmed Empire waist. Purse, shoes, flower earrings complete the outfit. Ken's her fashionable escort in pants and shirt accented by an ascot tie, brocade vest, Nehru-style coat. Shoes, socks included. Vinyl, 11½-inch tall Barbie and Ken come to you dressed in bright swimwear.
79 C 30443C—Shipping weight 3 pounds......Set $17.99

Julia Joins the Group

Barbie's newest friend and star of TV **$9.99** 8-piece gift set

Julia's a livin' doll, with Diahann Carroll's voice and sparkling good looks. Pull her ring and she talks. Her high-fashion outfit has knit skirt, jacket; satin bodice. Shoes, hanger. Vinyl, 11½-in. Julia wears a lamé jumpsuit.
49 C 30445—Wt. 1 lb. 7 oz......$9.99
Julia only. Dressed in jumpsuit.
49 C 30328—Shpg. wt. 10 oz..... 7.99

Barbie Dresses for a Special Occasion

Her lavish brocade suit is fur trimmed **$8.99** 8-piece gift set

Wow! Look at Barbie in her new evening outfit. The 2-piece brocade suit has a real mini-skirt and long jacket with fur-trimmed sleeves and gold-color chain closures. Snazzy hip-high boots are the perfect accessory. Vinyl Barbie stands 11½ inches tall and says many phrases when you pull her talking ring. She comes to you dressed in a flattering knit swimsuit.
49 C 30442—Shipping weight 1 lb. 4 oz.....$8.99

LOOK WHO'S TALKING

5 great conversationalists from MATTEL

"Hi! I'm Buzzy Bear"

Sears Exclusive **$8⁹⁹**

"Gimme a great big bear hug," invites this cuddly brown bear as his bright eyes jiggle under velvety lashes. Wears a washable collar and "mod" tie. 17½ inches high with floppy arms and legs. Says 10 different phrases when his ring is pulled. Acrylic plush.
49 C 40145—Shipping weight 3 pounds 11 ounces.... $8.99

"Coo coo"

Miss Peep®

A bundle of joy— and when you hug her, she coos with delight

$7⁹⁹

Here's a real-looking baby to hug and love. Just press her soft vinyl body and she makes delightful little cooing sounds . . cries when you pinch her arms. 18½ inches tall; molded hair. Dressed in a soft flannel kimono, diaper, booties. Wrapped in her own fluffy receiving blanket. Shpg. wt. 3 lbs. So easy to buy when you just use the phone.
49 C 30713......$7.99

Baby Go-to-Sleep "Mama"

Won't close her eyes till you rock her **$4⁹⁹** Each

(1 and 2) Rock her and she sleeps, tilt her and she cries "Mama". This bright-eyed baby has a soft, shredded foam-filled body; vinyl arms, legs, head; rooted hair. 14 inches tall.
1 Wears a nylon party dress, diaper, booties.
49 C 30688—Shpg. wt. 1 lb. 8 oz...... $4.99
2 Ready for bed in cozy flannelette sleepers.
49 C 30689—Shpg. wt. 1 lb 8 oz...... $4.99

Snuggle Softee "Mama"

22 inches BIG! Lightweight enough to carry all around

$7⁹⁹

She's a big baby, but filled with foam—so easy to lift and hug and hold. Cries "Mama" when you tilt her. Go-to-sleep eyes, rooted hair, chubby vinyl arms, legs make her look real. Wears play outfit, booties.
79C3069C-Shpg. wt. 4 lbs. $7.99

Outfits for 10 to 22-inch Baby Dolls

Playtime Outfit
2-piece snowsuit, 2-piece romper, blouse, playsuit.
49 C 30701—For 10-11 in. dolls. Wt. 12 oz...... $3.99
49 C 30702—For 12-13 in. dolls. Wt. 13 oz...... 3.99
49 C 30703—For 14-15 in. dolls. Wt. 14 oz...... 3.99
49 C 30704—For 16-17 in. dolls. Wt. 1 lb...... 4.99
49 C 30705—For 18-19 in. dolls. Wt. 1 lb. 1 oz...... 4.99
49 C 30706—For 20-22 in. dolls. Wt. 1 lb. 2 oz...... 4.99

Dress-up Outfit
Coat and bonnet, dress and panties, 2-piece jumpsuit.
49 C 30693—For 10-11 in. dolls. Wt. 12 oz...... $3.99
49 C 30694—For 12-13 in. dolls. Wt. 13 oz...... 3.99
49 C 30695—For 14-15 in. dolls. Wt. 14 oz...... 3.99
49 C 30696—For 16-17 in. dolls. Wt. 1 lb...... 4.99
49 C 30697—For 18-19 in. dolls. Wt. 1 lb. 1 oz...... 4.99
49 C 30698—For 20-22 in. dolls. Wt. 1 lb. 2 oz...... 4.99

Vinyl-covered Trunk

Wood frame, nickel-plated hardware, plastic handle. Hangers.

16x9x8 inches. 1 drawer.
49 C 30691—Wt. 4 lbs. 8 oz. $4.99

20x10x9 inches. 1 drawer.
79 C 30692C—Wt. 6 lbs.... 5.99

Once upon a time.. talking storybook dolls

"It's midnight!"

"Do any bears live here?"

"I've lost my sheep"

They're absolutely enchanting! Each doll says 8 phrases when you pull her talking ring . . comes with her own 16-page illustrated storybook

Each $6.99

3 little darlings . . each 11 inches tall, vinyl; rooted hair.

1 Cinderella. Ready to meet her prince in a gold lamé ball gown with sheer puff sleeves; gold-color headband. On her feet —clear-as-glass plastic slippers.
Shipping wt. 1 lb.
49 C 30423 . . . . . $6.99

2 Goldilocks. Such a pretty little maiden in her long cotton dress with print collar and pouf panels. Pantaloons. Shoes. Wt. 1 lb.
49 C 30425 . . . . . $6.99

3 Little Bo Peep. A real dear in a perky cotton dress with gingham bodice and "bustles"; pantaloons, shoes, bonnet. Wt. 1 lb.
49 C 30424 . . . . . $6.99

Goldilocks

Little Bo Peep

[3]

[1] Cinderella

[2]

Baby Small Walk

Our tiniest walking doll . . only 11 inches tall, yet she actually walks all by herself

$5.99 without battery

Just give her a gentle push and this grinning little girl toddles along like a real youngster. All vinyl; rooted hair. hair. Needs 1 "C" battery; order pkg. below.
Shpg. wt. 1 lb.
49 C 30021 . . . . $5.99

"C" Batteries. Pkg. of 6.
Shpg. wt. 12 oz.
49 C 46656—Pkg.$1.19

7-pc. Wardrobe. Skirt, blouse, jacket, shorts, flower basket, 2 hangers.
Shpg. wt. 6 oz.
49 C 30268 . . . .$1.99

"Hi . . . "

Talking Buffy

Repeats 8 phrases to Mrs. Beasley when you pull her talking ring

$7.99

She's freckle-faced and giggly . . loves her cloth-bodied Mrs. Beasley doll. 10 inches tall; vinyl; rooted hair. Wt. 1 lb.
49 C 30421 . . . .$7.99

"I love you"   "Go bye bye?"

Baby Small Talk

just pull her talking ring— she knows 8 phrases

[4]   [5]

Each $5.99

A little bundle of sunshine with wide eyes and a great big smile on her chubby baby face. She wears a sleeveless polka-dot dress trimmed with lace, daisies, and a pretty bow; matching panties. Jointed vinyl body, curly rooted hair. 10 in. tall.
(4) 49 C 30016—Shpg. wt. 1 lb. $5.99
(5) 49 C 30256—Shpg. wt. 1 lb. 5.99

8-piece Wardrobe. Includes play dress and panties, nightgown, 2 hangers, comb, brush, mirror.
49 C 30257—Shipping wt. 6 oz. $1.99

Baby Bouncy

Pick her up and she wiggles and jiggles

$6.99 swing not included

She's so active—waves her baby rattle, nods her head, swings her arms, and kicks up her heels. Dressed in a brushed nylon dress with lace-trimmed collar, attached panties. Vinyl; rooted hair; 11 inches tall.
49 C 30737—Shpg. wt. 1 lb. $6.99

Finally available... Happy memories thought lost for 45 years!

*Four new books from Windmill Press
reproduce rare original catalog pages from the legendary
Sears Christmas Wishbooks of the 1950's and 1960's*

BOYS' TOYS
OF THE FIFTIES & SIXTIES

If you were a boy growing up in the Fifties or Sixties, you'll surely remember these wonderful old Sears catalog pages from 1950-1969. Chock-full of classic toys like G.I Joe, Lionel trains, Marx playsets, James Bond spy gadgetry, Erector sets, Matchbox racers, slot cars, Tonka trucks, Roy Rogers pistols and more... with their original prices! 192 pages with thousands of illustrations.

GIRLS' TOYS
OF THE FIFTIES & SIXTIES

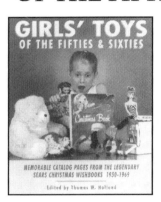

Destined to bring back happy childhood memories! This exciting book includes the best Sears Wishbook pages of toys and dolls from 1950 through 1969. Jammed with such classic toys as Barbie and Ken, Kenner's Easy Bake Oven, luxurious doll houses and kitchen sets by Marx, Twister, Mystery Date, Mouse Trap, Chatty Cathy and more with their original prices! 192 pages.

DOLL & TEDDY BEAR DEPARTMENT

A "Must Have" book for any one interested in the wonderful dolls and teddy bears sold by Sears from 1950-1969. This book is packed with original catalog pages of such classics as Barbie & Ken, Tiny Tears, Shirley Temple, Betsy McCall, Mme. Alexander, Betsy Wetsy, Miss Revlon, Chatty Cathy, Raggedy Ann, Kiddles and more. Cute teddy bears too, with original prices! 192 pages.

THE TOY TRAIN DEPARTMENT

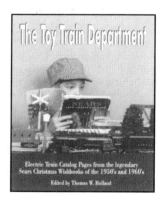

Electric trains were high on any boy's Christmas list during the Fifties and Sixties, and Sears sold the best. This neat new book contains every catalog page of toy trains sold by Sears from 1950 through 1969. The best and rarest are here, and beautifully illustrated: Lionel, Marx, American Flyer, Tyco and Revell trains and accessories in all gauges. 160 pages with the original prices!

EACH BOOK ONLY $19.95

SPECIAL OFFER: ANY TWO
BOOKS FOR JUST $35
ANY THREE BOOKS FOR $50
OR ALL FOUR BOOKS FOR $65 !

ADD $4.00 SHIPPING PER ORDER
Satisfaction Guaranteed

TO ORDER BY CREDIT CARD CALL (800) 470-5540

or send a Check or Money Order to:
Windmill Press
P.O. Box 56551 · Sherman Oaks, CA 91413